The Handbook of
Human Resource
Management
Education

The Handbook of
Human Resource Management Education

Promoting an Effective and Efficient Curriculum

Vida Gulbinas Scarpello

University of Florida

Editor

SAGE Publications

Los Angeles • London • New Delhi • Singapore

For information:

Sage Publications, Inc.
2455 Teller Road
Thousand Oaks, California 91320
E-mail: order@sagepub.com

Sage Publications India Pvt. Ltd.
B 1/I 1 Mohan Cooperative
   Industrial Area
Mathura Road, New Delhi 110 044
India

Sage Publications Ltd.
1 Oliver's Yard
55 City Road
London EC1Y 1SP
United Kingdom

Sage Publications Asia-Pacific Pte. Ltd.
33 Pekin Street #02–01
Far East Square
Singapore 048763

Printed in the United States of America

Library of Congress Cataloging-in-Publication Data

The handbook of human resource management education:promoting an effective and efficient curriculum/[edited by] Vida Scarpello.
      p. cm.
Includes bibliographical references and indexes.
ISBN 978-1-4129-5490-7 (cloth)
   1. Personnel management—Handbooks, manuals, etc.
2. Personnel management—Vocational guidance. I. Scarpello, Vida Gulbinas, 1940-

HF5549.17.H36 2008
658.30071'1—dc22   2007014601

Printed on acid-free paper.

07   08   09   10   11   10   9   8   7   6   5   4   3   2   1

Acquiring Editor:	Al Bruckner
Editorial Assistant:	MaryAnn Vail
Production Editor:	Sarah K. Quesenberry
Copy Editor:	Barbara Ray
Proofreader:	Joyce Li
Typesetter:	C&M Digitals (P) Ltd.
Marketing Manager:	Nichole Angress

Contents

Dedication

I dedicate this book to the industrial relations, psychology, sociology, and economics faculty at the University of Minnesota who taught me the disciplines they loved. As I earned both my Master's and PhD in industrial relations, there are too many professors to name. I would like to acknowledge several who influenced my thinking the most. In industrial relations it was Professors Thomas A. Mahoney, George T. Milkovich, and William F. Weitzel. In psychology it was Professors Thomas A. Bouchard, Marvin D. Dunnette, and my dissertation chair, John P. Campbell. In sociology, it was Professor Richard Hall.

I also dedicate this book to all HRM faculty who passionately transfer their knowledge, skill, and love of the field to their students and to all students who allowed them to teach them. Three little guys who bring joy to my heart and hope for the future also deserve recognition, Thomas Alexander Scarpello, Anthony Joseph Scarpello, and Paul Kazimeras Fagans.

Finally, I want to single out and acknowledge three HR friends and colleagues who directly or indirectly contributed to this book and are no longer with us.

Thomas A. Mahoney (Chapter 2)

Thomas J. Bergmann (Chapter 5)

Frederick S. Hill

The three of you are greatly missed. I counted on your friendship and your great interest in discussing all aspects of the HR field anytime I wished.

Tom Mahoney, I value you greatly as a teacher, mentor, and friend and am honored that your last lesson is within the pages of this book. That lesson extends beyond your chapter. Many of the authors of this book were taught by you or your students. Others were influenced by your writings, presentations, and personal exchanges throughout your career. Your last lesson echoes throughout this book. To use your own words, it challenges us all to "keep at it," till we develop an HR curriculum that results in satisfactory employment relationships for all stakeholders in the world of work.

Fred and Tom J., we shared the Minnesota experience and later became close friends and collaborators on several HR textbooks and articles. Tom J., you left me without revising your chapter—too quickly and unexpectedly. Fred, you and I had opportunities to talk after your terminal diagnosis. I had asked you, "now that you're going on a long journey and won't be back, what advice do you have for me about life?" I've never forgotten your answer. I thought you would give me some personal words of wisdom. Instead, you said, "fight for the field." Now I pass your words on to colleagues, students, and practicing professionals who are as passionate about the HR field as you.

—Vida Gulbinas Scarpello,
University of Florida

Preface

On Learning and Teaching

Learning is joy, teaching a privilege

to do both, a gift

nurture it, cherish it, pass it on freely from your soul

warming the hearts of all

The collection of works in this handbook is intended to aid discussion of the curriculum necessary to educate HRM students so they are successful in their future careers and contribute to their organizations and society by developing, maintaining, and innovating effective and efficient human resource management (HRM) practices. I am confident that the contents of the handbook provide a good first step to understanding current thought on HR education in the United States and the nature of HRM programs in educational institutions. The handbook's chapters also should help executives set selection criteria for HR jobs as well as inform HRM professionals about HRM educational programs.

This handbook is organized into nine sections. Some sections contain more chapters and others fewer. Some chapters are thought pieces, others report empirical research results, and still others present approaches to teaching HRM. The set of 23 chapters address the following content domains: (a) evolution of HRM and HRM education; (b) HR Master's programs in industrial relations and industrial and organizational psychology; (c) HR education in business schools; (d) new emphasis on international HRM education; (e) neglected topics in HRM education; (f) views of executives, labor leaders, and one Society for Human Resources Management

(SHRM) executive about the need for and content of formal HRM education; (g) HR success constraints; (h) HR success factors; and (i) the future of HRM education.

The idea for this book came from several sources. First, a large number of articles and books have been written on the topic of HR education and HR practice in the last 15 years. Many of those articles portrayed HRM in a very negative manner. Many articles were written by practicing professionals trying to justify their worth to their organizations. A 1996 article in *Fortune* was written by a professional writer. Many articles and books were written by academics who obviously had no expertise in the functional areas of HR or with functionally oriented HRM educational programs wherever they might be housed. Given the state of HRM practice and the lack of focus on organizationally relevant issues, some of these academics became unexpectedly credible with their audiences. Several even acquired status as HR experts and HR "gurus." My functionally educated HRM colleagues seemed to ignore these developments. At one level I understood why they didn't want to get involved in a debate over the field with people who didn't even understand it. Yet, it seemed that corporate executives and respectable practitioner organizations such as the Conference Board were agreeing with these writers. This led me to ask, "is there really an HR field as I know it? Is HR dead or just sleeping?"

These questions motivated me to organize the first HR Town Meeting at the Academy of Management meetings in Denver, Colorado in 2002. The theme of the town meeting was "Is HR Education Dead or Just Sleeping?"

I solicited 22 HR friends, who were highly committed to the field of HRM and to HR education, to write papers for the town meeting and to act as discussion leaders. Additionally, I asked each to answer the question "Is HR dead or just sleeping?" The answers below are representative of the answers I received:

> HR is currently on life support in Business Schools (although it appears to be alive and well in a small number of IR programs such as Cornell and Illinois). In business schools, it is hanging on because of extraordinary measures by some very committed people, inertia, and a certain amount of PR value vis-à-vis employers.

> I am definitely and strongly in the camp of "just sleeping." HR education needs some new life breathed into it. Creativity and innovation are critically important as is a willingness to throw out the old HRM way of thinking: that is, presenting functional HRM silos such as training and selection as discrete bodies of learning, while neglecting the strategic focus that is propelling the profession forward. Students need to be prepared to take on entry-level specialist roles, but also need the set of skills that enables them to become generalists and eventually strategic players in their chosen firm/agency.

HR education is merely sleeping, but if it doesn't wake up soon, it may as well be dead.

One colleague, however, had a different take on the issue:

> Many students of business administration, especially undergraduates, do not appreciate the importance of people-related business issues. This is not entirely their fault, because many have not yet had the kind of business experience that will force them to grapple with knotty issues involving people. So instead, they often focus their attention and their coursework on learning the technical skills necessary to master the important disciplines of managerial economics, accounting, finance, information systems, and marketing. They sometimes see "people-related business issues," or, as many curricula refer to them, "human resource" issues, as soft and squishy, the kind of issues that one need not take seriously. Conversely, many MBA and Executive MBA students have been exposed to people-related business issues in the course of their experiences in organizations, and they tend to apply themselves more seriously to understanding organizational behavior and the constraints that face operating managers in the employment context. To some extent, therefore, the answer to the question, "Is HR education dead or just sleeping?" is a function of the audience. At the same time, it is every bit as important to acknowledge that the marketing of the topic as well as its delivery in the classroom are also key considerations.

The 2002 HR town meeting was well attended, attesting to interest in the topic among HRM educators and was therefore a second motivating source for this book. Yet, it wasn't until 2005 that the article "Why We Hate HR," written by Keith Hammonds, the deputy editor of *Fast Company*, struck a chord with many HRM academics who agreed with him. The article, however, did not portray knowledge of HRM education or acknowledge the presence of highly professional HRM graduates in a variety of U.S. corporations. Missing was recognition of the strong commitment and expertise HRM graduates bring to their corporations, despite difficulties in getting professional HRM jobs without "previous" HR experience. Unfortunately, it's the lack of HRM education that contributes to employees' hating HR. As Hammond (2005) put it, "The really scary news is that the gulf between capabilities and job requirements appears to be widening. As business and legal demands on the function intensify, staffers' educational qualifications haven't kept pace" (p. 43).

I also had a third motivation for this book. As I approached retirement, I thought a lot about the field of HR as I know it, as I taught it for over 30 years, and as I interacted with business and unions in my consulting activities. In particular, I thought about my education in industrial relations at the University of Minnesota. There I learned that the field was multidisciplinary. I also learned to view teaching and practice in HR as a system. The relationship between the organization and its employees does not exist in a vacuum. HRM has a relationship with both the environment outside the organization and the environment within the organization. The external environment includes labor markets, labor unions, government, and society as a whole, its values and interests. The internal environment includes the organization's structure, strategies, culture, and workforce requirements, all of which are affected by the organization's interests. Achievement of organizational goals through people requires productive employee behaviors and performance, all of which are affected by the behavior of the organization and by individual employee and occupational interests. Thus, the role of HRM is to manage the human system in such a way that the interests of the organization, its employees, and society are considered in decision making. To achieve this objective, I learned that HRM should be an ethical practice.

The chapters in this handbook convey information about the state of major HRM educational programs and convey the perspectives of individuals whose knowledge, experience, and commitment to HRM education should help facilitate development of continuous improvement in HRM education and hence practice in the United States. Thirty-five individuals contributed to this effort. Twenty-nine are academicians, and five are former academicians. Four are consultants, one is the chief knowledge officer at SHRM, and one is currently managing a family full-time. The academicians come from a cross-section of large and small universities with varying emphasis on research and teaching.

Nine contributors earned their doctorates from the Industrial Relations Center at the University of Minnesota. This is not a coincidence, as they are friends and colleagues who shared the industrial relations adventure with me. Five earned their doctorates from the industrial relations (IR) programs at the University of Wisconsin, Cornell University, the University of Illinois, and Michigan State University. Five others earned their doctorates in industrial and organizational psychology (I/O) from such universities as Colorado State, the University of California at Irvine, Old Dominion, Purdue, and Rochester. Others earned their doctorates in management departments of a wide range of universities such as: Texas A&M, Louisiana State, SUNY-Albany, Ohio State, Georgia State, University of Iowa, University of South Carolina, and University of Washington. Some of these individuals also earned their Master's degrees from IR and I/O programs. Newer academics participated with their senior faculty mentors on some of the chapters. These contributors have either recently earned their doctorates or are in the process of earning them. The Master's-level and undergraduate preparation of the authors is also variable, as are their current employment situations, university positions, and practical experience. Biographical information about each author can be found at the end of the book. As will be seen from contributor biographical information, all are firmly grounded in the academic areas relevant to this book's focus, and many are similarly grounded in the world of business and HRM practice.

I thank all the authors for their contributions to this work. I sincerely hope that its contents stimulate further discussion of the professionalization of the HRM educational programs and practice. I also hope that this issue continues to be examined in further writings.

References

Stewart, T. A., & Woods, W. (1996, January 15). Taking on the last bureaucracy. *Fortune, 133*(1), 105–108.

Hammonds, K. H. (2005). Why we hate HR. *Fast Company, 97,* 40–47.

SECTION 1

Development of the HRM Field and HRM Education

The two chapters in this section provide an overview of the evolution of the HRM field and HRM education.

In Chapter 1, Scarpello traces the parallel evolution of HRM in business and psychology. The first part of the chapter discusses the evolution of HRM in business organizations, followed by the introduction of HRM in business schools. Next, Scarpello discusses the evolution of HRM in psychology. Three themes are evident throughout the chapter: (1) criticism of HRM practice, (2) criticism of HRM education in business schools, and (3) debate whether HRM is a specialized field of practice or a function of management.

In Chapter 2, Mahoney discusses the historical evolution of HRM from the point of view of one who has lived the experience. He sees the field of HRM as having evolved from industrial relations (IR) which he characterizes as an interdisciplinary field of study, research, and practice, with economics as one of its contributing disciplines. He further notes that "a particularly integrative conceptualization of HRM today was provided in 1984 by Michael Beer and associates and that the framework clearly casts HRM as a function of management" (p. 13). In discussing HRM education, Mahoney presents three models of education and gives suggestions for maximizing HRM's contribution to organizations.

Parallel Approaches to Development of the HRM Field and HRM Education

1

Vida Gulbinas Scarpello

Defining the field of human resource management (HRM) is not easy. Over the years the name has changed to reflect the activities conducted by its practitioners (e.g., *personnel* or *employee relations* in nonunion settings; *industrial relations* or *labor relations* in union settings). Most definitions, however, are relatively similar:

> HRM is the management function that deals with the acquisition, development, utilization, maintenance, development, and integration of individuals within the work place for the purpose of enhancing employee contribution to the effectiveness of the organization.

> HRM is a synthesis of perspectives from organizational behavior/ development, labor relations, and personnel administration. As a field of study, it is the study of all management decisions and actions that affect the nature of the relationship between the organization and employees. (Beer, Spector, Lawrence, Mills, & Walton, 1984)

In the 1995 *Handbook of Human Resource Management,* Ferris, Barnum, Rosen, Holleran, and Dulebohn define "human resource management" as the "science and practice that deals with the nature of the employment relationship and all of the decisions, actions, and issues, that relate to that relationship. In practice, it involves the organization's acquisition, development, and utilization of employees, as well as the employees' relationship to an organization and its performance" (pp. 1–2). There are multiple similar definitions; however, Ferris et al.'s (1995) definition is instructive for two reasons. When they note "this broad definition encompasses industrial relations (traditionally defined as the study of the employment relationship), as well as topics and issues that might conventionally be included under the rubrics of organizational psychology, organizational sociology, and strategic management" (pp. 1–2), they focus attention on the science of HRM. When they note that HRM "involves the organization's acquisition, development, and utilization of employees, as well as the employees' relationship to an organization and its performance," they focus on the practice of HRM.

The distinction between the science and practice of HRM is important. As a science HRM exists in many versions all of which have as their common denominator research on human beings within all types of work organizations at four levels of analysis: individual, group, organization, and society. Thus, multiple disciplines and fields of study claim HRM as their domain. For example, Kaufmann (2000) notes that HRM is "applied economics." Schneider (1999) and Korman, Kraut, and colleagues (1999) claim that it is "applied psychology." Indeed, scholars from diverse disciplines—economics, psychology, sociology, education, political science, law, anthropology, and applied fields such as health care, business, public administration, education, and others—work singly and jointly to deal with various employment issues such as labor-management conflict, excessive turnover, sabotage, social and economic inequality, labor mobility, health and safety of workers, work-family conflicts, pension reform, workforce diversity, and a host of pressing issues relevant to work and workers in contemporary societies. Thus, if we look at research, investigators in almost any discipline or field who conduct research on humans in employment relationships consider themselves HRM scholars. Yet, although HRM research informs HRM practice and HRM education, it is a mistake to assume that HRM researchers are also HRM educators.

The practice of HRM is a functional responsibility of an organization's management, like other functions of management such as finance, operations, and marketing. Indeed, the term "human resource" appears to have been coined by Peter Drucker in his book, *The Practice of Management* (1954). He presented in that volume three broad managerial functions: managing the business, managing other managers, and managing workers and work (p. 263). In his discussion of managing workers and work he noted that the worker is "the human resource" within the organization. Although comparable to other resources, the human differs from other resources in that "the human being . . . has absolute control over whether he works at all" (p. 264). This aspect of the human being has been of particular interest to managers, sociologists, social psychologists, psychologists, and economists focused on ensuring the efficiency and effectiveness of individuals and groups in work organizations. This interest is perhaps the reason for the multiple and parallel development of HRM practice and HRM education.

Historically, HRM practice and HRM education developed along three parallel paths: business, psychology, and industrial relations. This chapter discusses the evolution of HRM in business and psychology. In Chapter 2, Tom Mahoney further develops the evolution of HRM in business, and in Chapter 3, John Fossum examines the parallel evolution of industrial relations and HRM in industrial relations.

Evolution of HRM in Business

Ling (1965) notes that the first spark of any employment relationship can be gleaned from the apprenticeship systems of the late medieval period (circa 1450). Indeed, present-day benefits programs can be traced to this era. Nevertheless, the forerunner of the personnel function, the welfare secretary, originated in Europe and was introduced into U.S. industry during the 1890s. Although the U.S. never experienced the widespread industrial problems characteristic of much of the 18th and 19th centuries in Europe, similar problems in the U.S. motivated similar solutions. Labor disputes during the post–Civil War period, employer desires to thwart unions, and workers' living conditions and their effects on worker performance increasingly led employers to perceive that establishing welfare programs might benefit their businesses. These programs varied in complexity. For example, around 1800, factory owner Robert Owen taught his workers temperance and cleanliness. He also improved working conditions and refused to employ young children (Davis, 1957, p. 5). Some programs were more elaborate, requiring the development of company towns. Here, workers were typically provided with company housing, company stores, company school and apprentice programs, a savings and loan institution, a life and accident insurance program, a pension fund, a convalescent home, clubhouses, hospitals, dining halls, and a library. As welfare programs grew in scope, some firms hired so-called welfare secretaries to administer them. Eventually, the work evolved into the role and office of the employment manager.

This office later became known as the personnel management office. To a large extent personnel management performed the managerial functions of hiring, firing, disciplining, and rewarding employees and left management to focus on producing and distributing its products. This division of labor, in effect, removed management from the responsibility of managing its workforce.

The welfare secretary's transformation into personnel management led to the enactment of paternalistic human resources management practices. Yet, not all employers embraced paternalism. Some mistreated their employees. These actions led craftsmen and other best-off workers to join self-protection societies, which later became labor unions. Many employers fought the growth of unions through various means including securing court injunctions against union activities and forcing applicants to sign yellow dog contracts (i.e., promises not to join a union as a condition of employment). With the advent of the assembly line, employers sought other ways of gaining internal efficiency. The second part of this chapter discusses the use of psychologists for this purpose. Another method was to implement ideas and methods proposed by so-called classical management theorists, such as Frederick Taylor, Max Weber, and Henri Fayol.

Industrial engineer Frederick Taylor (1911/1947) proposed a philosophy that became known as Taylorism (later called scientific management) to explain the use of human effort. Taylorism seeks to maximize output with minimum effort through the elimination of waste and inefficiency at the individual operative level. Scientific management focused on rationalizing work and the workplace and on providing workers with monetary incentives to exert maximum effort. During the same period, sociologist Max Weber (the father of bureaucracy) suggested that organizational efficiency could be realized by managing the enterprise through use of legitimate (rational) rules and an authority structure. Weber (1924/1947) believed that an organization based on rational (legitimate) authority would be more efficient because continuity is related to formal structure and positions rather than to a particular person. Finally, French industrialist Henri Fayol (1916/1949) noted that efficiency could be realized by implementing 14 management principles, 10 of which focus directly on the management of the firm's human resources. Later, Fayol's principles became known as "principles of management." Because all three individuals focused on efficiency, following any one of their ideas produced the same result, i.e., the adoption of the functional organizational structure. Until the mid–20th century, organizations believed that the functional organizational form was the best way of organizing because it was the most efficient way. Although many of the principles of "fairness" in managing workers discussed by the classical management theorists apply to this day, their assumption that efficiency and effectiveness are synonyms is now known to be contrary to fact. Chapter 15 discusses organizational structures in greater detail.

The 1935 passage of the National Labor Relations Act (NLRA), which encouraged unionization as a matter of public policy, led to the growth of unions in America and the emergence of an HR function for the unionized workforces. As a general rule, personnel departments continued to perform counseling and administrative activities for the non-unionized workers, and industrial relations (IR) departments managed the collective bargaining agreement. World War II, however, slowed the growth of unions. The war years brought wage freezes and prohibition of strikes. By the end of the war, however, collective bargaining was firmly established in most of the important American industries (Barbash, 1976). The postwar years brought renewed union determination to recover the wage increases they had forgone. This led to an epidemic of postwar strikes and other labor unrest. The power of the unions and labor unrest prompted a vigorous antiunion movement that resulted in the 1947 passage of the Taft-Hartley Act, commonly referred to as the Labor-Management Relations Act. This act's basic objectives were to equalize the bargaining power between labor and management, protect individual employees against the union and against management, and protect innocent bystanders against negative consequences that could result from an interunion or a union-management conflict. The 1947 Act restricted unions in a way that paralleled the Wagner Act's restrictions on management. The two acts, along with the Landrum-Griffin Act (1959), are collectively called the National Labor Code.

During the mid-1940s to 1950s, unions represented about 47% of the U.S. labor force. Moreover, nearly 95% of all U.S. corporations had at least one unionized unit (Foulkes, 1980). Thus, unions began to pose a major decision-making constraint on U.S. corporations. To manage that constraint, corporations increasingly employed more educated personnel to manage their unionized workforces. To avoid unionization, large non-unionized firms began to function as if they were unionized (Foulkes, 1980). Indeed, through the 1970s the common characteristic of vice presidents of "personnel" of America's largest non-unionized corporations was their experience within the industrial relations and collective bargaining arena (Foulkes, 1980). Corporate leaders viewed such experience as contributing to the maintenance of a union-free environment because the heads of their personnel functions understood employee-related problems and were capable of effectively dealing with them before they exploded into unionization attempts.

In contrast to the practice of industrial relations, the practice of personnel management had its share of critics. Although Drucker (1954) viewed HRM as a management function, he disparaged the personnel management discipline of his day (pp. 273–288). He believed that practitioners (1) assumed people did not want to work, (2) looked on the function as a specialist's job rather than a key part of any manager's job, and (3) tended to "fire fight" and troubleshoot rather than focus on the positives and building harmony within the organization. Nevertheless, Drucker was hopeful. He answered his own question, "is personnel management bankrupt?" with a "no," choosing to see it as temporarily insolvent. Drucker saw the personnel management function as having the necessary expertise, being on the right track, but not yet knowing how to apply that expertise. Rather, the personnel function performed such chores as housekeeping, filing, and fire-fighting, and was destined to take over a cluster of unrelated activities such as accounting, office management, and the handling of administrative arrangements—a sort of staff office (Drucker, 1954, p. 287). Others also levied such criticism. For example, psychologists Dunnette and Bass (1963) noted that "like alchemists, personnel mangers have concentrated on the wrong problem, trying one technique after the other in a long search for a psychological touchstone to solve all human problems in industry" (p. 115). Moreover, personnel practices exhibited a pattern of "increasing stagnation and lack of significant innovation" (p. 116). Odiorne (1960), a management professor, suggested that too many personnel officers reflected the naïveté and continued practices of the 1920s.

Furthermore, the personnel function was rapidly regarded as entirely ancillary to the major purposes of the firm. By the 1960s, most observers were less than positive about the practice of personnel management.

HRM IN BUSINESS SCHOOLS

Probably the first academic interest in human resource management education occurred in the 1930s, with the development of business schools. In 1931 there was a material increase in the number of books on personnel management offered to business school instructors (Stockton, 1932). Nevertheless, most of those books suffered from lack of management theory and lack of standardized topics. Furthermore, the texts did not relate the company's personnel program to its business, the state of the firm's development, or the production and marketing functions. Only two of the books discussed wage theories, and all but one text ignored the trade union movement (Stockton, 1932). This state of affairs led Stockton to conclude, "personnel management still plays a subordinate role as a field of instruction in collegiate schools of business" (p. 220). He suggested that one reason for this state of affairs could have been the lack of properly trained instructors. Bossard and Dewhurst, in *University Education for Business* (1928–1929), had levied the same criticism. They pointed out that personnel instructors were recruited largely from men with either labor economics or psychology interests. Building on this observation, Stockton (1932) suggested

> It is safe to say that neither group has had the sort of training which would enable it to be thoroughly at home in the entire field. The future should see a type of instructor who is soundly trained in economic principles, labor economics, production, finance, marketing, insurance, statistics, business law, accounting, sociology, and psychology, and who has possibly had some practical experience handling personnel. (p. 223)

In the 1950s, business school curricula attracted another type of criticism. Critics, including executives of the Ford and Carnegie foundations and deans of business schools, held that businesses saw themselves only as economic entities, a view the critics saw as counterproductive for the U.S. economy. In response to these criticisms, the American Assembly of Collegiate

Schools of Business (AACSB) commissioned two studies on the state of business schools (see Gordon & Howell, 1959; Pierson, 1959). Among the studies' many recommendations for improving business schools was that the business firm "be seen not only as an economic activity but as an organization of people" (Haire, 1960, p. 271). That recommendation was of great interest to the developing HRM academic programs in psychology departments and in industrial relations centers.

Taken together, the 1959 reports by Gordon and Howell and Pierson motivated academic units outside business schools to develop personnel management majors at all levels, undergraduate through PhD. Within business schools, those reports prompted courses focused on teaching students about organizational behavior, which led to increased employment of psychologists in business schools.

Development of HRM in Psychology

The word "psychology" originated from the Greek word "psyche," which signifies the soul, the spirit, and the source of all vitality (Denmark, 1980). Today, it is defined as the study of behavior. In this context, behavior includes mental processes as well as observable actions. In the United States, industrial psychology began around 1901. To understand the development of industrial psychology and its relationship to other fields, it is useful to go back to the beginning of psychology in America. Among the early pioneers of industrial psychology was Walter Dill Scott (1903, 1908), who showed how psychology could be applied to advertising and selling (Viteles, 1932). He became the first psychologist to hold the title of professor of applied psychology at the Carnegie Institute of Technology, where the first graduate school of industrial psychology was established in 1915. Although professional interests of the early applied psychologists were quite diverse, they tended to concentrate on problems of personnel selection and placement.

From the field's inception, one of the chief objectives of industrial psychology was the improvement of efficiency in industry (Viteles, 1932, p. 8). This objective wedded the evolution of industrial psychology to the work of Frederick Taylor and the emerging scientific management and employment management (personnel) movements. Like Taylor, Scott attempted to maximize human efficiency by promoting competition, loyalty, concentration, and imitation (Saal & Knight, 1988, p. 13). Another key figure was psychologist Hugo Munstenberg, who, like Scott, was trained in Germany under Wilhelm Wundt, who is considered the father of psychology. Munstenberg came to Harvard at the invitation of William James. Contemporary psychologists note that Munstenberg's *Psychology and Industrial Efficiency* (1913) laid the foundation for research in personnel selection and training.

During the period prior to World War I, the field of industrial psychology had two influences: the work of Frederick Taylor and other industrial engineers (e.g., Lillian and Frank Gilbreth, 1917) and Munstenberg's work. The work of industrial engineers relied heavily on traditional experimental psychology for generalizations about human capabilities and limitations. This motivated Taylor and his colleagues to conduct time and motion studies to discover the best way to design and perform jobs. Munstenberg's work, on the other hand, was based on differential psychology, which is predicated on the uniqueness of individuals; some call him the father of American industrial psychology.

Munsterberg (1913) outlined three basic areas in which psychologists could serve industry:

1. Help find workers whose mental qualities were best suited for the work to be done.

2. Determine the psychological conditions most conducive to high performance.

3. Help produce the influences on human minds that are desired in the interest of business.

Although psychologists were beginning to be well respected by industry, it is widely recognized that the field benefited enormously from armed conflicts. Korman (1971) stated that "it took WWI to start the first great growth of industrial psychology in the country" (pp. 3–4). Dunnette and Borman (1979) claimed that April 6, 1917, the date the United States declared war on Germany, marked the beginning of the modern era of personnel selection. The successful use of psychological tests for military classification and placement during World War I familiarized the public with the efficiency of psychological testing in selection decisions. In 1921, Psychological Corporation was founded. This further brought the industrial psychologist into the view of businesses, as its purpose was to develop and distribute psychological tests and to provide consulting services to businesses and other work organizations in the public sector.

Nevertheless, during the late 1920s many managers became disenchanted with industrial psychology. Korman (1971) attributes this disenchantment to three problems:

1. Many of the selection tests were not very effective.

2. Many managers believed that ability tests totally ignored such factors as motivation and personality, which they deemed important to predicting performance.

3. Managers had seen industrial psychology as a tool to avoid unionization, and union growth was slowed in the affluent 1920s, making industrial psychology less relevant.

The disenchantment with industrial psychology opened the door to social psychology in the world of work. In a paper for the Ford Foundation Program in Economic Development and Administration, Mason Haire (1959) noted that there were three traditions within the field of industrial psychology. The first he called the field of personnel psychology, flowing from the tradition of individual differences; the second he called human engineering, which grew out of experimental psychology (used by Frederick Taylor); and the third he called industrial social psychology.

Haire (1959) noted that whereas the aim of the personnel psychologist is to find the right man for the job, the aim of the human engineer is to "make the job fit the man—any man" (p. 170). The aim of the social psychologist is to understand how the job may be rebuilt to maximize the use of human potential. Haire (1959) stated that unlike the human engineer,

> The social psychologist tries to arrange work situations to provide maximum motivational satisfactions and to structure groups so that their strengths are not barriers but aids to the accomplishment of the organization's productive objectives, and the like. (p. 717)

Haire further noted:

> The philosophy of the social theorist [industrial social psychologist] is a little harder to put concisely than the other two, but he stands quite far apart from them. The historical background is more complex. It includes some sociological traditions and a group of diverse psychological fields. The classic *Management and the Worker* (Roethlisberger & Dickson, 1939) marked the clear emphasis on certain aspects of group structure and social motivation. Moreno (1946) added others and Lewin (1938, 1947, 1951) and the group dynamicists still others. (p. 171)

Although Haire's distinctions among the psychology specializations are too simplistic today, they did focus on one continuing interest of industrial psychologists, that is, selection. In time, however, industrial psychology expanded to include "organizational and social psychology." Saal and Knight (1988) suggested that the single most important event during the 1920s and early 1930s to motivate development of industrial and organizational psychology came from the "Hawthorne studies."

In 1924, a group of Harvard psychologists headed by Elton Mayo (none of whom were industrial psychologists, but following Haire, may be labeled industrial social psychologists) began to study the effects of fatigue, lighting, music, and the like on worker productivity in GE's Hawthorne plant. The literature generally notes that the purpose of these studies was to establish the relationship between different levels of lighting and optimal working efficiency, but other variables were also studied. The effects of the lighting studies surprised everyone. Productivity seemed to increase or remain constant whether lighting was increased, decreased, or allowed to remain at a constant level. The results of additional studies during the next five years, conducted by Mayo and his colleagues, produced the same results. Together, the studies suggested that attention shown to employees by the experimenters positively affected their productivity. Siegel and Lane (1974) and others have noted that Hawthorne studies opened a new era of psychological research and ushered the human relations movement into industrial organizations.

One of the management pioneers of the human relations movement was Mary Parker Follet (1942). Her theory was that the fundamental problem of any organization is to build and maintain harmonious relationships between managers and workers. Those relationships would enable workers and managers to agree to pursue common goals. The human relations movement led to large-scale implementation of a wide range of training programs within industry, particularly the training of supervisors in human relations skills. As an aside, researchers today recognize that the Hawthorne studies were flawed in design. Franke and Kaul (1978) suggested that over 90% of the improvements in productivity could be explained by such factors as increased supervisory discipline, improved raw materials, and workers' anxiety about being laid off (remember that many of the studies were conducted during the Great Depression). An interview with one of the original participants many years later (see Daft, 2000) revealed that just getting into the experimental group meant a huge increase in pay (p. 51). Thus, money and job security may be the more accurate explanation for the results. Nevertheless, the Hawthorne studies contributed greatly to attention paid to social factors in work behavior.

Additionally, they led to the eventual merging of the human relations and industrial psychology schools of thought and the change in the field's name from industrial psychology to industrial and organizational psychology (Bass & Barrett, 1981). Eventually, some psychologists interested only in the organizational aspect of industrial psychology split from their "industrial" sisters and focused their efforts on organizational psychology (called organizational behavior in business schools).

As in World War I, industrial psychologists were in great demand during and after World War II. The U.S. Army used these psychologists to help develop various tests for separating new recruits into a few basic ability categories, develop simulators for pilot training, and develop assessment methods for applicants to the Office of Strategic Services (OSS). Much of this work was later transferred to industrial applications.

Korman (1971) described the decade following World War II as one of high growth for the field of industrial psychology. In 1945, the division of Industrial Psychology was established within the American Psychological Association. Nevertheless, industrial psychology came under criticism in the late 1950s and early 1960s. Dunnette and Bass (1963) noted that industrial psychology, like its "sister" profession, personnel management, became technique-bound. Furthermore, industrial psychologists applied their pet techniques and psychological instruments to various problems rather than spending time identifying appropriate solutions to actual business problems. Korman (1971) noted the following:

1. Industrial psychology had forfeited its status as a science by developing tools and techniques specifically designed to help personnel managers do their jobs, thereby becoming a technical assistant to management.

2. The tools and techniques industrial psychologists used were hopelessly outdated and based on assumptions about the workplace that were no longer valid.

3. Industrial psychologists permitted fads and popular ideas of the moment to dominate their activities and recommendations (p. 10).

These criticisms resulted in the field's self-examination, the results of which firmly established the field of industrial and organizational psychology (I/O psychology). In describing the development of organizational psychology, Leavitt (1961) pointed out that after World War II, engineering psychology, clinical psychology, and social psychology joined forces in coming to the aid of the "personnel man," the training director, and the general line manager. Gradually, the industrial psychologists joined with the human relations psychologists who in turn joined with game theorists, operations researchers, and computer people. Gilmer (1966) suggested that organizational psychology is a melding of traditional industrial-differential psychology and the newer concerns of organizational social psychology (p. 4).

In a report to the Ford Foundation, Haire (1959) stated that several themes characterize industrial social psychology. The first is the interest in group processes, flowing from the impact "of Lewin, Moreno, and the Mayo school . . . the second is the interest in the 'other,' through perception and detailed understanding of the world of experience of the subject . . . the third is the presence of a broad humanistic value which seems to run through the field" (pp. 177–178). Indeed, Haire went so far as to state that writings by Argyris (1957), Katz and Kahn (1952), and others "seem to imply . . . that it is possible *and advisable* to reduce the achievement of organizational goals in order to increase the achievement of individual need satisfaction" (p. 178). A fourth theme is the shift in the manner of dealing with motivation, particularly the focus of internal rather than external work rewards. Finally, Haire discussed the adoption of ideas from industrial sociological psychology to deal with problems related to group processes and group structures.

As industrial psychology and industrial social psychology were drawing closer together, the passage of the Civil Rights Act in 1964 again separated those psychologists who were interested in industrial psychology from those who were interested only in organizational psychology. For example, industrial psychologists played the major role in the drafting the Uniform Selection Guidelines (see Equal Employment Opportunity Commission, 1978), whereas their organizational psychology counterparts were not very interested in this topic. It is clear that the key distinguishing factor between psychologists who are attracted to industrial and organizational psychology, as opposed to those who are attracted only to organizational psychology, is the orientation toward managing behavior rather than just studying it. Because of their applied interests, many I/O psychologists work for governments as consultants to industry or as highly specialized staff within large corporations. Those whose interests are solely in organizational psychology consult in the areas of organizational development and change. I/O psychologists also teach in HRM programs within psychology departments, and some also maintain outside consulting practices. Still others work in business schools as faculty within management departments. Those with more applied interests teach HRM and organizational psychology (which in business schools is called organizational behavior), and those with more conceptual interests limit their teaching to organizational behavior. Although writers today suggest that various disciplines make up organizational behavior, all agree that psychology is primary (e.g., Schneider, 1985). The core of most definitions of organizational behavior would run something like this: "organizational behavior (OB) as a field of study represents the application of behavioral science concepts and methods to the *study* of human behavior in the organizational environment" (Organ, 1978, p. 2). Thus, OB focuses on the understanding of human behavior rather than on managing that behavior at work. Organizational behavior concepts are very important to the development of HRM programs. Murray and Dulebohn elaborate on this topic in Chapter 14. Klein, DeRouin, Salas, and Stagl discuss the current state of HRM Master's programs in psychology departments in Chapter 4.

Discussion and Conclusion

This chapter focused on two parallel sources of HRM development, HRM in business and business schools, and HRM within the field of psychology. Two questions surfaced in this chapter. First, is HRM a specialized field or is it a function of management? Second, if we assume it is a function of management, why don't business schools and managers pay enough attention to HRM?

IS HRM A SPECIALIZED FIELD OR A FUNCTION OF MANAGEMENT?

I believe HRM is both a specialized field and a function of management. As a specialized field, HRM, is practiced at four levels: (1) societal, (2) organizational, (3) group, and (4) individual. My view assumes that

HRM must work to satisfy the interests of stakeholders at all four levels to maintain a stable, satisfactory, and profitable relationship among those stakeholders. This, however, is no different than other functions of management that directly interact with the organization's business environment. For example, marketing must satisfy the interests of consumers as well as those of the organization. Finance must satisfy the interests of financial markets as well as those of the organization. Concern with the results of HRM decision making on individuals and groups within and outside the organization minimizes risks associated with disruptive external and internal events flowing from unmet employee and societal expectations. Thus, effective managerial decision making must take into account the HR constraints that may be imposed on it by its internal and external stakeholders (employees and society). As a function of management, HRM requires specialized knowledge and skill *and* business knowledge and skill, as do all other functions of management (e.g., accounting and marketing). Thus, in my opinion, all functional areas of business are specialized functions and require specialized knowledge and skill, along with more general business knowledge and skill. Early criticism of lack of business knowledge among HR faculty and HR practitioners still holds true to this day. In Chapter 21, Theeke focuses explicitly on this issue.

I also agree with Drucker's (1954) view that HRM is a management function. That is, each manager must be responsible for managing his or her direct reports. In a small organization, the manager must become an HR specialist (see Chapter 7, which describes HR education at the University of Colorado-Boulder). However, in large organizations, the HR function is the center of specialized expertise in the field of human resource management, much the same way as the finance function is the center of specialized expertise in the area of finance, even though individual managers are responsible for managing the financial aspects of their operations. E. Bakke (1958) articulated and elaborated on the dual role of HRM as a specialist and a management function. A sociologist by training and a multidisciplinary industrial relations scholar by practice, Bakke described HRM as an ignored managerial function although it was as important to business success as accounting, production, finance, marketing, and other managerial functions. Consistent with my education in the University of Minnesota Industrial Relations Center, Bakke noted the human resources function subsumes all personnel administration, industrial and labor relations, human relations (organizational behavior), human engineering, executive development, and the like. He further laid out seven points that detail why the HR function goes beyond the work of the personnel or industrial relations manager. Specifically:

1. The HR function is not a *special* function; it must meet the standards for all the other functions of management, which are to understand, to maintain, to develop, to employ or utilize effectively, and to integrate these resources into a working whole.

2. Levels of the HR function are not new gadgets or tools to be afforded when the really important functions are running smoothly or profitably. Rather, the management of HR must be done from the startup of any organization.

3. The objective of the HR function is not personal happiness but productive work and the maximum opportunity for all the company's people to utilize to the fullest possible extent all the skills they have relevant to making that work more productive.

4. The HR function includes not only the welfare and compensation activities associated with personnel and labor relations (union-management relations), but the human resources aspect of every working relationship between people in the company. It should improve the work process, work associations, and work opportunities of employees so as to reduce the need for rewards which compensate for boredom and hardship.

5. The HR function is not solely concerned with employees but with every person at all levels of the organization, including the CEO.

6. The HR function is necessarily performed by every person in the organization who is responsible for supervising others. This includes managers in a unionized environment. In such cases line management carries out basic HR functions within a framework of expectancies, controls, and other activities of the union.

7. The focus of concern for all HR effort must be the simultaneous achievement of the central and essential interests of the company and its people. The interests need not be the same but they must not be incompatible. (Bakke, 1958, p. 200)

IF HRM IS A FUNCTION OF MANAGEMENT, WHY DON'T BUSINESS SCHOOLS AND MANAGERS PAY ENOUGH ATTENTION TO IT?

Although there are a variety of answers to this question, one that I would like the reader to consider is proposed by Bohl, Slocum, Luthans, and Hodgetts in their 1996 article "Ideas That Will Shape the Future of Management Practice" published in *Organizational Dynamics*. These authors note:

The importance of human resources has been given considerable lip service over the years. However, few companies are walking the talk. Real world organizations and their managements continue to give priority to—and do quite well with—the functional and technological sides of the organization. But the human side continues to be downsized in importance as well as head count. (p. 8)

They suggest that the major reasons for this continued imbalance of things over people may have a lot to do with complexity. Although finance, marketing, technological processes, and information systems appear on the surface to be more complicated and challenging, they suggest this is not so. They reach this conclusion by appealing to Kenneth Boulding's classical work on the hierarchy of systems complexity (Boulding, 1956).

> Boulding points out that people and human organizations are one step below the ultimate of systems complexity in the entire universe. In his widely recognized scheme of things, cybernetic systems (today's information systems) are below the cell (the simplest living organism) . . . then, in increasing complexity come plants, animals, humans, and human organizations. The complexity culminates in transcendental systems (deities, time machines, and secrets of the universe). (Bohl et al., 1996, p. 8)

Complexity may also explain the reason why individuals obtaining PhDs in the same fields do not end up with the same scope and depth of expertise. Unfortunately, complexity produces ambiguity, which in turn promotes political behavior. Ambiguity allows entrepreneurial academics to seize the opportunity to establish academic programs and call them HRM or strategic HRM, even though the faculty of those programs acknowledge that they know little about HRM. Ambiguity also allows other academics to claim expertise in HRM simply by stating that they are "HRM" faculty, even when they might have never taught an HRM course or at best taught one course by reading the textbook ahead of their students. It allows academics to establish pseudo-credibility in IR or HRM when they research HR-relevant issues or even when they publish think pieces on HRM. Ambiguity as to the domain and content of HRM has also led many business school administrators to assume their OB and HRM faculty are interchangeable in the classroom.

Today's HRM educators vary widely in their expertise. The best are educated in all functional areas of HRM. Many are also educated in organization theory, design, development, behavior, labor economics, and collective bargaining. Many have MBAs and many have learned the essentials of business and accounting on their own. Many, however, do not understand and are not interested in economic principles, labor economics, collective bargaining, production, finance, marketing insurance, or accounting. Nevertheless, HRM students in business programs complete all required business courses, along with their HRM concentration courses.

Although I can criticize the education of HRM faculty, my experience teaching a variety of HRM and labor relations courses as well as organization theory, design, and development courses in five research universities over a 30-year period is that HRM faculty have broader and more in-depth expertise than other specializations in departments of management. Despite this, HRM is not an equal partner in design of business curricula in many business schools and is not yet a full partner in the management of organizations. In business schools it is the only function of management that is seldom represented in the core course requirements for all business majors. Lack of representation in business curricula clearly leads to misunderstanding of the field's knowledge base and potential contribution to organizational success. It results in less than optimal human resource management practices in employment settings. These practices can be improved significantly if business schools added a core HRM course requirement for all business majors and required faculty teaching HRM courses to be functionally trained in HRM. Practices can also be significantly improved if corporate executives gained some understanding of HRM education and demanded the same level of functional expertise of their HRM personnel as they do of all other functional specializations.

As the philosopher George Santayana noted, "those who cannot remember the past are condemned to repeat it."

Let's not wait another 76 years or more to read about the same criticism of HRM education and practice as we heard in 1932 and as we hear today.

References

Argyris, C. (1957). *Personality and organization*. New York: Harper.

Bakke, E. W. (1958). *The human resources function*. New Haven, CT: Yale Labor-Management Center.

Barbash, J. (1976). The labor movement after World War II. *Monthly Labor Review, 99*(1), 34–37.

Bass, B. M., & Barrett, G. V. (1981). *People, work, and organizations: An introduction to industrial and organizational psychology* (2nd ed.). Boston: Allyn & Bacon.

Beer, M., Spector, B., Lawrence, P. R., Mills, D. Q., & Walton, R. E. (1984). *Managing human assets*. Cambridge, MA: Free Press.

Bohl, D. L., Slocum, Jr., J. W., Luthans, F., & Hodgetts, R. M. (1996). Ideas that will shape the future of management practice. *Organizational Dynamics, 25*(1), 7–14.

Boulding, K. E. (1956). General systems theory. *Management Science, 2*(3), 197–208.

Bossard, J. H. S., & Dewhurst, J. F. (1931). *University education for business: A study of existing needs and practices*. Philadelphia: University of Pennsylvania Press.

Daft, R. L. (2000). *Management*. New York: Dryden Press.

Davis, K. (1957). *Human relations in business*. New York: McGraw-Hill.

Denmark, F. L. (1980). Psyche: From rocking the cradle to rocking the boat. *American Psychologist, 35*, 1057–1065.

Drucker, P. F. (1954). *The practice of management*. New York: Harper.

Dunnette, M. D., & Bass, B. M. (1963). Behavioral scientists and personnel management. *Industrial Relations, 2*, 115–130.

Dunnette, M. D., & Borman, W. (1979). Personnel selection and classification systems. *Annual Review of Psychology, 30*, 477–525.

Equal Employment Opportunity Commission. (1978). Uniform guidelines on employee selection procedures. *Federal Register, 43*, 38290–38309.

Fayol, H. (1949). *General and industrial management* (C. Storr, Trans.). London: Pittman. (Original work published in France 1916 or 1919)

Ferris, G. R., Barnum, D. T., Rosen, S. D., Holleran, L. P., & Dulebohn, J. H. (1995). Toward business-university partnerships in human resource management: Integration of science and practice. In G. R. Ferris, S. D. Rosen, & D. T. Barnum (Eds.), *Handbook of human resource management* (pp. 1–17). Cambridge, MA: Blackwell.

Follet, M. P. (1942). *Dynamic administration.* New York: Harper.

Foulkes, F. (1980). *Personnel policies in large non-union companies.* Englewood Cliffs, NJ: Prentice Hall.

Franke, R. L., & Kaul, J. D. (1978). The Hawthorne experiments: First statistical interpretation. *American Sociological Review, 43,* 623–643.

Gilbreth, F. B., & Gilbreth L. M. (1917). *Applied motion study.* New York: Macmillan.

Gilmer, B. (1966). *Industrial psychology* (2nd ed.). New York: McGraw-Hill.

Gordon, R. A., & Howell, J. E. (1959). *Higher education for businesses.* New York: Columbia University Press.

Haire, M. (1959). Psychological problems relevant to business and industry. *Psychological Bulletin, 56,* 169–194.

Haire, M. (1960). Business is too important to be studied only by economists. *American Psychologist, 15,* 271–273.

Kaufman, B. (2000). Personnel management: Its roots as applied economics. *History of Political Economy, 32,* 227–256.

Katz, D., & Kahn, R. L. (1952). Some recent findings in human-relations research in industry. In G. W. Swanson, T. M. Newcomb, & E. L. Hartley (Eds.), *Readings in social psychology* (2nd ed., pp. 650–665). New York: Holt.

Korman, A. K. (1971). *Industrial and organizational psychology.* Englewood Cliffs, NJ: Prentice Hall.

Korman, A. K. (1999). Motivation, commitment, and the "new contracts" between employers and employees. In A. I. Kraut & A. K. Korman (Eds.), *Evolving practices in human resource management* (pp. 23–40). San Francisco: Jossey-Bass.

Kraut, A. I., & Korman, A. K. (Eds.). (1999). *Evolving practices in human resource management.* San Francisco: Jossey-Bass.

Leavitt, H. J. (1961). *Toward organizational psychology.* Pittsburgh, PA: Carnegie Institute of Technology, Graduate School of Business Administration.

Lewin, K. (1938). The conceptual representation and the measurement of psychological forces. *Contributions to Psychological Theory, 1,* 4.

Lewin, K. (1947). Group decision and social change. In T. M. Newcomb & E. L. Hartley (Eds.), *Readings in social psychology* (pp. 330–344). New York: Holt.

Lewin, K. (1951). *Field theory in social science.* New York: Harper and Row.

Ling, C. (1965). *The management of personnel relations: History and origins.* Homewood, IL: Richard D. Irwin Inc.

Mayo, E. (1946). T*he human problems of an industrial civilization.* Boston: Division of Research, Graduate School of Business Administration, Harvard University.

Moreno, J. L. (1946). *Psycho-drama and socio-drama.* New York: Beacon.

Munsterberg, H. (1913). *Psychology and industrial efficiency.* Boston: Houghton Mifflin.

Odiorne, G. S. (1960). Company growth and personnel administration. *Personnel, 37,* 32–41.

Organ, D. W. (1978). *The applied psychology of work behavior.* Dallas, TX: Business Publications Inc.

Pierson, F. C. (1959). *The education of American businessmen.* New York: McGraw-Hill.

Roethlisberger, F., & Dickson, W. J. (1939). *Management and the worker.* Cambridge, MA: Harvard University Press

Saal, F. E., & Knight, P. A. (1988). *Industrial/organizational psychology: Science and practice.* Pacific Grove, CA: Brooks/Cole.

Schneider, B. (1985). Organizational behavior. *Annual Review of Psychology, 36,* 571–611.

Schneider, B. (1999). Is the sky really falling? In A. I. Kraut & A. K. Korman (Eds.), *Evolving practices in human resource management* (pp. 329–357). San Francisco: Jossey-Bass.

Scott, W. D. (1903). *The theory of advertising.* Boston: Small, Maynard.

Scott, W. D. (1908). *The psychology of advertising.* New York: Arno.

Siegel, L., & Lane, I. M. (1974). *Psychology in industrial organizations.* Homewood, IL: Irwin.

Stockton, F. T. (1932). Personnel management in collegiate business schools. *Personnel Journal, 11*(4), 220–226.

Taylor, F. (1947) *Principles of scientific management.* New York: Harper. (Original work published 1911)

Viteles, M. S. (1932). *Industrial psychology.* New York: Norton.

Weber, M. (1947). *The theory of social and economic organization* (A. H. Henderson & T. Parsons, Eds. & Trans.). Glencoe, IL: Free Press. (Original work published 1924)

Human Resource Management Education

2

Past, Present, and Future

Thomas A. Mahoney

What is being called HRM here today has had a long and checkered history. It originated under various influences, evolved in a variety of directions, and is still a quite varied body. It is still seeking some common identity and form and will continue to evolve in future years. The teaching of HRM in business schools is one specific component of the broad, overall body of HRM, and this chapter focuses primarily on that component while recognizing that scholarship and teaching in HRM take many different forms at the same time. Although not present at the beginning, I have been fortunate to live through the most productive and spirited period of its evolution as an academic focus and can speak personally of many of the stages I witnessed and experienced.

Various others have in recent years written about the history and evolution of what we know as HRM, each reflecting a different focus and bias (Dulebohn, Ferris, & Stodd, 1995; Kaufman, 1993). I draw from and affirm much of what they have observed but come at this task from my own personal bias and thus differ at times from their interpretations of the events and occurrences.

Evolution of Human Resource Management

Although unrecorded, the actual managing of human resources doubtless has occurred since the first organization of people into functioning units such as tribes. As tribes formed and, particularly, as they evolved from hunting and then farming, a division of labor undoubtedly arose with recognition of differing productivity of individuals and development of a form of division of labor in which different persons occupied different roles in the productive society. Craftspeople who could develop tools for farmers and be supported by the productivity of others engaged in farming doubtless emerged and a natural division of labor arose. In short, the division of labor emerged as the productivity of various crafts and occupations varied, and trade evolved to take advantage of these variations. Whether managed through the natural functioning of a market and a market allocation of productive roles, or the human resource management of a tribal leader, the issues of managing human resources emerged. However this evolved, it is likely that at some stage some leading influence in the farming tribe coordinated and supported this division of labor, performing the functions of a market within an organized group. And certainly there was managing of human resources in productive endeavors for centuries before 1900. Tribal leaders and, later, industrial leaders all managed groups of contributors who had to be allocated tasks and directed and motivated in their endeavors. The managing of human resources, whether through a functioning market mechanism or a directed body of leaders, has been with us since the earliest days of human development. Historically, HRM probably was the earliest evolved management function, predating other functions such as finance, accounting, and marketing.

Most of the historians of HRM begin with the 19th century, a period of rapid industrialization in the U.S., the emergence of large employing organizations with many varied roles for employees, the later organization of labor unions, and the development of collective bargaining in large industries. Earlier organizations were of independent craftsmen organizing and controlling product markets. As the markets grew and employers came to dominate activities, employees also banded into unions to bargain for their returns. At the same time managing organizations of employees doubtless involved the selection, training, organization, and motivation of workers. The early problems of organizing and leading collections of contributors toward a common goal and effort can be observed today in the attempts to unite fighting tribesmen in societies such as Afghanistan. Similar problems doubtless confronted leaders in the developing system of business and commerce.

The 20th century brought increasing attention to issues of managing organizations of people and saw the development of attempts to prescribe professional approaches to the management of people in work roles. F. W. Taylor (1895) and his efforts at "scientific management" exemplify early approaches to the organization of work roles and the training and motivation of workers. Another example was the Committee on the Classification of Personnel headed by Walter Dill Scott with the War Department in 1917;

their focus was on the assessment of individuals for differing work assignments. And the role of what was later termed personnel administration
(PA) was emerging in practice; the Boston Employment Managers Association was formed in 1911 and the National Association of Employment
Managers in 1919, later changing to the Industrial Relations Association
of America in 1920 and the National Personnel Association in 1922. One
of the earliest publications in the field was *Personnel Administration: Its
Principles and Practice* in 1920 by Tead and Metcalf.

At the same time, labor union organizations and collective bargaining
were growing as a reaction to employer practices. These efforts had been
put on hold during World War I but emerged again following the war.
These were termed "labor problems" and generally viewed independently
from the issues of scientific management and personnel assessment, which
were termed "personnel administration." So-called labor problems drew
the attention of economists, whereas personnel administration had drawn
the attention of industrial psychologists. Classical economics had no role
for labor unions, relying instead on the operations of the perfect market to
bring about appropriate wages and employment contracts. Instead, what
was termed "institutional labor economics" evolved to address issues of
collective bargaining, unemployment, and the like, phenomena at odds
with the image of the perfect market in classical economics. The label
"industrial relations" was applied to this group of issues, and research units
were established at Wharton, Princeton, and the University of Wisconsin in
the early 1920s to address these issues.

Thus emerged two related but relatively independent fields of practice
and analysis: personnel administration, which addressed the effective utilization of individuals in work organizations exemplified in the work of
Tead and Metcalf (1920), and industrial relations, which addressed what
was accepted as inherent conflict between the interests of employing organizations and employed workers exemplified in the work of Commons
(1921) and Slichter (1919). Later during the 1930s a third focus, human
relations, emerged with the work of Mayo (1930) and Roethlisberger and
Dickson (1939). That focus was directed at adjusting relationships within
work organizations to achieve a more harmonious relationship between
workers and employers. It was more closely related to personnel administration than to industrial relations, but it constituted a third branch in the
overall field of concern and study.

Research and teaching during the first half of the century proceeded
relatively independently in the several streams of labor economics and labor
relations, industrial psychology and personnel administration, and industrial sociology and human relations. There were occasional mergers of talent and interests around specific issues, but there was not much coordination
of efforts until the 1930s and 1940s. One example of early collaboration
was the Employment Stabilization Research Institute founded in 1930 at

the University of Minnesota to address issues related to the Depression of the 1930s and the resulting unemployment and welfare efforts. Academics from the varied disciplines of economics, psychology, law, and political science collaborated in the investigation of issues and development of efforts to address problems. These and related efforts were abandoned after Pearl Harbor as participants shifted to Washington to serve on the War Labor Board, the War Manpower Commission, and related bodies.

The collaboration of scholars from different universities in the war effort was continued in the Labor Market Research Committee of the Social Science Research Council, a group dominated by labor economists but also including industrial psychologists and sociologists. This collaboration and the increasing awareness of possible contributions of interdisciplinary efforts doubtless influenced the emergence of interdisciplinary organizations of faculty at various universities during the 1940s, organizations often labeled Industrial Relations Centers. Although sometimes administratively located within schools of business, these centers typically stressed their independence from any single discipline or focus. Collegiate schools of business management also were emerging and growing about this time and were not as established within the academic community as they appear today. Faculty concerned with industrial relations might hold joint appointments with a disciplinary unit (departments of psychology, economics, etc.) and the interdisciplinary center. Interdisciplinary research was conducted within the center, and instructional courses might be taught through the center or base disciplinary departments. Research efforts of the centers have been described as "eclectic and empirical" (Paterson & Yoder, 1955), stressing their independence from any single disciplinary body of theory and their focus on empirical research as opposed to theoretical elaboration.

The practice of personnel management and labor relations continued to develop over this period as exemplified in the different professional associations, certain of them later forming the American Management Association. These efforts were basically independent of academic links, although various texts on personnel administration began to appear (Tead & Metcalf, 1920; Yoder, 1938).

Many of the academic centers, typically called Industrial Relations Centers, appear to have been related through membership of scholars in the Social Science Research Council Committee on Labor Market Research and dominated by academics from labor economics, probably related also to their joint efforts in wartime agencies in Washington. The common label applied to these efforts was industrial relations. The Industrial Relations Research Association (IRRA) also emerged about this time from these collaborative efforts. Even the term industrial relations (IR) appears more reflective of labor economics interests than of industrial psychology or sociology interests. Nevertheless, most of these academic efforts tended to encompass concerns of labor market operations, collective bargaining and labor relations, labor legislation related both to social welfare and labor relations, and personnel administration within organizations. The scope of IR was viewed as encompassing all of these concerns, and PA was only one relatively small concern within the larger framework. Personnel administration and labor relations were clearly differentiated, however. Similarly, concerns for labor markets and labor legislation were viewed as concerns of social governance, whereas labor relations and personnel administration were concerns of respectively differentiated organizational responsibilities.

The collection of scholars from the different disciplines related to IR provided an exciting opportunity for both research and education. Every topic or issue for research and instruction had to be addressed by scholars from different disciplines, which often had different groundings and theories. Thus, for example, economists viewed wages as a dependent variable to be explained in terms of behavior, whereas psychologists viewed wages as an independent variable to be manipulated to affect behavior. Economics looked to market models to explain observed phenomena, whereas psychologists looked to individual analysis, motivation, and action. Sociologists tended to turn to models of group actions. Bringing the different theoretical approaches to bear on specific issues often resulted in richer research, in terms of both findings and lessons to be communicated. The emergence of IR as an organized interdisciplinary approach offered potential for increased development of knowledge and improved management of individuals. Scholars relying on traditional disciplinary models to explain observed phenomena had to take account of and merge explanations from the different disciplines. Industrial relations emerged as an interdisciplinary field that pulled together competing disciplines and thus a richer field for research and scholarship. As a graduate student in labor economics at that time and holding a research assistantship in IR, I found the interplay of disciplines in research endeavors quite exciting. The interaction with my colleagues in industrial psychology and sociology on research projects provided much more challenge and reward than the coursework required in the single discipline of labor economics.

Economics and Human Resource Management

Over the years, the discipline of economics and economic theory, as well as individual economists, have contributed to the evolution of HRM as a field of research and practice. As noted above, I view the field of HRM as having evolved from IR, an interdisciplinary field of study, research, and practice. Economics was one of the contributing disciplines. Over the years there have been some (e.g., Dunlop, 1957; Heneman, 1969; Somers, 1969) who sought to cast IR as a separate and distinguishable theory that evolved from related disciplines but might be viewed as a separate discipline. These efforts appear to have been abandoned, probably because of the difficulty of distinguishing a theory separable from the related contributing theories and disciplines. Each of the related disciplines has evolved separately over time, with IR and HRM continuing to use relevant developments as appropriate.

Early influences of economics appeared in the application of market concepts and models. Much of the early work in IR addressed issues of unemployment, wage determination, labor mobility, and the allocation of labor in terms of labor markets. Market concepts were predominant in early research and thinking, and they continue to influence thinking about issues such as wage determination, executive compensation, alleviation of unemployment, and recruitment of labor. The concept of a labor market continues to influence much thinking, research, and practice in HRM.

Early work in IR also recognized that the "perfect market" of classical economics was not always realized in practice. Much of the early work in IR addressed issues and problems inconsistent with the model of a perfect market. Thus, early research addressed issues of labor mobility, identifying barriers to mobility and patterns of mobility inconsistent with seeking the highest wage. The model of the perfect market was modified as work in IR identified inconsistencies.

One example of such modification was the identification of "wage contours" (Dunlop, 1957), where wage differentials for a single occupation persisted over time within a presumably single market, differentials inconsistent with the predictions of market theory. Researchers recognized that market behavior of employers and employees was constrained and influenced by tradition. This phenomenon is incorporated today in surveys by compensation consultants for establishing wage rates and levels.

Another example was the development of the concept of the internal labor market (Doeringer, 1967). It was recognized that much of the allocation of labor among occupations and jobs was accomplished within employing organizations without resort to the external labor market. Recognition of this phenomenon has influenced the development of career ladders, compensation bands, employee appraisal, and training and development efforts. The broad concept of the market is still employed but modified to accommodate employer practice. Today we have employers who rely totally on interaction within a broader labor market and others who isolate themselves from that market with the establishment and maintenance of an internal labor market.

Another example of the application of economic influences is the application of "agency theory" in the design and management of compensation contracts, particularly in the compensation of key executives. In short, the executive is cast as an agent of owners and compensation contracts are designed to align the executive's interests with those of owners. Although not as striking, compensation for all employees is viewed in the form of incentives to encourage employee action and behavior consistent with the interests of the employer. Thus, pension rewards, bonuses, stock options, and other forms of incentives are designed to promote specific actions and behaviors of all employees (Lazear, 1981). This represents a modification of the earlier market model in which wage rates were determined by behavior of workers in the labor market; it focuses more on employer free-dom to design compensation to motivate relatively specific behaviors. This is a modification of the early models of economics in which wages were viewed as a dependent variable and incorporation of influences from psy-chology in which wages were viewed as an independent variable manipu-lated to motivate behavior.

"Tournament theory" is another modification of traditional market analysis. Individual employees within employing organizations are cast as players in a tournament seeking positions in hierarchical organizations and the rewards associated with the positions (Lazear, 1981). Engagement in the analysis of problems and issues from industrial relations has pro-vided a rich field for the development of economic analysis and models to explain outcomes and behavior inconsistent with simple perfect market models.

Still another contribution from economics has been "game theory," the elucidation of models of competition between players where the outcomes are determined by the interacting choices of the players. This model has had applications in the understanding and design of behavior in all bar-gaining and negotiation interactions, notably collective bargaining. Most recently game theory has been employed in the study of strategic choices of enterprises, not merely those relating to HRM.

Elements of economic theory also have been applied to the design of labor market and social programs that affect but are not typically viewed as HRM. The economic model of markets certainly has influenced the design of unemployment compensation, the provision of education, espe-cially for welfare recipients, and labor legislation relating to collective bar-gaining. All of these affect the practice of HRM within organizations.

Nevertheless, it is difficult to find that economic theory has contributed much to current work in HRM. Labor economics, in particular, was an early influence on the development of IR, from which the field we know as HRM evolved. Economics did contribute by shaping an analytical focus on IR and, later, HR issues and practice. The field was more than a collec-tion of issues and problems; it was an opportunity to apply theoretical models in the understanding of observed problems and the shaping of actions and solutions. And HR continues to be a source of stimulation for economic analysis (Lazear, 1998). Recent research in labor economics explores the effects of piece-rate compensation, the impact of deferred compensation on individual behavior, and the phenomenon of wage com-pression and its sources and effects (Lazear, 1999). This research, however, contributes to understanding and thinking about HRM practices and issues, but it appears to have little direct and immediate effect on the teaching of HRM. It may explain or rationalize various HRM practices, but there appears to be little contribution to the development of new and innovative practice. Nevertheless, economics continues to be a major influence on scholarship and research in HRM.

A somewhat different contribution of economics occurred in the contribution of individual economists to the development of HRM as a field of study, particularly in the development of IR and institutions devoted to research, education, and service in the broad field of IR. As noted earlier, the institutionalization of IR as an academic field was heavily affected by labor economists who predominated in the development of IR centers and IR professional associations (Paterson & Yoder, 1955). Although assisted by academics from the broader behavioral sciences (Bakke, McGregor, Paterson, Likert, Whyte, Homans, and Shartle), the predominant names associated with the early centers of IR research and teaching were those of labor economists (Dunlop, Witte, Reynolds, Yoder, Schultz, Harbison, Derber, Myers, Kerr, Rees, Lester, and Schister). And the IRRA was initiated and dominated in its early years by labor economists. I can only speculate on why this occurred. Perhaps it was because the mid-century issues of concern included unemployment, labor unions, and collective bargaining, which were external to the firm and to which economics had contributed more than the behavioral sciences that focused on issues within the firm, the province of PA. PA was incorporated into IR as a subfield, but labor markets, labor relations, and labor legislation were predominant issues at the time.

A less tangible and more debatable contribution of the economics discipline might be an analytical emphasis within the IR and HR traditions. Economics, with its base in theoretical models and analysis, demands somewhat more rigor in analysis of issues than certain other disciplines related to IR and HR. Although labor economists abandoned the concept of a perfect market, they still sought the framework of a broad theoretical model (e.g., Dunlop, Somers, and Heneman). In consequence, issues are submitted to a more rigorous and critical examination in the light of existing theories and analyses, and proposed actions are more critically challenged than might otherwise be the case. This contribution is particularly relevant in an age of "model of the month" and "action/strategy of the month" proposals. The traditions of economics and economic analysis are particularly helpful in stabilizing thinking and action in a field increasingly prone to faddish change.

One additional contribution may have been the gradual change in labels and implicit change in focus with the evolution of HRM from PA. The implicit focus of PA and the actual practice of it were "administering" personnel within the employing organization, the selection, staffing, training, compensation, and discipline of employed personnel. The shift in label and practice from PA to HRM more clearly casts employed personnel as economic resources of the organization, analogous to capital, petroleum, land, copyrights, iron ore, and the like and to be managed as an economic resource while taking into account the unique aspects of humans. The field of HRM today certainly focuses on this paradigm more than did the field of PA in earlier years.

Industrial Relations Education

Education in the various concerns of IR was sometimes concentrated or coordinated through IR centers and sometimes diffused and lodged in different disciplines—labor market operations in labor economics, public policy in law, and labor relations and personnel administration in business or psychology.

Schools of business also were emerging and growing at the same time. They were viewed as professional schools drawing selected concerns of different disciplines for specialized professional education—corporate finance from economics, operations from industrial engineering—as well as developing special applied fields such as marketing and accounting. Although some schools likewise included personnel administration, many academics associated with IR resisted incorporation within the business curriculum, arguing that IR was more than PA and that IR itself embodied a profession, one that could be compromised by inclusion within the business curriculum. In consequence, various universities established separate schools of IR (e.g., Cornell University), whereas others established separate IR degrees administered by an IR faculty wherever they were located administratively (Kaufman, 1999). This resulted in a hodgepodge of foci for IR education, sometimes viewed as a management function and to be integrated with other management functions and sometimes viewed in isolation from various management functions.

Schools of business or management had emerged somewhat before the field of IR and grew substantially after 1950. Like IR, schools of management offered collections of applied knowledge from different disciplines (finance, accounting, marketing, operations). These collections were useful in the management of organizations, but they were not as integrated around issues as in IR. They were united only in that they addressed issues in the management of business organizations. Further, departments within the schools represented different disciplinary interests that were relatively independent of each other, however, and did not develop the interdisciplinary research and teaching efforts of IR. And each of these, interestingly, was related to a specific function and career within business organizations (e.g., finance, marketing, operations, accounting). The only thing uniting the disciplines and functions was their focus on the enterprise.

Business and management education was given a jolt in the early 1960s with the growth of the MBA degree and reports on business education (Gordon & Howell, 1959). These reports critically reviewed business management education and outlined recommended improvements, particularly in the MBA programs. One of these recommendations called for the introduction of the behavioral sciences into the curriculum. This provided the spark for the development of what today is commonly termed organizational behavior (OB). Recruits from the disciplines of psychology and sociology were brought into schools of business and management and developed courses in leadership, teamwork, communications, negotiation, and related subjects. Interestingly, these courses of study were viewed as related to skills every manager should possess and were not restricted to specific functions or careers within business organizations. This education began confusing education in IR, particularly HRM, within schools of business and management.

Management careers in industrial relations in 1960 were not as well developed or recognized as were careers in other management functions. Typically they were split between responsibilities for labor relations and responsibilities for personnel administration. Lacking any tradition of education for careers in human resources or personnel administration, these responsibilities often were assigned to general managers drawn from other functional careers. There was a professional association, the American Society of Personnel Administration, but, as implied in the title, it was often viewed as a body of "administrators" rather than a body of "managers." There was no single, well-accepted body of knowledge associated with the professional association.

Field of Human Resource Management

The field of HRM today as conceptualized in research, education, and practice differs notably from the historic antecedents of IR and PA. In many respects it has merged interests of labor economics, industrial psychology, human relations, and organization theory, with a particular focus on the management of organizations. Michael Beer and associates (Beer, Spector, Lawrence, Mills, & Walton, 1984) provided a particularly integrative conceptualization of HRM today. They cast the practice of HRM as managing the full utilization of human resources in the productive functions of an organization and the integrated management of everything dealing with human resources in a corporate context (Figure 2.1). HRM encompasses (1) the effective design of organizations, work systems, and tasks into roles for employees, individually and in teams; (2) managing human resource

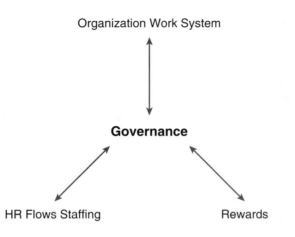

Organization Work System

Governance

HR Flows Staffing   Rewards

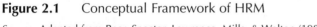

Figure 2.1   Conceptual Framework of HRM

Source: Adapted from Beer, Spector, Lawrence, Mills, & Walton (1984).

flows into and out of the organization, interacting with the labor market in the recruitment, later development, and allocation of employees to assignments; (3) the motivation and reward of employees for task performance; and (4) the governance and influence system of the organization, coordinating and negotiating with unions and professional associations of employees, and monitoring compliance with social policies relating to employment, compensation, safety, and the like. Such a conceptual framework provides for the integration of disciplines of economics, psychology, sociology, human relations, law, organization science, and operations in the utilization of human resources in a productive enterprise.

This conceptual framework casts HRM as an integrated management function, combining the management of human resources with other management functions such as finance, marketing, and operations. It is no longer a set of interacting practices as evolved in IR with various different and relatively independent disciplines focused on specific elements of HRM such as staffing, collective bargaining, training, and compensation. Rather, it provides a basis for integrating the entire scope of HRM in the strategic design and management of organizations. In terms of professional practice, this framework calls for the integration of efforts represented by segmented professional efforts such as the American Society for Training and Development, the American Compensation Association (now WorldatWork), the Human Resource Planning Society, and the Organization Development Network within some larger professional framework such as the Society for Human Resource Management. Each subprofession might continue a specific and limited focus, but it would be part of a larger, more integrated functional framework.

Emergence of HR Education

The introduction of OB into business and management curricula in the 1960s confused whatever education was offered in IR. Knowledge of labor markets, labor legislation, and collective bargaining was not viewed as essential for business management. And "personnel administration" was viewed as a semiclerical set of duties monitoring managerial actions. Over time the term "Human Resource Management" evolved to encompass the components of IR that applied in organization management, and ASPA changed its name to the Society of Human Resource Management. But what distinguished HR from OB?

In some schools HRM was clearly designed as a function of management equivalent to finance, marketing, and operations and was linked to specific careers in business management. MBA students might select HR as a field of concentration. OB, on the other hand, was focused on the knowledge and skills that every manager should possess, such as accounting, economics, and statistics, but not identifiable functions of management such as finance, marketing, and operations. In other schools OB and HRM were combined, with no clear distinction between them. HRM was conceptualized and taught as something every manager should know and practice in the managing of subordinate employees and focused more on individual managers in their spheres of operation than on the HRM effort of the total enterprise. In the former, HRM continued as an interdisciplinary field focused on specific problems and issues such as organization design, compensation design, staffing and selection, training and development, and workforce governance. In the latter, the distinctions among disciplines were merged and the focus was on the skills every manager should possess.

Education in HRM today thus takes various forms: (1) education in the broad field of traditional IR encompassing labor markets, collective bargaining, labor legislation, and PA where IR is viewed as a specialized field bringing together various disciplines to focus on specific issues and problems and where IR is viewed as a profession independent of the employing institution (business, government, or social agency); (2) education in HRM as a functional field of specialization in the management of organizations; and (3) education in the behavioral sciences for every manager of organizations, a combination of HRM and OB. Clearly the education provided in HRM today varies with its intended application. Education in HRM today thus appears to take one of three different forms (Figure 2.2).

1. Education in HRM within the IR model focuses on the management of human resources within the enterprise, as does education in HRM viewed as a specific function of enterprise management. However, it is cast within the broader model of IR and relates more to broader market and social concepts than to other functional fields of management. It implicitly assumes that the practice of HRM requires broad professional development and is

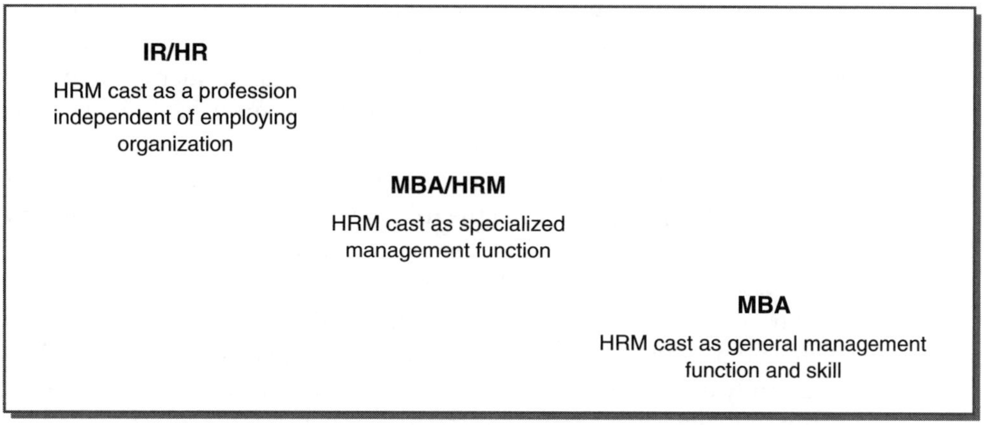

IR/HR

HRM cast as a profession
independent of employing
organization

MBA/HRM

HRM cast as specialized
management function

MBA

HRM cast as general management
function and skill

Figure 2.2   Models of Education in HRM

independent of the institutional setting (e.g., corporation, law practice, social agency). This education typically is found in academic units separate and differentiated from schools of business and management.

2. A second model is common within schools of management. It focuses on the practice of HRM within specific employing organizations and assumes a need to know how it relates to and affects other management functions such as finance, marketing, and operations. HRM is cast as a functional field within employing agencies, one requiring specialized education and development, but integrated with related functions of management.

3. The third model casts HRM as part of the behavioral sciences every manager should apply in the managing of subordinate employees and concentrates more on individual managers in their spheres of operation than on the HRM effort for the total enterprise.

It appears that part of the concern for the teaching of HRM stems from these different models of HRM and the intended applications of HRM knowledge. Which is the most appropriate focus for HRM education, particularly HRM education within schools of management?

HR Education in Schools of Management

The distinction sketched above between the two models of HRM education in schools of management relates critically to the role of HRM education in the curriculum of business or management schools. A common design of the MBA curriculum in such schools identifies some common core of knowledge every graduate should possess and specifies courses for that purpose. Students then concentrate their studies in at least one of several functional fields anchored in the core, which requires completion of specified courses of study. Typically, schools of management specify a core of knowledge to be obtained prior to functional specialization. They may also specify a core of skills required of every manager, such as communication, teamwork, and leadership, but not leading to a specialized functional education. Determining the role of HRM in management education can be viewed in the same manner, particularly at the MBA level. Is HRM to be cast as a core skill for all managers (e.g., leadership) or as core education as a base for functional specialization? If it is a core skill, each student would complete study in a general course in HRM, possibly combined with study of organizational behavior and management. If it is a core education for subsequent HRM functional specialization, each student would complete an introductory core course in HRM, independent of OB, providing a base for subsequent study of specialized topics (reward and compensation, staffing and selection, organization design, etc.) to complete a functional specialization.

Choice between these two alternatives raises the question of the role of HRM in organizations. Should HRM play a specialized role in the management of organizations or be distributed as a general role for all managers? Just as in the case of financial management, while recognizing that all managers must manage financial budgets, it is accepted that there is a separate, specialized role of financial management for the entire organization. If there is to be an overriding HRM program for the organization, then it appears obvious to me that HRM education must be cast as a special functional field of management rather than as a responsibility delegated and decentralized among all managers. It must be clearly differentiated from OB and from organizational management (OM), which are viewed as general knowledge and skills for all managers. Calls today for a strategic role for HRM in organizations clearly imply that there should be a clearly designated role for HRM in the organization, one that shapes the direction and contribution of HRM to the entire strategic endeavor and determines policies then to be applied by all managers in the organization. There must be a standard framework for HRM rather than a collection of the HRM practices of assorted general managers. To me, this provides the logic and structure of an HRM component in MBA core education and a specialized functional specialization in the MBA program.

Confusion in HRM Education

As noted above, one element in the confusion of foci in the design of HRM education in schools of management has been the competition among differing interests and disciplines in the design of HRM educational programs. In the early days of IR when research into applied issues was the predominant concern, competition among the disciplines of labor economics, psychology, and human relations was welcome. The competing views and hypotheses enriched research efforts and contributed to a better understanding of problems and concerns. To be sure, there was certain competition among the disciplines in the allocation of faculty positions and resources, but there was a recognition that contribution of all related disciplines was helpful to research efforts.

This framework began to change with the emergence of IR/HRM educational programs, particularly those within schools of management. Education, rather than research, became the raison d'être for the associated bodies of faculty. Faculty members understandably became more concerned with building empires of faculty and courses supportive of their own interests than with building bodies of competing interests and viewpoints for enriched research efforts. The emerging contradictions of viewpoints became more apparent beginning in the 1960s with the introduction of behavioralist approaches to the management curriculum. The behavioralist approaches, with their relatively micro foci, implicitly competed with the more analytical and macro foci of the more traditional IR/HRM approach.

Faculty members inevitably sought to enhance their roles in the educational body by creating courses of study utilizing their approach and by recruiting like-minded faculty for teaching them. As I am certain has occurred in other interdisciplinary bodies, this resulted in political competition for the allocation of resources. This competition appeared most obvious in the design of the core curriculum and overall orientation of the educational program. Most faculty prefer teaching courses in their own specialized research interests, courses advanced beyond the core program of management education, to interested students rather than teaching core courses to often uninterested and unwilling students. Yet these interested students would not be available unless turned on and recruited from the core course of study. This obviously creates competition in the design of the core curriculum and the design and teaching of core courses. Hence the political competition between faculty with micro-behavioral interests and faculty with macro-analytical interests.

In consequence, there are many different programs in education in schools of management that are offered under the label HRM. Perhaps the ultimate test will emerge on the basis of the placement and career experiences of MBA graduates. Just as MBA students traditionally have flocked to the finance concentration because of ease of placement with high salaries and advancement opportunities, they may well differentiate between the micro-behavioral and macro-analytical approaches to HRM on the basis of the same considerations. It appears in recent years that the micro-behavioral emphasis relates more to management consulting and general management placement and the macro-analytical emphasis relates more to professional HRM placement in organizations. Market tests of the future may well shape the ultimate preferred form of HRM education.

Viewed in this context, the question about the future role of HRM education in schools of management converts to a question about the future role of HRM in employing organizations. What is the likely role of HRM in the future in employing organizations? Is HRM to play a major functional role in employing organizations, strategically managing the contribution of human resources within the overall strategy of the organization (see Bates, 2002), or is HRM to be a skill that every general manager uses in the supervision of immediate subordinates (see Cohen, 2002)? The increasing recognition of the potential strategic contribution of the human capital resources of the organization would argue for a major functional role for HRM. The human resource potential of the organization must be viewed and managed as a whole to complement the other major resources of the organization. This is quite contrary to the conceptualization of HRM delegated to every individual manager. Individual managers, to be sure, must activate and conduct the overall HR strategy in the supervision of subordinates, but the sum of their efforts is unlikely to realize some overall strategic effort without a macro-structure of policies.

Thus, it appears to me that the potential contribution of HRM would be maximized with HRM cast as a major functional responsibility in organizations, a role consistent with the macro-analytical model of HRM education sketched above. Those engaged in HRM education might well wait for a market test of the survival of the alternative models of HRM education. I would recommend, however, that they engage in that market test, developing and promoting the macro-analytical model, demonstrating through the performance and contributions of graduates the potential contribution of HRM as a major strategic component of organization management. Let us form a closer alliance with the HRM profession to develop and realize the full potential contribution of HRM in the managing of organizations.

References

Bates, S. (2002). Facing the future. *HR Magazine, 47*(7), 26–32.

Beer, M., Spector, B., Lawrence, P. R., Mills, D., & Walton, R. (1984). *Managing human assets.* New York: Free Press.

Cohen, D. J. (2002). Human resources training: A key to enterprise success. *Perspectives on Work, 6*(1), 37–38.

Commons, J. (1921). *Industrial government.* New York: Macmillan.

Doeringer, P. (1967). Determinants of the structure of industrial type internal labor markets. *Industrial and Labor Relations Review, 20,* 206–220.

Dulebohn, J., Ferris, G., & Stodd, J. (1995). The history and evolution of human resource management. In G. Ferris, S. Rosen, & D. Barnum (Eds.), *Handbook of human resource management* (pp. 18–41). New York: Blackwell.

Dunlop, J. (1957). The task of contemporary wage theory. In G. Taylor & F. Pierson (Eds.), *New concepts in wage determination* (pp. 127–139). New York: McGraw-Hill.

Gordon, R., & Howell, J. (1959). *Higher education for business.* New York: Columbia University Press.

Heneman, H. (1969). Toward a general conceptual system of industrial relations: How do we get there? In *The role of industrial relations centers, proceedings of a regional meeting of the International Industrial Relations Association* (pp. 49–58). Madison, WI: IRRA.

Kaufman, B. (1993). *The origins and evolution of the field of industrial relations in the United States.* Ithaca, NY: ILR Press.

Kaufman, B. (1999). The evolution and current status of university HR programs. *Human Resource Management, 38*(2), 103–110.

Lazear, E. (1981). Agency, earnings profiles, productivity, and hours restrictions. *American Economic Review, 71,* 606–620.

Lazear, E. (1998). *Personnel economics for managers.* New York: Wiley.

Lazear, E. (1999). Personnel economics: Past lessons and future directions. *Journal of Labor Economics, 17,* 199–236.

Mayo, E. (1930). *A new approach to industrial relations.* Cambridge, MA: Harvard Business School Press.

Paterson, D., & Yoder, D. (1955). *Industrial relations research: Ten years of progress.* Minneapolis: University of Minnesota Press.

Roethlisberger, F., & Dickson, W. (1939). *Management and the worker.* Cambridge, MA: Harvard University Press.

Slichter, S. (1919). The management of labor. *Journal of Political Economy, 27,* 813–839.

Somers, G. (1969). *Essays in industrial relations theory.* Ames: Iowa State University Press.

Taylor, F. (1895). A piece rate system, being a step toward partial solution of the labor problem. *Transactions, 16,* 856–883.

Tead, O., & Metcalf, H. (1920). *Personnel administration.* New York: McGraw-Hill.

Yoder, D. (1938). *Personnel and labor relations.* Englewood Cliffs, NJ: Prentice Hall.

SECTION 2

HR Master's Programs in Industrial Relations and in Industrial and Organizational Psychology

Although HR programs exist in business schools, public administration departments, adult education departments, and virtually any department that wishes to call itself HR and does not encounter resistance from other departments in the university, two of the most recognized and strongest academic programs with HR content are in industrial relations (IR; housed within or outside business schools) and in industrial and organizational psychology (I/O; housed within psychology departments). These two programs focus primarily on Master's and PhD level education. Chapters 3 and 4 introduce the reader to MA and MS educational programs in HR within IR and I/O psychology. Familiarity with each type of program will provide insights into the similarities and differences between HRM graduates from IR programs and those from I/O psychology programs. As well, familiarity with these two programs will enable the reader to evaluate HRM graduate programs in business schools.

In Chapter 3, Fossum focuses on HR Master's programs in industrial relations. He starts his chapter by stating, "If IR Master's programs did not currently exist, in today's environment it's unlikely that one would be invented." Noting that understanding of the current state of IR Master's programs entails tracing the development of the IR field, his chapter first identifies the events, conditions, and actors that were instrumental for the development of IR and HRM programs. He then addresses the changing emphasis in the field and the current state of IR programs. Among Fossum's conclusions is the following: "Although HRM content of IR programs has increased, I think it's unlikely that IR programs will morph into HRM programs." He gives six reasons for this statement.

In Chapter 4, Klein, DeRouin, Salas, and Stagl focus on HR Master's I/O programs in psychology departments. They examine the extent to which graduate training in I/O prepares professionals to work in the field of HR. Through select interviews with HR professionals and a review of relevant literature on HR and I/O education, the authors develop five themes describing the disconnects between what is taught in, and what is desired from, I/O Master's-level programs in HR. Before they present their five themes, they briefly discuss training, education, and career opportunities for Master's-level I/O psychologists.

The Origins, Development, and Current State of Professional Master's Programs in Industrial Relations

3

John A. Fossum

Professional Master's degrees in industrial relations (IR) have been offered for over 60 years. As a field of inquiry and problem-solving, IR has been around for over 100 years. Like the issues it studies, the IR field is in constant ferment, with changing boundaries, new directions, issues emerging or becoming dormant, driven and defined by the academics and practitioners who study employment or implement new solutions to achieve their organizations' goals.

If IR Master's programs did not currently exist, in today's environment it's unlikely that one would be invented. The corporatist approach to employment that was advocated by the academics who founded the programs no longer exists. This approach emphasized a tripartite understanding of employment involving employers, employees and their representatives, and public policy. It emphasized the institutional setting that governs employment. Now, new Master's programs focusing on employment issues and problems would emphasize either human resource

AUTHOR'S NOTE: I thank John Budd for his helpful comments on an earlier version of this manuscript.

management (HRM) within employers or labor studies (LS) for union advocacy. Both are distinctly more micro-oriented than IR. If a Master's program continues to include industrial or labor relations in its degree title, it indicates that its faculty and constituent groups continue to support an understanding of the tripartite nature of employment for graduates to perform well in fulfilling demanding employment responsibilities. The market test of whether this approach is still valid is whether recruiters prefer to hire graduates from these programs.

In order to understand the current state of professional IR Master's programs, it is necessary to trace the development of the IR field, particularly during the periods in which professional Master's programs were initiated. It is also important to differentiate between the ways in which universities institutionalized the IR field and when and where degree programs were begun and internally located.

The development and maintenance of these programs is a function of their geographic location; their internal and external champions; the importance and quality of the research they produce; and their ability to construct, modify, and deliver a curriculum that is seen by students and employers as a better alternative for meeting their needs for developing or utilizing human capital than non-IR programs.

This chapter identifies the events, conditions, and actors that were instrumental for the development of IR Master's programs, the differences between approaches to professional development in IR and HRM programs, the changing emphasis in the field over time in relation to changes in the overall employment environment, and the current state of IR programs.

Universities' Role in the Specialization and Application of Knowledge

The modern Western research university is an evolutionary product of almost 1,000 years. From its initial roots in philosophy, theology, and history, new lines of inquiry and specialization were developed as the depth of knowledge increased and new methods were developed.

The development of economic theory in the 18th century (Smith, 1776/1976) was the genesis of the social science disciplines. As economics developed, the classical school elaborated the primary theoretical framework that underlies modern economics, i.e., the assumption that individuals make rational decisions among alternatives to maximize their utility, and that the use of resources in production will be a function of their relative costs and the value that they add. An institutional school also developed explaining how the various actors in an economy interact and how regulation can help markets overcome imperfections in information.

The systematic study of human behavior began in the 19th century. Beside observing and classifying behavior and its consequences, instruments were developed to measure latent traits. Relationships between these measures and actual behaviors enabled the estimation of construct- and criterion-related validity for the first time. With the mobilization that followed the U.S. entry into World War I, measures developed by psychologists were applied to more accurately classify what would be the optimal assignments for new recruits given the numbers of positions in various military jobs that were necessary to operate an armed force. Following the successful application of testing in World War I to improve performance, its use was extended more widely in employment. As a result, industrial psychology became a permanent applied branch of the broader discipline of psychology. Over time, advances in basic theory, measurement, and areas of behavioral inquiry have been added to the applied repertoire of industrial psychology as they have relevance.

While industrial psychology was developing, the field of sociology emerged. The study of organizations, the stratification of society and mobility within it, and the accumulation and exercise of power in hierarchical relationships were focuses of theory development and research.

These three disciplines—economics, psychology, and sociology—were the parents of the IR field. Presently, in most universities all three of these disciplines are usually located in a college of liberal arts or social sciences. But before the 1960s, many economics departments were housed in business schools, because the business schools had evolved from increasingly successful applications of economics to business problems.

THE DEVELOPMENT AND GROWTH OF PUBLIC HIGHER EDUCATION IN THE U.S.

Even before the American Revolution, private colleges had been established by religious bodies whose primary interest was the training of theologians and pastors. As the nation expanded and technology became more complex, an increasing demand emerged for higher education and the development of applied fields.

As the social science disciplines were being created by academics in Western universities, a watershed event took place that quickly affected the breadth and scope of public higher education in the U.S. In 1862, the Morrill Act was passed to foster the development of public state universities to provide broadly accessible and low-cost education in agriculture, engineering, classical liberal arts, and other applied fields. The act designated tracts of public land in each state from which the proceeds from their sale would pay for the establishment and support of public universities. The land-grant universities devoted relatively more resources to applied fields than the existing private universities, particularly in their development of agriculture and engineering degree programs and outreach activities.

The Development and Increasing Prevalence and Magnitude of Labor Problems in the U.S.

In the last three decades of the 19th century, vast entrepreneurial empires in natural resources, railroads, steel, and other basic industries were established. Owners of successful firms in these industries became incredibly rich. At the same time, employment conditions in mines, railway construction, steel, and textiles were very onerous. A ready supply of unskilled and unsophisticated labor was available from the increasing flow of immigrants from Europe. There were no laws and regulations to protect workers, and their political and economic bargaining power was low.

Unions began to develop after the Civil War, with the earliest unions being more interested in politics than collective bargaining. But in 1883, a group of skilled worker unions, with pragmatic goals to improve the wages and employment conditions of their members through collective bargaining, banded together to form the American Federation of Labor (AFL).

Between about 1880 and 1915, especially in Pennsylvania, Idaho, and Colorado, radical unions and both private and public militias engaged in increasingly escalating conflict. The economic power of miners was difficult to sustain during strikes because in most cases they were required to live in employer-provided housing in remote mining towns, and industrial action inevitably led to threats of eviction unless tenants went back to work.

In manufacturing, increasing capital intensity made it more important for employers to avoid work stoppages because opportunity costs would increase continuously during a strike. Employers used Pinkerton detectives, private armies, and court injunctions to quash any incipient union activity, and were largely successful outside of the railroad industry.

Then in 1913, Henry Ford revolutionized manufacturing by introducing the assembly line. "Fordism" rapidly deskilled manufacturing jobs and reduced production costs, allowing automobiles to be priced within the means of the mass market. Although Ford made news by implementing the $5 daily wage—substantially above competition—it was not an altruistic action, but rather a strategy to ensure a steady stream of applicants, reduce worker power, and enable the implementation of draconian internal discipline.

THE LUDLOW MASSACRE AND ITS PROGENY

In 1914, the tragic results of another episode in the recurring armed skirmishes between employers and employees in the mining industries shocked the nation and pricked the conscience of a prominent capitalist, John D. Rockefeller. Rockefeller owned the Colorado Fuel and Iron Company located in southeastern Colorado. Miners struck the company in 1913. As usual, an escalating spiral of violence ensued. Miners established a large tent colony in Ludlow where they lived with their families. In April 1914, Colorado national guardsmen rode into the camp. The miners grabbed their guns and took to the hills to divert the militia and to defend themselves. Some of the militia members pursued the miners while others strafed the camp with machine guns and later burned the tents and furnishings, indiscriminately killing hundreds in the process. Public outrage followed, a great deal directed personally at Rockefeller for his perceived hypocrisy for extolling Christian religious beliefs while tacitly permitting violent repressive tactics. As time went on, the Rockefeller Foundation and Clarence Hicks, a Rockefeller industrial relations executive, were instrumental in establishing employer organizations and funding university efforts to reduce and peacefully deal with industrial conflict.

Post–World War I: The Developing Study and Practice of Industrial Relations

Academics had been increasingly interested in employment problems from the advent of the 20th century. Kaufman (1993) has extensively examined the development of the IR field and notes that in its early stages the field was highly inclusive in terms of the types of problems to study and the disciplines that could contribute to solving problems and developing knowledge (Social Science Research Council, 1928). Early IR research units were established at Princeton and Pennsylvania, the former as an adjunct to the economics department, the latter as a unit within the Wharton School of business.

Kaufman (1993) identified two predominant developing approaches to IR during the 1920s, which he labeled the personnel management (PM) approach and the institutional labor economics (ILE) approach. The PM school originated among practitioners and was concerned with efficiency issues. The approach emphasized consistency in practice and attention to employee motivation and work design (Taylor, 1911). The ILE school consisted primarily of labor economists who argued that employers would not be able to implement progressive practices unless labor problems were ameliorated at the industry and economy levels. Thus, institutions and regulations needed to be developed in order for PM to have an additive effect.

Three employer-sponsored organizations were founded: the National Industrial Conference Board (NICB) in 1916, the American Management Association (AMA) in 1923, and Industrial Relations Counselors (IRC) in 1926 (Kaufman, 2003). These three completed research studies, provided training on employment issues for supervisors and managers, published practitioner-oriented books and manuals, provided consulting services on employment issues (particularly relating to unions), and basically adopted a PM approach to IR. On the academic front, in addition to Princeton and Wharton, Clarence Hicks helped to establish IR research units at Stanford, Michigan, MIT, and Cal Tech (Hicks, 1941). Of these, none is a land-grant university and only one is public.

EVOLVING INDUSTRIAL RELATIONS PROBLEMS FOLLOWING WORLD WAR I

During World War I, employees experienced a period of rising wages and increased interests in unionization. But several forces dampened the advance of unionization: the AFL's lack of interest in organizing the unskilled industrial workforce, a continuing surplus of unskilled immigrant laborers that permitted the implementation of the "drive system" (under which workers essentially owed their jobs to strict obedience to their supervisors who, in turn, were continually pressured to increase productivity), the lack of institutions guaranteeing the rights of employees to organize and bargain, and the development and implementation of welfare capitalism by some large employers (see Jacoby, 1997). The PM school's advocacy of increasing attention to moral values and worker welfare seemed to be gaining traction among larger employers with skilled workforces.

But the deepening economic disaster of the Great Depression brought the ILE school to the ascendancy. Its argument that the loci of employment problems were primarily at the industry and total economy levels seemed to be validated by the downward spiral of wages and employment practices as employers tried to cope with the continually worsening economic situation.

The 1930s saw the largest number of employment laws and regulations enacted during any single period in the U.S. These laws were aimed at enhancing income security and the ability to unionize. For the first time, unskilled employees had guaranteed rights to organize and a new set of labor unions under the Congress of Industrial Organizations (CIO) umbrella that immediately went to work to secure them.

The Norris-LaGuardia Act prohibited federal courts from enjoining a set of union activities that were defined to be, per se, legal. The Wagner Act designated collective bargaining as the preferred method for resolving industrial conflict and provided mechanisms for determining whether a majority of employees in an enterprise favored unionization. It created the National Labor Relations Board to resolve conflicts over representation and to prohibit employers from intimidating or threatening employees in their exercise of rights to organize and collectively bargain.

During the 1920s and 1930s, there were a few employers who introduced some degree of employee representation through company unions or employee committees (Jacoby, 1989). Others improved economic benefits and job security through higher-than-market wages, profit-sharing plans, the introduction of pension plans, and the development of internal labor markets. However, with the passage of the Wagner Act, company-sponsored unions and other similar representation plans were prohibited. The "exclusive representation" requirements in the Wagner Act guaranteed unions the rights to represent all employees in a bargaining unit if it won an election, but left employees without a guaranteed voice if it lost, thus encouraging an adversarial relationship between employers and unions in a "winner-take-all" contest. For the most part, conflict between employers, employees, and their unions reescalated during the 1930s. How the conflict would ultimately have been decided will never be known because World War II intervened.

Very quickly, employment in America underwent radical changes. Unemployment disappeared as millions of men entered military service. Manufacturing was retooled to support the war effort, aggregate demand rose quickly, and shortages of materials developed. Prices and wages rapidly increased. Rationing, wage and price controls, and no-strike regulations were quickly implemented. Women were rapidly recruited into the workforce, with many quickly learning to perform jobs that were previously exclusively reserved for men. Because wages were controlled, the only way that many employers could attract employees in a tight labor market was to develop and implement a variety of benefit programs. In unionized situations a variety of benefits such as pensions, vacations, and health insurance were negotiated. Because unions were forbidden to strike during the war, dispute resolution methods to deal with conflicts were developed. Many young academics from the social sciences were recruited to work in the War Labor Board. Arbitration was quickly expanded to cover intracontract disputes within labor agreements as well as its previous use for other types of contract disputes. The way in which employment problems were dealt with was consistent with the approach of the ILE school.

Even though there was substantial regulation, strong public support of the war effort, and no-strike requirements, industrial tension grew and several major strikes took place in defiance of the requirements. It was quite likely that the end of the war and the return to a peacetime economy would simply shift the focus of the conflict from the Axis powers to domestic employers and unions.

Postwar Industrial Relations and the Academy

Nineteen forty-six witnessed the greatest incidence of strikes America has ever experienced. Between August 1945 (when World War II finally ended in the Pacific) and August 1946, there were over 4,600 strikes involving almost 5 million workers who were idled for nearly 120 million workdays (approximately 1.62% of all available workdays in the economy). It was clear that chaos would ensue unless additional institutions and rules were created to deal with industrial conflict. The sophistication of the parties—both labor and management—would also have to quickly increase. Congress passed the Taft-Hartley amendments to the Wagner Act establishing symmetrical responsibilities for both labor and management by defining a set of union unfair labor practices to complement those already in place that regulated employer conduct, creating the Federal Mediation and Conciliation Service to provide assistance to deadlocked negotiators in reaching agreements, and providing mechanisms for the president to temporarily stop strikes and engage settlement procedures in situations where the security of the nation was threatened.

These changes came less than a dozen years after the Wagner Act. Both employers and unions had yet to develop substantial experience with negotiations and conflict resolution. But a cadre of young academics had gained experience and expertise in arbitrating disputes for the War Labor Board. When they returned to their universities following the war, they began to put in place programs to train practitioners, educate students, and conduct research in the collective bargaining process. Kaufman (1993) noted that within three years of the end of World War II new industrial relations units were started at Cornell (statutory college), Chicago, Minnesota, California-Berkeley, Yale, Illinois, Rutgers, Wisconsin, New York University, and Hawaii. Of these, seven were public and three were private, contrary to the previous mix of one public and six private. Additionally, several Catholic schools started programs, including Rockhurst, Loyola (Chicago), Manhattan, Seton Hall, and St. Joseph's (Philadelphia).

Employment had become substantially more complicated in the 20 years between 1928 and 1948. Employers now needed to comply with a host of regulations that didn't previously exist. Rapid and thorough unionization in basic industries spelled the end of the drive system's effectiveness. Managers and specialists with IR expertise were increasingly in demand. Universities that had begun IR programs responded to this demand by conducting and publishing research on industrial conflict and its resolution, developing curricula to be taught at the undergraduate and graduate levels, and providing practitioner-oriented training to employers and union representatives to better enable them to successfully negotiate and administer labor agreements.

ESTABLISHING THE INDUSTRIAL RELATIONS RESEARCH ASSOCIATION

As individual universities developed their specific programs, faculty members from several programs organized the Industrial Relations Research Association (IRRA) in 1947 to promote and disseminate applied research on collective bargaining and other employment issues. The IRRA strongly promoted the education of practitioners. It developed and sponsored local chapters in many locations across the U.S. and Canada and actively recruited practitioners from both employers and organized labor to join the organization as full members.

The IRRA's founders represented several social science disciplines, primarily economics, sociology, and political science, but its primary focus and its leadership came from the ILE school. It was several years after its founding before it was led for a year by someone with a strong connection with the PM school, Dale Yoder.

Several of the presidents of the IRRA during its first 20 years later became highly influential university leaders or public policy makers. Clark Kerr (1954) was the first president of the University of California system. John Dunlop (1960) was secretary of labor during part of Gerald Ford's term as president. Edwin Young (1965) served several years as the president of the University of Wisconsin system. George Shultz (1968) was first secretary of labor and later secretary of state in the Reagan administration. Ray Marshall (1977) was secretary of labor during the Carter administration. There is probably no other association of academics that has had such a large number of significant appointed public policy positions relative to its size.

THE LOCATION OF INDUSTRIAL RELATIONS IN THE UNIVERSITY STRUCTURE

Because IR is a multidisciplinary applied field, it had no clearly identifiable home or boundary as a discipline would. The organizational placement, structure, and programs that developed in each university were largely the result of the location of the disciplinary homes or financially responsible units to which the associated faculty were or had been permanently assigned. In addition, the activities of IR units varied across universities. The range of activities that might be undertaken by these units generally included research, degree programs in IR, and outreach activities to meet labor or employer needs.

The programs begun before World War II concentrated on applied research to address employment problems. Initially, many programs were attached to economics departments. Over time as the institutional labor economists that founded the programs retired, they were replaced by neoclassical labor economists who did not share the same problem-solving orientation toward research and opposed the extension of regulation as the most salient remedy for employment problems. The same occurred with jointly appointed faculty from other social science disciplines. As they retired or moved elsewhere, they were frequently not replaced by faculty members who had the same interests because the home departments made decisions that would support current disciplinary emphases or innovative new areas. Thus, programs that had not developed their own schools, institutes, or departments were increasingly at risk.

Following World War II, undergraduate IR majors and Master's degree programs were developed by industrial relations units in several universities with support from the Rockefeller Foundation, particularly in the public and private universities that initiated work in the field during that period. There were large differences across universities in the institutional arrangements surrounding these programs. At Cornell, a New York state statutory school was created within the mostly endowed university (Cornell, having been designated the land-grant university for the State of New York, also housed its agriculture school and some other applied units). At Illinois an Institute of Labor and Industrial Relations was created as a free-standing unit. At Wisconsin an Industrial Relations Research Institute was developed that reported to the dean of the College of Liberal Arts and was staffed by jointly appointed faculty from several disciplines across the colleges of business, liberal arts, and law. Rutgers established the Institute of Management and Labor Relations. California-Berkeley established an Institute of Industrial Relations, which had a primarily research and outreach charter. Minnesota's Industrial Relations Center was housed in the business school.

Over time, free-standing programs that offered degrees were more likely to survive because they were not subject to changes in a college's strategy and had built a growing alumni constituency. They do not face a situation in which a dean can reallocate faculty lines between departments and in which their yearly budgets are largely determined outside of their units. The leaders of most of the IR institutes and degree programs were ILE faculty.

Many of the graduate programs that are in operation today were initiated during the late 1940s and 1950s. From the end of the war through the mid-1950s, the unionized workforce grew in both absolute and relative size until somewhat more than one-third of U.S. employees belonged to or were represented by a labor union. From the late 1940s through the end of the 1960s, unionized employment relations followed a corporatist approach in which unions, employers, and the state jointly determined economic outcomes. Basically, the bargain permitted wages to increase at the same rate as productivity grew. Under this regime, inflation was modest and workers achieved real wage gains. At the same time, employers made reasonable profits but did not maximize profits. Practices initiated among unionized employers quickly spread to nonunion employers so there was increasing uniformity in employment conditions. Employment costs had essentially been taken out of competition. Thus, managers and specialists involved with employment needed expertise in how to operate the system within a set of institutionalized rules.

Most of the developing programs emphasized subjects of primary interest to the ILE school, such as collective bargaining, labor market institutions and regulation, contract administration, mediation and arbitration, and employment security programs. Subjects from the PM school were usually in the minority, but most often emphasized personnel administration and classical management and organization theory. Whereas both the

ILE and PM schools initially forwarded an inclusive perspective regarding issues and methods of research that would be included in IR, Kaufman (1993) noted that both went their own ways, with the ILE school, in particular, equating IR with employment problems in unionized environments, and the PM school adopting an approach that eventually evolved toward the present-day HRM approach.

The Evolution of IR Graduate Degree Programs Over the Past 30 Years

By 1974, there were 19 programs offering Master's degrees in industrial relations (Herman, 1974). Table 3.1 displays the names of the schools. Of these, 15 are public comprehensive universities. The program at Cornell is located in a New York state statutory school. Three are private, and of those, two are Catholic. Including Cornell, seven are in land-grant institutions. Five are located west of the Mississippi River.

Table 3.1   U.S. Graduate Programs in Industrial Relations in 1974

Alabama, University of	Michigan State University
American University	Minnesota, University of
Chicago, University of	North Texas State University
Cincinnati, University of	Rutgers University
Colorado, University of	St. Francis College
Cornell University	Oregon, University of
Illinois, University of (Champaign-Urbana)	Temple University
Iowa State University	Utah, University of
Loyola University (Chicago)	Wisconsin, University of (Madison)
Massachusetts, University of	

Source: Adapted from Herman, 1974.

Moving forward a decade to 1984, there were 25 Master's programs, as shown in Table 3.2. Eight of the programs that were offered in 1974 were not in existence in 1984 (Alabama, American, Chicago, Colorado, Massachusetts, North Texas State, Oregon, and Utah). Fourteen new programs had been created (Cleveland State, Georgia State, Indiana University of Pennsylvania [IUP], Kansas, New Haven, New York Institute of Technology [NYIT], Ohio State, Pace, Purdue, South Carolina, Wayne State, West Virginia College of Graduate Studies, West Virginia University, and Winthrop College). Of these 25, 20 are public. Of the 20 public programs, 10 are located at land-grant universities. Only Iowa State and Kansas are west of the Mississippi River. Thus, the public-private, land

Table 3.2   U.S. Graduate Programs in Industrial Relations in 1984

Cincinnati, University of	Ohio State University
Cleveland State University	Pace University
Cornell University	Purdue University
Georgia State University	Rutgers University
Illinois, University of (Champaign-Urbana)	St. Francis College
Indiana University of Pennsylvania	South Carolina, University of
Iowa State University	Temple University
Kansas, University of	Wayne State University
Loyola University (Chicago)	West Virginia College of Graduate Studies
Michigan State University	West Virginia University
Minnesota, University of	Winthrop College
New Haven, University of	Wisconsin, University of (Madison)
New York Institute of Technology	

Source: Adapted from Herman, 1984.

grant-non land grant mix was essentially unchanged from 1974, but the mix was substantially more eastern.

In 2007, 23 years later, there are 13 programs. Since the 1984 publication, three new programs have appeared (Penn State, Rhode Island, and University of Wisconsin-Milwaukee), whereas 15 programs no longer offer an IR degree or have ceased to exist (Georgia State, Iowa State, Kansas, Loyola, New Haven, Pace, Purdue, Rutgers,[1] St. Francis, South Carolina, Temple, Wayne State, West Virginia College of Graduate Studies,[2] Winthrop, and the University of Wisconsin-Madison). Of the 15 programs that stopped offering IR degrees between 1984 and 2005, six were located in states where union representation of employees is below the U.S. average. Of those that remain, *none* is located in a state with below U.S. average union representation. Only one of the private schools (NYIT) continues to offer an IR Master's degree. Of the 13 public programs, seven are in land-grant universities. Over the 31-year period between 1974 and 2005, only two programs based in land-grant universities were shut down: Iowa State and Wisconsin-Madison.[3]

Of the programs that ceased to operate, none was a freestanding unit prior to its termination. Most were housed in either economics departments or business schools. Within economics, as ILE scholars retired, they were routinely replaced by neoclassical economists (some in labor, some in other areas) who had little interest in institutional approaches in general and IR in particular. The others were in business schools. In those situations, names and emphases were often changed to eliminate industrial or employee relations from the title of the program, and as faculty who had primary interests in collective bargaining retired or left, they were not replaced or were replaced with new faculty whose interests were in HRM.

There are currently only six Master's programs that include IR or a similar name in their program or unit title that have relatively more than 75 full-time equivalent students: Cornell, Illinois, Michigan State, Minnesota, Ohio State, and Rutgers. All also have doctoral programs. All of the programs at land-grant universities have or did have attached outreach programs that provided services to labor or employer constituencies. Of the six, Cornell, Illinois, and Rutgers are in freestanding units.[4] Michigan State's program is within the School of Labor and Industrial Relations, which is a unit within the College of Social Sciences. Both the Minnesota and the Ohio State programs are located in departments within their universities' business schools, but they were originally created through multidisciplinary efforts and had already operated outreach activities before their permanent locations were determined. With the exception of Michigan State and Ohio State, all of these IR programs were created within 10 years of the end of World War II. Table 3.3 identifies the homes of all current IR Master's programs, the year each was established, the number of full-time equivalent students, the number of full-time tenured or tenure-track faculty with primary assignments in the degree program, and the number of semester credits required to complete each program. The six programs with the largest number of IR Master's students (Cornell, Illinois, Michigan State, Minnesota, Ohio State, and Rutgers) produce over 70% of the total.

Table 3.3   U.S. Graduate Programs in Industrial Relations in 2007

School	Year Established	FTE Students	FTE Core T/TT Faculty	Semester Hours in Program
Cincinnati, University of (Liberal Arts)	1975	50	2	53
Cleveland State University (Business)	1982	52	4.5	34
Cornell University[1] (freestanding)	1944	100[1]	50	48
Illinois, University of (freestanding)	1946	150	13	48
Indiana University of Pennsylvania (Business)	1977	50	5	42
Michigan State University (Social Science)	1966	125	17	36
Minnesota, University of (Business)	1953	170	13.75	48
New York Institute of Technology (Business)	1978	52	3	42
Ohio State University (Business)	1976	82	3.5	51
Penn State University (Liberal Arts)	1995	16	8	37
Rhode Island, University of (freestanding)	1983	20	2	39
Rutgers University (freestanding)	1976	90	12	39
West Virginia, University of (Business)	1957	42	4	42
Wisconsin-Milwaukee, University of (College of Letters and Science and School of Business)	1983	45	3	36

1. Cornell also enrolls approximately 650 undergraduate ILR majors.

ILE or PM: Which Paradigm Prevails?

Over the last 40 years there has been a plethora of label and content changes in courses and programs. Some are cosmetic and some are in response to the fact that the employment relationship has changed markedly. IR, labor relations, and employee relations are used to identify courses and programs far less frequently. Personnel is barely in the lexicon anymore, and HRM is ubiquitous. This is probably to be expected given that IR (or HRM for that matter) is not a discipline, but rather the study of a set of issues or problems connected with employment. The shift in emphasis is ultimately driven by the evolving pattern of demand for graduates of employment-oriented graduate programs. In the 20 years following the passage of the Wagner Act, labor unions became an increasingly important actor in the employment relationship, with approximately a third of the workforce covered by collective bargaining agreements, including virtually complete coverage of blue-collar production workers outside of the South. Over the following 50 years, unionization declined to cover approximately an eighth of the workforce, with perhaps one-twelfth of the private-sector workforce covered. The decline can be traced to a number of factors. It is primarily due to the relative increase in demand for employees with intellectual skills and abilities and the relative shift in industrial employment from goods to services. Secondary factors include the relative reduction in unionized employment due to globalization, the relative expansion of manufacturing in the generally anti-union South together with contraction in the generally pro-union North, the increasingly hard line that employers have taken in opposing union organizing and demanding contract concessions (Freedman, 1979, 1983), and the decrease in competition to organize and bargain for employees that resulted following the merger of the AFL and CIO in 1955.

As the 1970s were ending, employers began to opt out of the corporatist approach and seized the initiative in dealing with or avoiding unions. Politicians were decreasingly interested in intervening in labor-management conflict, so two legs of the corporatist stool collapsed. Employers' interests in specialists and managers in employment activities now shifted from accommodation and compliance with regulations to efficiency and profitability. How employment practices were implemented was now seen as a source of competitive advantage rather than a set of uniform processes across employers, supported by regulations that applied to all, that would take labor out of competition.

Several forces combined to change employment practices. First, the oil shocks in the 1970s focused attention on efficiency for both producers and consumers. In the short run, foreign goods were already more efficient and could meet consumers' needs more quickly than American operations could redesign and retool. Second, consumers recognized that besides being more efficient, many of the foreign goods were of substantially higher quality relative to price than what American producers built. Third, the rate of return to shareholders was at an unacceptable level. Inflation was rampant, and the stock market had been wallowing for almost 15 years.

The 1980s saw the end of the capital-labor accords (Gordon, 1997), the flattening of organizational structures, increasing decentralization, and the redesign of work and pay programs (Kochan, Katz, & McKersie, 1986). For employers, this meant that the demand for IR program graduate skills shifted from functional depth to problem-solving flexible generalist. The ability to understand business problems and to identify employment practices that contributed to firm performance was predicted to become increasingly important for IR graduates (Fossum, 1987). More responsibility for organizational change and consulting support to line managers was important. Less emphasis was placed on compliance and more on accommodating and promoting diversity.

The changes in emphasis in the field are apparent from the topics emphasized in mainstream personnel and HR texts that have been broadly used in these programs. Bear in mind that the texts were written by authors whose feet were generally in the PM (HRM) camp rather than in the ILE faction. Even so, the change in emphasis from a corporatist approach toward an organizational effectiveness or firm performance approach is apparent. The focus is increasingly shifted toward practices that are of benefit to the employer and away from those that are primarily oriented toward employee welfare.

Table 3.4 shows the changes in topics in Dale Yoder's personnel management text from its original edition in 1942 to its sixth edition in 1970 (Yoder, 1942, 1970). Although Yoder's text clearly reflects a corporatist perspective in the sixth edition, the shift from a labor problems approach in the original edition toward a PM (HRM) approach in the sixth edition is quite clear. Also included are the chapter titles of a personnel text widely adopted in MBA programs between 1960 and 1980 by Strauss and Sayles (1960, 1980).

A third part of Table 3.4 shows the chapter titles in the first editions of two widely adopted texts from 1974 and 1980 (Glueck, 1974; Heneman, Schwab, Fossum, & Dyer, 1980), and the chapter titles from a currently widely adopted text (Noe, Hollenbeck, Gerhart, & Wright, 2006). A comparison of the amount of coverage in Yoder's 1970 edition with these three shows how the IR influence has declined. In Yoder (1970), there was a four-chapter section on union-management relations topics. In Glueck (1974), unions were included as part of the environment close to the beginning, followed by a chapter on collective bargaining and group representation close to the end. In Heneman et al. (1980), there was a two-chapter section related to union-management relations near the end of the book. In Noe et al. (2006), there is one chapter near the end under a "Special Topics in HRM" section. The shift in emphasis over the 35-year period moves unions from an endogenous factor in the employment

Table 3.4   Evolution of Textbooks

Personnel Management and Industrial Relations

First Edition	Sixth Edition
Introduction (formal organizations)	Part I—Policy and Theory in Manpower Management
Background of Personnel Administration (history)	
Approaches to the Study of Industrial Relations (approaches of various disciplines, especially social sciences)	Introduction—The Management of People
	Management Goals and Policies
	Management's Theory Base
Statistical Tools for Personnel Administration	Theories of Work
Job Analysis, Description, and Classification	Part II—Organization and Administration
Recruitment and Sources	Theories of Organization
Selection (debunking conventional wisdom)	Major Problems in Organization
Selection (tests and measurements)	Administration: Styles of Leadership and Direction
Training for Industry	
Industrial Unrest	Part III—Staffing
Working Hours	Manpower Management Planning
Service Rating (performance appraisal)	Staffing Requirements
Wage Plans	Manpower Resources: Personnel Appraisals
Wage Policies	Sources and Recruitment
Promotion and Transfer	Selection Policy and Programs
The Health of Employees	Part IV—Training and Development
Interest and Morale	Development of Human Resources
Employment and Unemployment	Employee and Supervisor Development
Employment Stabilization	Manager Development
Employee Representation	Part V—Labor Relations Management
Collective Bargaining (history and organizations)	Union Theory, Policy, and Practice
Collective Bargaining (institutions and processes)	U.S. Labor Relations Policy
Personnel Services	Current Labor Relations Guidelines
Personnel Administration in the Public Service	Negotiation and Contract Administration
Personnel Records	Part VI—Maintaining Commitment
Personnel Research	Commitment and Morale
	Employee Communications
	Financial Rewards: Theory and Practice
	Wage and Salary Administration
	Employee Benefits and Services
	Part VII—Audits and Research
	Auditing Manpower Management
	Research in Manpower Management

Source: Dale Yoder, *Personnel Management and Industrial Relations*, Englewood Cliffs, NJ: Prentice Hall, 1942; and 6th edition, 1970.

Personnel: The Human Problems of Managment	
First Edition	*Fourth Edition*
Part I—The Components of the Personnel Problem	Part I—Individuals and Their Jobs
Meaning of Work	The Meaning of Work: Employee Needs and Satisfactions
Technology and Job Satisfaction	Motivating People to Work
Work Groups and Informal Organizations	Innovations in Job Design and Scheduling
The Impact of the Union	Part II—Groups, Supervisors, and Unions
Part II—Supervision	Supervisory Behavior: Balancing Structure and Support
Motivating People to Work	Group Behavior: Organization Consequences
General Supervision	The Supervisor as a Group Leader
The Supervisor's Use of Authority	The Impact of the Union
The Supervisor and the Group	Part III—Managerial Skills
Part III—Supervisory Skills	Communications: The Information Transmission Process
Communications	Communications: The Problem Solving Process
Interviewing: The Fine Art of Listening	Introducing Change: The Managerial Issues
Conference Leadership	Using Discipline for Effective Performance
Introducing Change	Part IV—Structure
Discipline	Decision-making and Organization Levels
Part IV—Organization	Information Flows Through the Hierarchy
The Impact of Hierarchy on Human Relations	Organization Design: Alternative Structures
The Supervisor: Man in the Middle	Managing the Personnel Function
The Impact of Specialization on Human Relations	Part V—Employee Development and Protection
Minimizing the Human Problems of Large Organizations	Manpower Planning
Personnel as a Staff Function	Selection Techniques
Part V—Manpower and Employee Development	Learning, Training, and Behavior Modification
Recruitment and Selection Policies	Minority Employment and Affirmative Action Programs
Promotion, Transfer, and Seniority Policy for Non-Managerial Employees	Women and Management
Technical Training	Employee Health and Safety
Management Development	Part VI—Management and Organization Development
Performance Evaluation	Managerial Career Planning
Management Training	Performance Appraisal & MBO
Part VI—Incentives for Effective Performance	Organization Development and Managerial Training
Wage and Salary Administration	Part VII—Compensation
Work Measurement Techniques	Wage and Salary Administration
Individual Incentive Systems	Employee Benefit Programs
Incentives for Group Participation	Incentives and Performance Standards
Safety	Organizationwide Participation and Productivity Sharing
Service and Benefit Programs	Part VIII—Conclusion
Part VII—Management's Responsibilities	Personnel Challenges and the Future
Management's Responsibilities in Dealing With People	

Source: From George Strauss and Leonard Sayles, *Personnel: The Human Problems of Management,* Englewood Cliffs, NJ: Prentice Hall, 1960; 4th edition, 1980.

(Continued)

(Continued)

Glueck	Heneman, Schwab, Fossum, and Dyer
Part I—Introduction	Part I—Personnel/Human Resource Management and Its Environment
Personnel Administration: An Introduction (model, history)	Overview and Model of Personnel/Human Resource Management
People and Personnel (aptitudes, personality, motivation)	External Influences (labor markets, laws, EEO)
Environment and Personnel (unions, locations, work)	Part II—Analyzing Individuals and Jobs
	Individuals in the Organization (ability and motivation)
Part II—Determining Personnel Needs	Job Analysis and Design
Employment Planning (job design, descriptions, satisfaction)	Part III—Assessing Personnel/Human Resource Management Outcomes
Part III—Attracting, Selecting and Assigning Personnel	Employee Performance
Attracting Personnel	Employee Satisfaction, Length of Service, and Attendance
Selection of Personnel	Part IV—Personnel Planning
Orientation of Personnel	Personnel Planning
Part IV—Career Development—I	Part V—External Staffing
Career Development and Counseling	Personnel Recruitment
Employee Evaluation and Promotion	External Staffing Concepts
Part V—Career Development—II	External Staffing Processes
Employee Training	Part VI—Internal Staffing and Development
Selection and Evaluation of Managers	Internal Staffing and Career Management
Managerial Obsolescence and Development	Employee and Organization Development
Part VI—Direct Compensation	Part VII—Compensation
Financial Compensation	Pay-Setting Processes
Part VII—Indirect Compensation	Benefits
Employee Benefits and Services	Impacts of Pay on Employees
Retirement and Pensions	Part VIII—Labor Relations
Employee Health and Safety	Labor Unions
Part VIII—Personnel and Groups of Employees	Labor-Management Relations
Affirmative Action Plans	Part IX—Safety, Health, and Hours
Collective Bargaining and Group Representation	Occupational Safety and Health
Part IX—Control of Human Performance	Hours of Work
Discipline and the Difficult Employee	An Integration
Evaluation and Research of Personnel Administration	

Source: Glueck, 1974; Heneman, 1980.

Human Resource Management: Gaining a Competitive Advantage

Human Resource Management: Gaining a Competitive Advantage (introduction and staging)

Part I—The Human Resource Environment
  Strategic Human Resource Management
  The Legal Environment: Equal Employment Opportunity and Safety
  The Analysis and Design of Work

Part II—Acquisition and Preparation of Human Resources
  Human Resource Planning and Recruitment
  Selection and Placement
  Training

Part III—Assessment and Development of HRM
  Performance Management
  Employee Development
  Employee Separation and Retention

Part IV—Compensation of Human Resources
  Pay Structure Decisions
  Recognizing Employee Contributions with Pay
  Employee Benefits

Part V—Special Topics in Human Resource Management
  Collective Bargaining and Labor Relations
  Managing Human Resources Globally
  Strategically Managing the Human Resource Function

Source: Raymond Noe, John Hollenbeck, Barry Gerhart, and Patrick Wright, *Human Resource Management: Gaining a Competitive Advantage*, 5th ed., Burr Ridge, IL: McGraw-Hill-Irwin, 2006.

relationship to an exogenous factor seen as having a decreasing effect on employment outcomes for both employers and employees. The consignment of collective bargaining to a special-topics grouping suggests that professional knowledge and skill in labor relations are no longer seen as necessary for a successful professional career in employment.

Differences and Similarities Between Programs

Table 3.5 displays the courses offered within and across the 14 current programs (Rutgers included). To create this table, I reviewed the course offerings for each program as posted on its current Web site. I made a list of all of the offerings across all of the schools. There is a lot of "customization" in course titles between schools. In constructing the table, I collapsed categories into similar topics if only one program gave a particular course (except in cases where the course was required). In some programs, more than one course is required or offered in a given area. I have made no notation of that in the table. In the table, *R* means *required,* *DE* means *department (or program)*

Table 3.5 Comparison of Current IR Program Course Requirements

	Cincinnati	CSU	Cornell	U-IL	IU-PA	Mich St.	U-MN	NYIT	Ohio St.	Penn St.	U-RI	Rutgers	WSU	U-WV	U-W-Mke
Alternative Dispute Resolution		OE						DE		DE	DE				DE
Arbitration		OE	DE		R		DE	DE			R(IR)			DE	
Benefits	DE			DE	DE		DE	DE			DE			R	DE
Business Strategy and HR	DE		DE	DE		R	R			R			OE	R	OR
Collective Bargaining	DE	OE	R		R	R	R	R				R	DE	R	R
Comparative HR			DE	DE											
Comparative IR		DE	DE	DE	DE		DE	DE		DE		DE(L)		DE	OE
Compensation	DE	R	DE	DE	DE	R	R	DE	R		R(HR)		OE	R	DE
Diversity	DE		DE				DE		R	DE		DE(L)	DE	DE	OE
Economics of Firm Performance				DE			DE							R	R
Employment Relations	DE	DE		R								R(L)			
Employment (Labor) Law	R	R	R	DE	R	R	DE	OR	R	R		R	R	R	R
EEO/AA			DE	DE				OE						R	
Ethics	DE			DE			DE							DE	
Financial Accounting				DE			OE					R-E		DE	
High Performance Work Systems				DE		DE						R(H)			
History and Foundations of HRM									R						
History and Foundations of IR			DE	DE						R	R(HR)				
HR and Business Functions	DE								R			R(H)			
HR Information Systems	DE	R	DE	DE		DE	DE	OR	R			DE(H)		R	
Industrial/Organizational Psychology		OE	DE	DE			OE								OE

	Cincinnati	CSU	Cornell	U-IL	IU-PA	Mich St.	U-MN	NYIT	Ohio St.	Penn St.	U-RI	Rutgers	WSU	U-WV	U-W-Mke
International HR	DE		DE	DE		DE	DE	DE				R(H)	DE	DE	DE
Introduction to HRM and/or IR		R	R				DE	R					OR		OR
Labor Economics	R	R	R	DE		R	DE	OR	R	R		R	R		OR
Labor History and Labor Movements		DE	DE			DE	DE			DE		DE(L)			OE
Labor-Management Conflict			DE		DE								OR	DE	
Labor Unions	DE		DE		R			DE		DE	R(IR)	R(H)	DE		
Metrics	DE		DE				R	OR				R(H)			
Negotiation	DE	DE	DE	DE	DE	DE		R	R					DE	OE
Organization Theory and Organizational Behavior	R		R	DE		R	R	R	R				DE	DE	OE
Organizational Development	DE	DE	DE			DE	OE		R			DE(H)	OE	R	OE
Performance Management		R		DE										R	
Personnel Economics			DE	DE			OE								
Public Sector HRM	OE	OE	DE		R			DE		DE	DE	DE	DE		OE
Public Sector IR	DE	DE	DE	DE	DE			DE		DE	R(IR)	DE(L)	DE	DE	DE
Research Methods	R	DE	DE	R	R	R	R	OR	R	R		R	OR		DE
Sociology of Work and Organization		OE	DE								DE		OE		
Staffing and Selection	DE	R	DE	DE	DE		R	DE	R			R(H)		R	R
Statistics	DE		R	R			R	R	R	R		R(H)			R
Training and Development	DE	R	DE	DE	DE	DE	R	DE	R			R(H)		R	

Source: From George Strauss and Leonard Sayles, Personnel: The Human Problems of Management, Englewood Cliffs, NJ: Prentice Hall, 1960; 4th edition, 1980.

Note: Cincinnati = University of Cincinnati; CSU = Cleveland State University; Cornell = Cornell University; U-IL = University of Illinois; IU-PA = Indiana University of Pennsylvania; Mich St. = Michigan State University; U-MN = University of Minnesota; NYIT = New York Institute of Technology; Ohio St. = Ohio State University; Penn St. = Pennsylvania State University; U-RI = University of Rhode Island; Rutgers = Rutgers University; WSU = Washington State University; WSU = Wayne State University; U-WV = University of West Virginia; U-W-Mke = University of Wisconsin-Milwaukee.

elective, OR means *required course offered by another department or program,* and *OE* means *elective offered by another department.* Rutgers has two programs, one oriented toward HRM and the other toward LS. Those courses that are HRM oriented have an *(H)* following, whereas LS-oriented courses have an *(L).* The same logic holds for the Rhode Island program.

There are some differences across programs in the extent to which courses are required. Ohio State and Rutgers have the largest proportion of courses that are required. Otherwise, approximately half to two-thirds of the credits necessary to graduate are in required courses. All of the programs require evidence of a certain level of skill in statistics or additional statistics courses as part of the program requirements. Most also have a research methods requirement. Most programs require microeconomics and general psychology as prerequisites for admission.

Beyond statistics and research methods, the courses that are required or included in the curriculum by two-thirds or more of the programs include collective bargaining, compensation, employment or labor law, human resource information systems, international HR, labor economics, organizational development, public-sector IR, staffing and selection, and training and development. Of these, the proportional mix between ILE and PM approaches is about even. Labor economics is generally taught from a neoclassical perspective, however.

Other courses that are required or offered by seven or more programs include arbitration, benefits, business strategy and HR, comparative IR, diversity, labor history and labor movements, labor unions, negotiations, organizational behavior, and public-sector HRM. Increasing numbers of programs are requiring some work in business-related areas (particularly accounting and financial analysis). Where programs are located outside of business schools this may require that they build their own courses because of difficulties in enrolling in MBA courses—especially if tuition differentials exist. On the other hand, it is important to avoid content dilution simply to maintain the production of credits within the program.

The Evolving IR Degree Program

Most of the IR graduate degree programs have substantially restructured over the last 30 years. Currently, only Cornell, IUP, Penn State, Rhode Island, and Rutgers have programs that either emphasize or enable a student to develop a concentration that would be oriented toward employment by a labor union. Of these, IUP, Penn State, and Rhode Island place a majority of their emphasis on topics that are more oriented to industrial relations from a union's perspective. The large majority of Cornell's graduates are oriented toward HRM careers. Its ability to offer a large number of labor-oriented courses is related to the large faculty size necessary to offer its very large undergraduate program.

As compared to faculty in disciplinary programs who discover new knowledge that may lead to future applications, faculty in applied programs most often study and evaluate current practice to test theories most often developed in disciplines. Curricula in applied programs respond to two things: the research and teaching skills and interests of its current faculty, and the changing patterns of employer demands for their graduates.

All programs have some required courses, and most identify one or more tracks or emphases for students, but most do not project an explicit model of what they are offering or trying to develop. Rutgers, Ohio State, and Minnesota are probably the most explicit. Rutgers and Ohio State have the programs with the greatest proportion of required courses in their curricula. Rutgers has also basically divided the HR and IR students, with only a few courses required by both programs. For many years, Minnesota has based its curriculum on an explicit model aimed at developing generalists. Early in 2005, its faculty developed a significant revision to its Master's program consistent with the model shown in Figure 3.1. This revision goes beyond the modification, elimination, or introduction of courses to broaden the base for learning to include extracurricular and work opportunities and experiences. Because many Master's students have little or no significant experience in human resources and industrial relations either as

The Minnesota Model of HRIR Success

The Minnesota Model is a partnership between faculty, students, and the broader HRIR community. The faculty and the HRIR community provide learning opportunities; students are responsible for developing their critical competencies through these learning opportunities in and out of the classroom.

Figure 3.1   The Minnesota Model of HRIR Success

Source: Adapted from The Minnesota Model of HRIR Success Model, developed by Theresa Glomb, John Budd, and Connie Wanberg.

undergraduates or in any previous employment and few have explicitly worked to develop leadership competencies, the revised program offers opportunities for students to enhance learning transfer through a variety of noncourse, noncredit activities. These include internship and part-time opportunities during summers and the two academic years of the program, the availability of alumni mentors and the opportunity during the second year to be a mentor to a first-year student, volunteer consultancies on HRM projects with public-sector and nonprofit organizations, and opportunities to attend professional development programs designed for practitioners.

The revisions also reorient the quantitative methods courses toward the design and evaluation of metrics and expand the economic analysis focus to emphasis managerial economics, accounting, and finance. More attention is paid to organizational and work-unit problem-solving through courses on change management, strategy, and ethics.

In general, IR programs are increasing the business-oriented content in their programs, either by recommending MBA program electives or by building more accounting, finance, operations, and marketing into their courses. More programs are offering HRM strategy courses that have explicit business content linkages. At the same time, some IR faculty are looking at employment and work more introspectively (Budd, 2004) and are developing ethics courses or other more in-depth explorations about what the relationships between employers, employees, and the society should be.

Although the emphasis in IR programs has moved increasingly toward HRM, they can be distinguished from HRM programs by their continuing attention to the role of public policy in employment, the desirability of a need for balance between employer and employee interests in the employment relationship, and ethical issues in the employment relationship. IR programs will continue to flourish to the extent that they maintain a problem-solving approach, identifying emerging employment issues and crafting solutions that improve the outcomes of all of the actors in the employment relationship—the same pragmatic, nondoctrinaire approach they took when they were first developed.

Conclusion

Although the HRM (PM) content of IR programs has increased, I think it is unlikely that IR programs will morph into HRM programs. There are several reasons for this conclusion.

1. IR programs include faculty members from several disciplines. Disciplinary interests in staffing will prevent the elimination of a multidisciplinary approach. Disciplinary survival trumps program survival at the margin. Self-interest will prevail.

2. There will continue to be a demand for students who have developed skills in collective bargaining negotiations and administration or for students who at least understand the goals and operations of labor unions. These programs are best able to supply this need.

3. Many of the IR programs include outreach activities in addition to their degree programs. Thus, they deal with opposing constituencies, one that favors HRM approaches and one that favors ILE approaches. Neither trusts the other very much. By their continued presence, outreach activities strengthen a program's position in a land-grant university and also require the program to include a diversity of viewpoints on employment.

4. The increasing inclusion of international and comparative courses in HRM and IR in IR program curricula enhances the importance of ILE approaches. Much of the study in this area aims to acquaint students with global institutional differences and how they influence employment practices and employee outcomes. More attention is paid to "what if" questions as they relate to public policy on employment.

5. From a market demand standpoint, although most students are hired by employers who operate using an explicit HRM approach, the evidence thus far suggests that for many of the nation's largest employers, HR-IR Master's programs that have evolved in what were originally IR programs remain the preferred source for hiring high-potential future HR professionals.

6. Understanding business problems and relating IR and HRM to business strategies requires a working knowledge of economic and financial analysis. These are available in MBA programs, but top-quality MBA programs require that students have several years of general business experience to be admitted. Thus, most MBA students' aspirations are beyond what employers are offering in HRM development programs. All else being equal, an employer will prefer an IR program graduate to an HRM program graduate because the IR student is much more likely to have been taught by at least some economists.

Notes

1. Between 1984 and 2007, Rutgers divided its programs into separate Master's in human resource management and labor studies. Collective bargaining subjects are no longer required of HRM students, and HRM is no longer required of LS students. Its HRM program, offered in the evening, is among the largest in both absolute numbers and full-time equivalents.

2. West Virginia College of Graduate Studies was merged into West Virginia University between 1984 and 2005.

3. Rutgers is a land-grant university. As Note 1 noted, its program was bifurcated into two separate programs that continue to operate. Thus, it is not included in the set that "shut down."

4. Rutgers's programs are also located in a freestanding unit.

References

Budd, J. W. (2004). *Employment with a human face: Balancing efficiency, equity, and voice.* Ithaca, NY: Cornell University Press.

Fossum, J. A. (1987). The evolving market for IR professionals: Meeting the needs. *Proceedings of the Industrial Relations Research Association, 40,* 482–489.

Freedman, A. (1979). *Managing labor relations.* New York: The Conference Board.

Freedman, A. (1983). *A new look at wage bargaining.* New York: The Conference Board.

Glueck, W. F. (1974). *Personnel: A diagnostic approach.* Dallas, TX: Business Publications.

Gordon, D. M. (1997). From the drive system to the capital-labor accord: Econometric tests for the transition between productivity regimes. *Industrial Relations, 36,* 125–159.

Heneman, H. G., III, Schwab, D. P., Fossum, J. A., & Dyer, L. D. (1980). *Personnel/human resource management.* Homewood, IL: Richard D. Irwin.

Herman, G. (1974). *Personnel/industrial relations/human resource management colleges: A directory.* Berea, OH: American Society for Personnel Administration.

Herman, G. (1984). *Personnel/industrial relations/human resource management colleges: A directory* (2nd ed.). Minneapolis: Industrial Relations Center, University of Minnesota.

Hicks, C. J. (1941). *My life in industrial relations.* New York: Harper.

Jacoby, S. M. (1989). Reckoning with company unions: The case of Thompson Products. *Industrial and Labor Relations Review, 43,* 19–40.

Jacoby, S. M. (1997). *Modern manors: Welfare capitalism since the New Deal.* Princeton, NJ: Princeton University Press.

Kaufman, B. E. (1993). *The origins and evolution of the field of industrial relations in the United States.* Ithaca, NY: ILR Press.

Kaufman, B. E. (2003). Industrial Relations Counselors, Inc.: Its history and significance. In B. Kaufman, R. Beaumont, & R. Helfgott (Eds.), *Industrial relations to human resources and beyond: The evolving process of employee relations management* (pp. 31–114). Armonk, NY: M. E. Sharpe.

Kochan, T. A., Katz, H. C., & McKersie, R. B. (1986). *The transformation of American industrial relations.* New York: Basic.

Noe, R., Hollenbeck, J., Gerhart, B., & Wright, P. (2006). *Human resource management: Gaining a competitive advantage* (5th ed.). Burr Ridge, IL: McGraw-Hill-Irwin.

Social Science Research Council. (1928). *Survey of research in the field of industrial relations.* New York: Author.

Smith, A. (1976). *The wealth of nations* (E. Cannan, Ed.). Chicago: University of Chicago Press. (Original work published 1776)

Strauss, G., & Sayles, L. (1960). *Personnel: The human problems of management.* Englewood Cliffs, NJ: Prentice Hall.

Strauss, G., & Sayles, L. (1980). *Personnel: The human problems of management* (4th ed.). Englewood Cliffs, NJ: Prentice Hall.

Taylor, F. W. (1911). *The principles of scientific management.* New York: Harper.

Yoder, D. (1942). *Personnel management and industrial relations.* Englewood Cliffs, NJ: Prentice Hall.

Yoder, D. (1970). *Personnel management and industrial relations* (6th ed.). Englewood Cliffs, NJ: Prentice Hall.

What We Should Know but (Probably) Never Learned in School

4

Thoughts on HR Education in Psychology Departments

Cameron Klein

Renée E. DeRouin

Eduardo Salas

Kevin C. Stagl

In today's business environment, human resources (HR) professionals must be armed with a broader and deeper set of competencies—not just mastery of traditional HR functions but also of interpersonal, teamwork, customer service, and information technology skills. These emerging competency requirements place incredible demands on the HR professional. In this chapter, we examine the extent to which graduate training in industrial and organizational (I/O) psychology prepares professionals to work in the field of HR. In order to accomplish this, we gathered information through both a review of the relevant literature on HR training and practice and an informal series of interviews with HR professionals. We used this information to develop five themes that summarize the state of the art of HR education in psychology departments.

A revolution in the field of HR has long been underway. Managers in this field now need to be prepared to handle not only traditional HR functions, such as developing compensation and benefits packages and administering training programs, but also more psychosocial and business-related functions, such as acting as liaisons between unions and management and linking HR strategies to organizational missions, visions, and strategies (Dyer, 1999; Hansen, 2002). The knowledge, skill, and affective competencies (KSAs) necessary to accomplish these diverse responsibilities require students of HR-related programs to be trained to a historically unparalleled level. Has HR education kept up with these changes? Not exactly. We agree with others (e.g., Dunnette, 1991; Chapter 13 of this volume) when we state that HR education programs are often discrepant from the practice of HR management.

For many practitioners, HR education is received in I/O psychology Master's programs. As Lowe (1993) points out, "better knowledge about the content of Master's-level industrial-organizational (I/O) psychology training and about its relevance for the jobs held by Master's graduates would be useful" (p. 27). Therefore, the education and training of students in I/O psychology Master's programs, and especially their preparation for careers in HR, constitute the focal point of this chapter.

In order to gain a practitioner perspective of requisite HR competencies, we conducted an informal series of interviews with several HR professionals in the United States. Specifically, our intention was to pinpoint some of the competency gaps between HR-related education and practice by interviewing eight HR professionals chosen for their subject-matter expertise in both HR education and practice. These professionals typically held Master's degrees in I/O psychology, HR/organizational development, or business administration and were either training coordinators in large organizations or senior HR managers or consultants. We asked our interviewees 34 semistructured questions designed to capture their thoughts, feelings, and attitudes toward the competency level of entering HR practitioners at their company and how important certain KSAs are to effective HR performance in their firm.

In addition, we reviewed the relevant literature on HR and I/O education to illuminate what researchers and academicians suggest are the most important competencies for HR graduates to possess. The findings from our review and interview process led us to develop and advance five themes describing the disconnects between what is taught in, and what is desired from, I/O Master's-level programs (see Table 4.1). These themes can be viewed as a set of challenges that mandate the joint cooperation of both academia and the business world to overcome. By balancing our discussion between a careful examination of the academic

Table 4.1   Thoughts on HR Education in Psychology Departments: Common Themes

Theme	Description
1: I/O psychology graduate programs should periodically conduct needs analyses of HR practice in organizations.	I/O Master's-level programs would benefit from a clear and comprehensive needs assessment that would enable the identification of the declarative and procedural knowledge competencies needed by managers in the HR field. Ideally, programs should periodically update the KSAs covered in their programs so that these competencies are relevant for HR practice at any particular time.
2: I/O psychology graduate programs need to emphasize how workplace environmental changes affect the competencies needed to effectively perform HR functions.	HR professionals face an increasingly complex set of issues in the daily practice of their jobs; thus, I/O psychology Master's programs should describe how technological advances, the development of an international workforce, and changing workplace demographics affect HR practice.
3: I/O psychology graduate programs need to emphasize (for those interested in practice) the importance of becoming true business players.	The role that HR departments play in organizations has shifted from a purely administrative function to one that includes becoming a true strategic player concerned with adding value to the organization; therefore, I/O Master's programs need to point out the importance of aligning HR strategies with organizational goals.
4: I/O psychology graduate programs need to teach graduates how to navigate corporate politics.	The potential for conflict over resources is great in organizations. Unfortunately, I/O psychology Master's programs typically do not emphasize the impact of corporate politics on HR management careers. It is likely that much of the individual development in this area will need to take place in internships and applied field courses.
5: I/O psychology graduate programs need to emphasize the importance of managing one's career and viewing HR education as a lifelong pursuit.	As new technologies are implemented and the nature of work continues to evolve, HR professionals will be required to learn skills that were not even recognized as important during their formal education. As a result, I/O Master's programs need to highlight the fact that HR practitioners will be expected to "learn constantly" and to take responsibility for their own development.

literature and the information obtained via practitioner interviews, we hope to reveal some of the most important gaps between I/O Master's education and practice. Thus, we expect this chapter will have value for both academicians and practitioners, although we emphasize practitioner training as the focal point.

Before we present our five themes, it is useful to briefly discuss education, training, and career opportunities in I/O psychology. I/O psychology is essentially "the application or extension of psychological facts and principles to the problems concerning human beings operating within the context of business and industry" (Blum & Naylor, 1968, p. 4). As such, it is intimately concerned with people in the workplace. The "I" side of I/O typically focuses on the individual as the unit of analysis and includes such topics as training, selection, individual assessment, performance appraisal, and job and task analysis. The "O" side focuses on issues that arise as a result of individuals being brought together in social collectives in order to accomplish a specific purpose. This side of I/O psychology concerns, for example, organizational theory and development, leadership, small groups and teams, motivation, employee attitudes, and career development.

Training and Education of Master's-Level I/O Psychologists

The main organizing structure for I/O psychologists is the Society for Industrial and Organizational Psychology (SIOP). Of particular relevance to the current discussion, SIOP has published guidelines for the education and training of Master's-level I/O psychologists (SIOP, 1994). Thus, in addition to acquiring competency in the core "I" and "O" areas briefly described above, I/O Master's program graduates are also expected to have knowledge of the history and systems of psychology and various fields of psychology (e.g., social, cognitive), as well as a high level of skill in research design, delivery, analysis, and evaluation. Additional Master's-level I/O psychology domains include career development theory, human performance and human factors, consumer behavior, compensation and benefits, and industrial-labor relations. Educational experiences in the latter areas are considered desirable but not essential to the training of I/O Master's students.

The competency domains SIOP endorses are meant to guide the curricular and pedagogic decisions made by faculty responsible for training I/O Master's students. However, not all Master's programs cover all domains, and even when they do, not all domains are covered equally. In order to present a clearer picture of this state of affairs, Table 4.2 includes SIOP's competency domains, their coverage in I/O Master's programs, and their level of importance according to a recent survey of I/O Master's graduates (Trahan & McAllister, 2002).

Table 4.2   Core and Desirable I/O Master's Level Competency Domains: Their Coverage and Importance

I/O Psychology Domain[a]	Mean Coverage of Domain in I/O Master's Programs[b]	Mean Importance of Domain in I/O Practice[b]
Core Competency Domains		
Ethical, Legal, and Professional Contexts	Not assessed	Not assessed
Measurement of Individual Differences	3.71	2.56
Criterion Theory and Development	Not assessed	Not assessed
Job and Task Analysis	4.05	3.77
Employee Selection, Placement, and Classification	3.78	3.66
Performance Appraisal and Feedback	3.70	3.31
Training: Theory, Program Design, and Evaluation	4.11	3.76
Work Motivation	3.74	3.24
Attitude Theory	2.68	2.78
Small Group Theory and Process	3.47	2.51
Organization Theory	Not assessed	Not assessed
Organizational Development	4.01	3.27
Desirable Competency Domains[a]		
Career Development Theory	1.96	2.64
Human Performance/Human Factors	2.44	2.32
Consumer Behavior	0.58	0.85
Compensation and Benefits	1.49	1.93
Industrial and Labor Relations	1.35	1.39

[a] SIOP, Inc. (1994).

[b] Trahan & McAllister (2002). Scale values ranged from 0 (not at all) to 6 (to a great extent).

The number of academic programs offering terminal Master's (MA/MS) degrees in I/O psychology has increased more than threefold (i.e., from 23 to 74) since 1986 (Rogelberg & Gill, 2004). A typical Master's degree program usually takes no more than two years to complete and requires both coursework and a thesis. Many programs also involve internships or field experience (84% require or encourage practica, and 79% require or encourage internships; SIOP, 1989).

Beyond classroom coursework, applied practice and skill development through the use of internships or field experience is often an important part of graduate training in I/O psychology. Internships serve to supplement the training provided by graduate faculty and expose students to the challenges of applying research-based strategies in the field. Likewise, applied field projects, in which students work together on projects for actual organizations, serve as effective techniques for training I/O psychology Master's students for work in the field, as these projects offer students the chance to gain "hands-on" experience in real business settings. Field experience, internships and applied field projects prepare students for a career in HR, a topic we address in greater detail in the next section.

Career Opportunities for I/O Master's Graduates

Graduates of I/O Master's degree programs typically work in both the private and the public sector and may have job titles such as training specialist, personnel systems analyst, executive recruiter, or compensation consultant (Berry, 1990). There are also several subspecialties in I/O psychology, including personnel psychology, industrial relations, organizational behavior, organizational development, vocational and career counseling, and engineering psychology (Muchinsky, 1990). Thus, practicing I/O psychologists may perform a wide variety of specific job duties (e.g., selecting, training, counseling, motivating, and evaluating personnel). Moreover, Schoonover (1998) sees HR professionals fulfilling three roles: HR product and service specialists, HR generalists, and HR strategists. I/O psychology Master's-level graduates must be prepared to carry out any of these roles.

THEME 1: I/O PSYCHOLOGY GRADUATE PROGRAMS SHOULD PERIODICALLY CONDUCT NEEDS ANALYSES OF HR PRACTICE IN ORGANIZATIONS

As the HR function continues to evolve, periodically assessing the degree to which I/O Master's education prepares students for work in the field is not only a good idea, it is essential to meeting current and future organizational needs in a globalized economy. As Giannantonio and Hurley (2002) point out, "If we are to have a clear picture of what HR curricula should include to prepare our students for HR in this millennium, academics must continue to work collaboratively with HR practitioners to gain their insights into the field of HR" (p. 509). This collaboration will provide academicians and practitioners alike with a better understanding of the necessary knowledge, skill, and affective competencies to include in graduate I/O training.

In order to identify what businesses really want from their graduates, I/O Master's programs must get a sense of what is relevant in a changing HR world. One way to do this is to conduct a "needs analysis." Such a needs analysis may include the following tasks: identification of the competencies needed for HR managers, specification of the training objectives, design of the training environment, determination of the optimal sequence for learning tasks and subtasks, selection of the most appropriate delivery methods, and periodic evaluation of the effectiveness of the educational training (with this information used to continually revise and improve the program). For example, Dyer's (1999) review found the following core competencies to be necessary for today's human resource managers: (1) the ability to be a business partner with others in the organization, (2) technical competence in HR functions (e.g., employee selection, compensation), (3) competence in organization development technologies (e.g., team building, organization design, reengineering), and (4) the ability to help an organization manage change effectively. Many of these ideas are echoed in our Theme 2 (next section), which discusses how workplace environmental factors affect the competencies needed by HR professionals.

Ideally, programs should periodically update the KSAs targeted by their curricula so that these competencies are relevant for HR practice at any particular time. As the HR function changes, the curriculum in graduate I/O programs should also change. Thus, I/O psychology Master's programs must be adaptive, just as good organizations are.

Although it appears somewhat obvious that continuous collaboration between I/O psychology Master's program faculty and HR practitioners would provide a good indication of what KSAs should be covered in I/O graduate programs, only one of our interview participants indicated that a graduate school had ever contacted their organization to inquire about how they may be better able to align their HR program with actual business needs. If the remainder of our interviewees had been contacted, they might have been able to inform I/O Master's program directors of the HR education skill gap they described to us. Specifically, the HR professionals in our survey indicated that HR graduates need more training in the following competencies: facilitating strategic change, positive conflict resolution, communication, teamwork, and customer relations. Although there is little doubt that these competencies are addressed in graduate training, there is limited evidence to suggest that graduates are adequately prepared to employ them on graduation.

The concerns of HR executives and professionals as described above suggest an important area for future research. Specifically, more research is needed that will elicit the opinions of HR executives about the most important competencies of HR employees (Giannantonio & Hurley, 2002) and, thus, the most important competencies for new I/O Master's graduates to possess. Although information about the coverage of SIOP's competencies in I/O Master's programs and their importance in HR practice is a good start (see Table 4.2), it remains critical that I/O Master's faculty continue to collaborate with HR professionals. Information obtained from these mutually beneficial collaborations will better enable I/O psychology graduate programs to prepare their students for the complex world of work they will encounter.

*THEME 2: I/O PSYCHOLOGY GRADUATE
PROGRAMS NEED TO EMPHASIZE HOW WORKPLACE
ENVIRONMENTAL CHANGES AFFECT THE COMPETENCIES
NEEDED TO EFFECTIVELY PERFORM HR FUNCTIONS*

Kraut and Korman (1999) outline five sets of workplace environmental forces that significantly influence HR management policy and practice. These workplace environmental forces include changes in demographics (e.g., workforce makeup, education, migration, birthrates), economics (e.g., wage rates, growth, competition), legal and regulatory issues (e.g., equal opportunity, labor relations), technology (e.g., communications, transportation, computers), and attitudes and values (e.g., work ethic, company loyalty) (referred to as the "Delta Forces of Change"). We found support for many of Kraut and Korman's Delta Forces of Change in our interviews with HR professionals and our review of the literature on HR practice. Thus, the following sections discuss the impact of several of Kraut and Korman's workplace environmental factors in addition to providing further examples of changes that may affect the practice of HR for new entrants in the field. Specifically, we discuss the influence of technological changes, the importance of interpersonal, teamwork, and customer service skills, and environmental changes relevant to HR education in I/O psychology graduate programs.

Technology

With regard to changes in technology, arguably one of the most important environmental factors influencing HR practice today, all but one of our interview participants noted the tremendous impact technological advances have had on the field of HR. Specifically, they pointed out how technology has changed the way they perform their jobs, providing new and unique methods of delivering training, presenting company information, and recruiting employees. Similarly, literature has suggested that organizations are increasingly moving into the area of "eHR" (i.e., electronic or Internet-based HR delivery) in an effort to efficiently handle routine, time-consuming employee inquiries (Hunter, 1999; Stone, 2003). For example, it is estimated that 70% of organizations now use Internet-based employee self-service systems to manage benefits and records (Cedar, 2001; Towers Perrin, 2001), and closer to 100% of firms use Web sites (either their own Web sites or commercial sites) to announce job openings (Cedar, 2001; Gueutal, 2003). In addition, 40% of organizations use Web-based portals to communicate HR policies and disseminate HR information (e.g., inform employees about pay practices and benefit offerings, including options under cafeteria benefit systems; Cedar, 2001; Towers Perrin, 2001). The professionals we interviewed generally agreed with these estimates, indicating that in their organizations, information technology aids in benefits information, application processing, compensation, training, and recruiting. In fact, many companies have made these systems entirely computer-based in an effort to provide more consistent information to employees and to free up important resources.

Horton (2000) suggested one of the greatest technological advances for HR practitioners is the use of Web-based training. In support of this argument, one HR professional we interviewed (a former Director of Human Resources of a large insurance company) described the way in which technology has allowed her current organization to launch an on-line corporate university, an impossibility without recent significant advancements in technology. Taken together, this research-based and anecdotal evidence combines to support the notion that computer and information technology skills are important for I/O Master's-level graduates to possess. In order to maximize the benefits of today's technology for HR, graduates must be prepared to understand, administer, and capitalize on these systems in their organizations.

Interpersonal Skills and Teamwork

Kaufman (1999) argues that HR's shift in emphasis from technical specialization to facilitation and consultation makes excellent communication, dispute resolution, and other interpersonal skills more important than ever. In support of this idea, one of our interviewees aptly pointed out that professionals in any management function who do not possess adequate interpersonal skills will fail, as the quality of their interactions with other employees and management will suffer. To combat this, HR practitioners must be capable of (1) relating to individuals at all levels in the organization on a daily basis, (2) giving effective feedback, and (3) defusing high-tension situations. It is important to remember that the underlying goal of HR management is to get the job done through people. Thus, without these requisite interpersonal capabilities, it will be difficult for HR practitioners to win over skeptics at all levels of the organization who debate the value of the HR function.

Because much work in organizations now requires the skills of multiple players, teams have become a fixture in many organizations. As shown in Table 4.2, small-group theory and team processes remain an important area of study for I/O Master's students. However, because HR professionals must work collaboratively and interdependently with outside departments on a daily basis, not only is it important that I/O Master's students receive training in how small groups operate but it is also important that I/O programs teach their students appropriate teamwork KSAs. One interviewee, currently a training director in a large automobile manufacturing plant, stated that teamwork is such a focus in her organization that it has been used as an organizing structure for employees. Thus, being able to leverage opportunities and minimize constraints to effective teamwork is an increasingly critical competency for I/O Master's graduates to possess. Unfortunately, although it is talked about and trained, our data indicate that it is still a challenge for most or all organizational members, not just staff. That is, although teamwork receives a fair amount of attention in most organizations and may even serve as an overarching organizing structure, entering graduates and current employees often have not developed these skills to an adequate level. Furthermore, even though many graduate courses are now organized around (or at least include) team-based projects, members of these classroom-based project teams often have different motivations, time frames, and capabilities than would be otherwise found in a typical organizational work team. Therefore, even the completion of a number of team-based school projects may not adequately prepare the I/O Master's graduate for a career in a team-centered environment on graduation.

Customer Service

For both HR executives and employees from the service sector, customer service skills are vitally important (Giannantonio & Hurley, 2002). This competency set includes being able to deal effectively with individuals having different backgrounds and experiences. It is important to remember that all businesses have customers, both internal (i.e., employees) and external (i.e., clients). As such, customer service skills are a core competency in all organizations, and are particularly relevant in the domain of HR. In support of this, one of our interviewees argued, "All your employees and prospective employees are the customers of HR, therefore good customer service skills are imperative." Another interviewee took this idea a step further, pronouncing, "For the HR staff, your employees are your biggest customer—modeling service to your employees emulates how service should be delivered to external customers." In short, HR professionals must work every day to satisfy the internal and external customers they serve.

Demographic, Legal, Political, and Economic Issues

In addition to technological changes and the increasing importance of interpersonal, teamwork, and customer service skills, demographic, legal, political, and economic issues also represent significant workplace environmental factors that must be addressed. Because HR professionals have to constantly adapt their HR strategies to changing environmental circumstances, it is no wonder that a recent survey of HR executives indicated that the most important issue facing HR executives today is managing change

(Giannantonio & Hurley, 2002). Considering both international developments (e.g., destabilized governments, conflicts on foreign soil) and changes occurring closer to home (e.g., continued layoffs and streamlining of American companies, increasing oil dependency, fluctuating economic markets), it is easy to see how the ability to manage change can be vital workplace competency for HR managers. On a more positive note, new technologies continue to make our lives easier, while the rising European Union (EU), Chinese, and other Asian markets continue to expand. Each of these changes may require a different organizational response (e.g., outsourcing, facilitating distributed or "virtual" work arrangements, training on new technology, dealing with downsizing). Determining the most appropriate response to changes in the workplace environment is the task of current and future HR practitioners.

THEME 3: I/O PSYCHOLOGY GRADUATE PROGRAMS NEED TO EMPHASIZE (FOR THOSE INTERESTED IN PRACTICE) THE IMPORTANCE OF BECOMING TRUE BUSINESS PLAYERS

I/O Master's program graduates that are inclined to go into practice must become true business players. They must understand not only the importance of developing strategic partnerships within and between organizations, but also how HR fits into the overall missions, visions, and strategies of workplace organizations. It can be argued that the role HR executives play in organizations has shifted from a purely administrative function to one of a business analyst concerned with adding value to the organization (Kaufman, 1999; Schuler, 1990). Because HR departments have traditionally been viewed as serving supportive roles in the organization rather than providing core operating functions (Mintzberg, 1979), the pressure to provide real value to the business is strong, and HR executives often find themselves struggling to prove the necessity of different HR functions and tasks.

As organizations are increasingly seeking competitive advantage through HR, today's HR manager must be able to position and utilize HR so that it is a recognized contributor to the firm's revenue and future growth (Kaufman, 1994). Aligning and positioning HR so that its contributions are recognized systemwide involves demonstrating how HR leads to substantial cost savings, positively affects revenue growth, and serves as a source of competitive advantage (Hunter, 1999). These outcome variables highlight the benefits of HR to key organizational stakeholders and speak to the importance of HR in carrying out an organization's mission, vision, and strategies.

As noted above, adding substantial value through the HR function is achieved only when HR practitioners become true strategic players.

Therefore, HR leaders need to develop more fully their capabilities to generate HR strategy and lead change (Walker & Reif, 1999). To contribute to strategic analysis, HR professionals need to remain informed about industry and market trends, workforce and demographic changes, competitor prices, and other forces relevant to the future performance of the business (Walker & Reif, 1999). Walker and Reif suggest that these goals are best accomplished by direct participation in the company's strategic management process (e.g., in strategic analysis, strategy formulation, and strategy implementation).

The HR professionals we spoke with also agreed that the alignment of HR strategy with organizational strategy is imperative to both HR and organizational success. In our interviews, all participants emphasized the need for HR to be aligned with organizational goals. However, as Van Eynde and Tucker (1997) pointed out, "One of the greatest shortcomings of human resource programs in academia is that students graduate without a comprehensive understanding of how the human resource function fits into and complements the overall strategy of the organization" (p. 401). Although they were referring directly to human resource management programs, this critique also applies to I/O psychology Master's-level education (e.g., most graduates of I/O psychology programs leave without a thorough understanding of the overall concept of compensation and the rationale for using different forms of compensation). Thus, our interview results support Van Eynde and Tucker's assessment. Only one of the HR professionals we interviewed actually reported taking a class in HR strategy, and several other interviewees noted the lack of emphasis on meeting strategic organizational goals. This apparent gap in the training of HR practitioners suggests that I/O psychology Master's programs would benefit from the addition of classes that emphasize the alignment of HR strategy with organizational objectives.

THEME 4: I/O PSYCHOLOGY GRADUATE PROGRAMS NEED TO TEACH GRADUATES HOW TO NAVIGATE CORPORATE POLITICS

Because organizations are made up of individuals and groups with different values, goals, and interests, the potential for conflict over scarce resources is great (Pfeffer, 1981). In order to maintain a stake in the allocation of these scarce resources, many organizational members engage in politicking. Farrell and Petersen (1982) define politicking as the collective set of actions one takes to influence, or attempt to influence, the distribution of advantages and disadvantages within one's organization. Organizational politics thus involve intentional acts of influence that are meant to protect or enhance the self-interest of individuals or groups (Allen et al., 1979).

The results from our interviews with HR professionals indicate that an understanding of how to navigate corporate politics is crucial to work success but, at the same time, is not always emphasized thoroughly enough in graduate-level HR training. One explanation for this apparent disconnect is the limited opportunity graduate students—in particular, I/O Master's students—receive for developing this competency in the classroom. Along these lines, a number of the HR professionals we interviewed felt that recent graduates get frustrated by the realities encountered in business. Some of these graduates learn a great deal about business from their educational experiences and are eager to put that knowledge to use. However, they are often unaware of the complexities and politics of corporate environments that regularly limit the solutions and ideas that can be implemented. On entering work organizations, these students often have impractical ideas and would clearly benefit from more realistic previews concerning their ability to influence their organization.

Compounding the difficulty of navigating corporate politics is the fact that corporate politics are often company-specific. That is, organizations vary in the degree to which political savvy is critical for obtaining resources. Understanding when and how to engage in politicking has thus become an important skill for I/O Master's graduates to possess. Although this skill can be taught to some degree in the classroom, it seems likely that much of the development in this area will have to take place in internships and within actual workplace settings (see Chapter 13 for more information on how to use internships and applied field courses in the training of HR management students).

THEME 5: I/O PSYCHOLOGY GRADUATE PROGRAMS NEED TO EMPHASIZE THE IMPORTANCE OF MANAGING ONE'S CAREER AND VIEWING HR EDUCATION AS A LIFELONG PURSUIT

As new technologies are implemented and the nature of work continues to evolve, HR professionals will be required to build and maintain competencies that were not even recognized as important during their formal education. Employees will be expected to keep abreast of new developments in the field and to drive their own self-development (Kemske, 1998). This self-development will need to occur at multiple points in HR professionals' careers and should be tailored to the needs of specific individuals (Barber, 1999).

Our interviewees echoed the importance of continuous development in the management of their own careers. Specifically, the overwhelming majority indicated that they received no formal training on how to manage their careers during their HR education. In fact, most of these individuals reported that the primary mode of development throughout their careers had been self-development and learning that resulted from life experience. There are, however, options for organizations that want to take a more proactive approach to promoting continuous learning.

One avenue with particular promise for enabling I/O Master's graduates to manage their careers is mentoring. Mentoring is "the process of an older, more experienced member of the organization assuming a paternal, guiding role with a less experienced protégé" (Hill, Bahniuk, Dobos, & Rouner, 1989, p. 356). Mentors may serve a variety of functions, including emphasizing the importance of being involved in professional organizations, providing developmental coaching and feedback, and directing newer workers to appropriate training and educational opportunities. Research evidence has demonstrated that mentoring relationships can be beneficial for protégés as they have been associated with increases in protégé pay, the number of promotions they receive, and their job satisfaction (Allen et al., 2004; Chao, Walz, & Gardner, 1992; Dreher & Ash, 1990; Fagenson, 1989; Scandura, 1992; Whitely, Dougherty, & Dreher, 1991).

Although mentoring may help HR professionals in their career development, most graduates understand that learning is a lifelong pursuit. However, they may not fully recognize the myriad of ways in which learning can occur. For instance, another area of development mentioned by many of the professionals we interviewed is the opportunity for special training and certificate programs. These programs can adopt a number of formats, including in-house training, off-site workshops, Web-based training and learning modules, and Society for Human Resource Management–sponsored continuing education opportunities. It is important that new I/O Master's graduates recognize the value of these opportunities for career advancement and readily identify and capitalize on them when they are provided. The need for HR graduates to continuously update their skills was echoed most succinctly by one of our interview participants who stated the oft-repeated maxim, "the only thing for sure is change." Realistically preparing graduates for this change before they leave school seems a useful endeavor indeed.

Concluding Remarks

In today's business environment, HR professionals must be armed with a broader and deeper set of competencies—not just in traditional HR functions but also in interpersonal, teamwork, customer service, and information technology skills. In addition to enlarging their skill base, they must also be cognizant of how the changing nature of work affects HR practice and how HR can contribute to overall organizational objectives and goals. These various competency requirements place incredible demands on the

HR professional that can potentially be met in I/O psychology graduate training. However, our review of the literature, combined with interviews of HR professionals, revealed that not all of these competency requirements are adequately covered in I/O Master's-level programs.

In this chapter, we identified five themes that, taken together, suggest that I/O psychology graduate programs would benefit from matching their curricula to the results of needs analyses conducted with HR professionals, including courses that emphasize the influence of workplace environmental forces on HR functions and requisite competencies, outlining how changes in the HR roles (e.g., in terms of acting as a strategic business partner) affect how HR is performed, providing instruction on how to network and navigate corporate politics, and teaching students how to manage their careers. However, because most terminal I/O Master's programs involve only two years of coursework, we fully acknowledge that there is a limit to the amount of information and KSAs that can be taught within these programs. It is important, therefore, that internships or applied field projects be used as much as possible to provide additional means of preparing I/O Master's students for work in the field.

As HR becomes a pivotal part of many workplace organizations, it is likely that HR functions and responsibilities will become even more demanding and challenging in the future. In fact, Kemske (1998) notes, "[HR] will move into a leadership position as organizations come to understand how much they depend on it" (p. 53). These changes in the functions and responsibilities of HR will require that HR professionals be equipped to take on new roles within organizations and to apply what they have learned in graduate training to novel situations. As a result, it is crucial that I/O graduate programs consistently evaluate the effectiveness of their course curricula. To accomplish this, HR academicians and practitioners must continue to communicate with each other and to work in partnership to develop educational opportunities that adequately prepare students for work in the field.

References

Allen, R. W., Madison, D. L., Porter, L. W., Renwick, P. A., & Mayes, B. T. (1979). Organizational politics: Tactics and characteristics of its actors. *California Management Review, 22*(1), 77–83.

Allen, T. D., Eby, L. T., Poteet, M. L., Lentz, E., & Lima, L. (2004). Career benefits associated with mentoring for protégés: A meta-analysis. *Journal of Applied Psychology, 89,* 127–136.

Barber, A. E. (1999). Implications for the design of human resource management—Education, training, and certification. *Human Resource Management, 38,* 177–182.

Berry, L. M. (1990). *Careers of I/O psychology alumni: Part II. Working with an I/O master's degree.* Paper presented to the convention of the Western Psychological Association, Los Angeles, April 1990.

Blum, M. L., & Naylor, J. C. (1968). *Industrial psychology: Its theoretical and social foundations.* New York: Harper & Row.

Cedar. (2001). *Cedar 2001 human resources self-service/portal survey: Fourth annual survey.* Baltimore, MD: Author.

Chao, G. T., Walz, P. M., & Gardner, P. D. (1992). Formal and informal mentorships: A comparison on mentoring functions and contrast with nonmentored counterparts. *Personnel Psychology, 45,* 619–636.

Dreher, G. F., & Ash, R. A. (1990). A comparative study of mentoring among men and women in managerial, professional, and technical positions. *Journal of Applied Psychology, 75,* 539–546.

Dunnette, M. D. (1991). Blending the science and practice of industrial and organizational psychology: Where are we and where are we going? In M. D. Dunnette & L. Hough (Eds.), *Handbook of industrial and organizational psychology* (Vol. 1, pp. 1–27). Palo Alto, CA: Consulting Psychologists Press.

Dyer, W. G., Jr. (1999). Training human resource champions for the twenty-first century. *Human Resource Management, 38,* 119–124.

Fagenson, E. A. (1989). The mentor advantage: Perceived career/job experiences of proteges versus non-proteges. *Journal of Organizational Behavior, 10,* 309–320.

Farrell, D., & Petersen, J. C. (1982, July). Patterns of political behavior in organizations. *Academy of Management Review, 7*(3), 430–442.

Giannantonio, C. M., & Hurley, A. E. (2002). Executive insights into HR practices and education. *Human Resource Management Review, 12,* 491–511.

Gueutal, H. (2003). The brave new world of eHR. In D. Stone (Ed.), *Advances in human performance and cognitive engineering research* (Vol. 3, pp. 13–36). Amsterdam: JAI.

Hansen, W. L. (2002). Developing new proficiencies for human resource and industrial relations professionals. *Human Resource Management Review, 12,* 513–538.

Hill, S. E. K., Bahniuk, M. H., Dobos, J., & Rouner, D. (1989). Mentoring and other communication support in the academic setting. *Group & Organization Studies, 14,* 355–368.

Horton, W. K. (2000). *Designing web-based training: How to teach anyone anything anywhere anytime.* New York: Wiley.

Hunter, R. H. (1999). The "new HR" and the new HR consultant: Developing human resource consultants at Anderson Consulting. *Human Resource Management, 38,* 147–155.

Kaufman, B. E. (1994, September). What companies want from HR graduates. *HR Magazine, 39,* 84–86.

Kaufman, B. E. (1999). Evolution and current status of university HR programs. *Human Resource Management, 38,* 103–110.

Kemske, F. (1998, January). HR 2008: A forecast based on our exclusive study. *Workforce, 77,* 46–55.

Kraut, A. I., & Korman, A. K. (1999). The "DELTA forces" causing change in human resource management. In A. I. Kraut & A. K. Korman (Eds.), *Evolving practices in human resource management: Responses to a changing world of work* (pp. 3–22). San Francisco: Jossey-Bass.

Lowe, R. H. (1993). Master's programs in industrial/organizational psychology: Current status and a call for action. *Professional Psychology: Research and Practice, 24,* 27–34.

Mintzberg, H. (1979). *The structure of organizations.* Upper Saddle River, NJ: Prentice Hall.

Muchinsky, P. M. (1990). *Psychology applied to work: An introduction to industrial and organizational psychology.* Pacific Grove, CA: Brooks/Cole.

Pfeffer, J. (1981). *Power in organizations.* Marshfield, MA: Pitman.

Rogelberg, S. G., & Gill, P. M. (2004). The growth of industrial and organizational psychology: Quick facts. *The Industrial-Organizational Psychologist, 42*(1), 25–27.

Scandura, T. A. (1992). Mentorship and career mobility: An empirical investigation. *Journal of Organizational Behavior, 13,* 169–174.

Schoonover, S. (1998). *Human resource competencies for the year 2000: The wake up call.* Alexandria, VA: Society for Human Resource Management.

Schuler, R. (1990). Repositioning the human resource function: Transformation or demise? *Academy of Management Executive, 4,* 49–59.

SIOP, Inc. (1989). *Graduate training programs in industrial/organizational psychology and organizational behavior.* College Park, MD: Author.

SIOP, Inc. (1994). *Guidelines for education and training at the Master's level in industrial-organizational psychology.* Arlington Heights, IL: Author.

Stone, D. (Ed.). (2003). *Advances in human performance and cognitive engineering research: Electronic human resource technologies* (Vol. 3). Amsterdam: JAI.

Towers Perrin. (2001). *HR survey.* Retrieved November 2001, from http://www.towers.com/towers/servicess-products/TowersPerrin/hrsurvey2001.htm

Trahan, W. A., & McAllister, H. A. (2002). Master's level training in industrial/organizational psychology: Does it meet the SIOP guidelines? *Journal of Business and Psychology, 16*(3), 457–465.

Van Eynde, D. F., & Tucker, S. L. (1997). A quality human resource curriculum: Recommendations from leading sector HR executives. *Human Resource Management, 36,* 397–408.

Walker, J. W., & Reif, W. E. (1999). Human resource leaders: Capability strengths and gaps. *Human Resource Planning, 22,* 21–30.

Whitely, W., Dougherty, T. W., & Dreher, G. F. (1991). Relationship of career mentoring and socioeconomic origin to managers' and professionals' early career progress. *Academy of Management Journal, 34,* 331–335.

SECTION 3

HR Education in Business Schools

Chapters in Section 2 described Master's-level HR programs in IR and I/O psychology. There is no comparable chapter on Master's-level HRM education in business schools. The reason for this state of affairs is variability in course offerings. As Cohen discusses in Chapter 18, accreditation bodies and faculty composition play a role in the development of all educational curricula. Graduate faculty field identification plays an even greater role in the development of *graduate* curricula in management departments of business schools than the role played by general faculty at the undergraduate level. Each department's faculty tries to maintain or increase its core course offerings, as these generate required student enrollment and thus provide additional resources for the department. Within management departments it is very difficult for a small group of faculty, such as HRM faculty, to get their course listed as "core." Compared to other departments in the college, faculty in management departments are field diverse (e.g., OB, HR, strategy, operations, and sometimes others). Although one "behavior" course is specified by the business school accreditation body (AACSB), the core course is typically an organizational behavior course. As a general rule, there are more OB faculty in business schools than HRM faculty. Consequently, the MBA and BBA core tends to include a course in organizational behavior, not in HRM. Within business schools, there also tends to be confusion among faculty and administrators as to the differences between OB and HRM. That confusion results in development of specialized Master's programs, using the label HRM, whose faculty are not proficient in the functional areas of HRM. Because of all of these reasons, Master's "HRM" graduates of business schools will vary in their HR expertise. This is less true for BBA graduates.

The undergraduate business HRM major is required to take all business core courses. As well, the undergraduate HRM major is normally taught by faculty who are functionally proficient in HRM. Thus, although there is no chapter specifically describing HRM Master's-level education in business schools, this section of the book contains three chapters on the topic of undergraduate HRM education in business schools. Recognizing a need to recharge HRM undergraduate education, Chapters 5, 6, and 7 discuss four approaches to educating undergraduates in business schools: University of Wisconsin-Eau Claire, Ohio University, University of Colorado, and Copenhagen Business School. The last approach is typical of the European approach to HRM.

In Chapter 5, Bergmann and Lester discuss key elements of a successful undergraduate educational program in HRM at the University of Wisconsin-Eau Claire and ways students can effectively learn and demonstrate their competencies. The chapter focuses on ways students can learn technical HR knowledge and skill and develop a range of other competencies necessary for job and career success. Besides functional HR courses, their HR curriculum emphasizes oral and written communication and includes one course in organizational change and also the capstone course in business strategy. The authors further emphasize the use of a wide range of curriculum delivery tools, including exercises, cases, projects, and a paid internship. Additionally, they discuss the advantages of SHRM student memberships and the value of the professional HRM certification exam.

Thacker starts Chapter 6 by suggesting that some major changes should be made in approaches taken to educate HRM majors in undergraduate business school programs. In describing the recommended changes, she presents a four-pronged approach to undergraduate HRM education at Ohio University: textbook, application, competency development, and integration. She explains through examples how all four elements are necessary and can be incorporated into the educational process through careful planning. Her teaching goal is to both ground the student in the required body of knowledge and test the application of that knowledge. Thacker notes that textbook knowledge acquisition is the first step in education, and this knowledge should be delivered by a professor with understanding of the material. Memorization and exposure to basic principles are also necessary steps before application can lead to effective learning.

In Chapter 7, Balkin and Schjoedt view HRM as an individual manager's responsibility. Even so, they describe two very different applications of Mahoney's Model 3. At the University of Colorado-Boulder, undergraduate HRM education is focused on preparing undergraduates to work primarily in small businesses and entrepreneurial ventures in which functional HRM skills are embedded within broader managerial roles. The Copenhagen Business School also focuses on developing individuals with general business competence. However, Copenhagen's HR preparation differs significantly from that of Colorado and other HR programs in the

United States. Specifically, the HR coursework consists of two electives, reading lists, thesis, and internship. The two HR courses are not functional and in the U.S. would be labeled organizational behavior courses. The students sample numerous HR topics rather than receive a comprehensive presentation of one or more HR functional areas. Chapter 7 presents relatively detailed descriptions of both approaches.

Developing Quality Human Resource Professionals

5

Identifying the Appropriate Undergraduate Curriculum, Applying Human Resource Competencies, and Validating Human Resource Competencies

Thomas J. Bergmann

Scott Lester

We believe that HRM education is embarking on a major transformation. By being cognizant of and responsive to the concerns of organizational leaders and established human resource professionals, we believe that educators can have a positive impact on the contributions of new practitioners entering the field. In this chapter, we examine the key elements of a successful undergraduate educational program in human resource management. We discuss ways that students can effectively learn and demonstrate their competencies to potential employers who are hiring for an entry-level position. More specifically, we focus on the following important issues in undergraduate HRM education: (1) an appropriate undergraduate curriculum for human resource management majors, (2) the value of an internship as part of the learning experience, (3) the advantages of being an active member in a student chapter of the Society for Human Resource Management (SHRM), and (4) the benefits of having majors prepare for and take SHRM's "Professional in Human Resources" certification exam as part of their educational process.

The questioning of the status of human resource management education is really not a new topic. Herbert G. Heneman, Jr. and others in the early 1980s questioned the appropriate educational background for individuals entering the HRM field. The issue arose at that time because the nature of the field was shifting from the study of labor-management relations, that is, primarily union-management relations, to employee relations that include both union and nonunion employment relationships (Heneman, 1999). This shift was due in part to the decreasing percentage of the unionized labor force and to the implementation of new management practices and a changing employment relationship.

So why are professionals and educators once again questioning the status of HRM education? As the new millennium gets underway, American business finds that it is witnessing significant changes in the employment relationship due to a variety of operating problems. Changes in the employment relationship are once again requiring human resource educators to examine the role human resources will play in the strategic direction of business and consequently the educational background required of human resource professionals to be active partners in the strategic decision-making process. We believe that, once again, human resource education is going through a major transformation that can have a positive impact on the human resource field.

The field of human resources faces serious challenges as it attempts to deal with a dynamic and often hostile business environment. As organizations face an increasingly competitive marketplace, management is analyzing all facets of the organization to reduce operating costs. Because labor cost makes up a significant percentage of most organizations' operating costs, it is an area that constantly comes under scrutiny. It has traditionally been the responsibility of the human resource department to design and implement an employee relations program that will enable the organization to recruit, develop, and retain the best employees without significant concern about other business issues—a silo approach.

There are some who believe the future of the human resource function will go the way of the dinosaur, that is, it will become extinct. They believe that individuals within the human resource unit have become a hindrance to the organization's ability to adapt to the changing workplace and that it has become at best an unneeded overhead expense. And with a silo attitude, that might very well be true. But there is increasing evidence that the human resource function is significantly changing and that it will continue to evolve (Barber, 1999; Heneman, 1999; Losey, 1999; Thacker, 2002).

Organizations must still be able to recruit and retain competent employees in a tight labor market in order to serve their customers in an efficient and effective way; if human resource professionals are educated to view the big picture of corporate strategy, they can assist the organization in the implementation and development of its strategic plan.

To be sought-after members of the evolving human resource profession, poised to be successful partners with members of the other business functional areas, students must be aware of the critical competencies they should develop while completing their undergraduate education. New human resource professionals whose value to the organization exceeds their cost will yield returns to the organization sooner and thus will be perceived a more valuable asset acquisition. It is critical that undergraduate students are able to demonstrate competencies because it will give them an edge over other applicants attempting to enter the field; they will be able to show their learning curve will be faster than the competition. How can students develop these competencies and demonstrate to potential employers that they possess them?

This chapter addresses three ways for undergraduate students to develop and demonstrate competencies to a potential employer who is looking to fill an opening for an entry-level human resource management position:

1. Successful completion of appropriate course work that incorporates sufficient background in the functional human resources areas along with an internship that can show the potential employer that the knowledge and skill gained in the university transfers to the workplace.

2. Active membership in a student chapter of SHRM that indicates both interest and interaction beyond the minimum.

3. Successful completion of SHRM's "Professional in Human Resources" (PHR) certification process to validate an individual's content knowledge in the functional human resource areas.

HRM Competencies and Curriculum

In recent years a number of articles have addressed the competencies, knowledge, and skills an individual must posses to be an effective human resource professional. Ulrich, Brockbank, Yeung, and Lake (1995) presented a framework for three domains of human resource competencies: knowledge of the business, human resource functional expertise, and managing change. The framework—a result of a survey of 12,689 individuals in 109 firms—found that human resource professionals were perceived as more effective if they could (1) demonstrate an understanding of how business actually operates beyond their own field (e.g., finance, accounting, strategy, technology, marketing-business knowledge), (2) transfer their specific knowledge into effective human resource practices (staffing, development, appraisal, rewards, organizational design, and communication), and (3) manage the organizational change process (e.g., analyzing and solving problems, leadership, building relationships, and establishing goals). In follow-up research by Brockbank, Ulrich, and Beatty (1999), two additional domains were added: cultural management (help firms deal with different mindsets) and personal credibility (integrate values and beliefs that build positive relationships with internal and external customers). Research by Losey (1999) identified an HR competency equation that includes intelligence, education, experience, ethics, and interest that can fit into the above framework by Ulrich et al. (1995) and Brockbank et al. (1999).

In designing an undergraduate curriculum it is essential to look at what the relevant literature identifies as the critical competencies that will be required of human resource professionals in the future. The literature indicated that becoming proficient only in human resource practices does not fully prepare an individual to be an effective professional. The future professional must have competencies not only in the traditional areas within human resources (e.g., staffing, development) but also the business functions (e.g., strategy, finance) to be able to understand and manage change (e.g., leadership, vision) and have personal credibility. The increased emphasis on the business functions and the management of change has resulted in increased training of practicing HRM professionals in the functions of business. This is evident in offerings by SHRM Academy. On June 22–23, 2002, the Academy provided a day-and-a-half-long course in either finance, individual and organizational change, or marketing or business strategy to 100 practicing HRM professionals. The success of the program resulted in a second offering on October 24–25 in Chicago (Clark, 2002). As long as there is demand, these offerings are continuing.

Where can one find information about the current state of practice, which can be useful to consider when developing an appropriate human resource curriculum? One approach is to be personally involved in practice. Another is to contact SHRM for information. SHRM is the largest professional organization devoted to the field of human resources. It has approximately 180,000 members and has developed a certification process to validate the human resource knowledge of its professionals. SHRM examinations focus on a common body of knowledge built around the following domains: strategic management, workforce planning and employment, human resource development, compensation and benefits, employee and labor relations, and occupational health, safety, and security (HRCI, 2002). These same issues are usually the content of introductory textbooks in HRM, although depending on the author's perspective, some of the topics are not included. Thus, it is useful to examine the content of SHRM examinations as well.

Business executives have complained about the poor communication skills of most college-degreed applicants in general, and human resource applicants have been no exception. It is critical for students who wish to obtain an entry-level HRM position to develop their oral and written communication skills. Most universities require a freshman English composition course; however, that by itself is totally inadequate. It is important for students to take additional written communication courses, especially those designed to focus on business communication, such as business report and memo writing. Papers written for all business courses should be reviewed for appropriate grammar, sentence structure, and style.

Oral communication also needs additional attention. Students should take a number of oral presentation courses to improve their presentation skills and their interpersonal communication skills. Such courses, designed for business, emphasize conducting meetings and leading team projects as well as making presentations to an audience. The emerging human resource professionals will not fulfill their true potential by solely understanding the functional areas. They must also be able to communicate their ideas effectively, in a manner that allows colleagues to understand the reasoning behind the human resource policies and practices that are being suggested or implemented. We also believe that students should experience and use advanced business technologies in their communication courses because this is what they will be expected to do for their employer.

Seven years ago the University of Wisconsin-Eau Claire's (UW-Eau Claire) College of Business doubled the written and oral communication course requirements for all business majors. In addition, upper-level business courses significantly increased the number of technologically enhanced activities required as part of regular course requirements. For example, students learned to create professional-level presentations using presentation software and experienced classes conducted with electronic meeting software. The feedback from recruiters has been overwhelming positive. They have told us that our students present themselves better than other students, and this has resulted in an increased desire by recruiters to interview on campus. Even when other institutions were experiencing a drop in recruiters, UW-Eau Claire was seeing a significant increase.

Academics and others who continuously interact with the business community indicate the importance of the undergraduate curriculum not only reflecting the common body of knowledge as identified by SHRM, but also including basic course work in the various functional areas of business and courses that will permit students to understand and champion organizational change (Brockbank et al., 1999; Losey, 1999). In fact, 42% of human resource professionals surveyed in the United States identified the management of change as the most critical competency for being effective in their jobs (Ulrich et al., 1995). HRM majors at UW-Eau Claire are required to take a course in organizational change as well as complete a capstone course in business strategy that forces them to integrate their human resource knowledge with their understanding of other business functions. However, sending students through lecture courses (even with PowerPoint) in each of these areas will not provide them with the competencies required to be successful. A successful educational program must take steps to increase the transfer of knowledge from the classroom to the business environment. Several approaches can facilitate this transfer process.

First, the course design must require the students to apply the theories, principles, and concepts being taught to a variety of business situations. Just as the human resource professional must become an active partner with line managers at all levels and assist them in increasing the competitive advantage of their unit and the organization as a whole, the educator should design application exercises, cases, and projects such that the students learn not only how to apply human resource practices, but also how to fit them into a larger business context (Barber, 1999; Brockbank et al., 1999). Activities would include a combination of human resource practice applications and larger projects that force students to consider external factors such as product and labor market issues, both domestic and global, cost constraints, and other financial and strategic issues (Barber, 1999; Thacker, 2002). This increased strategic emphasis will enable the professionals to increase their personal credibility, as they can view employee issues from a broader perspective and thus are able to integrate human resource strategies better with organizational goals and strategies.

Building partnerships with local companies can improve both the curriculum and the practical value of course projects. Universities can invite respected professionals from their community to serve on an advisory board (Thacker, 2002). These individuals can provide feedback about the strengths and deficiencies of previous graduates in the field. Two benefits of this feedback are (1) increased knowledge of the types of applied projects that would benefit students and (2) the likelihood that the advisory board will be willing to give students access to their companies to complete the applied projects they recommend.

And yet, coursework is not enough, even with the best cases and other activities that require students to apply content specific practices in a variety of situations while considering both the short-term and long-term impact on all organizational units and the organization's goals. If at all possible, students need real-world practical experience so they can observe these human resource practices in action and view the impact these practices have on the strategic direction of the organization. One of the most effective methods for students to gain this experience is through a paid internship. We emphasize paid internship because it has been our experience that unpaid internships do not provide the student with the in-depth experience they need. An organization that pays interns is more diligent in finding meaningful work, as opposed to low-level clerical tasks that do not permit interns to gain the experience potential employers value. This does not mean that all unpaid internships should be rejected. Indeed, some organizations provide the students with relevant experience even though they will not or cannot pay the interns.

It has been our experience that a student who has been on an internship does better on examinations, provides more pertinent information during classroom discussion, does a better job on cases and other applied activities, is a more effective leader in team activities, and has a broader perspective in reviewing course materials. Even though we have not kept official records, many years of observation indicate that UW-Eau Claire students with internships generally interview better and receive more job offers, both in human resources and in other management jobs. These observations are in line with national figures regarding the benefits of internships. For example, employers rated internships as one of the most effective tools for identifying and recruiting candidates for full-time positions. Furthermore, those employers who were surveyed indicated that they made job offers to 57% of their interns and 62% of these offers were accepted (Gold, 2001). By gaining work-related experience during college, graduates are more likely to be employed within their fields of study and are able to secure employment more quickly following graduation (Kysor & Pierce, 2000). In summary, the literature and our experience indicate that potential employers wish entry-level human resource professionals to have experience before starting a job. Internships provide students with the opportunity to fulfill this entry-level job requirement.

Participation in Student Chapter of SHRM

College campuses that are serious about educating potential undergraduates for entry-level HRM jobs have active student chapters of the Society for Human Resource Management. The purpose of these chapters is to increase student awareness of the field of HRM. In a way, the chapter experience provides students with a "realistic job preview" without actually having a job in the field. This is accomplished by having the student group engage in such activities as conducting projects for the local professional SHRM chapter (e.g., wage and benefits surveys, review of local performance appraisal practices), having guest speakers from the local professional SHRM chapter make presentations and engage students in dialogue on relevant human resource topics, and coordinating resume and interviewing workshops in which professionals critique students' resumes and run them through mock interviews.

Student chapters of SHRM are relatively small in comparison to some other students groups (e.g., American Marketing Association, Student

Accounting Association). Therefore, students have a good opportunity to take on a leadership role. One competency that has been identified as important for the HR professional is that of leadership, and student SHRM chapters provide students with the opportunity to take on an officer's role, committee chair position, or special project chair. The ability to come into an interview and provide concrete examples of tasks an individual was able to accomplish in a student group usually impresses interviewers, who are familiar with how hard it is to lead and motivate college students with conflicts among school, jobs, and an active social life.

SHRM student leadership also provides students with experience in leading a relatively diverse work team. Most campuses are more diverse than the community from which many of the students originate. Students have an opportunity to lead committees that consist of individuals from diverse backgrounds, a more likely representation of the diversity they will experience in a work setting. By interacting with the local professional chapter of SHRM, the leaders of the student chapter will also gain valuable experience in sharpening their communication skills and other business skills. One additional benefit is that active membership and leadership in SHRM demonstrates to potential employers that the students are truly interested in the HRM field and are willing to contribute to the field by taking leadership roles. We have found that well over 50% of the officers seek out and attain human resource internships and over 50% of the officers obtain human resource professional positions by graduation or shortly thereafter.

The Value of SHRM Certification Examination

The issue of validating an individual's knowledge is more critical for a student with limited or no human resource experience than it is for someone who has been practicing in the profession for years. Even beyond completing the appropriate coursework and gaining initial experience either through a human resource internship or through a leadership role in the local student SHRM chapter, there is a method by which students can validate their knowledge in the field—the PHR certification exam. This is not strictly a student examination. Professionals without formal training in human resources, but with experience, often use the certification process offered by SHRM to validate to employers that they have an adequate background in the total human resource function. By passing SHRM certification test they can demonstrate that they have the technical background to perform the job, thus improving their marketability. For students, it may even be more important to use SHRM certification test to validate their knowledge. During times of documented university grade inflation, employers can use this test to level the playing field for all applicants and ensure that the applicant has at a minimum the technical human resource knowledge necessary to perform the job.

SHRM certification test that college students are eligible to take is the Professional in Human Resource Management (PHR). Current students are permitted to sit for the PHR for a reduced price but must complete the Human Resource Certification Institute Student/Recent Graduate Verification Form prior to the examination. Students passing the examination cannot use the PHR designation until after they have obtained two years of exempt human resource work experience, provided an official transcript documenting graduation, and paid the remainder of the examination fee (HRCI, 2002). We have found that employers have a very positive view of students passing the PHR examination and look at it as something that makes the applicant distinct from many other applicants. This distinction may be particularly advantageous for graduates as employers continue to increase their use of online recruitment methods. Specifically, certifications serve as a tool to help companies narrow down their applicant pool for a human resource position to more manageable numbers (Cohen, 2001). Since spring of 1999, 106 management majors at UW-Eau Claire have taken the PHR examination and 86 have passed, giving us an 81% pass rate. This pass rate is above the national average of 66% of all individuals taking the PHR certification examination.

The certification test provides faculty one additional piece of information regarding curriculum design. As mentioned earlier, it breaks the material into six functional areas. For each of the six functional areas it provides the percentage of the PHR examination that each area will make up, thus providing a weighted importance for each area based on judgment of SHRM professionals. It should be noted that the percentages for the areas differ on the basis of whether an individual is taking the PHR or the Senior Professional in Human Resource Management (SPHR, which is not available to students). The following is the percentage coverage of each of the functional areas for the PHR test: strategic management (12%), workforce planning and employment (26%), human resource development (15%), compensation and benefits (20%), employee and labor relations (21%), and occupational health, safety, and security (6%; HRCI, 2002). We are not saying that an undergraduate human resource curriculum must parallel the percentages just listed, but that the content areas and percentages can be used as general guidelines on what SHRM identifies as important for entry-level positions.

Summary

The field of human resources is a very competitive one in which more individuals are seeking positions than there are openings. Thus, to be considered legitimate applicants for entry-level positions, undergraduate students must be properly prepared. The demand on professionals is changing. If the field is going to survive it must adapt to the demand placed on it or it will die, as some have predicted. One significant change is the increase in business knowledge competencies that will be required of human resource professionals in the future. Curricula should be designed to provide students with adequate education in such areas as accounting, finance, and technology so they can be more active partners with line managers who are attempting to design and implement strategies that will accomplish organizational goals as efficiently and effectively as possible. Human resource professionals also need to have training in the area of organizational change. The business curriculum should place a greater emphasis on both written and oral business communications. The ability to communicate effectively is a critical skill when it comes to successfully managing change initiatives. The student must still be well versed in the traditional functional areas of human resource practices (e.g., staffing, training, performance appraisal, compensation) because those are the skills they will likely apply in their initial assignments. Students can validate this knowledge by passing SHRM's PHR examination. In addition, students must demonstrate that they can transfer this knowledge to the work environment and that they possess the leadership skills to influence behaviors. This can be accomplished via human resource internships, part-time human resource jobs, and leadership positions in student SHRM groups.

References

Barber, A. E. (1999). Implications for the design of human resource management—Education, training, and certification. *Human Resource Management, 38,* 177–182.

Brockbank, W., Ulrich, D., & Beatty, R. W. (1999). HR professional development: Creating the future creators at the University of Michigan Business School. *Human Resource Management, 38,* 111–118.

Clark, M. M. (2002). Academy gives HR pros business tips. *HR News, 21*(1), 4.

Cohen, D. (2001). Is certification in your future? *HR Magazine, 46,* 296.

Gold, M. (2001). Colleges, employers report on experiential education. *Spotlight, 24,* pp. 2, 4.

Heneman, R. L. (1999). Introduction: The need for a supply side examination of the human resource profession. *Human Resource Management, 38,* 97–98.

Human Resource Certification Institute (HRCI). (2002). *HRCI 2002 certification information handbook.* Alexandria, VA: Human Resource Certification Institute and Professional Service, Society for Human Source Management.

Kysor, D., & Pierce, M. A. (2000). Does intern/co-op experience translate into career progress and satisfaction? *Journal of Career Planning & Employment, 60,* 25–31.

Losey, M. R. (1999). Mastering the competencies of HR management. *Human Resource Management, 38*, 99–102.

Thacker, R. A. (2002). Revising the HR curriculum: An academic/practitioner partnership. *Education + Training, 44*, 31–39.

Ulrich, D., Brockbank, W., Yeung, A. K., & Lake, D. G. (1995). Human resource competencies: An empirical assessment. *Human Resource Management, 34*, 473–495.

The Critical Components of HRM Undergraduate Preparation

6

Textbook, Application, and Competency Development

Rebecca A. Thacker

Two big problems with undergraduate HRM education are that students do not readily integrate the various core functions of HRM (e.g., how performance appraisal should be closely intertwined with compensation), and students are not forced to apply their learning in meaningful ways. As a result, students are unprepared for the challenges of real-world HRM. This lack of preparedness has had an unfortunate consequence in both the academic and practitioner communities, and the relevance of HRM as an academic discipline has been called into question.

We are at a point in the evolution of the academic side of HRM education that some major changes should be made in the approaches taken to educate undergraduate HRM students. This chapter suggests a four-pronged approach to undergraduate HRM education to include textbook, application, competency development, and integration. Figure 6.1 shows the model that explicates this approach.

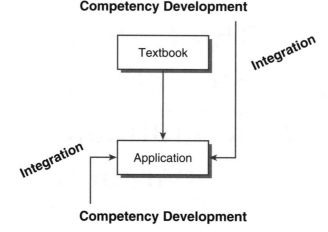

Figure 6.1   Four-Pronged Approach to Undergraduate HRM Education

Textbook Learning

Textbooks do a marvelous job of informing the students of the important principles that underlie the practice of good human resource management, such as different performance appraisal methods, different methods of job analysis, and different job evaluation methods. As well, one can learn about the phases of the training model, the purposes and responsibilities of career development, the advantages and disadvantages of different recruiting methods, and the choice of selection methods available.

Although this is just a sample of what undergraduate HRM textbooks contain, the important point is that the information in textbooks lays an important and necessary foundation for HRM undergraduate education. The textbook information should be delivered by a professor with understanding of the material, as some of it is difficult for students to grasp on their own, e.g., selection test validation strategies. It is simply not possible for undergraduate students to read an HRM textbook on their own and understand the practice of HRM. It is also not possible for textbook reading and professorial explanation alone, regardless of how well delivered, to provide the students with enough of a grasp of the principles to walk into an organization and begin to apply them. That is where the next prong of the approach, application, comes into play.

A word about written cases first. Cases can enhance textbook learning, but are not truly "application." Cases usually provide such a limited amount of information that students are left with more questions than they answer, which often leaves them frustrated. Useful cases present short written scenarios that allow undergraduates to reflect on a particular chapter's topic and in a meaningful, albeit artificial manner reinforce the foundation principles. Good undergraduate HRM textbooks provide short case scenarios that help to cement the textbook learning. Again, this is a useful part of the learning process and lays the groundwork for the next step, application.

Application

Without application, students' learning is of the traditional variety. The pedagogy of traditional learning has led us to the point that we question whether HRM education is dead or simply sleeping. Heinich (1984; as reported in Savery & Duffy, 1995) describes traditional learning as valuing replicability and control. Application, on the other hand, relies on learning that links cognition and action in a direct manner. Professors switch roles from that of a teacher and lecturer to a facilitator of learning. For the students, problem solving, information gathering, and critical thinking skills become important.

Memorization and exposure to basic principles are necessary first steps before application can lead to effective learning, and with textbook learning, these steps have been accomplished. However, application calls on students to tolerate ambiguity, as the "right answer" does not immediately present itself; indeed, there may be more than one right answer.

Here are examples of the difference between *textbook learning* and *application*.

Textbook learning: Using the completed job analysis (shown in the end-of-chapter material) for the job of Supervisor of Maintenance, identify the job specification questions and the job description questions. Then, referring to the sample job description on p. XXX as a guide, write the job description for this position.

Application: Identify a job for which you can conduct a job analysis. Choose a job analysis method, ensuring that you have both job description and job specification questions. Justify your choice of this particular job analysis method. Complete the job analysis. Once the job analysis is completed, write the job description for that position.

Textbook learning: Using the textbook and the assigned readings on Strategic HRM, write a definition of Strategic HRM. Using bullet points, describe the characteristics of an HRM department that is operating in a strategic manner. Do the same for an HRM department that is operating in a traditional manner.

Application: Identify a real-world HRM department that you will be allowed to analyze. Analyze this department. Is it operating in a strategic or a traditional manner, or a combination of both? Support and justify your reasoning in a written report. Make a presentation to the HR manager and your professor summarizing your conclusions.

Competency Development

Although there is no standard set of competencies for HR managers, examples of generally agreed-on competencies include the following:

Interpersonal skills: Active listening, coaching, communicating well both orally and in writing, displaying an understanding of the human concerns and emotions that accompany organizational problems.

Presentation skills: Use of visual aids to enhance presentations, speaking before an audience.

Negotiation skills: Ability to mediate, resolve conflicts.

Team skills: Participate effectively as a team member.

Information technology skills: Ability to use information technology to enhance efficiency and effectiveness for the individual, HR function, or organization.

Troubleshooting skills: Ability to anticipate and recognize problem and crisis situations, help others to understand that problems exist.

Along with application projects, include the opportunity to develop a competency or two. For example, in the job analysis "application" scenario above, the professor has an opportunity to stress the use of interpersonal skills, as the student must be an active listener and a good oral communicator to complete the job analysis properly. The second example involving strategic HRM emphasizes the "presentation skills" competency.

Integration

Integration requires creativity and innovation, as students should be exposed to problems that involve contemplation of more than one HRM function and require further development of one or more competencies. Obviously, integration requires thinking beyond the classroom and the textbook, as the need for crossing functions and incorporating competencies would suggest. Some ideas include the following:

- Go to an actual company for a project. For example, in designing a pay-for-performance plan for a department of a small company, students are forced to look at the performance appraisal system, work design, and job analysis systems.

- Use what's handy and easily accessible. For example, have the HRM students design a recruiting problem for the student SHRM chapter, implement it, and then follow through to see if their ideas have increased the number of chapter members. They will delve into recruitment, planning, and incentives.

- Use your college or university's HRM department for an analysis of whether the department is traditional, strategic, or a combination thereof. In its totality, this kind of project spans many HRM functions: planning, compensation, performance appraisal, training, and development.

Integration is simpler if the faculty map out the learning outcomes for each integrative project ahead of time, ensuring that there are sufficient numbers of projects such that each HRM function is addressed at least once in an integrative manner, i.e., in the presence of other HRM functions. As well, mapping out the competencies that each project is to address is helpful to ensure proper exposure and development for each competency. A matrix approach makes this task easier (see Figure 6.2).

	Project 1	Project 2	Project 3	Project 4
HRM Functions				
Job analysis	X		X	
Performance appraisal		X	X	
Compensation			X	X
HR planning	X	X		
Recruiting		X		X
Strategic HRM	X			X
Competencies				
Interpersonal skills	X	X		
Presentation skills	X		X	X
Negotiation skills		X		
Team skills			X	X
IT skills	X			X
Troubleshooting skills		X	X	

Figure 6.2   A Sample Matrix

If a "live" project with a real company is not possible, another option is to choose a company or current business problem with enough available information that students can delve sufficiently into the project to understand the big picture. In other words, although the project is not "live," it is grounded in a real-world business problem. An example would be to ask students to study the issue of whether stock options should be used as an incentive for company executives and whether backdating has a positive or negative effect on executive performance. Plenty of information is made public on the topic (e.g., company annual reports, SEC filings, *Wall Street Journal* articles), and the topic is certainly timely.

Integrative Roles for HRM Professionals

The importance of partnering with HRM professionals to enhance the integrative nature of the project should not be underestimated. HRM professionals are able to provide a link among different HRM functions, forcing students out of the "functional silo" mentality and encouraging thought about the ramifications of student suggestions. Identifying project experts for each of the newly created projects will also enhance the transfer of the students' learning to the real world. Here are some suggestions for integrating HRM professionals as project advisors into student projects while the projects are ongoing:

- As online advisors who answer questions from the students during a project (relational electronic databases are particularly helpful).
- As on-site facilitators if the project is designed as a "live," on-site project.
- As project development advisors who work with the faculty to develop the project into a practical and meaningful student experience.

Conclusion

This chapter has emphasized that HR education needs a much better grounding in the practical and the applied, although the textbook has its role to play as well. The body of HRM knowledge needs to be instilled in the minds of undergraduate students before they apply it. Application is critically important; it calls on the professor to be both creative and tolerant of ambiguity, much as we ask our students to be. The development of competencies that will serve the students well in the HRM professional world is also a necessary component of HRM education, and can easily be incorporated into the educational process through careful planning. The end result is a student who is both grounded in the required body of knowledge and tested in its application.

References

Heinich, R. (1984). The proper study of instructional technology. *Educational Communications and Technology, 35,* 67–87.

Savery, J., & Duffy, T. (1995). Problem based learning: An instructional model and its constructivist framework. *Educational Technology, 35,* 31–38.

Teaching HR to Undergraduate Students

7

The Colorado and Copenhagen Business School Approaches

David B. Balkin

Leon Schjoedt

"Is HR education dead or just sleeping?" This question provides a challenge to "traditional HR," and it provides an opportunity to consider the recent advances made in HR, as well as a way to stimulate discussion and exchange of ideas between HR scholars. Our brief answer to this challenging question is similar to the remarks of Mark Twain after reading his own obituary in a newspaper, which can be expressed as "the demise of HR has been greatly exaggerated."

This brief answer does not provide an illustration and reason for our position that traditional HR education has adapted to a changing business environment. The business environment and globalization have not been kind to the practice of traditional HR. The field of HR has been forced to rethink its assumptions as large corporations and their headquarter staffs, the traditional location of HR jobs, have been flattened and downsized, and business processes have been deconstructed and pushed out into the market because of information technology advances related to the Internet. In many cases functional HR departments have disappeared. Many HR services have been outsourced and are now delivered by specialized service companies that focus on providing recruiting, training, or benefits administration services to clients. As a reaction to this changed business environment, universities that have provided specialized degrees that prepare students for jobs in functional HR departments have noticed a decline in the interest from employers who seek students to fill traditional HR jobs that are becoming more scarce, and, in turn, a decline in enrollment numbers of students wishing to sign up for HR courses. The decline of interest in traditional HR from both employers and students has led to the question: "Is HR education dead or sleeping?"

It is our position that HR skill requirements have been reconfigured and redistributed into the roles of managers, entrepreneurs, individual employee contributors, teams, and HR generalists as a reaction to the changing business environment and work structures of the 21st century. We believe that university HR programs need to stop grieving for the loss of the traditional HR jobs that have disappeared and deal with the reality that HR exists in different forms and is now embedded within different organizational roles. This chapter describes two approaches to undergraduate HR education that deal with the new reality facing the practice of HR: the first is at the University of Colorado and the second is at the Copenhagen Business School. Each program aims at developing students with HR and business skills that prepare them to function within a broader context of a contemporary business organization and its needs.

The University of Colorado Approach to Teaching HR to Undergraduate Students

The University of Colorado at Boulder has built on its well-known programs in entrepreneurship to restructure the design of its undergraduate program in HRM in a way that takes into account the needs of its students and the firms that employ them. Boulder, Colorado is a major center of entrepreneurship in the United States with many technological start-up companies and entrepreneurships in the area due to the close proximity to the University of Colorado, a major research university, as well as national scientific laboratories such as the National Center for Atmospheric Research (NCAR) and the National Institute of Standards and Technology (NIST). Also, large local employers such as IBM, Storage Tech, and Sun Microsystems have been responsible for creating spin-offs that resulted in the formation of many new companies in the area. Many of the students enrolled in the undergraduate program in business also have career plans to remain in Colorado and participate in the growing entrepreneurial economy of the state and of Boulder in particular. Because of the interests of the students and the university location in the center of a hotbed of entrepreneurship

activity, the faculty at the University of Colorado redesigned the undergraduate HRM program in the late 1990s to focus on preparing its graduates to work in small businesses, entrepreneurial ventures, and larger
companies where human resource management skills are embedded within
the broader roles of managers.

The philosophy of the Colorado approach is to create effective managers who know how to "manage people." This is opposed to producing a
functional human resource specialist that some of the well-known "stand-
alone" HR programs such as Cornell, Minnesota, Illinois, and Michigan
State tend to focus on. These specialized HR programs focus more on the
needs of large corporations. They also focus to a greater extent on graduate education and on developing high-level technical HR skills in their students. These skills are used to design HR policies and programs as well as
manipulate HR information, rather than provide delivery of HR to employees, which is done by managers and HR generalists. Few large, corporate
employers recruit at the University of Colorado for HR skills. Additionally,
the majority of our students aim to remain within Colorado because of its
attractive quality of life. The University of Colorado approach therefore
aims its undergraduate HR program at smaller businesses and attempts to
provide students with broad skill sets in both business and human resources.

BUSINESS SKILL SET

The business skill set requires that Colorado HR students have some
basic understanding of general business skills, which include financial and
managerial accounting, finance, marketing and consumer behavior, operations management, business law and ethics, and strategic management.
The business skills set provides a student with an understanding of functional business disciplines in an organization so that the people management problems can be solved within the context of making a contribution
to the mission and goals of the business and its functional units. For example, a Colorado HR graduate working in a bank as a manager is more likely
to be a quick study and understand that targeted HR services provided by
the manager to front-line bank tellers are going to translate into better
quality customer service given to clients, who will be receiving service
from more satisfied employees.

HUMAN RESOURCE MANAGEMENT SKILL SET

The HRM skills taught in the Colorado HR program are fashioned from
the perspective of the managers and HRM generalists who are expected to
deliver human resource services to employees within their units (in the case
of managers) or to other managers and employees in different functional

groups (in the case of human resource management generalists). The instruction focuses on providing technical content along with cases and experiential training exercises that encourage the students to learn how to apply the HRM skills as managers or HR generalists. This means an emphasis on the implementation of HR policies and practices, rather than on the technical details of the HR policy choices.

Two courses that all HR students take prior to enrolling in their HR content courses are (1) "Critical Leadership and Management Skills" and (2) "Quality Management." The leadership and management skills course provides students the opportunity to obtain hands-on experiences in applying HR tools such as job interviews, performance appraisals, disciplinary actions, and the rewarding and recognition of employees after they make significant contributions. A focus of this course is to develop and deepen the students' "people skills" so they are able to provide better HR services as managers or as HR generalists. The quality management course teaches HR students how to align HR services with product or service quality. It gives students some tools that help them develop the most effective performance measures for HR services.

The students next select three out of four HR courses that have been designed to provide necessary knowledge and skills to successfully earn the certification in human resources from SHRM, the principal professional society in the field. The four HR courses available to Colorado undergraduate students are the following:

- "Employee Relations" covers employment law, workforce diversity, employer and employee rights and responsibilities to each other, employee involvement and empowerment, disciplinary procedures, workforce health and safety, and working with the union in an employment setting.

- "Hiring and Retaining Employees" covers job analysis, recruitment and selection, performance evaluation, workforce planning, and employee assessment and testing.

- "Employee Reward Systems" covers theories of motivation as applied to pay; the legal environment of pay; base salary management and its tools such as job evaluation, pay surveys, and pay structures; policies that link pay incentives to productivity at the individual, group, and organization-wide levels; coverage of government mandated and voluntary employee benefits; and the application of nonmonetary rewards.

- "Training and Development" examines how to develop and deliver an effective employee training program. It explores individual, team, and organization-wide development programs. Topics include skills training, team-building, and managing change.

Each of the HR courses focuses on using HR knowledge to "manage people," which reflects the philosophy of the Colorado approach explained earlier. As a way of illustrating the Colorado approach, we will take the "Employee Reward Systems" course and present some examples of skills that students are taught in this course:

- Learning and applying the Hay Job Evaluation method to accurately classify the worth of a set of job descriptions that represent benchmark positions in the market.

- Developing skills on how to use data gathered from pay surveys available on the Internet and elsewhere to develop pay scales for jobs correctly classified by job evaluation.

- Learning how to apply the pay laws such as the FLSA to correctly classify exempt and nonexempt jobs with respect to overtime and minimum wage provisions, as well as to differentiate between "employee" and "independent contractor" legal statuses for purposes of pay rates and eligibility for group benefits.

- Learning to apply knowledge of merit pay systems, so that pay is allocated fairly with the use of pay differentials, in order to provide levels of rewards corresponding to excellent, average, and below-average employee performance.

- Knowledge of diverse, qualified retirement plans that pertain to small businesses and self-employed individuals, including IRAs, 401(k)s, and Keogh profit-sharing plans.

As this illustration shows, the emphasis of the University of Colorado approach is to put students in the role of a manager who is expected to deliver various HR services to employees so that these services are aligned with company strategies and goals.

The Copenhagen Business School Approach to Teaching Undergraduate HR

Teaching HR to undergraduates in Denmark and in the United States is fundamentally different, which is largely due to the very different goals and stakeholders of higher education. In Denmark, the government funds university-level education (i.e., no tuition is paid by the individual student). Therefore, costs and benefits to society are considered important to the outcome of degree programs. The bachelor's program in business is scheduled to take three years and consists of four semesters of foundation coursework, one semester with electives, and a final semester to complete and defend a thesis.[1] Also, during the program multiple research projects are conducted as part of a course or as independent requirements for the earning the degree. On graduation, the individual is expected to function as a qualified partner in business and in furthering society, as well as have international business competence. This means that the bachelor's program in business focuses on developing an individual with general business competence in analyzing business-related problems, making recommendations, and making business decisions. As this brief introduction suggests, project-based research studies in which theory is applied to real-world situations function as an important aspect in developing individuals into competent business graduates. Also, it shows that the undergraduate program is a generalist program with an opportunity for the individual to develop an emphasis by focusing the electives and thesis on a particular area of interest, such as HR.

At the Copenhagen Business School (CBS) several opportunities exist for a student to develop an emphasis in HR. First, the student may take additional courses at CBS. The course catalog for electives is very extensive and includes courses offered in Danish and in multiple other languages including English. The elective course catalog includes the following HR-related courses: "HRM in Europe," "Personnel Strategy and Labor Law," "Negotiation Strategy and Tactics," "European Labor Law," "International Negotiations," "Crisis Management," and "International Management." Four of these HR-related courses are offered in English: "HRM in Europe," "European Labor Law," "International Management," and "International Negotiations." The course descriptions for "HRM in Europe" and "International Negotiations" are provided in the Appendix. Notice the innovative exam for the course in international negotiations, which consists of a role-play that is videotaped and a written analysis that is to be turned in within 24 hours. Second, the student may participate in an exchange program and complete coursework at the host university, e.g., University of Minnesota. Third, the student may complete a practicum (similar to an internship) that will be the basis for the bachelor's thesis. Whereas the first two opportunities are traditional approaches to teaching HR at CBS, the third approach to teaching HR is an educational innovation at CBS because this approach places a very heavy emphasis on action learning and integrates the practicum with the later bachelor's thesis. This educational approach is under evaluation (audit) at the Ministry of Education for its potential for continued use. Therefore, the remainder of this section will focus on the practicum and the bachelor's thesis, as well as two examples of bachelor's theses that were based on practica.

PRACTICUM AT COPENHAGEN BUSINESS SCHOOL

The practicum is based on students being confronted with the real world of business through a six-month internship in a viable company. To avoid conflicts of interest, the basis for the practicum is not employment with the organization, but the student may be compensated for time and expenses and may seek employment on completion of the practicum. Rather, the practicum provides the student with an opportunity to identify a practical business problem or situation, apply theoretical knowledge to this problem, and make recommendations to the company on how to solve the problem under investigation. This develops the student's theoretical knowledge and competence in using this knowledge and expands the student's experience and network for a career in the business world. For the company, the practicum provides an opportunity for problem identification, analysis, and recommendations for future actions made on the basis of sound research, as well as access to new knowledge and outside perspectives to the organization under the guidance of a faculty member. Any type of organization, including government agencies, can participate as a partner in the practicum. Prior to starting the practicum an agreement is established that covers what work assignments the student needs to complete, contact person at the organization, which department at CBS is the host department, and the project advisor. The student, the advisor, and the contact person develop a plan for the practicum and its execution. The written reports, including the bachelor's thesis, may be treated as confidential. The practicum program is supported by leading organizations in Danish business, such as Dansk Industri, AIESEC, FUHU, Finansrådet, and Dansk Handel & Service, as well as the Danish Ministry of Education. If the student chooses a practicum, the bachelor's thesis is required to be based on the practicum. The examination of the bachelor's thesis based on a practicum consists of the bachelor's thesis and an oral defense of the thesis.

THE BACHELOR'S THESIS

The bachelor's thesis may be completed by an individual or as a group of no more than three students. Whether the bachelor's thesis is completed by an individual or as a group affects its length and the time allocated for the oral defense. If the bachelor's project is completed by one, two, or three students, then the thesis may not exceed more than 60, 80, and 100 pages and 30, 45, and 60 minutes for the oral defense, respectively. An executive summary in English of no more than one page is required for all bachelor's theses. The advisors, a lead and a supporting advisor, and an external examiner evaluate the thesis and the oral defense.

The thesis needs to fulfill some basic requirements. In addition to the requirements of a conventional bachelor's thesis, the thesis based on a practicum needs to include a description of the organization in which the practicum took place and of the practicum itself, i.e., the work, work processes, and problem areas in the organization. This description may not exceed 10 pages. The problems identified in the organization then form the basis for the bachelor's thesis.

The thesis contains a clear and concise problem statement that will be examined. The problem statement addresses the issue under investigation, the theoretical foundation, and empirical basis for the study. The problem statement needs to be approved before further progress is made. The problem statement is presented in a thesis proposal (five to eight pages for an individual, and seven to 10 pages for a group of two or three students) that includes the rationale for the problem statement, the problem statement, limitations for the study, and a preliminary outline for the study.

The bachelor's thesis is based on theory, which forms the basis for the investigation. Theory selection needs to be related to the problem under investigation and is required to be discussed explicitly, including how theory can assist in solving the problem. Also, theory has to be linked to empirical data (either quantitative or qualitative) gathered as part of the project, which requires that research methods be discussed explicitly. The research methods are an integral part of the bachelor's thesis. This method section needs to explain how the theory, methods, and empirical data are related. The thesis reaches a conclusion, which may include recommendations, on the basis of the empirical findings.

The second author, while employed at CBS, functioned as an advisor for multiple bachelor's theses. To provide the reader with a sense of the types of the problems that students examine as part of their bachelor's theses, we will outline two examples.

TWO EXAMPLES

First, a group consisting of three students who were earning a degree in business administration and modern languages (English and Japanese) chose to address a problem with implementing management by objectives (MBO) as a performance appraisal instrument in a Japanese subsidiary of a multinational pharmaceutical company. These three students visited the parent company in Sweden to understand the situation and problem from the perspective of the headquarters. The problem from the parent company's perspective was that the implementation of MBO as a performance appraisal instrument did not work as well as in other subsidiaries. Then they went to Japan for an extended period to collect data—both quantitative and qualitative—that formed the basis for their analysis. The students found that the Japanese employees understood the purpose and use of MBO in performance appraisal, but had issues with setting and discussing goals with their superiors. On the basis of coursework, data collected, literature review, and understanding of the differences between Eastern and Western culture, the students concluded that the HR innovation of using MBO as a basis for performance appraisal in this particular company was incompatible with the Japanese culture and that this incompatibility was the root course for the unsuccessful implementation of MBO in the Japanese subsidiary. The students recommended that the parent company be culturally sensitive when implementing HR changes. The company abandoned the MBO initiative in Japan as a reaction to the students' bachelor's thesis.

Second, a group of three students were asked by a multinational Danish team-based company to conduct an audit of an HR initiative designed to improve employees' basic skill level in Danish, English (the corporate language), and math. The target was to increase the skill level through classes during working hours so that all employees would have at least an eighth grade level in Danish and English reading and comprehension and math skills (nine years of school is required by law). The students conducted multiple interviews with employees at several departments located in greater Copenhagen. On the basis of a social-constructivist paradigm, the students found that the employees were very interested in improving their skills as individuals. However, the local unions representing the employees had problems with the HR initiative despite the fact that no employees would be laid off as a result of failing the tests or classes provided during work hours to improve their skills. The students discovered that some employees did not understand why the company was seeking to improve their skill levels, and they communicated this lack of understanding to their local unions. After further investigation, the students concluded that the company's communication of the program was faulty. Specifically, the company had communicated the language initiative to employees through posters displayed in virtually every room in the company but had not clarified the process it would use to achieve its goals nor allowed employees to ask questions about the initiative and its implementation process. In discussing these findings with the vice president of HR, the students suggested that employees needed an opportunity for two-way communication about the HR initiative. Subsequently, both large-group (25 employees) and small-group sessions were held to present the HR initiative and to answer questions. The students also found that a significant number of employees would not discuss their low skill levels in large groups. On the basis of this information, the company trained some employees to be team leaders. These employees explained the company's vision of the HR initiative and the process of implementation to their peers. They also answered their peers' question. In this way, the employees who had felt uncomfortable asking questions related to their skill levels in large groups could ask these questions of another employee with whom they were comfortable. The end result of this project was that the company informed the students' faculty adviser that it had modified its HR initiative on the basis of the students' recommendations at one plant and, because of its success there, was planning to implement the modified HR initiative at their other plants and offices.

As this description of the practicum and the related bachelor thesis suggests, action learning is a high priority that develops the student's business competence and takes the human element into consideration in theory, in practice, and in integrating theory and practice. Besides coursework in HR and HR-oriented projects, the innovation consists of the training and development of students' knowledge, skills, and competence by using action learning. The human element becomes central to the students' perspective of business administration at Copenhagen Business School.

Note

1. As an illustration of the workload for a three-year bachelor in business program, the second author completed in excess of 160 semester credits to earn a bachelor of science in business administration and economics at Southern Denmark Business School.

Appendix

This appendix presents two HR course descriptions listed on the Copenhagen Business school website. Both courses are offered in the Department of Organization and Industrial Sociology (IOA).

COURSE: HUMAN RESOURCE MANAGEMENT IN DENMARK'S COPENHAGEN BUSINESS SCHOOL

Examination:

Four-hour written open-book examination. Alternatively, the students may in the spring semester choose to combine this course with writing of a bachelor project.

Aim of the Course:

Recent dramatic changes in the European business community increase the need for professional and personal development of the work force. Human resource development has become a strategic factor, and the strategic emphasis is particularly seen in knowledge-based and service-oriented organisations. Rather than selling physical products, these organisations provide service, know-how, systems, etc. The production has an immaterial nature and the development and selling of these "products" require an intensive use of high-level human competence. This explains why not only functional expertise, but also personal characteristics become vital when organizations select and deploy the employees.

The HR strategy is no longer merely a passive reflection of and adjustment to the business strategy. On the contrary, the HR strategy has a proactive role and may have a heavy impact on the business strategy, as this one is reflecting the areas where the organization has or can develop human competence and professionalism.

Course Content:

The course aims at analyzing and interpreting the way human resources are dealt with in various European countries. The course will focus on the following subjects:

- The (missing?) link between business strategy and HRM
- Recruitment and selection
- Training and development
- Developing the international manager
- Management development
- Flexibility of the workforce
- Remuneration
- HRM and cultural differences
- HRM planning

Teaching Methods:

The course will be based on lectures, student presentations of selected studies, and case discussions.

Course Readings:

Chris Steyaert/Maddy Janssens. Human and inhuman resource management; Saving the subject of HRM. *Organization*, Vol. 6, No. 2, 1999.

James Bowditch/Anthony Buono. *A primer on organizational behavior.* John Wiley & Sons, pp. 85–119, 1997.

Geert Hofstede. *Cultures and organizations—Software of the mind.* McGraw-Hill, Chapter 1 and 3, 1997.

Per Darmer. Is it here, there, everywhere?, LOK paper, No. 4, 2001.

Nan M. Sussman. Repatriation transitions: Psychological preparedness, cultural identity, and attributions among American managers, *International Journal of Intercultural Relations, 25,* 2001.

Hugh Fasken. Moving spouse, www.ftexpat.com, August 2001.

Dominique Hammond, Dangerous liaisons, *People Management,* May 31 2001.

William Isaachs. *Dialogue and the art of thinking together,* Doubleday, pp. 17–37 1999.

Ian Roberts. Remuneration and reward, Chapter 13 in Beardwell & Holden, *Human resource management.* Pitman, 1997.

Jeffrey Pfeffer. Six dangerous myths about pay, *Harvard Business Review,* May-June, 1998.

Michael Armstrong/Helen Murlis. *Reward management: A handbook of remuneration strategy and practice,* Kogan Page Limited, 1999.

Kate Purcell/Terence Hogarth/Claire Simm. *Whose flexibility,* Joseph Rowntree Foundation, York, pp. 20–45, 1999.

Jörgen Sandberg. Why some perform better than others, Paper presented in Brussels, October 19–21, 1995.

Robert S. Kaplan/David P. Norton. Using the balanced scorecard as a strategic management system. *Harvard Business Review.* January-February 1996.

Richard Lynch. *Corporate strategy,* Chapter 12. Prentice Hall. London, 1997.

Michael Arthur/Kerr Inkson/Judith Pringle. *The new careers,* Sage, London, pp. 1–21, 1999.

Kerr Inkson/Michael Arthur. How to be a successful career capitalist, *Organizational Dynamics,* Vol. 30, No. 1, 2001.

Chris Brewster/Henrik Holt Larsen. *Human resource management in northern europe,* Blackwell, 2000.

COURSE: INTERNATIONAL NEGOTIATIONS

Examination:

The final examination is a combination of participating in a role-play and writing an analysis of this play within 24 hours. Thus, the examination resembles the role playing and discussions in class. The major idea is to demonstrate the ability to understand what is going on during a negotiation. The written part will be guided by a set of questions.

Aim of the Course:

Commercial and business negotiations taking place in different cultural contexts and languages are becoming increasingly common. Negotiating with foreigners, or discussing issues involving instruction of people from other cultures, requires skills in both communications and interpretation, taking into consideration different social behaviour patterns, nonverbal behavior, etc. It is possible within the time allocated to teach how to master international negotiations, not to discuss all types of problems that may occur during such negotiations. Yet we hope to increase the students' awareness and understanding of these problems. The course offers an introduction to how to cope with cultural differences and to identify stereotypes and misunderstandings between both parties. Being conscious about one's own reactions may prove to be the most productive element. The course deals with norms of and techniques for negotiation and how these differ from country to country.

Course Content:

The course combines systematic description and analysis, including role-plays involving students of various nationalities. The students are expected not merely to reproduce the texts, but to engage themselves in persuasive arguments. The performed role-plays are subsequently used to analyze problems related to this type of negotiations. Class discussions are supplemented with group work and analyses of written or video recorded business cases. Apart from classes and reading assignments, the mixed composition of the student group will offer multiple examples of complex interaction between cultures that may disclose some of the hidden, yet important cultural stereotypes and partial misunderstandings.

Teaching Methods:

Class discussions and role-playing will demonstrate the course that only comprises a few lectures. The course also includes observation and analysis of videotaped negotiations. The students are expected to make themselves acquainted with models and concepts through readings assignments. Reading matters are not summarized in class, but form the basis for the students' comments and criticism and for the subsequent written analysis of the final role.

Course Readings:

A collection of articles and cases on negotiation techniques and inter-cultural differences in management is provided.

SECTION 4

New Emphasis on International HRM Education

As organizations increasingly operate in global markets, HRM activities become more and more complex. To increase the knowledge base of HRM professionals and managers working in international settings, business schools are starting to offer courses in international HRM and courses with an emphasis on managing international HRM activities. The three chapters that follow (Chapters 8, 9, and 10) focus on how the international HRM course is taught to graduate students and in one case, undergraduates at three different universities. Of note is the fact that all three authors have considerable professional experience in international HRM.

In Chapter 8, Hundley presents his approach to teaching a graduate class in international HRM. He bases his course on the idea that global businesses confront two basic problems: (1) localization, the need to adapt its practices to meet market conditions specific to different regions and nations and (2) integration, the need to coordinate regional and national activities and resources to achieve optimal levels of efficiency. The class seeks to build skills and expertise in HRM that will contribute most effectively to organizational success in balancing localization and integration problems.

In Chapter 9, Frayne calls her international HRM course "Managing People in Global Markets." Although consistent with Hundley's orientation, Frayne uses the contingency model as the underlying framework for the course and focuses on the relationship between HRM and organizational performance with respect to three managerial roles, builder, aligner, and navigator. Currently, she teaches this course to undergraduates.

In Chapter 10, Cascio, like Frayne, calls his graduate course "Managing People in Global Markets." Two issues underlie his course content: (1) what current and future HR professionals and general managers should know about the economic, legal, and cultural aspects of the countries in which they conduct their activities and (2) which HR knowledge and skills cross national borders and which apply only to the nation in which HR is practiced. Cascio's chapter also addresses the question of how the above two issues could be incorporated in an HR curriculum in an efficient manner, or whether they should be incorporated.

The Graduate Class in International Human Resource Management

8

Strategies and Tactics

Greg Hundley

Faculty in North American universities who teach a graduate class in international HRM are likely to find themselves with students drawn from more than one population, each with distinctive learning objectives and assumptions about international business. Students who are primarily concerned with developing skills and expertise as human resource managers are likely to view HRM in terms of its subfunctions (staffing, compensation, and so on) and are interested how functional tools and HR practices should be developed for or adapted to different national settings. Students who have a generalist orientation or a primary interest in a non-HR specialty will be more concerned with how their people management responsibilities (such as performance management, employee motivation, and leadership) are affected by international assignments. Those with exposure to a major multinational corporation will be concerned with the integration of business processes across national borders and the extent to which management practices can be transferred globally. Perhaps because of a greater interest in the behavioral sciences, the HR specialists give greater weight to the need to adjust HR practices and policies to accommodate differences in national cultures. The different views may also reflect the different experiences of class participants. Students with study-abroad experiences assign greater importance to the adaptation of management

practices to cultural differences, whereas guest speakers, particularly consultants, lean toward uniform application of best practices (typically, their
own) across national boundaries.

The instructor will also approach the class with his or her own set of
assumptions. She or he may see international HR in terms of the human
resource management problems confronting managers from the "home
country" who have been assigned responsibilities in one or more foreign
subsidiaries. Although this view encompasses one set of issues confronting
the international manager, such as those related to expatriate assignments, it
gives short shrift to many others and is particularly misleading insofar as it
encourages the view that solutions to international HR problems lie in dis-
covering how HR practices are uniformly affected by national cultures and
institutions. Although HR practices and policies may be affected by nation-
specific factors, these effects are profoundly conditioned by the nature of the
business and the way that it competes in the global marketplace.

My course is premised on the idea that the business that is trying to
compete internationally confronts two basic problems: first, *localization,*
where the business seeks to adapt its practices to meet market conditions
specific to different nations and regions; and second, *integration,* where
the activities and resources of different national or regional operations are
coordinated to achieve optimal levels of efficiency. Accordingly, the class
seeks to build the skills and expertise in HRM that contribute to the organization most effectively in localizing and integrating its business activities. The main media for instruction are articles and cases designed to
present the problems and issues within several rather arbitrarily defined
HR "functional" areas. Some very useful materials are provided in
Mendenhall and Oddou (2000), but other articles and cases available from
Harvard Business School Publishing can be assigned as well. Dowling and
Welch (2005) can be used as supplementary readings that focus on specialist tools and problems of international HR, or as a text supporting discussion of case materials. Evans, Pucik, and Barsoux (2002) is a promising
alternative text for a class that is oriented toward the human resource policy issues of the global corporation.

Introduction

I have found it useful to have the students read an account of an attempt to
transfer management practices across borders. An excellent vignette is provided by William Ouchi's (1981) legendary work on Japanese management,
Theory Z, which describes the negative reactions of a group of female production workers to the proposed replacement of their traditional Japanese
seniority-based pay system with individual piece rates. Two questions elicit
a number of important issues that will remain throughout the course:

(1) given the attachment of the Japanese workers to age- and seniority-based pay, how can we possibly expect the Japanese facility to achieve high levels of productivity? Why shouldn't the American company install a similar (Japanese-style) compensation system in its U.S. facilities? (2) Given that the events described occurred more than 20 years ago, would you suppose that things will always remain the same in Japanese plants, and the type of compensation systems used in Japan would remain so distinctively different from those used in the U.S.?

The role of national culture in determining the acceptance of management practices is quickly raised. This is also an excellent time to introduce the debate between the convergence hypothesis, which predicts that forces of industrialization and globalization will cause management practices to converge on the most technically efficient, and the divergence hypothesis (perhaps more accurately, the "nonconvergence" hypothesis), in which best practice is determined by national culture and the broader sociocultural and economic systems.

The students may also be reminded that despite the American emphasis on individualistic pay-for-performance, many U.S. companies continue to succeed with Japanese-type pay systems (seniority based, equal pay for doing the same job, etc.) and that many scholars view individualistic pay-for-performance with some reservations. This theme of different practices within nations as well as differences between nations will reemerge with the later discussion of international compensation decisions

Organizational and Strategic Framework of International HRM

International HRM must be understood within the context of a particular organization and the conditions affecting how it does business internationally. Accordingly, students should discuss the motivations for extending their business across borders and how the organization has chosen to compete in international markets. Useful frameworks are provided by the structural evolution approach of Vernon's (1966) lifecycle model, in which firms first go international to market domestic excess production, then develop an international departments to promote exports, then move manufacturing and product development activities offshore to more efficiently exploit local market conditions. On the basis of Perlmutter (1969), the multinational firm is often characterized by alternative "states of mind"—ethnocentric (each foreign subsidiary mirrors the parent's business model), polycentric (relatively autonomous foreign subsidiaries controlled by performance standards), or geocentric (all subsidiaries contribute to organizational success by both succeeding in its own market and contributing to the wider organization). Bartlett, Ghoshal, and Birkinshaw (2004) see alternative "strategic mentalities"—the traditional multinational, a federation of business units dedicated to serving a range of different market positions, to the ideal of a transnational mindset in which firms meet the imperative of global competitions by becoming both more local and more global in their orientation, recognizing the need to simultaneously achieve global efficiency and local national responsiveness and to develop and exploit knowledge across the worldwide organization.

Two readings provide an excellent basis for developing the linkages between business strategy and human resource management. "Global Strategy and Its Impact on Local Operations: Lessons from Gillette Singapore" (Kanter & Dretler, 2000) describes the complexities of merging disparate corporate cultures in a distinctive multicultural setting as part of the development of a successful global business. "Managing the Global Workforce: Challenges and Strategies" (Roberts, Kossek, & Ozeki, 2000) outlines several HR strategies for human resource development—the development of a cadre of globally oriented internationalists who can operate across international borders—awareness-building assignments, SWAT teams, and virtual solutions. The articles canvass many of the issues regarding what it means to be a global corporation and demonstrate why this is important aspiration for top management stakeholders and what it means for HRM. This is a good time to invite the students with expertise in the various HR functions to consider how HRM is key to the implementation of a firm's global strategy, and how the HR department should be involved (if at all) in the alternative human resource development strategies.

The Roles of National Cultures

Dimensions of cultural values, often those of Hofstede (1983, 1991), have become a ubiquitous in international management classes. Although Hofstede's original four dimensions (individualism/collectivism, power distance, risk avoidance, masculine/feminine) and his classifications of more than 60 nations on these dimensions may offer some guide to practice, it is best that these dimensions are viewed as prospective indicators of facets of national culture that *may* be important to management practice. To emphasize this point, I resort to other instruments that enable class members to evaluate their own cultural values on other well-established dimensions of national culture and compare them to other groups.

Globesmart is a Web-based cross-cultural training program that provides a 20-item instrument, "The Peterson Cultural Style Simulator," that is scored online and provides scores on four dimensions of cultural style (equality or hierarchy orientation, direct/indirect communication style, individual or group focus, task/relationship emphasis). It enables the individual to see their own profile and compare it to the profile for 30 countries available in the database and for the class as a whole. Students have been very responsive to this instrument and are struck as to the variation within the student group and, in some cases, how much their profile may differ from that of specific nations. The lessons are that cultural values do vary and that practitioners may underestimate the magnitude of the differences. Students are encouraged to think of the practical usefulness of the dimensions, while at the same time encouraging a discussion of whether or not there might be "missing dimensions," for example, use of time, long-term or short-term orientation, and bases for fairness (universalistic versus particularistic).

I have found it useful to have students perform self-assessment of cross-cultural style using other instruments. This has been most frequently accomplished by having them complete Triandis's (1996) INDCOL instrument, which distinguishes between vertical and horizontal individualism and collectivism. Consistent with previous work about cultural effects, the INDCOL schema assumes values relevant to decision making in organizational and economic life can be arranged along an individualistic-collectivistic dimension, in which individualists emphasize independence of the self and collectivists emphasize interdependence with others. Vertical cultures emphasize differences between people and accept hierarchy as natural whereas horizontal cultures accept equality as a given and support the equal division of rewards and resources. Although many writers have assumed that collectivist values also support hierarchy (as in the case of East Asian countries with a strong Confucian heritage), there are examples where collectivist values and horizontal values coexist. The horizontal-vertical distinction has been found to explain why some cultures such as China's will under certain conditions (such as an overriding group interest) accept or even embrace individual reward differences whereas others will not (Chen, Meindl, & Hunt, 1997). The online Cultureactive instrument based on Lewis's (1999) model of cross-cultural communication is another instrument that has worked well in class and has a track record in corporate settings.

Students should be encouraged to grapple with a number of questions. Do the commonly used dimensions of culture used adequately capture the important characteristics of a national culture? What about cultural variations within nations as well as across boundaries? What about the importance of regional, occupational, and sociodemographic variations in culture? This is also an excellent time to raise the increasingly important issue of managing groups and teams drawn from a variety of national cultures and occupational cultures (Soderberg & Holden, 2002).

Case studies of the effects of national culture work best when students are required to consider cultural factors in conjunction with other forces affecting management practices, thus avoiding easy recourse to cultural differences as the primary explanation of management problems. "The Anstrichehof Infrared Coating Corporation—AICC" (Zanzi & Lemieux, 2000) requires a disentangling of the forces of organizational culture and organizational life cycle from the obvious influences of national culture. The relationship between organizational and national cultures in (for most westerners at least) a more culturally distant setting is addressed in the case *Establishing an "ECL" Culture in China: Organizational Difference or National Difference* (Wong, Chan, & Ho, 2001).

Recruitment and Selection

International staffing issues cover a wide area. A critical decision at the outset of internationalization involves whether or not to use expatriates. "The International Assignment Reconsidered" (Boyacigiller, 2000) provides a model to guide this decision, arguing that the decision to expatriate is based on the interplay of a number of factors, including cultural distance, complexity, and the need for integration between subsidiary and headquarters. Classroom discussion is facilitated by the in-class assignment of a mini-case describing businesses in alternative national settings and inviting student groups to recommend decisions as when to make expatriate assignment and when to use locals.

Most jobs are filled by local country nationals, and staffing decisions are affected by a variety of demographic and economic attributes of labor markets. A particularly interesting case is "Precision Management of Japan" (Mendenhall & Oddou, 1995), which details the problems of a U.S.-based company and a Japanese company in establishing a joint venture in Japan. Although it is now an older case, it is particularly useful in that it requires the student to think about the wide-ranging effects of a complex of institutional and cultural forces on recruitment and selection as well as the special issues confronting joint-venture partners. The case poses a number of special dynamic issues, in which recruitment problems and possibilities will be shaped by a numbers of labor market changes, such as the aging population, shortages of young engineers, increasing numbers of engineers looking for second careers, increasing numbers of women seeking employment, and other changes in Japanese culture and labor markets. Because nearly 20 years have elapsed since the events described in this case, student discussion can be directed toward whether or not the changes have taken place and their implications for HR management in general.

The HR specialist may be somewhat disappointed with the lack of in-depth consideration for selection tools in these materials, as few cases are concerned with selection criteria for foreign assignments. However, *Sealed Air Taiwan (A)* (Paine, 2005) deal with selection of a sales manager in cross-cultural context, including the importance (or otherwise) of American assessments of personal fit to corporate culture.

Expatriation

Although international HR involves much more than expatriation, discussion of expatriate experience is still important. The stylized facts of North American expatriate practices are that expatriate assignments are made in an ad hoc fashion, with the ill-prepared expatriate being dogged by work-family issues on a grand scale, and then encountering reentry problems as the expatriate experience is found not to fit in well with his or her long-term career goals. Expatriate assignments still raise a range of interesting work-family and gender issues that may overwhelm the promising expatriate. "Catskill Roads" (Ritchie & Hawkins, 2000) raise these issues in a personal way from the perspective of a family confronting the decision making of multiple expatriate assignments, posing the inevitable work-family conflicts and career compromises. The expatriate assignment provides a particularly interesting setting for raising gender issues in management, including the particular challenges and opportunities confronting women managers working in national cultures in which the role of women is thought to differ substantially from those in the West. *Ellen Moore (A): Living and Working in Korea* (Lane, Nichols, & Ellement, 1998) provides scope for exploring gender issues in a global work environment, the special issues of managing international teams, and working in and managing global alliances. These are pressing concerns as the still low (though increasing) utilization of women in international assignments may be another part to the glass ceiling to top management advancement.

Employee and Management Development

The drive toward globalization places a premium on management development. Indeed, executive development and succession planning are often undertaken separately from the traditional HR function. I have found it especially useful to consider the management development practices of companies of non-U.S. origins, exposing class members to management development practices outside the U.S., and providing a much less MBA-centered view of management development. To this end, *LG Group: Developing Tomorrow's Global Leaders* (Black, Morrison, & Chang, 1998) poses the management development issues confronting the mammoth Korean *chaebol* after the Asian financial crisis in the late 1990s, including definition of skills for global managers who will serve as both localizers and integrators, the delivery of management education worldwide, and the need to develop effective supporting mechanisms, including the involvement of non-Koreans in corporate governance.

Local conditions, especially in countries that are culturally distant from headquarters at earlier stages of industrialization, may play a determinative role in employee and management development. For example, "Management Development: An African Focus" (Jones, 2000) challenges students to devise ways of developing managers in a hierarchical paternalistic culture that might otherwise inhibit information sharing and employee involvement that are part of effective management skills. Cross-national differences in the role of management and human resource management are now especially salient. "Management Development in Europe: A Study in Cultural Contrast" (Lawrence, 2000) describes how differing conceptions of what management is (and where managers come from) produce sharp distinctions in the role of management between France, Germany, Britain, and the United States, and how these distinctions lead to differences in the role of human resource management. Brewster and Larsen (1995) highlight the regulatory, economic, and other institutional factors that produce widespread differences in the roles of human resource managers and HR department in various European countries. Javidan, Stahl, Brodbeck, and Wilderan (2002) provide a provocative account of the role of top management resistance to Western management training and organizational development practices.

Compensation and Benefits

Arguably, in no other area is the tension between local and global considerations more problematic. On the one hand, local compensation levels are a primary driver of management decision making for firms seeking to establish cost-efficient global supply chains, and the view that local pay methods are predetermined by national culture retains many adherents. On the other hand, "Rethinking International Compensation" (Milkovich & Bloom, 2000) mounts a major challenge to the view that local factors dominate in the design of pay systems, arguing that organizational uniformity in compensation practices is important to the creation of the "global mindset" characteristic of the globally competitive company. Milkovich and Bloom (2000) provide an excellent basis for deeper analyses of local versus global differences, as students are asked to develop the implications for globalizing companies discussed previously in the course or in other international management classes, or that may be under consideration in the major project assignment in this class. It also provides a model for crafting a global compensation strategy that recognizes the practical constraints posed by national differences in institutional frameworks while enabling the design of a reward system that strengthens organizational culture, attracts individuals whose values fit with those of the company, and enables managers to reward employees on the appropriate performance criteria.

The case *Five Star Beer—Pay for Performance* (Golden & Gleave, 1998) is especially useful in that besides raising the issue of pay-for-performance in culture that might be considered inimical to performance-based pay, it introduces several other factors that affect the design of financial reward systems. These include the type of job (production worker, manager, and sales), the presence or absence of supporting systems (such as performance measurement), other structural and organizational factors, and institutional legacies (specifically, the management styles of state-owned enterprises characteristic of China's socialist system for the previous half-century).

Despite the recent pressures toward global uniformity, there is no doubt that national institutions affect compensation practices in very significant ways. This is especially true in the area of employee benefits, where there is considerable cross-national variation in the way that benefits considered part of the employer-provided benefits package in the U.S. are provided. These benefits include retirement income and health care insurance, which in nearly all other industrialized countries are provided through public programs and funded through payroll and income taxes. Institutional details cannot be comprehensively dealt with in an international HR class, but students need to be made aware of them and develop skills in devising policy for the management of international benefits. To this end, "High Technology, Incorporated: The International Benefits Problem" (Andre, 2000) introduces the huge task that a multinational company faces in providing competitive benefits to employees who work in a number of national locations throughout their career, funding these benefits on a cost-efficient basis and assigning these costs across international businesses.

An understanding of international compensation must be built on a foundation that students have not previously developed. These include introduction to compensation basics, including the concepts of relative pay levels, pay mix (balance between forms of pay—base salary, individual and group pay for performance), economic benefits (insurance, retirement income, and health care coverage), and job-based pay systems; and introduction to national social and income security systems, exchange rate determination, and the impact of exchange rates and other macroeconomic factors on business performance.

Employee and Labor Relations

National differences in institutional frameworks loom large for employee and labor relations. The one constant in managing across countries is that employee and labor relations environments in most countries differ significantly from those in the United States. Business school and HR students in the United States are not likely to appreciate the complexities that these pose for HR management as most MBAs and many HR students assume that they are able to manage in a relatively unconstrained way, except for the relatively predictable constraints (enforced by the HR department and legal advisers). "Labor Relations at EuroDisneyland" (Black & Gregersen, 2000) describes the employee relations problems encountered by the U.S. entertainment icon when replicating its theme park abroad, even in an environment characterized by relatively little cultural distance. Globalization means that employee and labor practices in some regions can readily affect the company in other regions, as portrayed in *Hitting the Wall: Nike and International Labor Practices* (Spar & Burns, 2000), which provides an account of the consequences of Nike's labor practices in Indonesia and the company's attempts to deal with the resultant adverse publicity and preserve markets. Frenkel and Scott (2002) can be used to promote discussion about the alternatives available to organizations such as Nike and their competitors as they resolve the conflict between cost-effectiveness and market image.

Integrative Project

A team project on the human resource management issues faced by a hypothetical company commencing operations in a foreign location serves as medium for integrating course materials and applying learning to the team. The written report should encompass the major functional areas of human resource management—recruitment and selection, training and development, labor and employee relations, and performance management and compensation—and explain how the recommendations support the organization's business strategy. Some guidance in the choice of the project is recommended in order ensure that students choose a topic that is neither too large (that is, spans a region of diversity in national institutions and markets) nor trivial in terms of human resource management challenges. For example, a whole continent (except for Australia) would be too broad, although a smaller region, such as some selected countries of Southeast Asia, could be considered. Students can be permitted to choose a company that is familiar to them (for example, a past or present employer) but the international initiatives that are understudied should be new. There is less value to describing and evaluating a set of current practices.

In all cases, students are required to describe that organization's business and relevant aspects the business strategies occasioning the entry into the new market. Analysis should be guided by consideration of national culture(s), institutions, and formal laws governing HR and the employment relationship. The paper should identify relevant aspects of national culture and describe how cultural attributes affect management practices in general and HR practices in particular. The relevant aspects of employment laws relating to such matters as labor standards, minimum wages, methods of compensation, fair employment practices, equal employment opportunity, and occupational safety and health should be described and discussed. Other important institutions to be analyzed include labor unions, education systems, employer associations, the military, and political parties.

Very small teams (one to three members) are best, serving to minimize free-rider problems and, more importantly, providing each individual with the experience of integrating all the important elements of international human resource management: business strategy, national culture and institutions, and the full complement of human resource functions.

The integrative case can require a considerable amount of time. Thankfully, for shorter courses, there are now several cases that can be used to engage students in the design of a human resource strategy and policies for overseas operations. One recent case is *GTI in Russia* (Grachev, Smith, & Bobina, 2003), in which the vice-president of a U.S.-based sign manufacturer must recommend a human resources strategy for possible entry in the Russian market including plans for expatriate assignment, selecting, and compensating as well as coming up with training needs and outlining the organizational culture.

Conclusion

The acquisition of the skills and knowledge that enable HR practitioners to most effectively contribute to business success global markets presents special challenges. Although it may be tempting to focus on building cross-cultural awareness and mastering institutional detail required to inform decision making about the adaptation of HR practices to specific national contexts, future global HR specialists and managers alike are better served by a course that develops the skills and analytical frameworks that inform how human resources can be developed and managed to contribute both to successful adaptation to local markets and to the effective integration of worldwide activities.

References

Andre, M. (2000). High Technology, Incorporated: The international benefits problem. In M. Mendenhall & G. Oddou (Eds.), *Readings and cases in international human resource management* (3rd ed., pp. 230–234). Cincinnati, OH: South-Western College Publishing.

Bartlett, C. A., Ghoshal, S., & Birkinshaw, J. (2004). *Transnational management: Text, cases, and readings in cross-border management* (4th ed.). New York: McGraw-Hill-Irwin.

Black, J. S., & Gregersen, H. B. (2000). Labor relations at EuroDisneyland. In M. Mendenhall & G. Oddou (Eds.), *Readings and cases in international human resource management* (3rd ed., pp. 300–309). Cincinnati, OH: South-Western College Publishing.

Black, J. S., Morrison, A. J., & Chang, Y. C. (1998). *LG Group: Developing tomorrow's global leaders* (case no. 9A98G009). London, Canada: Ivey.

Boyacigiller, N. A. (2000). The international assignment reconsidered. In M. Mendenhall & G. Oddou (Eds.), *Readings and cases in international human resource management* (3rd ed., pp. 125–132). Cincinnati, OH: South-Western College Publishing.

Brewster, C. (1995). Toward a European model of human resource management. *Journal of International Business Studies, 26,* 1–21.

Brewster, C., & Larsen, H. H. (1992). Human resource management in Europe: Evidence from ten countries. *International Journal of Human Resource Management, 3,* 409–434.

Chen, C. C., Meindl, J. R., & Hunt, R. G. (1997). Testing the effects of vertical and horizontal collectivism. *Journal of Cross-Cultural Psychology, 28*(1), 44–70.

Dowling, P. J., & Welch, D. E. (2005). *International human resource management: Managing people in a multinational context* (4th ed.). Cincinnati, OH: South-Western College Publishing.

Evans, P., Pucik, V., & Barsoux, J. L. (2002). *The global challenge: Frameworks for international human resource management.* New York: McGraw-Hill/Irwin.

Frenkel, S. J., & Scott, D. (2002). Compliance, collaboration, and codes of labor practice: The Adidas connection. *California Management Review, 45*(1), 29–49.

Golden, B., & Gleave, T. (1998). *Five Star Beer—Pay for performance* (case no. 8A9BC04). London, Canada: Ivey.

Grachev, M. V., Smith, P., & Bobina, M. A. (2003). *GTI in Russia* (case no. 903C08). London, Canada: Ivey.

Hofstede, G. (1983). National cultures in four dimensions: A research-based theory of cultural differences among nations. *International Studies of Management and Organization, 13,* 46–74.

Hofstede, G. (1991). *Cultures and organizations: Software of the mind.* London: McGraw-Hill.

Javidan, M., Stahl, G. K., Brodbeck, F., & Wilderan, C. P. M. (2002). Cross-border transfer of knowledge: Cultural lessons from Project GLOBE. *Academy of Management Executive, 19,* 59–76.

Jones, M. L. (2000). Management development: An African focus. In M. Mendenhall & G. Oddou (Eds.), *Readings and cases in international human resource management* (3rd ed., pp. 155–168). Cincinnati, OH: South-Western College Publishing.

Kanter, R. M., & Dretler, T. D. (2000). Global strategy and its impact on local operations: Lessons from Gillette Singapore. In M. Mendenhall & G. Oddou (Eds.), *Readings and cases in international human resource management* (3rd ed., pp. 4–17). Cincinnati, OH: South-Western College Publishing.

Lane, H. W., Nichols, C. E., & Ellement, G. (1998). *Ellen Moore (A): Living and Working in Korea* (case no. 97G029). London, Canada: Ivey.

Lawrence, P. (2000). Management development in Europe: A study in cultural contrast. In M. Mendenhall & G. Oddou (Eds.), *Readings and cases in international human resource management* (3rd ed., pp. 169–183). Cincinnati, OH: South-Western College Publishing.

Lewis, R. D. 1999. *When cultures collide.* London: Nicholas Brearley.

Mendenhall, M., & Oddou, G. (Eds.). (1995). *Readings and cases in international human resource management* (2nd ed.). Cincinnati, OH: South-Western College Publishing.

Mendenhall, M., & Oddou, G. (Eds.). (2000). *Readings and cases in international human resource management* (3rd ed.). Cincinnati, OH: South-Western College Publishing.

Milkovich, G. T., & Bloom, M. (2000). Rethinking international compensation. In M. Mendenhall & G. Oddou (Eds.), *Readings and cases in international human resource management* (3rd ed., pp. 200–212). Cincinnati, OH: South-Western College Publishing.

Ouchi, W. G. (1981). *Theory Z: How American business can meet the Japanese challenge.* New York: Avon.

Perlmutter, H. V. (1969). The tortuous evolution of the multinational corporation. *Columbia Journal of World Business, 4* (1): 9–18.

Paine, L. S. (2005). *Sealed Air Taiwan (A)* (case no. 9-305-094). Cambridge, MA: Harvard Business School Publishing.

Quelch, J. A., & Brown, H. (2001).Ten steps to a global human resource strategy. In M. R. Czinkota & I. A. Ronkainen (Eds.), *Best practices in international management* (pp. 207–220). Fort Worth, TX: Harcourt College.

Ritchie, J. B., & Hawkins, A. (2000). Catskill roads. In M. Mendenhall & G. Oddou (Eds.), *Readings and cases in international human resource management* (3rd ed., pp. 513–523). Cincinnati, OH: South-Western College Publishing.

Roberts, K., Kossek, E., & Ozeki, C. (2000) Managing the global workforce: Challenges and strategies. In M. Mendenhall & G. Oddou (Eds.), *Readings and cases in international human resource management* (3rd ed., pp. 18–39). Cincinnati, OH: South-Western College Publishing.

Soderberg, A.-M., & Holden, N. 2002. Rethinking cross cultural management in a globalizing business world. *International Journal of Cross Cultural Management, 21,* 103–121.

Spar, D., & Burns, J. (2000). *Hitting the wall: Nike and international labor practices* (case no. 9-700-047). Cambridge, MA: Harvard Business School Publishing.

Triandis, H. C. (1996). The psychological measurement of cultural syndromes. *American Psychologist, 51,* 407–415.

Vernon, R. 1966. International investment and international trade in the product cycle. *Quarterly Journal of Economics, 80* (2): 191–207.

Wong, G., Chan, S., & Ho, M. (2001). *Establishing an "ECL" culture in China: Organizational difference or national difference?* (case no. HKU156). Hong Kong: University of Hong Kong.

Zanzi, A., & Lemieux, P. (2000). The Anstrichehof Infrared Coating Corporation—AICC. In M. Mendenhall & G. Oddou (Eds.), *Readings and cases in international human resource management* (3rd ed., pp. 95–99). Cincinnati, OH: South-Western College Publishing.

Managing People in Global Markets 9

Colette A. Frayne

Developments during the last decades of the 20th century have produced what may be termed an era of globalization. As business has continued to globalize, one of the most challenging aspects has been how a firm manages its human resources to sustain a competitive advantage.

Scholars from several disciplines are addressing these issues—coming at them from the perspective of strategy, cross-cultural management, international business, organizational theory, sociology, and HRM (Evans, Pucik, & Barsoux, 2003). It appears that the traditional boundaries between academic disciplines and functional areas (e.g., HRM and strategy) are becoming more highly integrated and that the globalization of business is having a significant impact on HRM and organizational performance (Dowling, Welch, & Schuler, 1999). This chapter presents an integration of various approaches to designing and delivering courses on the topic of international human resource management. It presents the key role of the international HRM professional, implications for training and development in organizational settings, and future challenges regarding managing people in global markets.

Approaches to International HRM

The field of international HRM is generally characterized by three broad approaches (DeCieri & Dowling, 1999). Initial approaches in this area emphasized a cross-cultural approach to examining human behavior in organizations. Another approach studies comparative HRM practices within and across countries. A third approach focuses on various functional aspects of HRM in multinational firms. However, a recent undertaking by Evans, Pucik, and Barsoux (2003) integrates the orientations of strategy, culture, and HRM and presents international HRM from a general management rather than a functional perspective. These authors suggest using an organizational systems perspective and argue that we must consider implementation of various HRM strategies within a context of conflicting needs of the organization, such as local responsiveness versus global integration, coordination versus control, and short-term profitability versus long-term innovation. This orientation expands the traditional curricular focus to be more comprehensive and interdisciplinary, drawing on multiple theoretical perspectives and clearly promoting a general management view. The theoretical rationale draws on fit and contingency theory, the resource-based view of the firm, and different contextual schools (comparative management, institutional theories from political science), while building links to social capitalism and network theories, as well as theories of organizational learning (Evans et al., 2003). This approach clearly fits with recent demands of scholars and practitioners that international HRM be interdisciplinary and focused on contributing to firm performance.

Course or seminars designed to teach students and managers about HRM in international settings have been identified at different schools as well as within different organizational settings. The courses are usually designed to introduce students to the nature of managing human resources in international, multinational, global, and transnational firms. The purpose of the courses is to provide students with an in-depth understanding of the basic problems inherent in international HRM. The intention is either to prepare the students for further work in the field or to give them a sound basis for understanding the international corporate dimensions of their own careers—sometimes both. Using Evans et al.'s (2003) framework, I developed a course titled "Managing People in Global Markets." The overall framework stipulates that the relationship between HRM and organizational performance must be separated into three different faces or roles, namely, "the builder," "the aligner," and "the navigator" who steers through the dualities confronting organizations today. This course, which is composed of case studies, readings, videos, and projects, has been designed to reflect an integrative strategic approach to understanding and practicing international HRM. I have introduced adaptations of this course and its foundations in organizational settings in an attempt to develop an awareness and capability amongst line managers, senior managers, and professionals within the international HRM division.

Conceptualizing and Designing a Course or Seminar in International HRM

The "Managing People in Global Markets" course is designed for students of international management and general management, rather than for specialists in HRM. The course is intended to introduce students to the major issues associated with managing people in the context of the global marketplace. The emphasis is on skill development. In this regard, an effective manager must demonstrate fluency in the theories and concepts required to achieve congruence between an organization, its environment, its organizational systems and structures, the key tasks that the organization has to perform, and the organization's human, technological, financial, and other resources. Yet, conceptual skills alone are not sufficient. An effective manager must also demonstrate the skills required to manage the task, people, structures, and systems, as well as the ability to apply those skills to complex situations. This course uses the case-study method as a primary pedagogical approach, in an effort to create an environment conducive to active and participative learning, as opposed to more passive lecture-based instructional approaches.

PEDAGOGICAL OBJECTIVES FOR THE COURSE

I have various objectives for this course:

- To facilitate students' understanding of the impact of cultural differences on the management of people in multinational organizations.

- To enhance students' ability to assess the impact of global conditions on the strategic management of human resources in the context of overseas subsidiaries, acquisitions, and joint ventures and alliances.

- For the student to compare and contrast critical human resource issues in the contexts of domestic and international operations and the stages of a firm's internationalization.

In order to increase students' awareness of the complexity of managing multinational operations, I continuously ask them to identify key environmental, strategic, and organizational variables that influence international operations, how these variables interact, and how these variables affect the management of an organization's human resource capabilities. This course was designed for graduate students and practicing managers; however, I am teaching it to an upper-division undergraduate class. The course materials are complex and rigorous and certainly present challenges to any audience, particularly to undergraduates. After a discussion of the course, I will discuss adaptations of the course for organizational settings and the difficulties faced as we continue to confront the multitude of challenges that are posed by the development of international HRM professionals.

OUTLINE OF THE COURSE

The course is divided into four modules:

1. Historical Overview of HRM and Global Competition
2. Foundation Components of HRM
3. Aligning or Changing HRM Practices
4. Leveraging HRM Capabilities

I use the term "module" to reflect focused learning on a specific topic within the overall course. These modules vary in length and depth, depending on the overall topic area being addressed, and are discussed in greater detail in the following sections. I use the term "course" when referring to my courses designed for university students, and "seminar" when referring to modules offered through organizational settings.

MODULE 1: HISTORICAL OVERVIEW OF HRM AND GLOBAL COMPETITION

Module 1 provides a historical overview of human resource management and global competition, building, aligning, and leveraging HRM capabilities. The overview seeks to establish the scholarly disciplines inherent to the design of the course, including HRM, strategy, cross-cultural management, international business, international economics, and trade theory. The interdisciplinary nature of international HRM is distinguished from traditional HRM, and I highlight the changing role of HRM in international organizations. I have found Harry Lane's (1999a) article, "Implementing Strategy, Structure, and Systems," to be very useful for students in the beginning phase of this course. This reading provides students with a framework for assessing the various elements of an organization's design. This module also emphasizes the need for students to understand and assess the importance of cultural biases that may exist in an organization's normal modes of operation. Culture and context, central to the entire course, are presented so that students focus on being aware of the cultural assumptions underlying their systems and practices and the implications of their use in other countries and cultural contexts. The contextual issues considered extend beyond the realm of national or organizational culture and challenge the student to simultaneously balance these variables with the external context of the firm, its international context and stage of internationalization, the business strategy context, and the key structures, tasks, and mode of operation in the business environment. In this way, students are continuously challenged to examine the cultural and noncultural contextual variables and their impact for the HRM context within the firm.

In organizational settings, this module requires each participant to understand the industry context within which the organization operates— a need to understand the changes in the environment that are affecting changes in the organizational strategy, structure, and systems of the firm. Key to designing this module is to challenge the participant to consider the critical link between a firm's or business unit's strategy and the "fit" of the other elements of an organization's design in relationship to the human resource management function. I often present Lane's (1999a) organizational design framework as a basis for each participant to map the current organization and assess (within the elements of the framework) where changes in internationalization of the firm can result in subsequent changes needed in managing people. A critical analysis often gives managers insight into what type and level of employee is required in the international context and what "bench strength" the firm has when attempting to accomplish its key tasks.

MODULE 2: FOUNDATION COMPONENTS OF HRM

Module 2 introduces the first face of building HRM—getting solid foundations of selection, development, and performance management into place. I use the *Lincoln Electric: Venturing Abroad* case (Bartlett, 1998) to illustrate getting the basics of human resource management into place and ensuring internal coherence. This case has been used traditionally to show how human resource management can contribute to sustainable business performance. The largest manufacturer of welding equipment in the world, Lincoln Electric motivates its employees in the United States through its incentive and performance appraisal system. The company enjoyed unrivaled growth and prosperity until they decided to embark on a bold strategy for internationalization, under the guidance of a management team that had never worked outside the United States. The *Lincoln Electric: Venturing Abroad* case sets the foundation for the entire course by raising many important issues about how HRM contributes to organizational performance as a company goes international. Issues and concepts raised in the case include those of core competencies, culture-bound management practices, and the need to adapt, transfer, or create new systems as a company operates in one country versus another. Students get to see international acquisitions as a growth strategy, the duality of control versus coordination during the process of internationalization, and the overall importance of developing managers with international experience. I teach this case over a four-hour time block and complement the case study by showing a video of an interview with Lincoln Electric's former CEO, Donald Hastings, and NBC's Leslie Stahl from an excerpt of the television program, *60 Minutes* (CBS, 1992/1994). The video is excellent and brings the plant, the workers, and Cleveland, Ohio, into your classroom.

This case also works well in organizational settings. The critical theme within this module is one of understanding "fit" between the elements of the organizational design model as well as the pragmatic issues of internal consistency between the human resource management function and the other strategic functions within the firm. Many of the firms that I have worked with internationally often appreciate the key learning in this case, namely, the link between HR and performance in international firms; the "power" of strategy-structure-systems fit; the motivations, mentalities, and means of internationalization; and the complications when national confronts organizational culture.

MODULE 3: ALIGNING OR CHANGING HRM PRACTICES

Module 3 introduces the second face of "aligning HRM"—aligning or changing HRM strategy and internal practices so as to implement that business strategy effectively. The relationship of HRM with the organization's business strategy is key and is seen as a critical partnership. During this module, I emphasize the role of strategic HRM and the importance of fit with the external environment. I use the *Colgate-Palmolive: Managing International Careers* case (Rosenzweig, 1994) to illustrate the critical issues of HRM and career development as the firm's activities span nations and continents. Colgate-Palmolive, the U.S.-based consumer products company best known for its toothpaste and detergents, has long emphasized overseas experience for its managers. In the 1980s, Colgate-Palmolive developed a comprehensive policy regarding expatriate assignments, which addresses many personal, financial, and logistical concerns. By the 1990s, a new problem emerged: dual careers and the reluctance of some prospective expatriates to accept these critical international assignments. By examining these topics, students are exposed to the many issues involved in the management of international careers, as well as to the impact of social and environmental trends driving the company to reexamine this policy and its emphasis on international experience as a prerequisite for promotion to top management. Can a firm with 65% of its sales in international markets, that sells consumer products that must be adapted to local tastes and customs, not alter its expectations that managers obtain international experience through these types of assignments? The case provides a rich discussion of expatriate management, dual careers, business strategy, and the link between HRM strategy, international markets, and competence development. I also teach this course over a four-hour time period and end with a brief lecture on dual careers and the critical role that expatriates can play for a global firm.

The issues of dual careers as well as what constitutes dual-career families or couples is a key challenge facing organizations today. In a seminar setting, having managers share their concerns regarding expatriate assignments or any type of international assignments has been a useful lens for participants to identify challenges that they and their employees face, as the need to develop human resource talent often outpaces the developing global strategy being pursued. This module is often a foundation or basis for developing a multitude of training programs consistent with a firm's strategy and stage of firm internationalization. Recent work in China and the rest of the Asia Pacific region confirms that the need to identify, train, and maintain internationally skilled and internationally minded talent remains a key challenge and often an obstacle to further growth and performance of many firms.

To further "round out" the module on aligning capabilities, I continue the examination of global staffing and the key role of expatriation management. The *Marconi Telecommunications in Mexico* case (Lane, 1999b) allows the students to study personal accounts of expatriation, adjustment, and repatriation in the context of a firm that has continued global expansion through acquisitions while perhaps outdistancing its ability to staff the acquired companies in Mexico, Chile, and other parts of Latin America. We once again revisit the systems framework provided in Module 1 by Lane (1999a) and examine the role of fit between strategy and systems as Marconi embarks on a global strategy with implications for its human resource capabilities. Continuing with an examination of the systems model and the concept of fit, the *ABB Poland* case (Frost & Weinstein, 1998) provides a wonderful means of examining international strategy, structure, and staffing in acquisitions, as well as the need to manage change initiatives in the newly acquired Polish companies. The students struggle with issues of national versus organizational culture, how to implement changes, and how to maintain the matrix structure and mind-set of ABB with a host of companies in an ex-Soviet bloc area. We conclude this module and the *ABB Poland* case analysis with a discussion of the challenges of transferring systems within another organizational entity—international joint ventures—and we address the continued difficulty of adaptation versus creation of new systems to fit the strategy, culture, or administrative heritage of either the foreign parent company or the host country partner. Throughout this module, I introduce various regions of the world (e.g., Latin America, Poland, Russia, Southeast Asia) so that the students are continuously challenged to think about HRM practices in a context of country comparisons, issues of globalization and localization, and stages of the firm's internationalization. I expect that the students will prepare each case with a clear recognition of the country or region in which the case is depicted. I challenge the students to use current Internet sources, newspapers, magazines and Culturegrams (www.culturegrams.com) to understand the HRM practices particular to the country or region of study. When we do the ABB Poland case, for example, I provide them with the article "Business Success in Eastern Europe: Understanding and Customizing HRM" by Kirizov, Sullivan, and Tu (2000). This article gives the students a good grasp of the disparate and complex factors that influence human resource practices in some of the former communist countries.

A key component of this module in organizational settings is the aspect dedicated to the management of change. Most of the seminars delivered involve the need for the strategic alignment of a firm's human resource management practices with its strategic focus and organizational structure. Many line managers are charged with implementation of new business strategies but often lack the skills required to effectively assess and implement the changes needed from an HRM perspective. The change framework provided in the ABB Poland case allows managers to assess the key elements for consideration during a change process, including the skills needed for an effective change agent or change team.

MODULE 4: LEVERAGING HRM CAPABILITIES

The final module of the course focuses on leveraging HRM capabilities. The emphasis in this module is on the development of organizational capabilities for competitive advantage. It highlights the tensions between the "dualities" that international organizations face, including short-term results versus long-term profitability and global integration versus local responsiveness pressures. Each of the cases that I have selected for this module focuses on a different stage of leveraging HRM capabilities. The *Bristol-Compressors, Asia Pacific* case (Morrison & Black, 1998b) focuses on the efforts of the president of the Asia-Pacific region and his management committee as they try to increase the quality and quantity of managers in the region. Lack of management bench strength is viewed as a critical problem for Bristol Compressors, and the students are faced with action alternatives that balance training current managers, recruiting locals, or returning to the use of expatriates. Continuing with the theme of leveraging capabilities, students are exposed to cases in China (*Mabuchi Motor Co., Ltd.*; Beamish & Goerzen, 1998); Vietnam (*HCM Beverage Company*; Black & Morrison, 1998a); Indonesia (*Building Products International*; DiStefano & Everett, 1999); and Korea (*LG Group: Developing Tomorrow's Global Leaders*; Black & Morrison, 1998b). Each of the cases exposes the students to different cultural contexts, different phases of leveraging capabilities (e.g., managing, protecting, and steering), and different phases of HRM activities (e.g., training and development programs; crisis management programs; and global leadership development, recruitment, and selection). The focus of this module is truly integrative and is supported with readings dealing with the global manager and with the challenges of aligning the functional areas with the global strategies.

After completing the fourth module, I conclude the course with an integrative review and summary of the key concepts, frameworks, and learning points. To promote active involvement and interaction in this final review and learning session, I require the students to bring their three most important learning points from the course and to share them during the class discussion. Not only does discussion of these learning points promote active involvement of the students in the context of a review session, it also allows for additional concepts to be raised and for concepts to be discussed in greater depth and with further emphasis on integration.

The learning from this session enables me to reflect on the challenges and successes that I have experienced in teaching this course. The key challenge for me is presenting each module and clearly articulating the keen differences between the three faces of HRM in international firms. For each face, I highlight four main areas, namely, the activity, the focus, the theory, and the role of HRM within each distinct face. For example, during the Building HRM face, the activity involves getting the basics in place; the focus is on internal coherence; the theory is one of fit from an internal organizational design perspective; and the role of HRM is that of a builder. It often takes students some time to understand each of the faces, and the challenge for me is to highlight these four main areas throughout the selection of cases that I use. The key success for me in teaching this course is my preparation and selection of the various cases for each of the modules as well as the corresponding readings and activities. Through the extensive use of relevant, current, and meaningful case studies, I find that the student leaves the course with a richer appreciation of the HRM challenges that are involved in the process of internationalization. They also understand the need to operate in an increasingly global and complex environment in which people are considered a precious and sustainable competitive advantage.

Organizational Field Project

As an additional integral means of applying concepts from the course, I ask student groups to complete a field project that examines in some detail the management challenges of globalization. The student team conducts this project on an organization that they select; it incorporates analysis, critique, and recommendations. In order to place responsibility on the students for accessing and interpreting both primary and secondary data sources for the chosen organization, interviews and firsthand data are required in this project. The field project tests the students' deeper understanding of how an organization actually manages the global workforce and how well each of the students is able to integrate the materials and learning that we have collectively developed throughout the course. Most importantly, this project is intended to help the students internalize and integrate the issues discussed in the course in a practical, useful, and career-enhancing way. Past students have reported that they learned an enormous amount about the organization that they were interested in as well as knowledge of current global management challenges. Critical skills of how to collect data, conduct analyses, and apply the knowledge that they have gained in this course are also important to project success.

I also use these projects within organizational seminars as a basis for managers to transfer their training learnings and outcomes back to the workplace. I use the same guidelines described above and also encourage the organization to allow these projects to be graded within some type of certificate program within the company. On completion of the field projects, seminar participants give presentations to the company's top management team as a basis for organizational learning and discussion. The field projects provide the managers with a practical and effective way to apply the knowledge generated during the seminar and a means to share that knowledge with colleagues within and across business units and functions.

Personal Learning Journals

Coupled with the field project, a final and perhaps potent form of organization learning resides in the requirement for each student to keep a personal learning journal as we proceed through the course. The purpose of this journal is to ask each student to reflect on the daily learning in the class and ask the question, **"What does all of this really mean for me as I try to enhance my ability to effectively manage and work with others?"** After each session, students are asked to draw on the session's mix of cases, readings, role plays, discussions, simulations, and the like, and apply these various instructional activities to their own personal learning objectives for the course as well as their ability to maintain and enhance their overall effectiveness as global managers. I ask the student to do this reflection after *EACH* class. The student, via integration and prioritization efforts, should strive to translate this reflection into *AT LEAST* one journal entry for each class session topic and activity. For example, if a class session consists of a case, a reading, discussion, and a lecture, the student will have at least four entries for that day. Each entry should reflect a significant discovery, insight, connection, guideline, observation, concern, or other kind of learning that integrates session context or experience with the student's own current or future managerial reality.

It is within these entries that students often reflect on another key aspect of culture, namely, individual variations and interpretations of their own cultural beliefs, norms, values, and perspectives. This activity often aids the student in making sense of the various challenges presented in the cases when national culture confronts organizational culture. Rather than broadly interpreting cultural differences and making generalizations across cultures or countries, students are able to personalize such learning on the basis of individual cultural backgrounds and experiences. Three or four entries per class session, multiplied by 17 classes (based on a quarter system), means that the student should possess at least 50 entries by the end of the course. Each student is required to prepare an essay based on a review and integration of the journal entries. The essay should reflect their ability to sort out, integrate, and interpret their own entire collection of entries throughout the course. This essay provides the students with the opportunity to synthesize their learning from this course and apply the learning to their personal managerial effectiveness and their career.

I strongly advocate the use of personal learning journals within organizational settings. Two of the organizations within the Asia Pacific region have implemented learning journals throughout each training module conducted with the organization. Each manager is encouraged to review his or her journal every two weeks and monitor learning objectives and outcomes based on personal competencies and goals as well as those set within the framework of a performance appraisal or coaching session. During each session of the organizationally based module, I invite participants to share their learning points and describe how these learnings can enhance the development of international considerations of human resource management throughout the firm.

Conclusions

Managerial development is the single biggest challenge presented by increased globalization of firms and markets. Developing tomorrow's generation of global managers requires the creation of a global mind-set and the specific task of developing leaders for the future. These challenges only serve to heighten the need to conceptualize, design, and deliver courses on managing human resources in international firms that emphasize a broader perspective of what operating internationally involves. The course discussed in this chapter is one effort to meet this important educational and managerial challenge. Adaptation, modification, and transfer of this course throughout organizational communities have also enhanced our ability to develop a cadre of international managers and HRM professionals responsible for ensuring the quality and abundance of talent required as firms continue to expand into global markets—developing as well as developed.

References

Bartlett, C. (1998). *Lincoln Electric: Venturing abroad* (case no. 398-095). Cambridge, MA: Harvard Business School.

Beamish, P. W., & Goerzen, A. (1998). *Mabuchi Motor Co. Ltd.* (case no. 98M034). London, Canada: Ivey.

Black, S., & Morrison, A. (1998a). *HCM Beverage Company* (case no. 98C003). London, Canada: Ivey.

Black, S., & Morrison, A. (1998b). *LG Group: Developing tomorrow's global leaders* (case no. 98G009). London, Canada: Ivey.

CBS Video. (1994). *Lincoln Electric* (aired November 8, 1992) [Television broadcast]. New York: CBS, Inc.

DeCieri, H., & Dowling, P. (1999). Strategic human resource management in multinational companies: Empirical developments. In P. M. Wright, L. D. Dyer, J. W. Boudreau, & G. T. Milkovich (Eds.), *Research in personnel and human resource management: Strategic human resource management in the twenty-first century.* Stamford, CT: JAI Press.

DiStefano, J., & Everett, D. (1999). *Building Products International—A crisis management strategy* (case no. 9A99C002). London, Canada: Ivey.

Dowling, P., Welch, D., & Schuler, R. (1999). *International human resource management: Managing people in a multinational context.* Cincinnati, OH: South-Western College Publishing.

Evans, P., Pucik, V., & Barsoux, J. (2003). *The globalization challenge: Frameworks for international human resource management.* New York: McGraw-Hill Higher Education.

Frost, A., & Weinstein, M. (1998). *ABB Poland* (case no. 98C011). London, Canada: Ivey.

Kirizov, D., Sullivan, S. E., & Tu, H. S. (2000). Business success in Eastern Europe: Understanding and customizing HRM. *Business Horizons, 43*(1), 39–43.

Lane, H. (1999a). Implementing strategy, structure, and systems. In H. Lane, M. Maznevski, & J. DiStefano (Eds.), *International management behavior: Text, readings, and cases* (pp. 181–205). Cambridge, MA: Blackwell.

Lane, H. (1999b). *Marconi Telecommunications Mexico* (case no. 8A98C09). London, Canada: Ivey.

Morrison, A., & Black, S. (1998b). *Bristol Compressors, Asia-Pacific* (case no. 98M001). London, Canada: Ivey.

Rosenzweig, P. (1994). *Colgate-Palmolive: Managing international careers* (case no. 394-184). Cambridge, MA: Harvard Business School.

Educating the HR Professional and General Manager on Key Issues in International HRM

10

Wayne F. Cascio

This chapter considers three key issues relevant to educating the HR professional and general manager on key issues in international HRM. One, what should HR managers and general managers know about the economic, legal, and cultural aspects of countries in which they conduct their activities? Two, which HR knowledge and skill have the potential to cross national boundaries, and which, by necessity, focus on the nation in which HR is practiced? Three, how can this knowledge be incorporated into HR curricula in an efficient manner—or should it be incorporated?

To start, I call my course "Managing People in Global Markets" instead of "International HR." I do this because I have found that the phrase "Human Resources Management" appears to be a bit sterile to some students. Later on I will describe in more detail exactly what topics I cover in this course, and how I teach it, but for the moment, the main point is that, in my view, the marketing of an HR course is every bit as important as is its delivery in the classroom. "Managing People in Global Markets" focuses attention on the people-related business issues involved in global markets rather than just the "people" issues.

Student responses to the course's title have been quite positive. Students tell me that they are excited about learning the nuances of managing people in global markets. Generally, they understand that businesses operate in foreign as well as domestic markets, and many aspire to work overseas at some time in their future careers. Thus it makes good sense to them and focuses their attention on the people-related business issues involved in global markets.

The Specific Area of International HR

PEDAGOGY

I will describe in some detail my approach to teaching a graduate-level international HR course, "Managing People in Global Markets." I teach that course in two different ways, depending on whether it is a semester-long course (roughly 16 weeks) or an eight-week, four-hours-a-week Executive MBA course.

In a semester-long course, I begin by asking the students to place themselves into country-specific or region-specific groups. They do this within the first two weeks of the course. Although they may begin with a region-specific interest, such as Latin America, Eastern Europe, Scandinavia, or Southeast Asia, generally students will agree among themselves to focus on a particular country in which they are collectively interested.

During the first month or so of the course, their job is to collect information related to the broad topic of "Doing Business in [country of interest]." This information should include data relevant to the economy, geography, political system, customs, and key regulations or laws in that country. Each group then makes a (roughly) 30-minute presentation about its country. The presentations tend to be lively, incorporating posters, maps, brochures, short videos, and colorful slides. The purpose is to educate all class members (as well as the professor!) about the country they will be studying in more detail throughout the semester. Their overall task is to prepare a report by the end of the semester that includes two major sections, "Doing Business in [country of interest]" and "HR Practices in [country of interest]" By the time the students finish their first presentation, many have also finished the first sections of their end-of-term reports.

While the students are collecting information about doing business in their country of interest and reading introductory articles about international HRM and what makes it different from purely domestic HR, I spend the first few classes lecturing about the broad outlines of the topic and personally conducting some short business cases relevant to the subject of managing people in global markets.

During the remainder of the term I cover a different aspect of international HRM each class (as described more fully in a subsequent section) using both case and lecture formats. Each student group or team that made a country-specific presentation is also required to take responsibility to present a case. For the first hour or so of each class, student groups present their assigned cases.

In doing so, I encourage them to be creative and to involve the class through role-plays, debates, small-group caucuses, and plenary discussions. I tell the students that their job is not to know all the answers, but rather to ask provocative questions that will challenge the rest of the class to participate.

I tell them that a common gauge of a successful presentation is whether it drew each member of the class into the discussion. It's amazing how creative the student presenters can be in drawing their normally reticent classmates into the discussion when they know that they are being evaluated, at least partially, on the basis of their ability to do so! On the day of their major case presentations, they are also responsible for submitting a 15–20-page report that explores underlying issues in the case in more depth.

Students also expect that prior to each class I will provide audience handouts for my PowerPoint presentations. I make the entire presentation available to them electronically just before each class. They want to hear a lecture on the topic of interest, because normally that lecture is punctuated with colorful stories and situations to illustrate the topic. Students then take notes on the audience handouts that I provide.

Near the end of the term, each student group makes a final 30-minute presentation on HR practices in their chosen country. I tell them that by the time I finish listening to their presentations and reading their reports, I want to feel like an "insider" in the country of interest. Generally, these final presentations are even more colorful. They include role-playing, skits, games, and well-developed PowerPoint presentations that are handed out to the rest of the class. They usually include food as well. It is important for students to understand the cuisine and customs of the country in question, and the student groups have lots of fun preparing (or sometimes purchasing) native foods from their chosen countries. Students really enjoy learning about eating habits and foreign foods, and these sessions are quite involving.

In summary, with respect to course requirements, there are no formal, written tests per se. Rather, each student group is responsible for making three presentations:

1. A presentation on "Doing Business in [country of interest]."

2. A presentation that describes HR practices, such as recruitment, selection, performance management, compensation, and labor relations in the country of interest.

3. A presentation, class discussion, and a formal write-up of a preassigned case.

In addition to the three presentations, there are two major written requirements for the course: (1) a formal report on the preassigned case and (2) the country-based report that combines the "Doing Business in . . ." and "HR Practices in . . ." information.

Each student's total grade for the course is based on the following: case presentation (15%) and write-up (15%); "Doing Business in . . ." presentation (15%); "HR Practices in . . ." presentation (15%); the country-based report (20%); and class participation (20%).

EXECUTIVE MBA COURSE, "MANAGING PEOPLE IN GLOBAL MARKETS"

I structure the eight-week Executive MBA term similarly, except that student groups do not make a formal "Doing Business in . . ." presentation. Rather, because of the time constraints, it is a case-based course in which each student group is responsible for preparing two 20-page reports, corresponding to two preassigned cases. Each student group also is responsible for conducting a (roughly) one-hour presentation on one of those cases. During the remainder of the class I lecture on a selected topic. On class days when a particular group is not responsible for preparing a major-case report, the group is responsible for handing in a four-page synopsis and recommendation for action of the assigned case for the day.

These courses build on my firm belief that although there is a core of theory-based, content-related information that students should know, they also will have to demonstrate skills in oral presentation and report writing if they are to succeed in business. I try to structure my course so that it addresses all three of these concerns.

In a nutshell, HR education is definitely not dead, at least the way I teach it. I try to involve students in the collective education of everyone in the class (including me), and I emphasize that everyone has something to contribute. Students generally respond with interest, enthusiasm, and a zest for learning more. Routinely, they will tell me (or my Dean) that they never knew that people-related business issues could be so interesting. More importantly, they feel prepared to address the kinds of practical employment issues that they will face after graduation.

What Should HR Managers and General Managers Know About the Economic, Legal, and Cultural Aspects of Countries in Which They Conduct Their Activities?

This brings us to the question of topics to address. The topics, in my opinion, should not focus exclusively on the management of expatriates. Rather, to be inclusive and to recognize the fact that host-country nationals and third-country nationals (e.g., a German working for a United States–based multinational in Spain) may also make up an overseas workforce, it is important to address some key issues that will help managers "size up" any culture. I begin by defining the word "culture."

CULTURE AND ITS ROLE

I emphasize continually to HR professionals and prospective general managers that when doing business overseas, companies need to consider the impact of culture on international HR management. But what is culture? **Culture** refers to characteristic ways of doing things and behaving that people in a given country or region have evolved over time. It helps people to make sense of their part of the world and provides them with an identity. Culture affects virtually every aspect of beliefs, attitudes, and behavior. Thus, the very first thing that firms need to understand about doing business in a given location is the impact of culture on business practices.

For ease of exposition, I use a systematic framework of 10 broad classifications to help HR professionals and general managers assess any culture and examine its people systematically. This framework does not consider every aspect of culture, and by no means is it the only way to analyze culture. Rather, it is a useful beginning for cultural understanding. The framework is composed of the following 10 factors (Harris, Moran, & Moran, 2004):

- Sense of self and space
- Dress and appearance
- Food and eating habits
- Communication: verbal and nonverbal
- Time and time sense
- Relationships
- Values and norms
- Beliefs and attitudes
- Work motivation and practices
- Mental processes and learning

Here is a very brief description of each of these factors.

Sense of Self and Space

Self-identity may be manifested by a humble bearing in some places, and by macho behavior in others. Some countries (e.g., the United States) may promote independence and creativity, whereas others (e.g., Japan) emphasize group cooperation and conformity. Americans have a sense of space that requires more distance between people, whereas Latin Americans and Vietnamese prefer to get much closer. Each culture has its own unique ways of doing things.

Dress and Appearance

This includes outward garments as well as body decorations. Many cultures wear distinctive clothing—the Japanese kimono, the Indian turban, the Polynesian sarong, the "organization-man-or-woman" look of business, and uniforms that distinguish wearers from everybody else. Cosmetics are more popular and accepted in some cultures than in others, as is cologne or after-shave lotion for men.

Food and Eating Habits

The manner in which food is selected, prepared, presented, and eaten often differs by culture. Most major cities have restaurants that specialize in the distinctive cuisine of various cultures—everything from Afghan to Zambian. Utensils also differ, ranging from bare hands to chopsticks to full sets of cutlery. Knowledge of food and eating habits often provides insights into customs and culture.

Communication: Verbal and Nonverbal

The axiom "words mean different things to different people" is especially true in cross-cultural communication. When an American says she is "tabling" a proposition, it is generally accepted that it will be put off. In England, "tabling" means to discuss something now. Translations from one language to another can generate even more confusion as a result of differences in style and context.

Nonverbal cues may also mean different things. In the United States, one who does not look someone in the eye arouses suspicion and is called "shifty-eyed." In some other countries, however, looking someone in the eye is perceived as aggression. Just as communication skills are key ingredients for success in U.S. business, such skills are basic to success in international business. There is no compromise on this issue; ignorance of local customs and communications protocol is disrespectful.

Time and Time Sense

To Americans, time is money. We live by schedules, deadlines, and agendas; we hate to be kept waiting, and we like to "get down to business" quickly. In many countries, however, people simply will not be rushed. They arrive late for appointments, and business is preceded by hours of social rapport. People in a rush are thought to be arrogant and untrustworthy. The lesson for Americans doing business overseas is clear: *Be flexible about time and realistic about what can be accomplished.* Adapt to the process of doing business in any particular country.

Relationships

Cultures designate human and organizational relationships by age, gender, status, and family relationships, as well as by wealth, power, and wisdom (Harris & Moran, 1990). Relationships between and among people vary by category—in some cultures the elderly are honored; in others they are ignored. In some cultures women must wear veils and act deferentially; in others the female is considered the equal, if not the superior, of the male. Before going overseas, it is crucially important to understand how to address the various kinds of relationships in the country of interest.

Values and Norms

From its value system, a culture sets **norms of behavior**, or what some call "local customs." One such norm is that in Eastern countries business people strive for successful business outcomes after *personal* relationships have been established, whereas Westerners develop social relationships after *business* interests have been addressed. International managers ignore such norms at their peril (Ralston, Gustafson, Elsass, Cheung, & Terpstra, 1992; Schweitzer & Kerr, 2000).

Beliefs and Attitudes

To some degree, religion expresses the philosophy of a people about important facets in life. Whereas Western culture is largely influenced by Judeo-Christian traditions and Middle Eastern culture by Islam, Oriental and Indian cultures are dominated by Buddhism, Confucianism, Taoism, and Hinduism. In cultures where a religious view of work still prevails, work is viewed as an act of service to God and people and is expressed in a moral commitment to the job or quality of effort (Ibrahaim, 1994). In Japan, the cultural loyalty to family is transferred to the work organization. It is expressed in workgroup participation, communication, and consensus (Harris & Moran, 1990).

Work Motivation and Practices

Knowledge of what motivates workers in a given culture, combined with (or based on) a knowledge of what they think matters in life, is critical to the success of the international manager. Europeans pay particular attention to power and status, which results in more formal management and operating styles in comparison to the informality found in the United States ("Employee Motivation," 1989). In the United States individual initiative and achievement are rewarded, but in Japan managers are encouraged to seek consensus before acting, and employees work as teams (Howard, Shudo, & Umeshima, 1983).

Mental Processes and Learning

Linguists, anthropologists, and other experts who have studied this issue have found vast differences in the ways people think and learn in different cultures. Whereas some cultures favor abstract thinking and conceptualization, others prefer rote memory and learning. The Chinese, Japanese, and Korean written languages are based on ideograms, or "word pictures." On the other hand, English is based on precise expression using words. Western cultures stress linear thinking and logic, that is, A, then B, then C, then D. Among Arabic and Oriental cultures, however, nonlinear thinking prevails. This has direct implications for negotiation processes, and is the kind of information that future general managers need to know.

Human Resource Management Activities of Global Corporations

Initially, it is important to address a fundamental question: is this subject worthy of study in its own right? The answer is yes, for two reasons: scope and risk exposure (Dowling, 1999; Dowling & Welch, 2005). In terms of **scope,** I emphasize that there are at least five important differences between domestic and international operations. International operations have:

1. More functions, such as taxation and coordination of dependents.

2. More heterogeneous functions, such as coordination of multiple-salary currencies.

3. More involvement in the employee's personal life, such as housing, health, education, and recreation.

4. Different approaches to management, because the population of expatriates and locals varies.

5. More complex external influences, such as from societies and governments.

Heightened **risk exposure** is a second distinguishing characteristic of international HR management (Bussey, 1998; Kissel, 2004; Pasquarelli, 1996). A variety of legal issues confront companies in each country, and the human and financial consequences of a mistake in the international arena are much more severe. On top of that, terrorism is now an ever-present risk for executives overseas. I also include a special section of the course titled, "How to Stay Safe Abroad," based on Jossi (2001) and Bensimon (1998). Thus far student reaction to it has been quite positive.

After addressing the issue of culture, and the scope and risk exposure that characterize international HR, I then examine nine key areas that HR professionals and general managers should know about. The nine areas are organizational structure, workforce planning, recruitment, staffing, orientation, cross-cultural training and development, international compensation, labor relations (including international labor standards), and repatriation. The following sections contain brief summaries of each of these areas.

Organizational Structure

I emphasize how businesses tend to evolve from domestic (exporters), to international (manufacturing and some technology resources allocated outside the home country), to multinational (allocating resources among national or regional areas), to global (treating the entire world as one large company) organizations (Briscoe & Schuler, 2004; Reynolds, 1995; Sheridan & Hansen, 1996). I also emphasize that organizational structure directly affects all HR management functions from recruitment through retirement. Thus, effective HR management does not exist in a vacuum but is integrated into the overall strategy of the organization. Indeed, from the perspective of strategic management, the fundamental problem is to keep the strategy, structure, and HR dimensions of the organization in direct alignment (Bartlett, 1986; Schuler, Dowling, & De Cieri, 1993).

Workforce Planning

This issue is particularly critical for firms doing business overseas. They need to analyze both the local *and* the international external labor markets as well as their own internal labor markets in order to estimate the supply of people with the skills that will be required at some time in the future. Six other key issues in international HR planning are (Cascio, 1993; Dowling & Welch, 2005):

1. Identifying top management potential early (Spreitzer, McCall, & Mahoney, 1997).

2. Identifying critical success factors for future international managers.

3. Providing developmental opportunities.

4. Tracking and maintaining commitments to individuals in international career paths.

5. Tying strategic business planning to HR planning and vice versa.

6. Dealing with multiple business units while attempting to achieve globally and regionally focused (e.g., European, Asian) strategies.

Recruitment

Broadly speaking, companies operating outside their home countries follow three basic models in the recruitment of executives: (1) they may select from the national group of the parent company only, (2) they may recruit only from within their own country and the country where the branch is located, or (3) they may adopt an international perspective and emphasize the unrestricted use of all nationalities (Briscoe & Schuler, 2004; Dowling & Welch, 2005). Each of these strategies has both advantages and disadvantages.

International Staffing

Assuming the task is to select expatriates, I emphasize that selection criteria for international jobs cover five areas: *personality, skills, attitudes, motivation,* and *behavior* (Cascio, 1991). When success is defined in terms of completing the expatriate assignment, and also supervisory ratings of performance on the assignment, evidence indicates that three personality characteristics are related to ability to complete the assignment. These are extroversion and agreeableness (which facilitate interactions and making social alliances with host nationals and other expatriates), and emotional stability. Conscientiousness is a general work ethic that supervisors "see" in their subordinates, and this affects their performance ratings. Expatriate assignments require a great deal of persistence, thoroughness, and responsibility—all of which conscientious people possess and use (Caligiuri, 2000). A final issue that I address is the applicability of U.S. labor laws to multinational employees.

Orientation

Orientation is particularly important in overseas assignments, both before departure (initial and predeparture sessions) and after arrival. Formalized initial orientation efforts—for example, elaborate multimedia presentations for the entire family, supplemented by presentations by representatives of the country and former expatriates who have since returned to the United States—are important. After all, approximately 80% of international assignees are accompanied by a spouse, children, or both (Shaffer, Harrison, Gilley, & Luk, 2001).

Cross-Cultural Training and Development

To survive, cope, and succeed, managers need training in three areas: the culture, the language, and practical, day-to-day matters (Bhawuk & Brislin, 2000). Female expatriates need training on the norms, values, and traditions that host nationals possess about women, and also on how to deal with challenging situations they may face as women (Caligiuri & Cascio, 2000). Reviews of research on cross-cultural training found that it has a positive impact on an individual's development of skills, on his or her adjustment to the cross-cultural situation, and on his or her performance in such situations (Black & Mendenhall, 1990; Harrison, 1992). Evidence also indicates that training should take place prior to departure and also after arrival in the new location. Formal mentoring for expatriates by host-country nationals also shows organizational support, and it can help to improve both language skills and the ability to interact effectively (Kraimer, Wayne, & Jaworski, 2001).

International Compensation

Compensation policies can produce intense internal conflicts within a company at any stage of globalization. Indeed, few other areas in international HR management demand as much top-management attention as does compensation. I address three major issues in this area: expatriate salaries, benefits, and adjustments in pay.

The principal problem with respect to salaries is straightforward: *salary levels for the same job differ among countries in which a global corporation operates.* Compounding this problem is the fact that fluctuating exchange rates require constant attention in order to maintain constant salary rates in U.S. dollars. I discuss three types of expatriate compensation plans typically found during this stage of development (Reynolds, 1995): localization, "higher-of-home-or-host" compensation, and the balance sheet.

In terms of benefits, I emphasize that benefits may vary drastically from one country to another, and I provide examples from Mexico, Russia, and Vietnam. I also emphasize that global corporations commonly handle benefits coverage in terms of the "*best-of-both-worlds*" benefits model. That is, wherever possible, the expatriate is given home-country benefits coverage, for example, with respect to pensions and medical coverage (Overman, 2000). However, in areas such as disability insurance, where there may be no home-country plan, the employee may join the host-country plan. I also note that most U.S. multinationals also offer various types of premiums and incentives. Their purpose is to provide for the difference in living costs (that is, the costs of goods, services, and currency realignments) between the home country and the host country.

With respect to adjustments in pay, I highlight not only the substantial differences that exist in performance-appraisal practices in different countries and cultures, but also that research indicates that there are important similarities in reward-allocation practices across cultures. The most universal of these seems to be the *equity norm*, according to which rewards are distributed to group members on the basis of their contributions (Kim, Park, & Suzuki, 1990). In general, the more expatriates perceive that the methods the parent organization uses to plan and implement decisions are fair (procedural justice), the better their adjustment and performance in overseas assignments (Garonzik, Brockner, & Siegel, 2000).

Finally, I emphasize that as the international operations of multinational firms evolve, they begin to introduce local and regional performance criteria into their pay plans, and they attempt to qualify the plans under local tax laws. They do this to create stronger linkages between executives' performance and long-term business goals and strategies, to extend equity ownership to key executives (through stock options), and, in many instances, to provide tax benefits (Sheridan & Hansen, 1996).

Labor Relations in the International Arena

I believe that it is important to stress that labor relations structures, laws, and practices vary considerably among countries (Budd, 2005). Unions may or may not exist. Management or government may dictate terms and conditions of employment. Labor agreements may or may not be contractual obligations. Management may conclude agreements with unions that have little or no membership in a plant or with nonunion groups that wield more bargaining power than the established unions do. And principles and issues that are relevant in one context may not be in others, for example, seniority in layoff decisions or even the concept of a layoff (Gatley, 1996; Gaugler, 1988).

I also cover three other issues in this area: (1) how unions constrain the choices of global companies, (2) problems that global companies present to unions, and (3) international labor standards in areas such as child labor, forced labor, discrimination in employment, health and safety, adequate wages, and freedom of association.

Repatriation

This is the final topic that I cover in my treatment of international HR. The problems of repatriation, for those who succeed abroad as well as for those who do not, are well documented. I stress that all repatriates experience some degree of anxiety in three areas: personal finances, reacclimation to the U.S. lifestyle, and readjustment to the corporate structure (Black & Gregersen, 1991; Whitman, 1999). They also worry about the future of their careers and the location of their U.S. assignments. I emphasize that possible solutions to these problems fall into three areas: planning, career management, and compensation. I then describe what leading companies are doing to address each of these concerns.

Which HR Knowledge and Skills Have the Potential to Cross National Boundaries, and Which, by Necessity, Focus on the Nation in Which HR Is Practiced?

To some extent, I have answered this question in the preceding sections. Although a great deal of HR knowledge and skill have the potential to cross national boundaries, there are certain areas that, by their very nature, are country specific. These include cultural practices, for example, with respect to conducting meetings, handling conflict, and social conventions. They also include country-specific labor laws and required benefits, such as Social Security and healthcare contributions. The major international accounting firms regularly publish updated regulations that cover almost all countries, and HR professionals and general managers should at least be aware of the existence of these sources.

How Can Non-Country-Specific and Country-Specific Knowledge Be Incorporated Into HR Curricula in an Efficient Manner—or Should It Be?

In previous sections I have explained my approach to teaching content relevant to international HR, and which content I incorporate into the curriculum. With respect to country-specific information, such as employment laws and cost-of-living data, it seems to me that the best service we can provide to students is to tell them where to find that information, rather than focusing narrowly on just one or a few countries. For example, they should be encouraged to consult sources such as the International Benefit Guidelines, published annually by William M. Mercer, Inc. (www .MercerHR.com), the International Foundation of Employee Benefit Plans (www.ifebp.org), or consulting firms such as Runzheimer International (www.Runzheimer.com).

Conclusion

Educating the HR professional and the general manager on key issues in international HRM is an ongoing challenge. Certainly the depth of coverage of international topics will vary depending on the length of the course in question. At the very least, however, participants should understand the crucial role that culture plays in the international arena, particularly key aspects of culture that will enable them to understand and appreciate nuances across countries. Some of these aspects include sense of self and space, dress and appearance, food and eating habits, verbal and nonverbal communication, time and time sense, relationships, values and norms, beliefs and attitudes, work motivation and practices, and mental processes and learning.

Finally, it is important to understand how domestic and international HR differ with respect to issues such as scope and risk exposure, organizational structure, workforce planning, recruitment, staffing, orientation, cross-cultural training and development, compensation, labor relations, and repatriation. Given the rapid proliferation of technology and globalized business operations, managing people across multiple borders and time zones will become the norm rather than the exception in the years ahead. We need to begin educating HR professionals and general managers about these issues now.

References

Bartlett, C. A. (1986). Building and managing the transnational: The new organizational challenge. In M. E. Porter (Ed.), *Competition in global industries* (pp. 367–404). Boston: Harvard Business School Press.

Bensimon, H. F. (1998, August). Is it safe to work abroad? *Training & Development, 52*(8), 20–24.

Bhawuk, D. P. S., & Brislin, R. W. (2000). Cross-cultural training: A review. *Applied Psychology: An International Review, 49,* 162–191.

Black, J. S., &, Gregersen, H. B. (1991). When Yankee comes home: Factors related to expatriate and spouse repatriation adjustment. *Journal of International Business Studies, 22*(4), 671–695.

Black, J. S., & Mendenhall, M. (1990). Cross-cultural training effectiveness: A review and a theoretical framework for future research. *Academy of Management Review, 15,* 113–136.

Briscoe, D. R., & Schuler, R. S. (2004). *International human resource management* (2nd ed.). London: Routledge.

Budd, J. W. (2005). *Labor relations: Striking a balance.* Burr Ridge, IL: McGraw-Hill/Irwin.

Bussey, J. (1998, February 26). An evening at gunpoint in Mexico. *The Wall Street Journal,* pp. B1, B6.

Caligiuri, P. M. (2000). The big five personality characteristics as predictors of expatriates' desire to terminate the assignment and supervisor-rated performance. *Personnel Psychology, 53,* 67–88.

Caligiuri, P. M., & Cascio, W. F. (2000). Sending women on global assignments. *WorldatWork Journal, 9*(2), 34–40.

Cascio, W. F. (1991, September). *International assessment and the globalization of business: Riddle or recipe for success?* Keynote address prepared for the National Assessment Conference, Minneapolis, MN.

Cascio, W. F. (1993). International human resource management issues for the 1990s. *Asia-Pacific Journal of Human Resource Management, 30*(4), 1–18.

Catlin, L. B., & White, T. F. (2001). *International business: Cultural sourcebook and case studies* (2nd ed.). Cincinnati, OH: South-Western.

Dowling, P. (1999). Completing the puzzle: Issues in the development of the field of international human resource management. *Management International Review, 39,* 27–43.

Dowling, P., & Welch, D. (2005). *International dimensions of human resource management* (4th ed.). Mason, OH: South-Western College Publishing.

Employee motivation in Germany. (1989, March). *Manpower Argus, 246,* 6.

Garonzik, R, Brockner, J., & Siegel, P. A. (2000). Identifying international assignees at risk for premature departure: The interactive effect of outcome favorability and procedural fairness. *Journal of Applied Psychology, 85,* 13–20.

Gatley, S. (1996). *Comparative management: A transcultural odyssey.* London: McGraw-Hill.

Gaugler, E. (1988). HR management: An international comparison. *Personnel, 65*(8), 24–30.

Harris, P. R., & Moran, R. T. (1990). *Managing cultural differences* (3rd ed.). Houston, TX: Gulf.

Harris, P. R., Moran, R. T., & Moran, S. V. (2004). *Managing cultural differences* (6th ed.). Amsterdam: Elsevier.

Harrison, J. K. (1992). Individual and combined effects of behavior modeling and the cultural assimilator in cross-cultural management training. *Journal of Applied Psychology, 77,* 952–962.

Howard, A., Shudo, K., & Umeshima, M. (1983). Motivation and values among Japanese and American managers. *Personnel Psychology, 36*(4), 883–898.

Ibrahim, Y. M. (1994, February 3). Fundamentalists impose culture on Egypt. *The New York Times,* pp. A1, A10.

Jossi, F. (2001, June). Buying protection from terrorism. *HRMagazine, 46*(6), 155–160.

Kim, K. I., Park, H. J., & Suzuki, N. (1990). Reward allocations in the United States, Japan, and Korea: A comparison of individualistic and collectivistic cultures. *Academy of Management Journal, 33,* 188–198.

Kissel, M. (2004, May 13). Americans consider terror risks before taking jobs abroad. *The San Diego Union-Tribune,* p. A18.

Kraimer, M. L., Wayne, S. J., & Jaworski, R. A. (2001). Sources of support and expatriate performance: The mediating role of expatriate adjustment. *Personnel Psychology, 54,* 71–99.

Overman, S. (2000, March). Check the vitality of health care abroad. *HRMagazine, 45*(3), 77–84.

Pasquarelli, T. (1996, October). Dealing with discomfort and danger. *HRMagazine, 41*(10), 104–110.

Ralston, D. A., Gustafson, D. J., Elsass, P. M., Cheung, F., & Terpstra, R. H. (1992). Eastern values: A comparison of managers in the United States, Hong Kong, and the People's Republic of China. *Journal of Applied Psychology, 77,* 664–671.

Reynolds, C. (1995). *Compensating globally-mobile employees.* Scottsdale, AZ: American Compensation Association.

Schuler, R. S., Dowling, P. J., & De Cieri, H. (1993). An integrative framework of strategic international human resource management. *Journal of Management, 19*(2), 419–459.

Schweitzer, M. E., & Kerr, J. L. (2000). Bargaining under the influence: The role of alcohol in negotiations. *Academy of Management Executive, 14*(2), 47–57.

Shaffer, M. A., Harrison, D. A., Gilley, K. M., & Luk, D. M. (2001). Struggling for balance amid turbulence on international assignments: Work-family conflict, support, and commitment. *Journal of Management, 27,* 99–121.

Sheridan, W. R., & Hansen, P. T. (1996, Spring). Linking international business and expatriate compensation strategies. *ACA Journal, 5*(1), 66–79.

Spreitzer, G. M., McCall, M. W., Jr., & Mahoney, J. D. (1997). Early identification of international executive potential. *Journal of Applied Psychology, 82,* 6–29.

Whitman, M. F. (1999). *Antecedents of repatriates' intent to leave the organization: Repatriation adjustment, job satisfaction, and organizational commitment.* PhD dissertation, University of Sarasota.

SECTION 5

Neglected Topics in HRM Education

Clearly, there are many neglected topics in HRM education. The topic itself is large enough to warrant a separate book. This section focuses on three neglected topics. Although financial compensation is central to effective HRM practice, other rewards often are ignored. Chapter 11 deals with this issue. Although ethics is at the core of HR value, often this topic is not integrated across the HR curriculum. Chapter 12 focuses on HR ethics. Although a large body of HR-relevant academic research exists, it is not incorporated into HRM practice, and changes in HR practice often do not influence HR research and education. Chapter 13 presents a model of transfer of knowledge within the HRM field.

In Chapter 11, Newman acknowledges that "money matters." Nevertheless, he suggests other things that also matter are largely ignored. His chapter looks at what we know about applicants and the role of rewards in making job-choice decisions. Because wages have commanded the most attention, he focuses on other rewards and their impact on job-choice decisions.

In Chapter 12, Deckop proposes that HRM inherently involves ethical issues because HRM and ethical issues share at their core the treatment of people. Recognizing that ethics typically doesn't command treatment in HRM textbooks, Deckop provides a basic overview of conceptual tools that can be used to analyze the ethical aspects of HRM decisions. He suggests that HRM education cannot be complete without exposure to philosophical principles and theories about the treatment of humans.

In Chapter 13, Stone, Lukaszewski, and Stone-Romero present a model of the transfer of knowledge in the field of HRM and argue that there is a reciprocal relationship between HR practice, research, and education. They note that current problems in the system prevent results of research from being incorporated into HR practice and changes in practice from influencing HR research and education. Their chapter highlights how the transfer of knowledge system could become more integrated. They give examples of how changes in HR technology might influence research and education in the field. The authors provide suggestions for generating new research in HR and for revitalizing HR education systems.

Rewards 11

From the Outside Looking In

Jerry M. Newman

Money matters. Henry Ford indelibly printed this message on the minds of students and practitioners of compensation back before World War I. Pay a man $5.00 a day (when the going rate is $2.20!), Henry reasoned, and it doesn't matter how onerous the job is! People will flock to the opportunity. Unfortunately, the message worked too well. For more than 50 years, money "compensated for" everything else that was wrong with jobs. Perhaps as a consequence, our level of sophistication about money far exceeds our knowledge of other rewards. Salary surveys are routine business practices, because money matters in being competitive. Merit pay, although routinely criticized as ineffective, is still a regular part of compensation practice, in part because money matters. When we change other parts of our HR system, we ask, would or should this influence pay? Such thinking gave rise to skill-based pay, as efforts to make systems more flexible carried recognized changes in compensation practices. Largely ignored in this pattern of thinking, though, is what we should do about the other rewards in organizations. Certainly we recognize that other aspects of the corporate contract are rewarding. Most of us don't take a job, and go to work day after day, just because of money. Indeed, the increased interest in total compensation and total rewards suggests that, at the least, we recognize that other things besides money matter. But our level of sophistication in understanding what these rewards are, how they influence important behavioral decisions of employees, and how they interact in any systems perspective of HR, are seldom explicit subjects of discussion amongst compensation people. Nowhere is this more true than in the job-choice process. Do applicants make job choices on the basis of a rational assessment of rewards available? Probably not. The process is not entirely rational, and the role of rewards in the decision process is, at best, murky (Steel, 2002). Is it any wonder that most turnover occurs in the first 18 months of employment (Jackson & Schuler, 2003)?

This chapter looks at what we know about applicants and the role of rewards in making job-choice decisions. Because wages have commanded the most attention in prior looks at this question, the focus here is on other rewards and their impact on applicant decision making.

Rewards in Organizations: Nonpecuniary Ways to Entice Applicants

Arguably there are 13 different rewards (Table 11.1) in organizations (Milkovich & Newman, 2008). Our practical knowledge of these rewards is far better developed for money than it is for the remaining 12 rewards. We know, for example, that job applicants pay particular attention to pay in their job search process. Cable and Judge's (1994) study of applicant decision making showed that several pay system characteristics were generally related to organizational attractiveness. Pay level, not surprisingly, had a strong impact. Higher paying organizations were more attractive. Other pay characteristics mattered too. Fixed pay (lower variable component) and individual-based (not team) rewards were also more attractive.

Money is an expensive way to motivate applicant, and subsequently employee, behavior. When Henry Ford decided to pay $5.00 a day, people lined up around the block for a chance at a job that paid more than twice the going rate. In the early 1900s, these wages could be passed on to consumers. Today, though, globalization means heightened competitiveness, and identifying ways to cut costs while still rewarding desirable behavior is a critical element of corporate success. If we can identify rewards that satisfy applicant and employee needs more efficiently than money, the advantages are apparent. As a first step toward this goal, let's look at what we know about rewards and the role they play in attracting applicants to firms.

Using Rewards to Attract Applicants

What do applicants know about organizations when they scan for jobs? The question matters because we know that larger applicant pools allow organizations to be more selective in the hiring process. Empirically, we know that applicants pay attention to corporate reputation. The top 100 companies to work for regularly have very large applicant pools. For example, at Lincoln Electric and Southwest Airlines it's not uncommon to have over 200 applicants for each job. And both companies acknowledge that the ability to be picky and select top people is a key element in success. Where does this organizational reputation and attractiveness come from? Presumably a key element in attractiveness comes from the rewards offered. Employees at Lincoln Electric acknowledge that they applied there because of pay. With bonuses, pay at Lincoln Electric is 20–30% higher than market wages (Hodgetts, 1997). If you were to ask the same question of Southwest Airlines workers, though, pay would hardly be the deciding factor. Pay, by corporate edict, is designed to be no more than competitive. Workers are attracted here because of such intangibles as a fun work environment coupled with wide latitude in delighting customers. How important are these nonmonetary rewards in general? Let's take it as a given that money matters. Studies regularly indicate that money factors into every decision equation (Feldman & Arnold, 1978). Beyond this, though, there is at least anecdotal evidence that things other than money matter. For example, the dot-coms have become much less popular since the much-publicized downsizings and closures, but at what level does job insecurity become a factor in attractiveness? Does it require widespread industry collapse before job security assumes a prominent role in job selection? Similarly, anecdotal evidence suggests that part of General Electric's attractiveness to applicants comes from its well-known policies and practices in developing employees. During his reign as CEO at GE, Jack Welch used to promote the concept of "career security" as an important reward coming from GE employment. Job security isn't guaranteed, but GE employees build up leading-edge skill portfolios that serve them well in career moves outside GE. Are these anecdotes reinforced by scientific evidence?

Much of the research about the role of rewards in attracting employees has a conceptual basis in person-organization fit models of selection (Kristof, 1996) in general, and in particular Schneider's attraction-selection-attrition (ASA) framework (Schneider, 1987). ASA portrays selection as involving several phases. First, people select companies! They find organizations differentially attractive, partially as a function of fit between individual preferences or needs and organizational characteristics such as systems (including reward systems) and structures (Kristof, 1994). Thus, people don't randomly appear at the doorstep of an organization. Rather, individuals select themselves into (and out of, for that matter) organizations (Durham, 2000). Second in Schneider's model is the traditional portrayal of selection: organizations selecting candidates who have desired characteristics thought to influence organizational success. Finally, the attrition phase of ASA predicts turnover as a function of poor fit. High hopes built during attraction and selection are dashed, with either employees or the organization, or both, not finding their needs met.

We know relatively little about how people select companies compared to how companies select people. A number of studies suggest applicants adopt a need-based strategy for selecting companies (Bretz, Ash, & Dreher, 1989; Cable & Judge, 1994; Turban & Keon, 1993). Frequently these studies look at applicant needs being satisfied by establishing a fit between individual values or goals and attitudes with organizational values, goals,

Table 11.1   Rewards in Organizations

1. Compensation (money!)	Wages, commissions, and bonuses
2. Benefits	Vacations, health insurance, pensions, profit sharing, and other indirect pay
3. Social environment	Friendly workplace
4. Job security	Stable, consistent position
5. Status/recognition	Respect, prominence due to work
6. Work variety	Opportunity to perform different tasks
7. Workload	Right amount and distribution of work
8. Work importance	Work is valued by society
9. Authority/control/autonomy	Ability to influence others; control own destiny
10. Feedback	Receive information on one's performance feedback
11. Advancement	Chance for promotions
12. Development	Opportunity to acquire new skills
13. Work conditions	Hazard-free work situation

and norms. Relatively few studies look specifically at the fit between employee needs and the organization's rewards, as listed in Table 11.1. As stated, compensation matters. In the following sections we look at the remaining 12 rewards in Table 11.1 to identify how important they are for attracting applicants to companies.

EMPLOYEE BENEFITS

Employee benefits represent a huge expense to companies with little evidence that applicants pay attention to this costly job feature. One early study (Huseman, Hatfield, & Robinson, 1978) found that MBA students ranked benefits last of six rewards in their ability to attract job applicants (advancement, salary, job responsibilities, prestige, location, benefits). The ranking improves somewhat when benefits choices are given, as in flexible benefits packages (Cable & Judge, 1994). A later study (Barber & Roehling, 1993) ranked benefits as one of the top factors in job choice, along with salary and location. This was particularly true, though, when benefits were advertised as "generous." This apparent conflict in the importance of benefits might be partially cleared up by a study out of the military. Brown (1987) found that educational benefits had a much larger impact on the number of recruits than did military wages. Because the military focuses many advertisements on the educational opportunities from enlisting, some experts speculate that a key element in reward attractiveness (and benefits in this example) may be their visibility. From this perspective, the omnipresent attractiveness of wages may be linked to their natural visibility advantages. Along with a job offer comes some announcement of wages. With the ready availability of occupational wage data on, amongst other sources, the Internet, it's easy to judge the "competitiveness" of the offer.

Information about other rewards is less likely to appear in a job offer (except, perhaps, for benefits data), and is certainly less amenable to comparative evaluation from other data sources. From the outside looking in, this shortage of information about other rewards is likely to lessen their impact in the decision process.

SOCIAL ENVIRONMENT

There is little data on the relationship between the social environment of an organization and attraction of applicants. Judge and Bretz (1992) measured applicant value orientation, including concern for others. People with this value orientation were attracted to companies that emphasize concern for others (Judge & Bretz, 1992). Kristof (1994) speculates that a social need may be best satisfied in environments with strong team-based structures. Certainly companies such as Southwest promote the importance of concern for others and the "fun work environment." It's unclear, though, that this is a typical focus of recruitment literature.

JOB SECURITY

Job security (stability) seldom is mentioned as a factor in attraction to a firm or an industry (Rau & Hyland, 2002). In one of the earliest studies on job choice, Jurgensen (1978) asked individuals to indicate the sources of job attraction. When describing others, pay clearly led the list of important characteristics. When asked to describe themselves, though, individuals placed job security at the top of the list (along with promotion opportunity, type of work, and company characteristics). Indirect evidence also suggests that risk-averse people highly value security. Cable and Judge (1992) note that risk aversion is linked to decidedly lower importance attached to wages in job-choice decision. They speculate this may mean that individuals who dislike risk may willingly sacrifice higher wages for more stability in wages (more allocation to fixed pay, less to variable).

STATUS AND RECOGNITION

We know a lot about status and recognition as factors in retention and motivation of employees. Considerable economic research shows that employees will trade higher wages for more status (Frank, 1984; Schaubroeck, 1996). And recognition programs are a much acclaimed and inexpensive way to motivate employees (Milkovich & Newman, 2008). There is no data, however, suggesting that job choices are influenced by status or recognition. Applicants are not usually privy to information about internal recognition programs or job status differentials. Such communications are geared to current employees.

WORK VARIETY

Much like status and recognition, work variety is not something typically communicated in the preemployment exchange. Therefore, its effectiveness in attracting applicants is unclear. As evidence that work variety is well hidden in the search process, one study of workers transitioning between jobs found the biggest, and most pleasant, surprise in the level of work variety (Hutt & Parsons, 1981).

WORKLOAD

A growing body of evidence, typically catalogued under family-friendly practices and flexible work schedules, indicates that workload can be a powerful attraction reward for applicants (Davenport & Pearlson, 1998; Lee, MacDermaid, & Buck, 2000). Some sources label it a rising star in attracting highly desirable applicants who are not interested in traditional work relationships (JobTrac, 2002). Research in this area argues that workers face role conflicts, particularly between work and family life. Many of these role conflicts could be alleviated with different kinds of work hour configurations, including reduced hour (job sharing) and flexible schedules. Indeed, research shows that people with high role conflict are more likely to prefer flexible work arrangements (Rau & Hyland, 2002). Preferences for more flexible work schedules were also found to be more prevalent among females, older workers, and those preferring companies with a team orientation (Judge & Bretz, 1992).

I recently worked undercover as a crewmember in seven fast-food stores during 14 months (Newman, 2007). I regularly found that hours of work in low-wage jobs were an important currency for attraction. One McDonald's regularly paid more than a dollar below market, but attracted good workers because of, in part, a sophisticated software program that built schedules around preferred workdays during the week and requested hours per day and hours per week.

WORK IMPORTANCE

What little data exist on work importance as a factor in job attractiveness is related to corporate social performance. Companies that are environmentally friendly, committed to diversity goals, and active in community relations are rated more attractive (Backhaus, Stone, & Heiner, 2002).

It appears that this effect translates into favorable job decisions only for applicants who have multiple job choices (Albinger & Freeman, 2000). To the extent that number of offers correlates with applicant qualifications, though, this may be just the people companies want to attract.

AUTHORITY/CONTROL/AUTONOMY AND FEEDBACK

These rewards do not appear to play a role in job choice of applicants. Again, the failure of organizations to communicate such rewards makes it difficult to assess their possible impact on applicant decision making. However, observations suggest that these rewards may relate to turnover decisions among professional and managerial employees.

ADVANCEMENT

In two early studies of job choice, advancement opportunity (viewed as promotion to a higher level job) was reported as one of the top rewards in job-choice decisions (Jurgensen, 1978; Zedeck, 1977). The value of promotion opportunities increased when they were perceived as merit based. As organizations downsize and de-layer, fewer opportunities for promotions arise. Coupled with the large numbers of baby boomers "clogging up" the ranks of middle management, many reward experts lament the lessening availability of promotion opportunities as a reward (Schuster & Zingheim, 1992).

DEVELOPMENT

For the past 15 years I have been conducting polls of MBA students and managers, both in the U.S. and in such countries as Singapore, Indonesia, and China. These polls ask about reward importance for accepting a job, focusing on the 13 rewards outlined earlier. During that period of time, one reward has steadily increased in importance, now regularly scoring fifth or sixth in attractiveness out of the 13 rewards: developmental opportunities. Certainly, people such as Jack Welch, past president of General Electric, perceive development opportunities as a major competitive advantage for those companies that can regularly enhance employee training experiences. Noting that job security is a promise destined for disappointment, Welch trumpeted career security. GE offers career security for applicant hopefuls, he argued, because they provide the kinds of training and developmental experiences that make GE employees highly sought after the world over. Although this suggests that development opportunities as a reward ought to be prized by job applicants, there is little hard data to evaluate this claim.

One study reported that people with high achievement value (described in part by seeking opportunities to learn new skills) are more likely to seek organizations where development opportunities are more prevalent (Judge & Bretz, 1992).

WORKING CONDITIONS

Recent articles report that military recruiters are having difficulties meeting recruitment targets (Arndorfer, 2005). There is considerable evidence that workers pay attention to extreme working conditions, and either demand higher wages as compensation or choose other lines of work. Over the past several decades, the legal environment has forced firms to improve working conditions. As a consequence, this factor has become less important in job-choice decisions.

Some Caveats About Rewards

More than 20 years ago, Wanous (1980) decried the lack of knowledge about job-choice decisions. Since that challenge was issued, there has been some effort at studying how applicants choose companies. But the research volume is but a trickle in comparison to work on that other selection phenomenon, how companies chose applicants. As a consequence, we still do not know if rewards other than money play an important role in applicant decision-making processes. As an example, consider the following observation (Rynes, Brown, & Colbert, 2002): "People tend to understate the importance of pay to their decisions due to social desirability considerations and lack of self-insight" (p. 94). Rather than appear to be motivated by crass materialism, this view says people downplay the importance of money in reporting their choice factors in deciding where to work. This appears to suggest that other rewards are actually less important than some of the studies we reported on would indicate. Whether this is true depends on a better understanding of the selection process job applicants undergo in deciding what job to accept.

Breaugh and Starke (2000) outline a model of the way applicants formulate job expectations and decide if a job is appropriate. One part of this process involves comparisons between perceived abilities and job requirements. The second part, and the focus here, is a selection decision based on rewards: do job rewards match individual needs and wants? This is a classic selection question, but unlike organizational selection decisions, we know relatively little about individual decision processes. Clearly part of the process involves collection of data about rewards. This is relatively easy with monetary rewards. Multiple sources, some independent of the company, are available for arriving at accurate wage data. After all, salary surveys are ubiquitous. The Internet mounts numerous sites (e.g., www.bls.gov) reporting wages to be expected for specific jobs. Because multiple sources of wage information are available, this increases credibility of this data (Harkins & Petty, 1981), and credibility regularly has been linked to a greater impact in decision making (Stiff, 1994).

For other rewards, visibility a priori is much less apparent. For example, for a number of years I have run a compensation survey for the geographic area surrounding my home institution. By all accounts people think the survey is very detailed. We give considerable information about wage rates, wage ranges, expected changes in base wages, size of variable pay increases, shift differentials, union differentials, and so on. This wage-related information takes up about 80% of the survey space. Most of the rest of the survey covers competitive benefits levels: dollar amounts, expected changes in costs, and specifics on a wide variety of benefits and types of coverage. We ask nothing about competitive levels on other rewards—nothing. And in my experience this survey is not all that different from other professionally developed surveys around the country. How hard would it be to report competitive levels of other rewards? For example, what is the involuntary layoff rate for competitor companies? What is the average work week by job, and what percent of the workforce are on alternative, family-friendly work schedules? What percentage of the workforce was promoted during the past year? How much money was spent per employee on development efforts? None of these questions are asked. At least one study reports that this lack of breadth in reward information makes selecting a company difficult. Engineering students not only reported a lack of information across the reward spectrum, but also indicated that this deficiency made the offending organizations less attractive (Maurer, Howe, & Lee, 1992).

Not only is breadth of information important, but also depth. Applicants pay more attention to specific reward information. General information is devalued because of the uncertainty that is created. Indeed, Breaugh and Starke (2000), following an extensive review, recommended that companies provide specific information personalized to needs of applicants. Although more time consuming and potentially costly, such efforts pay off in much more systematic processing of company information. For example, most of the studies reported here on rewards noted that making a reward more visible increased its *reported* importance in the decision process. One study (Barber & Roehling, 1993) noted that the act of informing applicants that a benefits package was particularly generous, placing the target company as above average relative to competitors, increased the importance of benefits. In general, current models of job search report that applicants selectively attend to the most concrete data and companies that provide such data (Steel, 2002).

Finally, the accuracy of information, in addition to depth and specificity, matters. There has been renewed interest recently in realistic job previews (RJPs). As considered within the context of this chapter, RJPs involve corporate sources providing greater and more accurate information, not just about wages and benefits, but about the wide variety of rewards in organizations. Recent studies indicate that giving both positive and negative evidence about what to expect after accepting a job offer enhances attitudes toward a company (Ganzach, Pazy, Ohayun, & Brainin, 2002). Meta-analysis results for RJPs (Phillips, 1998) indicate that applicants who received realistic previews were significantly more likely to stay with a firm than when no RJP was given. Similarly, Ganzach et al. (2002) found that both RJPs and giving applicants training in decision making (to help them make rational decisions about job choice) led to increased preentry commitment.

Beyond increasing the amount and accuracy of reward information, companies also are beginning to experiment with feedback to applicants about the accuracy of their perceptions of fit (Dineen, Ash, & Noe, 2002). We can thank the Web for providing aids to applicants in their decision-making processes. Recently, companies have been putting value and reward questionnaires on the Web to permit applicants opportunities for self-assessment of fit. Texas Instruments, for example, asks questions such as the following (with the scaling from strongly agree to strongly disagree), to both convey rewards and values prevalent at TI, and to help applicants more systematically assess how close a fit exists.

I prefer . . .

1. Work that allows me free time to pursue my outside interests.

2. A job where my success depends upon the close cooperation of team members.

3. A job that provides opportunities for rapid movement up the management hierarchy.

4. Work that allows me to control my own activities.

5. A job where I must continually learn in order to improve my capabilities.

Notice how these statements map onto the rewards outlined in Table 11.1. At the end of the questionnaire applicants receive a "fit score" that is intended to suggest how well personal and corporate profiles match. Not only does the survey give information about important characteristics of jobs at Texas Instruments, but it also allows applicants to systematically assess whether their needs are aligned with these reward configurations. Such steps by companies have been shown to increase the attractiveness to applicants (Dineen et al., 2002).

Conclusions

The tale told here is a simple one. Turnover is highest in the first 18 months of employment, by a considerable margin. Applicants enter a firm with little information about rewards. They know their wages, have some idea of benefits, and understand their jobs at perhaps the most basic level. Once inside a firm, other rewards, or lack thereof, become more evident. Sometimes the discovery is agreeable. Too often it is not. The review of 13 rewards in this chapter suggests that employees are attracted by other rewards, particularly when they appear to be greater than the norm. Money will always matter in employment decisions, but we need to better understand the roles of other rewards. Do people flock to places like Lincoln Electric because the cultures are so strong and well communicated that the structure of all rewards is more evident? We don't know the answer. Essentially, we don't know how applicants process information about rewards, both in the job-choice stage and through the initial stages of hiring. Given the cost of turnover for some employers and the untapped potential of nonmonetary rewards for most, perhaps it's time we direct our efforts to understanding this component of the selection and socialization process.

References

Albinger, H. S., & Freeman, S. J. (2000). Corporate social performance and attractiveness as an employer to different job seeking populations. *Journal of Business Ethics, 20*, 88–99.

Arndorfer, J. (2005). War puts damper on army minority recruitment. *Advertising Age, 76*(9), 18.

Backhaus, K. B., Stone, B. A., & Heiner, K. (2002). Exploring the relationship between corporate social performance and employer attractiveness. *Business and Society, 20*, 28–41.

Barber, A. E., & Roehling, M. V. (1993). Job postings and the decision to interview: A verbal protocol. *Journal of Applied Psychology, 78*(5), 845–852.

Breaugh, J. A., & Starke, M. (2000). Research on employee recruitment: So many studies, so many remaining questions. *Journal of Management, 26*, 405–434.

Bretz, R. D., Jr., Ash, R. A., & Dreher, G. F. (1989). Do people make the place? An examination of the attraction. *Personnel Psychology, 42*(3), 561–570.

Brown, D. (2003). Packaging pay, benefits offerings. *Canadian HR Reporter, 16*(17), 9–13.

Cable, D. M., & Judge, T. A. (1994). Pay preferences and job search decisions: A person-organization fit perspective. *Personnel Psychology, 47*, 317–348.

Davenport, T. H., & Pearlson, K. (1998). Two cheers for the virtual office. *Sloan Management Review, 39*(4), 51–65.

Dineen, B.R., Ash, S. R., & Noe, R. A. (2002). A Web of applicant attraction: Person-organization fit in the context of web-based recruitment. *Journal of Applied Psychology, 20,* 723–734.

Durham, Y. (2000). An experimental examination of double marginalization and vertical relationships. *Journal of Economic Behavior & Organization, 42*(2), 207.

Feldman, D. C., & Arnold, H. J. (1978). Position choice: Comparing the importance of organizational and job factors. *Journal of Applied Psychology, 63,* 706–710.

Frank, R. H. (1984). Independent preferences and the competitive wage structure. *The Rand Journal of Economics, 15*(4), 510–561

Ganzach, Y, Pazy, A. Ohayun, Y., & Brainin, E. (2002). Social exchange and organizational commitment: Decision-making training for job choice as an alternative to the realistic job preview. *Personnel Psychology, 20,* 211–234.

Harkins, S. G., & Petty, R. E. (1981). The multiple source effect in persuasion. *Personality and Social Psychology Bulletin, 7,* 627–635.

Hodgetts, R. M. (1997). Discussing incentive compensation with Donald Hastings of Lincoln Electric. *Compensation and Benefits Review, 29,* 60–66.

Huseman, R., Hatfield, J., & Robinson, R. (1978). The MBA and fringe benefits. *Personnel Administration, 23*(7), 57–60.

Hutt, R., & Parsons, D. (1981). Getting the drift of graduate mobility. *Personnel Management, 13*(3), 29–32.

Jackson, S. E., & Schuler, R. S. (2003). *Managing human resources through strategic partnerships.* Mason, OH: South-Western College Publishing.

JobTrac (2002, May/June). *Non Profit World, 20,* 48–53.

Judge, T. A., & Bretz, R. D. (1992). Effects of work values on job choice decisions. *Journal of Applied Psychology, 77*(3), 261–271.

Jurgensen, C. E. (1978). Job preferences (what makes a job good or bad?). *Journal of Applied Psychology, 50,* 479–487

Kristof, A. (1994). Person-organization fit: An integrative review of its conceptualizations, measurement, and implications. *Personnel Psychology, 49*(1), 1–50.

Lee, M., MacDermaid, S., & Buck, M. (2000). Organizational paradigms of reduced-load work: Accommodation, elaboration, and transformation. *Academy of Management Journal, 43*(6), 1211–1226.

Maurer, S. D., Howe, V., & Lee, T. W. (1992). Organizational recruiting as marketing management: An interdisciplinary study of engineering graduates. *Personnel Psychology, 45,* 807–833.

Milkovich, G. T., & Newman, J. M. (2008). *Compensation* (9th ed.). New York: McGraw-Hill.

Newman, J. M. (2007). *My secret life on the McJob: Lessons from behind the counter guaranteed to supersize any management style.* New York: McGraw-Hill.

Phillips, J. M. (1998). Effects of realistic job previews on multiple organizational outcomes: A meta-analysis. *Academy of Management Journal, 41,* 673–690

Rau, B., & Hyland, M. A. (2002). Role conflict and flexible work arrangements: The effects on applicant attraction. *Personnel Psychology, 55*(1), 111–136.

Rynes, S. L., Brown, K. G., & Colbert, A. E. (2002). Seven common misconceptions about human resource practices: Research findings versus practitioner beliefs. *Academy of Management Executive, 16*(2), 92–103.

Schaubroeck, J. (1996). Pay status hierarchy and organizational attachment. *Journal of Economic Psychology, 17*(5), 579–590.

Schneider, B. (1987). The people make the place. *Personnel Psychology, 40,* 437–453.

Schuster, J. R., & Zingheim P. K. (1992). *The new pay.* New York: Lexington Books.

Steel, R. P. (2002). Turnover theory at the empirical interface: Problems of fit and function. *Academy of Management Review, 27*(3), 346–360.

Stiff, J. B. (1994). *Persuasive communication.* New York: Guildford.

Turban, D., & Keon, T. L. (1993). Organizational attractiveness: An interactionist perspective. *Journal of Applied Psychology, 78*(2), 26–33.

Wanous, J. (1980). *Organizational entry: Recruitment, selection, and socialization of newcomers.* San Francisco: Jossey-Bass.

Zedeck, S. (1977). An information processing model and approach to the study of motivation. *Organizational Behavior and Human Performance, 18,* 47–77.

Conceptual Tools for Studying the Ethics of Human Resource Management

12

John R. Deckop

Highly visible corporate scandals have increased attention on the ethical aspect of business decision making. Higher education and business schools in particular have been the focus of some of this attention. Many wonder if business schools are partly to blame for the displays of greed that have come to light, which have caused the downfall of prominent corporations and lowered investor confidence in financial markets. Business schools and universities are examining their curricula to determine whether students receive adequate training in the ethical aspect of decision making, to complement the training in the various functional areas of business.

At first glance, the field of HRM appears to have little involvement with the high-profile scandals, which have typically involved accounting and financial malfeasance. However, digging a little deeper often reveals that HRM issues are not far beneath the surface. For example, at Enron, a cutthroat HRM culture was developed that put tremendous pressure on employees to meet financial objectives or face termination, and selection, promotion, and performance appraisal practices contributed to the disaster (Gladwell, 2002). Incentive systems, including executive compensation practices, were a critical factor in explaining why executives in a number of firms made unethical decisions (Cassidy, 2002).

HRM inherently involves ethical issues. The term "resource" itself implies the use of the organization's employees as a means to an end (Greenwood, 2002). The morality of and limits to this use of individuals is the nature of ethical analysis. Academic literature has evidenced an increasing focus on the topic of ethics and HRM, and faculty teaching HRM should not find it difficult to stay abreast of this issue. For example, the January/February 2001 issue of the journal *Human Resource Management Review* was devoted to ethics and HRM, some thought-provoking books on this topic have been written recently (e.g., Deckop, 2006; Gravett, 2003; Winstanley & Woodall, 2000), and numerous analyses from a critical theory perspective have been done in our field (e.g., Greenwood, 2002; Townley, 1994). It is likewise important that HRM students and professionals develop and maintain constant awareness of the ethical aspects of HRM decision making.

Unfortunately, the treatment of ethics in HRM textbooks, and thus presumably most HRM coursework, is spotty at best. Few if any introductory HRM textbooks include a chapter on ethics. The same is generally true for textbooks covering specialized areas of HRM, such as staffing or compensation. A survey of the table of contents of a typical HRM management text often reveals at best a couple of mentions of ethics. A few (e.g., Gomez-Mejia, Balkin, & Cardy, 2007) present a more comprehensive treatment of ethics in the form of sidebars that discuss the ethical angle to the topic being covered. Although useful and necessary, the integration of ethics into specific HRM topics is limited if students do not have more fundamental conceptual tools to analyze the ethical aspects of business decisions. Although such tools are sometimes discussed in a separate business ethics course, or in texts in other areas (e.g., management, marketing), students may not have received adequate exposure to this topic prior to their HRM course. In any case, students and professionals may benefit from a discussion of the fundamentals of ethical analysis that is applied particularly to HRM.

This chapter provides a basic overview of conceptual tools, drawn primarily from philosophy, that can be used to analyze the ethical aspect of HRM decisions. HRM faculty can discuss these tools when incorporating ethical analysis into their courses, and students and practicing professionals can use them as bases for making ethical decisions. I will pay particular attention to *how* these tools can be used, not just what they are.

Before discussing tools for ethical decision making in HRM, I will address some common objections to teaching ethics in HRM or in business schools in general.

Ethics cannot be taught. The variation on this is that we learn the difference between right and wrong as children, and cannot be taught it in college or elsewhere. A rejoinder to this argument is that ethical decisions in business often involve complex issues far removed from the lessons of childhood. Has any child learned the appropriate level to set the risk of Type II error in a personality test? Are children taught whether market rates are more or less fair than job evaluation in determining pay equity? In childhood, and throughout life, we learn about morality and develop an understanding of right and wrong. We also learn to add, subtract, multiply, and divide. But that does not mean we have the tools to set up an accounting system for an organization. We learn this in school. We learn as we grow and mature how to relate to people. Education provides a way to apply our past learning—and perhaps acquire more—in order to become better leaders, managers, and coaches.

In the same way, ethics education can help students and managers become better decision makers. Ethics education can act as an awareness raiser so that individuals can realize the ethical implications of their decisions. It can also help individuals to think through the ethical angle to a decision, so they can better arrive at decisions consistent with basic values learned through their moral development.

The purpose of business organizations is to maximize profit—end of story. The implication of this belief is that employees, when faced with a decision, should always choose the course of action that maximizes profit. Alternatively, we can frame this as the beginning, not the end, of the story. Profit maximization is just one perspective on the role of business in society, and I will discuss later, decision making to always maximize profit is consistent with some philosophical bases for ethical decision making. But it is inconsistent with others. Examining the validity of this argument through ethical analysis allows one to take an informed position on this issue. Failure to critically examine this issue results in a belief based on assumption and inertia.

The vast majority, if not virtually all coursework in business schools, including HRM courses, reflects the assumption, either explicitly or implicitly, that profit maximization is the objective. The content is devoted merely to the means of getting there. Business students cannot help but focus on the good of the shareholders to the exclusion of other stakeholders. For example, an Aspen Institute study of around 2,000 students from 13 top business schools revealed that the process of moving through an MBA has a strong influence on values development: The proportion of those who believed that maximizing profits for shareholders was the prime responsibility of a company went up from 68% to 82% by the end of the first year (Aspen Institute, 2002). Ethical analysis that visits the assumption of profit maximization brings some balance to the topic and accomplishes a basic goal of education, which is to broaden horizons.

On a related note, in practice, profit maximization is a difficult rule to apply in every instance. Even strong believers in the principle of profit maximization can usually conceive of instances where alternate decisions should be made. For most individuals, the issue is more a matter of where to draw the line between company interests and the harm it may cause to others. Ethical analysis can help in figuring this out. In other ethical dilemmas, firm profit is not really the issue. Issues related to the treatment of fellow employees and questions of honesty often have no direct relation to firm performance. Again, exposure to fundamental principles of ethical decision making can assist one in making the best decision.

The existence of ethical problems in business is overhyped. It is often pointed out that even when business scandals are making front-page news, accusations typically involve only a very small percentage of firms. And in day-to-day business life, it is argued, very few decisions involve ethical issues.

However, when a large firm loses vast amounts of market value or declares bankruptcy because of ethical problems, the impact, as well as lessons that need to be learned to prevent future occurrences, can be significant. Beyond this, well-publicized ethical problems can shake investor confidence and create a fundamental mistrust in corporate behavior and financial markets that may last well after the stories disappear from the newspapers (Eichenwald, 2002).

In a way, it is an empirical question of whether ethical issues are common in daily business life. A 1997 survey of 1,300 executives, managers, and rank-and-file employees revealed that 48% respond to job pressure by performing unethical or illegal activities, and over half (58%) were asked in the past year to do something they believed was either illegal or unethical (McShulskis, 1997). These numbers do not support the view that ethical problems are rare in business. They may even be an underestimate, given that employees—especially those who have not received training in business ethics—may not even be aware of the ethical implications of their decision (O'Leary-Kelly, 2001).

Theoretical Bases for Analyzing the Ethical Aspect of a Decision

Philosophers have pondered ethical questions for millennia, and have developed numerous theoretical perspectives to aid in ethical decision making. The range and depth of philosophical theories on ethical decision making can be daunting. So much so that, arguably, presenting all the major philosophical perspectives and their nuances is likely to fail from a pragmatic standpoint because there is no way most students can absorb, much less apply on a day-to-day level, so much material.

So I will restrict this analysis to the two "dominant" (Beauchamp & Bowie, 1997) philosophical perspectives on ethics, utilitarianism and universalism, and will deal with only the most general features of these theories. Things will be complicated a little, in that I will also discuss a third theoretical perspective that is a subset of utilitarianism: profit maximization.

The goal is to provide three perspectives (utilitarianism, profit maximization, and universalism) on ethical decision making that can actually be easily remembered, taught, and used in daily decision making. Later, I will overview other perspectives, including theory that challenges these dominant perspectives.

UTILITARIANISM

The Theory. Utilitarianism, developed primarily in the 19th century, can be understood by the common phrases "The greatest good for the greatest number" and "The ends justify the means." The utilitarian believes that the potential outcomes of a decision should be analyzed to see who benefits and who is harmed. The decision that results in the most total benefit compared to harm is the best decision. The utilitarian is often portrayed figuratively as holding a scale, with the benefits on one side being weighed against the harm on the other.

A critical aspect of this theory is that a decision can result in harm to some individuals and still be the most ethical course of action. As long as benefit versus harm is maximized, "the ends justify the means." This has direct implications for HRM. As mentioned earlier, the term "resource" implies using employees as a means to an end. So from a utilitarian perspective, an organizational downsizing, for example, would be ethical as long as the good that comes from it, perhaps in the form of long-term company health and shareholder value, outweighs the harm to dismissed and current employees and other stakeholders.

Some Criticisms of the Theory. One criticism of utilitarianism is that the ends may not always justify the means. Universalism, the other dominant ethical theory to be discussed below, argues that humans have inherent worth and thus fundamental rights that should not be violated under any circumstances. Thus, for example, whereas a utilitarian may defend drug testing, a universalist might argue that drug testing fundamentally violates an employee's right to privacy. Another example relates to sweatshops—a utilitarian would argue that exceedingly poor treatment of employees can be justified if the benefits to the firm and the community it resides in are large enough. A universalist might disagree, arguing the exposing employees to extremely dangerous conditions is not justified under any circumstances.

Another criticism of utilitarianism relates to potential self-serving biases of the person making the decision. The utilitarian decision maker in theory should weigh the benefits and harm to all affected parties without bias. That may be difficult to do if the decision maker has a significant stake in the decision. Owners of sweatshops often reply that poor working conditions are necessary to stay competitive and provide jobs for the community. Is this true, or just what the owner tells himself as self-justification for getting rich? Similarly, a supervisor may fire a subordinate with whom she has a conflict, telling herself that this termination is good for the company, when in reality the decision may be self-serving. And even when the decision maker attempts to be unbiased with respect to self-interest, a variety of decision-making biases can nevertheless result in unethical decisions when attempting a utilitarian solution (e.g., Messick & Bazerman, 1996).

PROFIT MAXIMIZATION

The Theory. Profit maximization is not the name of a theory, but rather the ethical prescription of what has been termed "neoclassical economics" (Hosmer, 2006). The clearest explanation of profit maximization as an ethical imperative is probably the article by Milton Friedman (1970) titled "The Social Responsibility of Business Is to Increase Its Profits." Profit maximization is actually a subset of utilitarianism, because Friedman and other neoclassical economists argue that if all firms strive to maximize profits (subject to certain conditions, as discussed below) then the overall societal welfare, in terms of benefit versus harm, will be maximized (Hosmer, 2006). Why is this so? The explanation of this requires a detailed economic analysis, which is usually covered in basic economics courses. As Hosmer (2006) suggests, it may make sense to simply accept these economic arguments, as they are rigorously derived given the assumptions that underlie the model.

Profit maximization is a powerful basis for ethical decision making because it is so simple to apply. Choose the course of action that maximizes firm profit. It is most often cited as a basis for decision making in the context of the role of business in society. Friedman argued that firms are unethical if they, for example, engage in pollution control beyond the requirements of the law, if it hurts profits, or if they hire the hardcore unemployed in order to contribute to the social objective of reducing poverty. In both cases, Friedman argues, the decision maker is spending someone else's money (e.g., shareholders, customers) without their consent. Profit maximization can also be applied to more mundane, everyday decisions. Should a certain employee be terminated? The answer would be yes if, in the decision maker's judgment, the action is in the best interests of the firm. It would not matter if the employee was only marginally a subpart performer, or if the termination would result in severe problems for the employee and his family.

The part about the theory that has not been discussed thus far is the assumptions. They are critical, because the degree to which the assumptions are met has direct implication as to whether profit maximization can be considered an ethical decision basis. What are these assumptions? Again, these are covered in a basic economic course. For example, there must be perfect competition, all information needed for a decision must be known, all individuals must act rationally, all workers must be homogeneous in terms of their labor input, and so on. The way Friedman framed the issue may be more straightforward. A business should maximize profits "so long as it stays within the rules of the game, which is to say, engages in open and free competition without deception or fraud" (Friedman, 1970, p. 124). Actually, this sounds straightforward, although the most common criticism of this profit maximization as an ethical decision basis relates to the interpretation of these assumptions.

Some Criticisms of the Theory. Profit maximization is considered a subset of utilitarianism because, as mentioned, the theory states that if all firms seek to maximize profit, the overall welfare of society will be maximized. But the assumptions that must be met for the theory to apply have undertones of other ethical perspectives. When Friedman says "without deception or fraud," he is sounding like a universalist, who would claim that some actions (e.g., deception) are inherently wrong. He also states in his article that profit maximization should be subject to "the basic rules of society, both those embodied in law, and those embodied in ethical custom" (p. 33). How does one define or identify ethical custom? Using a common philosophical metaphor, this puts the theory on a "slippery slope," because without a clear standard of "ethical" (which from a tautological perspective puts us back at the beginning of all this discussion) almost any decision could be supported or criticized using this theory. Those decision-making biases discussed above with respect to utilitarianism in general also apply here. Self-serving and other biases may well affect whether a decision maker in a given instance determines that there is free competition, or no fraud.

Another main criticism of profit maximization is that as a utilitarian theory, it could support doing significant harm to individuals in the name of profit (i.e., the ends justify the means). This, of course, has particular implication for HRM, because the design of policies in most any area (e.g., selection, compensation, discipline, training) may involve doing harm to some in order to benefit the firm and hence profits.

UNIVERSALISM

The Theory. Universalism is probably most associated historically with Immanuel Kant, who wrote (primarily) in the 18th century. Two key statements are commonly associated with it: "Never treat another exclusively as a means to an ends," and "Act such that you would be willing that others do the same in similar circumstances." This second statement, which Kant labeled the "categorical imperative," bears resemblance to what in Christianity is called the Golden Rule, or "Do unto others as you would have them do unto you." In fact, this principle is not limited to Christianity; it is a fundamental tenet in every major religion in the world (Parliament of the World's Religions, 1993).

Universalism directly challenges utilitarianism, in that the first statement above contradicts the principle that the ends justify the means. It implies that employees have inherent worth, and that a firm or manager that views employees purely as a means to make profit or some other objective is acting unethically.

The second statement above, the categorical imperative, gets at notions of reversibility and hypocrisy (Schumann, 2001). Consider an action by a manager—lying to an employee about her chances of promotion in order to prevent her from quitting the firm. The universalist would oppose this because a world where all firms lied about such things would mean that employees, including this one, would not believe anything about promotions in the first place, and as such, the intent of the action (to retain the employee) would not be realized. In other words, if everyone did what this manager did, he would not benefit from his action.

The categorical imperative can be considered a way to test whether you are correctly applying the "don't treat employees as a means" principle (Hosmer, 2006). The categorical imperative implies that unless an action is morally right for others to do, then it is not morally right for you to do. As such, all humans are of equal value. Treating people exclusively as a means to an end denies the inherent worth of the individual and denies them fundamental rights.

Much of the application of universalism and related theories, in the context of HRM, is devoted to the identification of fundamental employee rights. There are numerous articles and books that proceed from a rights perspective and define what is and is not ethical treatment of employees. Many ethicists go so far as to claim that HRM as commonly practiced in firms is inherently unethical, because HRM policies typically have the ultimate objective of employee productivity, and good treatment of employees (or lack thereof) is considered only as a means to affect productivity (e.g., Greenwood, 2002).

Some Criticisms of the Theory. A strict application of the categorical imperative is considered by many to be difficult to apply in practice (Hosmer, 2006). For example, lying is prohibited. But probably everyone lies at least occasionally, and few of us would consider all lies to be unethical. Supervisors are often trained to provide supportive feedback to their subordinates, and it may be effective in some circumstances to restrain brutal honesty when discussing performance with an employee who has difficulty grasping something. Most of us would think that the dishonesty is justified by the outcome—protecting the employee's feelings of self-worth. This would be a utilitarian way to look at the issue.

Universalism also suffers from the same potential of self-serving biases that the other ethical theories face. The categorical imperative asks the decision maker to situationalize the problem. That is, under similar circumstances, would I be willing to make it a "universal law" for others to do the same? A universalist decision maker can be tempted to justify almost any action by situationalizing the action in restrictive fashion. For example, an HR manager might be tempted to skew a job evaluation to slot a job in a higher pay grade, which, let us say, would benefit the HR manager politically in the organization. Without situationalizing the problem, the action would not be justifiable because if all HR managers biased their job evaluation results when it was convenient to them, job evaluation would not establish a rational pay structure for the firm, which is one of its key objectives. So it would not be used, and this HR manager could not benefit from her action. However, she could tell herself that she will do it only this one time. Thus, she could rationalize that if there were a world where all HR managers biased their job evaluation results only once in their careers, then the intent of her action would still be realized. The limited occurrence of the practice would still mean that employees and firms would trust the validity of job evaluation. This may be so, but most of us would consider her action unethical.

Applying the Theories in Everyday Decision Making

The purpose of ethical training in HRM is not to learn the concepts in order to get questions right on an exam, or to impress others by dropping the names of impressive-sounding theories. It is to affect everyday decision making. The three theories presented above—utilitarianism, profit maximization, and universalism—are simple enough in their basic principles that they can be easily remembered after this book is closed.

Perhaps the next step after reading the theories is to think about which fits best with one's moral or religious upbringing and education. Which of these theories makes the most sense as a basic rule of organizational life? If you had to pick one to characterize your concept of what is right, which would it be? This theory can be the individual's "home base" theory. It is the first one to turn to when assessing the ethicality of a decision. It is applied to the situation, and if what it says to do makes sense, the decision maker acts accordingly.

However, its application may not make sense for a variety of reasons. Many people, in understanding the criticisms of the various theories, are reluctant to commit to using one theory in all circumstances. The theory may not provide a clear guide to action in a given case. Or there might be a competing ethical principle that makes more sense in a given circumstance.

So it is also fine to be willing to apply other theories in situations in which the home base theory does not make sense. Philosophers, as proponents of one or another of these theories, might object, but until the philosophers or management theorists can identify one set of ethical principles we can all agree on, each of us has the responsibility to develop an ethical framework for ourselves, one that we can live with and use.

Next, I will discuss each theory in terms of how it might be used as a home base theory, and how it might be modified in given circumstances.

Let us say utilitarianism is the home base theory. The decision maker believes in weighing the consequences of a decision against all affected stakeholders to the decision. It is acceptable if decisions cause harm to some, as long as the benefit that others receives outweighs the harm.

However, in thinking through a particular decision, one might ask a question along the lines of universalism: "Does my decision violate an employee's fundamental rights as a human?" The answer may be no to this. A termination may be justified, assuming that employees do not have an automatic right to continued employment in a firm.

Alternatively, one may answer yes to this question. Perhaps a firm has decided to downsize a group of employees. This may be an ethical decision on a utilitarian basis. However, let us say top management proposes to not notify affected employees about the downsizing until the day of termination. This action may also be acceptable from a utilitarian standpoint, if one believes that the benefit to the firm from this practice will outweigh the harm to employees. However, one may decide that this action, given the situation, is inherently wrong, because it violates fundamental rights of affected employees. In this instance, the decision maker could recommend that employees receive ample notice of the downsizing, even while the decision maker otherwise makes decisions on a utilitarian basis.

Let us say profit maximization is the home base theory. One believes that the objective of business decision making should be to maximize the long-term profitability of the organization. It can be an easy guide to apply, and it can be argued that it is an employee's duty to make decisions that benefit the firm, subject of course to the assumptions of the theory. But as with utilitarianism, the question may arise: "Are there instances where the best interests of the firm should take second place in my decision making?" "Are there instances where the harm caused to employees cannot be outweighed by any amount of profit?" This issue comes up, for example, when the ethicality of sweatshops is considered. More and more, production has shifted to countries in which labor standards afford workers and their communities little protection from harmful practices, such as dangerous working conditions and environmental pollution (e.g., Varley, 1998). Should a U.S. firm operate in another country using what would clearly be considered inhumane treatment of workers by U.S. standards? Even if so, should a firm provide only the absolute minimum in protection to workers and their communities dictated by the law in that country (often almost none) in order to maximize profit? Many who believe in profit maximization as a general principle would answer no to one or both of these questions. One might instead argue that the firm should treat workers as humanely as possible, while still allowing for a reasonable profit. This would be a utilitarian solution, one that does not conform to strict profit maximization.

At a more mundane level, HR managers face issues of employee treatment every day. Although the best interests of the firm may be one's basic orientation, there may be situations in which a more utilitarian solution is appealing, such that the shareholders of the firm (the ultimate beneficiaries of profit maximization) are considered but one stakeholder to the decision. And, from a universalist perspective, there may be certain actions that one would not be willing to do under any circumstances, simply because the actions are inherently wrong.

Let us say universalism is the home base theory. One may have a developed a strong Golden Rule (or its equivalent in other religions) orientation, and live, or try to live, by some basic rules. Do not lie. Do not break promises. Do not steal company property. Good treatment of employees is not necessarily a means to benefit the company or other stakeholders in this view, but fundamentally the right thing to do. Universalism is the home base theory, but as with the others, it may not be possible or practical to apply it in all circumstances.

To exercise universalist principles, one must either choose to work in a firm that has similar values, or be willing to constantly challenge HRM policies or actions that are considered wrong. It may be difficult to consistently practice universalistic principles in the workplace. We all have different value systems, and honest assessments of an HRM policy even by two universalists might contradict. For example, Grossman (2001), in applying universalistic principles, suggests that incentive pay is a basic individual right. Conversely, Heery (1999) argues that incentive pay, and the risk it imparts to employees, can represent a fundamental injustice.

It may be difficult for an employee to find a firm to work for that has exactly the same universal values. One cannot quit every time the firm does something, or asks one to do something, that is inconsistent with one's principles. Though one's home base theory is universalism, it may be necessary to search for a utilitarianism or profit maximization solution in some circumstances.

DRAWING LINES

As mentioned above, universalists cannot fight every fight, every time they see something in their firm that they consider unethical. This same argument applies to other ethical theories. We cannot try to change things, or quit, every time our ethical principles are violated. Thus, living up to one's ethical principles at work is also about learning where to draw the line—how bad things must get to speak out, or quit.

And, most importantly, it is important to think about where these lines should be drawn *ahead* of time—as in an educational environment versus the real world. Otherwise, the pressure of the situation may result in drawing a line in a place that looks reasonable at the time, but later is perceived as unethical (e.g., McCoy, 1997). The single-minded pursuit of a goal, say getting a project accomplished, can blind individuals to the ethical consequences of some of the decisions made along the way. Sometimes decisions must be made within a very short time frame, maybe even a split second. Perhaps financial or family pressures make it extremely difficult to do what ethical principles dictate. In all these situations, it is helpful to have thought through ethical principles ahead of time. Each of the three ethical theories discussed above share one common criticism: all can easily be misapplied if the decision maker engages in self-deception. The pressures of a situation may cause one to apply self-serving biases that appear acceptable in the short run, but in the long run result in damage to one's firm, career, or self in terms of staying true to ethical principles.

Other Ethical Perspectives

There are numerous other ethical perspectives that can serve as conceptual tools for ethical decision making. Some challenge the dominant perspectives discussed above, and other complement these perspectives. This section discusses two categories: justice theories and the theories related to the duty to care.

JUSTICE

The goal of justice theories is to analyze whether a procedure, outcome, or both, is inherently fair (Thorne McAlister, Ferrell, & Ferrell, 2003). Note that theories of procedural and distributive justice are frequently discussed in HRM textbooks, and are often based on philosophical concepts of justice. However, the use of these theories in HRM textbooks, as well as in academic HRM research, is mainly as a means to the ends of employee productivity (Greenwood, 2002). Justice, as a principle worthy of realization in its own right in HRM decision making, has not received significant attention in HRM texts.

Many justice theories relate to the distribution of wealth in society. For example, John Rawls's theory of distributive justice asks the decision maker, when thinking about what is right, to wear a "veil of ignorance" with respect to personal characteristics, such as race, family background, special talents, and the like. Then, one should make a decision that reflects this impartiality to personal circumstances. Rawls argues that if we do this, our decisions would be to distribute economic goods and services equally, unless an unequal distribution would work to everyone's advantage (Beauchamp & Bowie, 1997). The focus of this perspective is often on the disadvantaged in society, and many of its implications point to the need for a more egalitarian distribution of wealth both in society and within firms. However, Rawls does not argue for complete equality. For example, differential compensation practices, such as incentive systems for entrepreneurs, would be acceptable as long as the result was improved job opportunities for the least advantaged members of society (Beauchamp & Bowie, 1997).

Another justice theory can be termed "contributive liberty" (Hosmer, 2006). In contrast to theories of distributive justice, such as Rawls's theory, this theory, developed by Robert Nozick, focuses on an individual's right to liberty in the process of decision making. As such, it relates to procedural, not distributive justice. From a resource allocation perspective, this theory emphasizes the role of free markets, which, it argues, result in the fairest allocation of resources. This theory represents a companion of sorts to profit maximization. Whereas profit maximization argues that market mechanisms produce the most societal welfare, contributive liberty argues for the inherent justice of free markets.

All the theories up to this point focus on the individual—her rights, and the duties of the decision maker with respect to these rights. Another justice-based theory, communitarian theory, focuses instead on the *community*. Rather than discuss the rights of the individual versus the government or the firm, communitarian theory stresses the development of communal values and how those values should affect the individual (Beauchamp & Bowie, 1997). One aspect of this theory is that too much focus on individual rights obscures the responsibility the individual has to the collective. As a member of a community (the firm), an employee thus has the responsibility to be, among other things, part of establishing a workplace that is fair and just (Barrett, 1999).

THE DUTY TO CARE

Most well-known and established ethical theories, including all the theories discussed thus far, focus on the development of an abstract set of ethical principles based on rights and justice. There is no role for sensitivity to others, emotion, and relationships for their own sake in these theories. Even universalism, with its focus on "doing unto others," emphasizes the development of abstract principles not specifically related to particular individuals.

The duty to care is a label for several theories developed from a feminist tradition that emphasize character traits that are valued in close personal relationships, such as sympathy and compassion (Beauchamp & Bowie, 1997). One aspect of this work is to address societal inequality of women, and how laws, and even ethical theories developed by men, have contributed to this (Grimshaw, 1986).

Another focus is to advocate ethical decision making based on care. One prominent example is the work of Carol Gilligan (e.g., Gilligan, 1982). She asserts a framework of care and compassion, traits often associated with women, as underlying moral reasoning and ethical duty. Gilligan argues that a decision based on caring and concern for others can be as ethical, or more ethical, than a decision based on adherence to a set of abstract principles.

This relates to duties in a variety of areas in the workplace (Beauchamp & Bowie, 1997). HR managers should exhibit sensitivity to employees' personal problems not because it may result in a more productive employee or protect against a lawsuit, but because it is the right thing to do. We have the duty to be sensitive to the points of view of others. When there are conflicting rights, this sensitivity can help in finding solutions in which all parties' voices and perspectives are heard. Feminist thinking and the duty to care also involve metaphors in the workplace. Metaphors more commonly associated with men, such as sports and war, often reflect competition and conflict. Metaphors more commonly associated with women, such as relationships and family, are often seen as "soft" and not as important, despite the fact that these orientations may be correct (Beauchamp & Bowie, 1997). Although HRM in some firms represents this soft side, it is often under pressure to adopt a more "hard," business-oriented perspective. From the perspective of the duty of care, the question is if HRM does not exhibit this soft side, will anyone in the organization?

Conclusion

One view of the role of business education is that it should provide the conceptual tools necessary for business decision making. The ethical aspect of HRM decision making, particularly conceptual tools, are not well represented in HRM textbooks and, most likely, curricula.

Faculty should incorporate these tools in their HRM classes, and students and practicing professionals should apply them, for several reasons. Without exposure to a number of ethical principles, profit maximization may end up as an individual's default principle, because most HRM coursework and business coursework in general proceeds from this framework. Although profit maximization can be an ethical principle for decision making, many find, once exposed to other principles, that a singular focus on profit maximization is not consistent with their moral or religious values.

Without conceptual tools for ethical decision making, short-term pressures of the situation may result in choosing the path of least resistance. The more difficult path, however, may be the one that represents the more ethical road, and the one that in the long term is best for all, including the decision maker.

And finally, HRM and ethical issues are inherently intertwined, because they share at their foundations the treatment of people. An HRM education cannot be complete without exposure to philosophical principles and theories about the treatment of humans. HRM faculty, students, and practicing professionals have the responsibility to learn and master these tools for making ethical decisions.

References

Aspen Institute. (2002). *Where will they lead?* Aspen, CO: Institute for Social Innovation Through Business.

Barrett, E. (1999). Justice in the workplace? Normative ethics and the critique of human resource management. *Personnel Review, 28*(4), 307–318.

Beauchamp, T. L., & Bowie, N. E. (1997). *Ethical theory and business* (5th ed.). Upper Saddle River, NJ: Prentice Hall.

Cassidy, J. (2002, September 23). The greed cycle. *New Yorker, 78,* 64–77.

Deckop, J.R. (2006). *Human resource management ethics.* Greenwich, CT: Information Age Publishing.

Eichenwald, K. (2002, October 6). Even if heads roll, mistrust will live on. *The New York Times,* p. 1.

Friedman, M. (1970, September 13). The social responsibility of business is to increase its profits. *New York Times Magazine,* pp. 32–33, 122–124.

Gilligan, C. (1982). *In a different voice: Psychological theory and women's development.* Cambridge, MA: Harvard University Press.

Gladwell, M. (2002, July 22). The talent myth: Are smart people overrated? *New Yorker, 78,* 28–33.

Gomez-Mejia, L. R., Balkin, D. B., & Cardy, R. L. (2007). *Managing human resources* (5th ed.). Upper Saddle River, NJ: Prentice Hall.

Gravett, L. (2003). *HRM ethics: Perspectives for a new millennium.* Cincinnati, OH: Atomic Dog Publishing.

Greenwood, M. R. (2002). Ethics and HRM: A review and conceptual analysis. *Journal of Business Ethics, 36*(3), 261–278.

Grimshaw, J. (1986). *Philosophy and feminist thinking.* Minneapolis: University of Minnesota Press.

Grossman, W. (2001). Resolving human resource dilemmas through international human resource management: A transaction cost economics perspective. *Human Resource Management Review, 11,* 55–72.

Heery, E. (1999). Risk, representation, and the new pay. *Personnel Review, 25*(6), 54–65.

Hosmer, L. T. (2006). *The ethics of management* (5th ed.). Boston: McGraw-Hill.

McCoy, B. H. (1997). The parable of the sadhu. *Harvard Business Review, 75*(3), 54–61,

McShulskis, E. (1997). Job stress can prompt unethical behavior. *HR Magazine, 42*(7), 22–23.

Messick, D. M., & Bazerman, M. H. (1996). Ethical leadership and the psychology of decision making. *Sloan Management Review, 37*(2) 9–22.

O'Leary-Kelly, A. M. (2001). Sexual harassment as unethical behavior: The role of moral intensity. *Human Resource Management Review, 11,* 73–92.

Parliament of the World's Religions. (1993). *Towards a global ethic.* Chicago: Council for a Parliament of the World's Religions.

Schumann, P. L. (2001). A moral principles framework for human resource management ethical analysis. *Human Resource Management Review, 11,* 93–111.

Thorne McAlister, D. T., Ferrell, O. C., & Ferrell, L. (2005). *Business and society* (2nd ed.). Boston: Houghton Mifflin.

Townley, B. (1994). *Reframing human resource management: Power, ethics, and the subject at work.* London: Sage.

Varley, P. (1998). *The sweatshop quandary: Corporate responsibility on the global frontier.* New York: Investor Responsibility Research Center.

Winstanley, D., & Woodall, J. (2000). *Ethical issues in contemporary human resource management.* New York: St. Martin's.

A Model of the Transfer of Knowledge in Human Resources Management

13

Dianna L. Stone

Kimberly Lukaszewski

Eugene F. Stone-Romero

This chapter presents a model of the transfer of knowledge in HRM and argues that there are reciprocal relations among HRM practice, research, and education. However, current problems in the transfer of knowledge prevent (a) the results of research from being incorporated into HRM practice and (b) changes in practice from influencing HRM research and education. Thus, we explain how the transfer of knowledge system can become more integrated, using examples of how changes in HRM technology influence HRM research and education. In addition, we offer suggestions for generating research in HRM and revitalizing HRM educational systems.

Academicians in the field of HRM are concerned with facilitating the transfer of knowledge between research and practice (Baldwin & Ford, 1983;

Dunnette, 1991; Latham & Daghighi Latham, 2003). However, there is often a discrepancy between the goals of academicians (e.g., generating and disseminating scientific knowledge) and the goals of HRM practitioners (e.g., increasing the effectiveness of organizations; Latham & Daghighi Latham, 2003). For example, although research suggests that HRM practitioners should evaluate recruitment yield ratios, fewer than 5% of companies actually calculate them (Bernardin & Russell, 1998). Likewise, research shows that situational or structured interviews are more valid than unstructured interviews, but only 18% of companies use situational interviews (Bernardin & Russell, 1998). Similarly, in spite of the fact that performance appraisal research indicates that traits should not be included on rating forms and that rater training enhances the effectiveness of ratings, 75% of firms still include traits on rating forms, and fewer than 24% train raters (Bernardin & Russell, 1998). Thus, it is clear that much research-based knowledge is not being used in organizations. In addition, many academicians (Dunnette, 1991) contend that HRM research is often barren because it is divorced from the reality of organizational contexts. Similarly, we believe that HRM educational programs are often inconsistent with the practice of HRM. As a result, some academicians have lamented that HR education has become stagnant, and questioned whether "HR education is dead or just sleeping" (Scarpello, 2002).

It should be evident from the above that there is a growing concern about the transfer of knowledge among HRM research, education, and practice. For instance, the examples just noted suggest that there are barriers in the transfer of knowledge system that prevent scientific knowledge from being used in organizations (Dunnette, 1991), and there are obstacles that prevent changes in HRM practice from influencing both research and education (Latham & Daghighi Latham, 2003). For example, although there have been numerous changes in HRM practice in recent years (e.g., globalization, increased use of technology, outsourcing), relatively little research has focused on these and other critical issues facing HRM practitioners. In addition, HRM educational curricula continue to focus primarily on functional processes rather than the issues that actually confront organizations. Thus, the primary purposes of the chapter are to (a) present a model of the reciprocal relations among HRM research, education, and practice, and (b) illustrate these relations with reference to the impact of technology on HRM.

Model of the Reciprocal Relations Among HRM Research, Education, and Practice

Figure 13.1 shows relations among HRM research, education, and practice. Note that the figure is based on the model of the scientific method (Stone, 1978) and consists of the following elements: (a) the observation of real-world

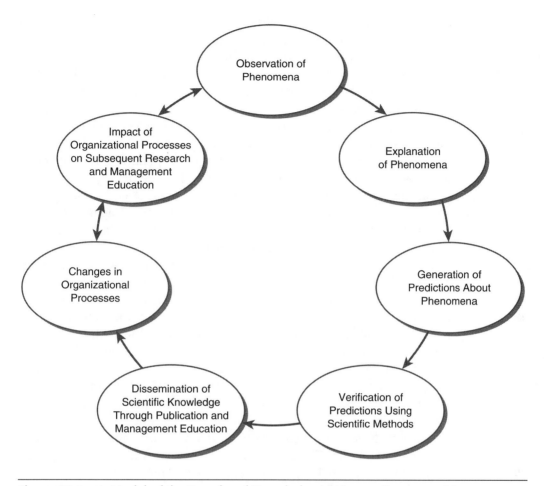

Figure 13.1   A Model of the Transfer of Knowledge in Human Resources Management

phenomena in organizations, (b) the formulation of explanations of the phenomena, (c) the generation of predictions about the phenomena, (d) the verification of those predictions using scientific research, (e) the dissemination of research-based knowledge through publication and management education, (f) the resultant changes in organizational processes and practices, and (g) the impact of such processes and practices on subsequent research and management education.

As can be seen in Figure 13.1, the model suggests that scientists observe phenomena (or facts) in organizations and formulate explanations of them. For example, they may observe that an organization has a high turnover rate and develop explanations of its causes and consequences using inductive reasoning, theory, and the findings of previous research. Second, scientists may explain the high turnover rate by arguing that employees with low levels of job satisfaction and pay will be more likely to leave organizations than those with high levels of job satisfaction and pay. Third, having formulated this tentative explanation, the scientists then use deduction to predict what would happen in the real world if their explanations are correct (Stone, 1978). For instance, if the turnover rate is negatively related to job satisfaction and pay levels, then increases in pay may serve to both increase satisfaction and decrease turnover.

Next, scientists test or verify their predictions using research that is based on the scientific method. Fifth, once the predictions are verified, the scientists disseminate the new knowledge through (a) publications in scientific journals and (b) the education of current and future managers. Although researchers often argue that practitioners do not read scientific journals, we believe that they have no real need to do so (Latham & Daghighi Latham, 2003). The reason for this is that the findings of scientific research are translated into practice through management education (e.g., classroom instruction, textbooks) that typically considers the results of relevant research. Thus, education is a critical component in the transfer of knowledge from research to both education and practice, and managers who are educated in HRM should be more likely to use scientific knowledge to enhance the effectiveness of their organizations than those who are not. As noted above, our model suggests that changes in organizational practices should serve as the basis for future research and education in the HRM field. For example, along with others (Dunnette, 1991; Latham & Daghighi Latham, 2003) we believe that issues that HRM practitioners face on the job often influence research and education in the HRM field.

Analysts have long focused on the transfer of knowledge between research and practice (Dunnette, 1991); however, scant attention has been paid to the influence that practice may have on HRM research and education. Thus, in the following sections we focus primarily on these relations and provide examples of how changes in HRM practice, especially changes in technology, may influence both HRM research and education.

How Changes in HRM Practice Influence Research

During the last decade, technology has had a profound effect on the way workers are managed in organizations For instance, results of recent surveys reveal that 70% of large firms now use Web-based self-service systems to manage benefits and records, 80% use Web-based recruiting, and 40% use Web-based portals to communicate HRM policies (Cedar, 2002; Towers Perrin, 2001). Although there are numerous reasons for using technology to facilitate HRM processes and practices, academicians and practitioners contend that technology (a) streamlines such processes and practices, (b) facilitates communication, (c) reduces costs, (d) increases the ability of organizations to adapt to change, and (e) enables organizations to attract, motivate, and retain critical employees (Cardy & Miller, 2003; Gueutal, 2003; Stone, Stone-Romero, & Lukaszewski, 2003, 2006). Despite the fact that most large organizations use technology to facilitate HRM processes and practices, relatively little research has considered the impact of Web-based systems on organizations and their key stakeholders (e.g., nonmanagerial and managerial employees; Stone et al., 2006). Thus, we believe that the advancement of knowledge in HRM hinges on an integration of HRM practice, research, and education, and below we describe how changes in organizational practices can influence HRM research and education. In particular, we consider the influence of technology on HRM processes and practices (e.g., recruitment, selection, training, and compensation), HRM research, and HRM education.

RECRUITMENT

The increased use of HRM technology has influenced the recruitment process in at least three ways. First, many companies now use the Internet to post job openings and facilitate internal and external recruiting. For example, results of a recent survey by the Cedar Group (2002) indicated that in 1997, 53% of large firms used the Internet to recruit, and almost 100% of large firms use Internet recruiting (Stone, Lukaszewski, & Isenhour, 2005). Second, representatives of organizations argue that HRM technology has enhanced the recruitment process because it reaches a broad range of applicants and facilitates applicant tracking. The online tracking of applicants makes it possible to (a) assess the effectiveness of recruitment sources (e.g., newspaper ads, Internet job postings), (b) track the costs of recruitment (e.g., advertising, travel expenses, labor costs), and (c) examine the success rates of applicants (e.g., second interviews, references checked, successful placements made; Kavanagh, Gueutal, & Tannenbaum, 1990). Third and finally, online recruitment systems give companies the ability to (a) identify current employees who have the requisite skills for new job openings and (b) store the resumes of individuals who may meet future job needs.

RESEARCH ISSUES—ONLINE RECRUITMENT

Many HRM practitioners argue that the use of online recruitment benefits organizations by reaching a wider range of job applicants and reducing the overall costs of recruitment. However, little research has directly examined the effectiveness of online recruitment systems, and no research has examined the extent to which contextual factors influence the effectiveness of online recruitment (Isenhour, Lukaszewski, & Stone, 2006; Stone et al., 2005). However, even if research shows that online recruitment is more cost-effective than traditional recruitment methods, it may lead to a number of dysfunctional consequences. For example, some researchers (e.g., Stone et al., 2003) have argued that online recruiting may have an adverse impact on members of protected groups (e.g., African Americans, Hispanic Americans, people with disabilities, older workers) because relative to members of dominant groups, they have less access to computers and may be less able to use new computer technology. Furthermore, Web-based systems or voice response systems may screen out minorities or women because they identify people by name or accent, and names and accents often yield information about an applicant's ethnicity or sex. Interestingly, recent research showed that applicants with "white-sounding" names (e.g., Emily, Greg) were 50% more likely to be contacted for job interviews than those with black-sounding names (e.g., Lakisha, Jamal; Bertrand & Mullainathan, 2004). However, the same research revealed that there were no differences between the rates at which male and female applicants were contacted for interviews (Bertrand & Mullainathan, 2004).

Likewise, some researchers maintain that online recruitment systems have the potential to invade personal privacy (Stone et al., 2006). One reason for this is that data in such systems can be merged or networked with data from other systems, and individuals can be permanently stigmatized in the process (Stone et al., 2005). For example, when an applicant applies for a job online, the data from the person's resume can be used to gather additional information that may or may not be job related. Similarly, the data can be released to others without the applicant's consent. For example, a recent study revealed that Hotresumes.com sold 4,500 resumes and e-mail addresses to other companies without the knowledge or consent of the data subjects (Dixon, 2003).Thus, research on Web-based recruitment systems can help organizations (a) identify potential problems with such systems and (b) find ways of resolving these problems before they have a negative effect on an organization's ability to attract talent. In addition, research on these systems may help society monitor a firm's compliance with employment laws.

SELECTION

In recent years, HRM technology has changed the selection process in several ways. First, it allows organizations to scan resumes for keywords in order to assess applicants' qualifications for job openings. As a result, the screening process can be greatly streamlined, and the cycle time for filling job requisitions can be substantially reduced. Resume-scanning systems can quickly eliminate applicants who (a) do not meet the basic job requirements or (b) lack relevant skills. In addition, Web sites, kiosks, and voice-response systems can be used to conduct online testing or screening, especially in cases when organizations have large numbers of job applicants. Thus, resume-screening systems and voice-response systems may increase the timeliness and efficiency of the selection process.

Second, the use of HRM technology in selection may increase the reliance on selection rules, helping to reduce biases in selection systems (Kehoe, Dickter, Russell, & Sacco, 2005). Interestingly, HRM technology may require that selection decisions be based on objective rules rather than subjective assessments of potential performance that are predicated on such variables as attractiveness, race, sex, and age. In addition, it can help organizations monitor the ratio of majority and minority candidates who are offered jobs. Moreover, the systems can trigger a warning when there are highly discrepant hiring rates for groups of applicants (i.e., there is evidence of adverse impact).

Third, some HRM analysts (e.g., Gueutal, 2003; Ulrich, 2001) have argued that intelligent Web-based systems can be used to assist managers in the selection process. For example, such systems can be used to generate both (a) a profile of an applicant's strengths and weakness prior to an interview and (b) a set of interview questions based on the profile. Fourth, HRM technology can be used to provide job applicants with a virtual preview of an organization and realistic information about one or more jobs. Fifth, and finally, it can assist with the evaluation of the overall selection process (Kavanagh et al., 1990; Stone & Gueutal, 2005). For example, a human resources information system (HRIS) can be used to monitor the criterion-related validity, cost, and utility of various selection procedures (e.g., interviews, tests, assessment centers).

RESEARCH ISSUES—SELECTION

Although technology is increasingly being used to facilitate the selection processes, research is needed to both examine the effectiveness of electronic selection (e-selection) systems and identify the consequences of using them. Likewise, research is needed on the contextual issues and boundary variables that may affect the acceptance and utility of such systems. For example, researchers have argued that there are a number of critical issues that should be considered when implementing e-selection systems, including legal issues, channels used to access the systems, data management, privacy considerations, and reactions of applicants and managers (Kehoe et al., 2005; Stone et al., 2003).

One important concern with the use of resume-scanning systems is that they may eliminate qualified candidates if they do not make use of the right keywords. Thus, research is needed to examine the impact of these systems on the effectiveness of the selection process (Mohamed, Orife, & Wilbowo, 2002). Another concern is that managers may object to e-selection systems when their ability to offer jobs to candidates is limited by the systems. In addition, applicants may be reluctant to apply for jobs if inflexible e-selection systems prevent them from revealing all of their job-related skills and abilities (e.g., interpersonal or communication skills). Similarly, the use of e-selection systems (e.g., complex Web-based systems, kiosks, or voice-response systems) may reduce the size of the applicant pool if applicants lack the ability to use them. These and other issues need to be examined through research before organizations replace traditional systems with e-selection systems.

TRAINING AND TRAINING RESEARCH ISSUES

The use of online or distance learning is one of the most dramatic changes in HRM practice in recent years, and has been implemented primarily because of its convenience, flexibility, and cost savings (Kosarzycki, Salas, DeRouin, & Fiore, 2003). For example, private-sector, governmental, and educational organizations use distance learning to deliver training and convey knowledge about both declarative and procedural issues. Typically, training courses are delivered to remote sites using a variety of media including videoconferencing, interactive TV, Internet and Web-based training, audiotapes, and videotapes. Interestingly, online training systems have been implemented widely without the benefit of adequate research on their effectiveness (Kosarzycki et al., 2003).

Despite its obvious cost advantages, research shows that distance learning is not always more effective than traditional forms of instruction (Alavi, Yoo, & Vogel, 1997), and it may even be detrimental to organizations and learners if not implemented properly. In addition, surveys by the American Society for Training and Development (ASTD & Masie, 2001) show that 62% of employees prefer classroom training to distance learning. Although there may be a number of reasons for the problems associated with distance learning, researchers have argued that one is that the effectiveness of distance learning has not been demonstrated through rigorous study. Unfortunately, distance learning is often nothing more than a simplified adaptation of other training tools and methods. Thus, organizations would benefit greatly from a set of guidelines that could be used to design and assess the effectiveness of distance learning programs (Salas, Kosarzycki, Burke, Fiore, & Stone, 2002).

COMPENSATION AND BENEFITS

HRM technology has long been used for the processing of payroll and is increasingly being used to help manage compensation and benefit systems. For example, HRM technology enables managers to model the effects of changes in compensation and incentive systems and choose the most effective such systems for attracting and retaining employees. In addition, HRM technology can be used to inform employees about pay practices and benefits offerings using employee self-service systems (ESSs). This use is important because pay and benefits account for more than 80% of all costs in service establishments. Moreover, benefits alone account for more than 40% of such costs, and employees are often unaware of the value of benefits offered by an organization (Bergmann & Scarpello, 2001; Cascio, 1998). Thus, technology is an effective online tool for communicating pay and benefits information and benefits options to employees or job applicants.

With respect to specific benefits, HRM technology facilitates the use of cafeteria-style benefit systems by allowing employees to select or change their benefit options online. In fact, one of the primary advantages of ESSs is that employees have greater control over their benefits options, and the results of a 2001 survey by Towers Perrin revealed that 60% of companies used such systems. In addition, research shows that 57% of the firms surveyed in North America used Web-based portals to provide benefits and other HR information to employees (Cedar, 2001). Many organizations have chosen Web-based ESS applications in an effort to decrease HRM costs. In this regard, a survey by the Cedar Group (2000) showed that ESSs often resulted in 80% cost savings over traditional communication systems.

RESEARCH ISSUES—COMPENSATION AND BENEFITS

Although there is widespread use of online compensation and benefits systems, most such systems have been implemented without the benefit of sound research (Dulebohn & Marler, 2005). Thus, research is needed to assess the effectiveness of these systems and identify the boundary variables that may influence their effectiveness in organizations. Likewise, research is needed to assess the unintended consequences of using these systems, including the degree to which they transfer work from HR professionals to other employees. For example, if an employee has just gotten married, she may want to add her spouse to her benefit plan. Traditionally, an employee would contact an HR professional to make the change in benefits; however, the use of online benefits systems requires employees to make these changes themselves. Thus, the use of such systems or ESSs may simplify the work of HR professionals but increase the workload of other employees. As a result, research is needed to assess employees' satisfaction with and use of such systems. The primary reason for this is that if employees either cannot or choose not to use online systems, the systems will not meet their intended objectives (e.g., enhancing the satisfaction and retention of employees).

SUMMARY

It is clear from the above that technology has had a dramatic impact on the practice of HRM, propelling it in several new directions. However, most new HRM systems have been implemented without the benefit of sound research on (a) their acceptance by users and (b) their effectiveness.

However, we believe that the value of technology-related changes in HRM practices should be assessed with rigorous research. In addition, partnerships should be formed between practitioners and academicians to facilitate such research. Unfortunately, at present there appears to be considerable distrust between academicians and practitioners, and some analysts have noted that these two groups have radically different interests (Latham & Daghighi Latham, 2003). For example, practitioners often pursue broadly defined objectives and focus on complex issues that are too "messy" to be addressed easily by traditional research methods (Dunnette, 1991). In addition, practitioners typically have little time for reflection, and may not be able to analyze the causes of HRM problems they face because they have to cope with a multitude of simultaneous demands (e.g., layoffs, turnover of critical employees, outsourcing). Furthermore, academicians often view practitioners as focusing on very short-term objectives that affect only the bottom line (e.g., cost issues). At the same time, practitioners frequently regard academicians as pursuing only narrowly defined, esoteric issues that have the potential to lead to publications in scientific journals. In addition, many practitioners view the research process as too slow and too far removed from the real world to have value in assessing the effects of changes in HRM practice. Likewise, practitioners often perceive that research is not applicable in their particular context and that the application of scientific knowledge will not help them gain a competitive edge in the marketplace.

Not surprisingly, we believe that sound scientific research can greatly benefit practice by examining the effectiveness of new HRM systems, assessing the consequences of new HRM practices, and investigating the contextual factors that may influence individuals' responses to new HRM systems, processes, and practices. However, we also believe that research would have a greater impact on organizations if it both (a) focused on basic knowledge and (b) helped to solve the key problems the confront organizations. Thus, we recommend that partnerships be formed between academia and industry so that academicians can learn firsthand about the challenges that face HR practitioners (Dunnette, 1991; Latham & Daghighi Latham, 2003). In addition, we maintain that such partnerships can facilitate the reciprocal transfer of knowledge between academia and industry. This strategy appears to work well in the field of medicine because the results of research are crucial to individuals' health and well-being; however, the transfer of knowledge from research to practice continues to be problematic in the HRM field. Apart from the influence of practice on research, we believe that (a) changes in practice should be incorporated into the design and delivery of HRM educational programs, and (b) the associated transfer of knowledge is critical to the revitalization of HRM education. Thus, we next consider how changes in HRM practice can influence the design and delivery of HRM educational programs.

How Practice Can Influence the Design and Delivery of HRM Educational Programs

Given recent changes in HRM practice, we believe that if they are to survive and thrive, HRM educational programs should operate as open systems so as to reflect the changes in the field. For example, in view of the critical role that technology plays in today's organizations, we contend that one way to revitalize HRM educational programs is to incorporate technology and other recent HRM trends into them. Unless HRM educational programs adapt to environmental changes, they will lag behind the needs of industry and will ultimately cease to be beneficial to either students or organizations. In addition, we believe that the results of research on HRM technology should be incorporated into HRM educational programs so that graduates can use the relevant knowledge to enhance the effectiveness of organizations.

The development or improvement of HRM educational programs should be based on sound training guidelines (Goldstein, 1993). Consistent with extant models of training, such programs should be based on a needs assessment that identifies the declarative and procedural knowledge that is needed by HR practitioners. For example, educators can partner with practitioners to identify the competencies that are needed by HR managers. Once training objectives have been specified, the training environment must be designed to achieve them. At this point, educators should work with practitioners to analyze the design of the overall training program and determine the optimum sequence for learning subtasks. Once training objectives are determined and the substantive content of training is specified, educators should select the most appropriate methods for conducting the training. Finally, educators should work with employers to evaluate the effectiveness of training in terms of such criteria as learning, transfer of learning, and benefits to organizations. Then, educators should use the information gained to continually revise and improve training programs. Below, we offer suggestions for designing and developing educational programs that take into account the critical role that technology plays in HRM practice.

STRATEGIES FOR INCORPORATING HRM TECHNOLOGY INTO THE HRM CURRICULUM

A number of strategies can be used to build HRM technology into the HRM curriculum. In the following sections, we discuss the formation of partnerships with industry to identify needed skills and competencies of HRM professionals. In addition, we consider the use of learning techniques that (a) engage the trainee, (b) clearly illustrate desired skills, and (c) allow for active trainee participation. In particular, we provide examples of methods that can be used to educate and train HRM managers and professionals. Note that each of the methods assumes that training programs are evaluated constantly and changed to meet the needs of relevant stakeholders. In addition, we assume that, whenever possible, training is based on the results of scientific research.

GUIDELINES FOR DESIGNING AND DELIVERING HRM EDUCATION PROGRAMS

Form Partnerships With Industry

As noted above, one strategy that can be used to conduct a needs assessment and identify the competencies that are needed in the field of HRM is for educators to form partnerships with representatives from industry. In particular, faculty can work with industry partners who can identify the declarative and procedural knowledge needed in the HRM field, and thus assist faculty in the development of training objectives. In addition, the industry partners might identify the challenges facing HRM professionals, and these can be used to guide relevant research, the results of which can be used to revise training programs in a timely fashion. Finally, the faculty can solicit feedback from industry partners about the degree to which training programs meet relevant objectives. The resulting feedback can then be used to continually improve the effectiveness of the programs.

Use Training Techniques That Clearly Identify Skills Needed on the Job

HRM educational programs should include courses that both convey the relevant declarative knowledge of the field and allow for active student participation in learning. Among the strategies that can be used to build HRM skills and incorporate HRM technology into educational programs are (a) the analysis of the offerings of HRM software vendors, (b) the design and development of HRM databases, (c) the use of case studies and role plays, (d) the use of field projects in industry, (e) the involvement of students in professional organizations, and (f) the use of oral briefings to assess learning. Examples of each of these strategies are offered below.

Conduct Software Vendor Analyses

One way to help students understand how technology supports HRM functions is to have them conduct a software vendor analysis. This involves an assessment of the strengths and weaknesses of the software offered by various vendors (e.g., PeopleSoft, SAP, Oracle). Given that HRM professionals often have to select and purchase HRM software, a software vendor analysis should help stimulate this process and familiarize students with available software. For example, students can be instructed to select an HRM application or functional area (e.g., applicant tracking, benefits, payroll) and research the software that can be used to assist with these HRM functions. They can then obtain information and demonstration copies of products and present analyses of their strengths and weaknesses to a class. Their analysis also might include a critical review of the product's functionality, price, and special features. The use of software vendor analyses in HRM education can provide students with valuable information about HRM technology and help them build analytical skills that are needed on the job.

Develop Databases or Web-Based Applications

Another strategy that can be used to provide students with knowledge about HRM technology is to have them develop a HRM database or Web-based application. Given that HRM technology is a key part of the HRM function today, it is imperative that HRM professionals understand HRM systems. Thus, one strategy for developing this understanding is to have students develop a relational database for a specific HRM process (e.g., training enrollment, benefits tracking). For example, student teams can be given a scenario describing a fictitious client and detailed specifications on the requirements of the database. After it has been designed, students can demonstrate the use of the database and asked to run specific queries to show its functionality. A database project can be a very effective way of showing students how an HRIS is designed and how it can aid managers in their work. It may also reinforce the students' understanding of the key principles underlying relational databases and modern HRM systems. In addition, students can be asked to construct a Web-based interface for the database so that it can be used to facilitate such HRM system goals as recruitment, benefits, and training.

Another strategy is to train students on the use of an actual HRIS software product. Several major systems vendors (e.g., PeopleSoft, SAP) have formed partnerships with colleges or universities and provide licenses for the use of their products in HRM educational programs. In addition, the same firms often provide training for faculty. Software training can be beneficial for students because it reinforces the skills needed on the job and allows them to see the functions of a HRM system in action. For example, students can learn how to use software to perform such tasks as (a) enrolling a new hire in a benefits program, (b) giving an employee a raise, and (c) promoting a worker. The assumption in using the software during training is that knowledge of one software product will transfer to others in actual work settings.

Case Scenarios and Role-Plays

Case scenarios and role-plays may be useful mechanisms for increasing students' understanding of technical HRM applications. For example, in the area of compensation and benefits, it is sometimes difficult to grasp complex concepts and techniques. Therefore, role-plays and applied projects (e.g., in compensation, benefits, and staffing) may allow students opportunities to apply and integrate the knowledge derived from classroom settings. For instance, a project could present students with a scenario about a fictitious company that needs a new compensation or staffing system. Student teams could then prepare a formal plan with specific recommendations for change. In addition, they could develop an interactive expert system to show how the changes would affect such outcomes as overall labor costs. Moreover, the students could make recommendations for ways of using HRM technology to increase the efficiency and effectiveness of systems for assisting with such functions as compensation and staffing.

Field Projects

In addition to the strategies described above, one of the most effective strategies for teaching HRM and HRM technology may be the use of real-life field projects. Two types of field projects that can be used are (a) consulting projects and (b) applied field research projects. The *consulting field project* might involve a team of students who are assigned a short-term consulting project. There are a number of ways of implementing such projects; one is to require students to work in industry one day per week for one or two semesters. Consulting field projects can focus on any topic area in HRM or HRM technology. These field projects may be quite beneficial for learning because they allow students the opportunity to gain "hands-on" experience working on an HRM project in a real company. Consulting field projects might focus on such tasks as the design of an applicant tracking database, the development an employee handbook, the conduct of a software vendor analysis, or the development of a Web site for an HR department. As a result of their work on the field project, students should be able to apply HRM concepts in a real context to facilitate an understanding of the dynamics of work in actual organizations. Although consulting field projects are often similar to internships, they are unique in that they provide students with regular access to faculty mentors who can facilitate work on the projects and help them develop skills. Students can also be required to report project progress during a class meeting in order to share the knowledge they have gained with other students.

The second type of project is an *applied field research project*. It requires student teams to conduct applied research in industry for two semesters (e.g., turnover studies, evaluations of the effectiveness of HRM practices). Faculty members facilitate such projects by contacting companies about sponsoring relatively short-term research. Then team members meet with company representatives to learn about project goals. Prior to conducting the research, the team conducts a review of the literature on the topic and selects the methods that will be used to conduct the research. Then the team presents its research plan to the sponsor, who reviews it and makes suggestions for changes. Once the research plan has been accepted by the sponsor, the team is asked to conduct the study during the second semester. Then, the student team is responsible for (a) preparing a report that summarizes the results of the study and (b) making two presentations. The first is to the professor and classmates. Class members are asked to provide feedback to team members, and it is incorporated into the second presentation, which is made to the sponsor.

Applied research projects can be very beneficial to both students and sponsoring organizations. For example, students can learn to (a) conduct applied research, (b) work in a team, (c) deal with the political issues that surface during their work with the employees of the sponsoring organization, and (d) sell research-based recommendations to organizations. Year-long applied research projects further enhance students' oral and written communication skills, project management skills, and sense of self-efficacy. The same projects are useful to sponsoring organizations because they can (a) answer important HRM questions, (b) evaluate the effectiveness of HRM interventions, (c) help organizations implement or improve HRM processes, and (d) provide sponsors with an opportunity to assess the abilities and performance potential of potential new hires.

Involve Students in Professional Associations

Another means of ensuring that students understand potential work roles in the HRM profession is to involve them in professional associations and have them attend conferences. For example, students may benefit from joining the student chapter of the Society for Human Resource Management (SHRM) at their college or university. They also can attend its local meetings to keep abreast of current HRM issues and learn professional norms and competencies. In addition, students can learn about the profession by attending regional or national conferences of professional societies. For instance, students can attend meetings of SHRM or the International Association for Human Resource Information Management (IHRIM). The latter society is primarily concerned with the impact of technology on HRM.

Use Oral Briefings Rather Than Traditional Tests

Finally, instead of using traditional written tests, HR educational programs can use oral examinations or briefings to assess students' knowledge in a role-play context. For example, students can be divided into teams and given a scenario describing a company and a meeting that will take place between newly hired HRM professionals and HRM executives. Faculty and alumni can play the roles of executives (e.g., vice president of HRM, CEO) and conduct a meeting with students who play the roles of newly hired professionals in the field. Students can be asked applied questions about HRM and the role of technology in HRM. After the briefings are completed the faculty can provide feedback to students about such matters as their declarative knowledge, procedural knowledge, and presentation skills. Oral briefings can help students identify strengths and weaknesses in their HRM-related knowledge, skills, and abilities, as well as their interpersonal skills. In addition, briefings can assist faculty in pinpointing areas of HRM training programs that are in need of improvement. Furthermore, briefings are often a more effective method of preparing students for the types of situations they will encounter in the workplace than are written tests. One reason for this is that they allow students to integrate a number of critical skills (e.g., critical thinking, analytical, oral communication).

Summary and Conclusions

In summary, we believe that changes in HRM practice should affect the design and delivery of HRM educational programs. In particular, we contend that HRM educational programs should operate as open systems in order to adapt quickly to environmental changes and remain viable. Although a number of strategies can be used to achieve this objective, we believe that academia and industry should form partnerships for a number of purposes, including the identification of the competencies needed by HRM professionals. Likewise, training techniques should be designed to clearly reflect the relevant skills and competencies needed in organizations, and these skills should be incorporated in simulations that actively engage students in the learning process. In addition, we believe that IIRM theory and research should be incorporated in training programs so that future HR professionals can use scientific knowledge to promote organizational effectiveness. Finally, we believe that HRM educational programs should adopt a continuous improvement philosophy and gather feedback from employers and industry partners to constantly increase program effectiveness.

We presented a model designed to facilitate the transfer of knowledge between HRM research, education, and practice, and noted how HRM practice should influence both HRM research and educational programs. In addition, we used changes in HRM technology to illustrate how changes in practice can both facilitate research and revitalize HRM educational programs. We hope that our model will help to promote knowledge transfer among HRM academicians, researchers, and practitioners. As a result, there should be improvements in both organizational effectiveness and the welfare of employees.

References

Alavi, M., Yoo, Y., & Vogel, D. R. (1997). Using information technology to add value to management education. *Academy of Management Journal, 40,* 1310–1333.

ASTD & the Masie Center (2001). *E-learning: "If we build it, will they come?"* Alexandria, VA: ASTD.

Baldwin, T. T., & Ford, J. K. (1988). Transfer of training: A review and directions for future research. *Personnel Psychology, 41,* 63–105.

Bergmann, T. J., & Scarpello, V. G. (2001).*Compensation decision making* (4th ed.). New York: Harcourt College Publishers.

Bernardin, H. J., & Russell, J. E. (1998). *Human resource management: An experiential approach* (2nd ed.). Boston: Irwin/McGraw-Hill.

Bertrand, M., & Mullainathan, S. (2004). *Are Emily and Greg more employable than Lakisha and Jamal? A field experiment on labor market discrimination* (NBER Working Paper 9873). Washington, DC: National Bureau of Economic Research, Inc.

Cardy, R. L., & Miller, J. S. (2003). Technology: Implications for HRM. In D. Stone (Ed.), *Advances in human performance and cognitive engineering research* (pp. 99–118). Greenwich, CT: JAI Press.

Cascio, W. F. (1998). *Managing human resources: Productivity, quality of work life, and profits* (5th ed.). Boston: Irwin/McGraw-Hill.

Cedar Group. (2000). *Cedar 1999 human resources self-service/portal survey: Second annual survey.* Baltimore, MD: Author.

Cedar Group. (2001). *Cedar 2000 human resources self-service/portal survey: Third annual survey.* Baltimore, MD: Author.

Cedar Group. (2002). *Cedar 2001 human resources self-service/portal survey: Fourth annual survey.* Baltimore, MD: Author.

Dixon, P. (2003). *Resume database nightmare: Job seeker privacy at risk.* Retrieved October 15, 2003, from http://www.privacyrights.org

Dulebohn, J. H., & Marler, J. H. (2005). e-Compensation: The potential to transform practice? In H. G. Gueutal & D. L. Stone (Eds.), *The brave new world of eHR: Human resources management in the digital age* (pp. 166–189). San Francisco: Jossey-Bass.

Dunnette, M. D. (1991). Blending the science and practice of industrial and organizational psychology. Where we are and where we are going. In M. D. Dunnette & L. Hough (Eds.), *Handbook of industrial and organizational psychology* (Vol. 1, pp. 1–27). Palo Alto, CA: Consulting Psychologists Press.

Goldstein, I. L. (1993). *Training in organizations: Needs assessment, development, and evaluation* (3rd ed.). Monterey, CA: Brooks/Cole.

Gueutal, H. G. (2003). The brave new world of eHR. In D. Stone (Ed.), *Research in human performance and cognitive engineering research* (pp. 13–36). Greenwich, CT: JAI Press.

Isenhour, L. C., Lukaszewski, K. M., & Stone, D. L. (2006, October). *e-Recruitment: Research at the intersection of technology and talent acquisition.* Paper presented at the annual meeting of the Western Business and Management Association, Las Vegas, NV.

Kavanagh, M., Gueutal, H. G., & Tannenbaum, S. (1990). *Human resource information systems: Development and application.* Boston: Kent.

Kehoe, J., Dickter, D., Russell, D., & Sacco, J. M. (2005). E-enabled section. In H. G. Gueutal & D. L. Stone (Eds.), *The brave new world of eHR* (pp. 54–103). San Francisco: Jossey-Bass.

Kosarzycki, M., Salas, E., DeRouin, R., & Fiore, S. M. (2003). Distance learning in organizations: A review and future needs. In D. Stone (Ed.), *Research in human performance and cognitive engineering research* (pp. 69–98). Greenwich, CT: JAI Press.

Latham, G., & Daghighi Latham, S. (2003). Facilitators and inhibitors of the transfer of knowledge between scientists and practitioners in human resources management. Leveraging cultural, individual, and institutional variables. *European Journal of Work and Organizational Psychology, 12*, 245–256.

Mohamed, A. A., Orife, J. N., & Wilbowo, K. (2002). The legality of key word search as a personnel selection tool. *Employee Relations, 24*, 516–522.

Salas, E., Kosarzycki, M. P., Burke, C. S., Fiore, S. M., & Stone, D. L. (2002). Emerging themes in distance learning research and practice: Some food for thought. *International Journal of Management Review, 4* (2), 1–18.

Scarpello, V. (2002, August). *The first HR town meeting: Is HR education dead or just sleeping?* Presentation at the annual meeting of the Academy of Management, Denver, CO.

Stone, D. L., & Gueutal, H. G. (Eds.). (2005). *The brave new world of eHR.* San Francisco: Jossey-Bass.

Stone, D. L., Lukaszewski, K., & Isenhour, L. C. (2005). e-Recruiting: Online strategies for attracting talent. In H. G. Guetal & D. L. Stone (Eds.). *The brave new world of eHR: Human resource management in the digital age* (pp. 22–53). San Francisco: Jossey Bass.

Stone, D. L., Stone-Romero, E. F., & Lukaszewski K. (2003). The functional and dysfunctional consequences of human resource information technology for organizations and their employees. In D. Stone (Ed.), *Advances in human performance and cognitive engineering research* (pp. 37–68). Greenwich, CT: JAI Press.

Stone, D. L., Stone-Romero, E. F., & Lukaszewski, K. (2006). Factors affecting the acceptance and effectiveness of electronic human resource systems. *Human Resource Management Review, 16*(2), 229–244.

Stone, E. F. (1978). *Research methods in organizational behavior.* Santa Monica, CA: Goodyear Publishing.

Towers Perrin (2001). *2001 HR Service Center Survey.* Retrieved November 15, 2001, from http://www.towers.com/servicesproducts/TowersPerrin/hrsurvey2001.htm

Ulrich, D. (2001). From e-business to e-HR. *International Human Resources Information Management Journal, 5*, 90–97.

SECTION 6

Micro- and Macro-Organizational Concepts Relevant to HRM

The two chapters in this section discuss psychological and organizational concepts about the behavior of people and organizations relevant to HRM education and practice.

In Chapter 14, Murray and Dulebohn suggest that effective human resource policies, programs, and procedures recognize and take advantage of psychological principles that underlie employee and organizational performance. They provide a tutorial of psychological theories that they believe have had a substantial influence on the practice of HRM or have the potential to help define the next era of HRM practice. They focus on three HRM activities—staffing, compensation, and performance management—present the theories relevant to these activities, and identify some of the implications of each theory for HRM. They discuss the theoretical perspectives of interactional psychology and the behavioral notion of "fit," attribution theories, organizational justice theories, expectancy theory, reinforcement theory, the job characteristics model, and goal-setting theory.

In Chapter 15, Scarpello focuses on fundamentals of organizational forms. If HRM is to become a legitimate and respected function of management then it follows that its policies, plans, and programs should support the organization's goals and strategies as well as the employees whose work implements those strategies and achieves those goals. To match HRM practice to the needs of the organization and its units requires matching

HRM practice to the needs of the organizational form in which HRM activities take place. The chapter is divided into three sections. The first section examines the functional structure and its modifications. The second section examines research on the determinants of the organization's structure and presents a conceptual framework for understanding structural variations. The third section discusses implications for HRM.

Some Psychological Concepts Essential for Human Resource Managers

14

Brian Murray

James H. Dulebohn

Why is the study of behavior important for human resource managers? Simply put, it's because effective human resource policies, programs, and procedures recognize and take advantage of the behavioral principles that underlie employee and organizational performance. Practitioners, whose ultimate goal may be to recruit and retain top talent, to provide meaningful benefits and compensation, or to develop a high-performing workforce, however, often design and implement programs through trial and error or respond blindly to the influence of "best practices." Unfortunately, these managers seem unaware of the theoretical foundations that explain why some programs succeed and others fail. For the benefit of these HR managers, HR professionals, and would-be professionals and their organizations, we identify those behavioral theories and principles that are based on well-developed conceptual and empirical research, and, we believe, are essential to HRM.

Fully informing a human resource manager about all of the behavioral theories would require a book, or perhaps several books. There is, therefore, some risk and inherent deficiency in summarizing an entire body of relevant theory into a chapter of essentials. There is, likewise, the risk of offending one reader or another because we have not identified a favorite theory as "essential." However, there are some theories that many of us might agree have had a substantial influence on the practice of HRM, or have the potential to define the next era of HRM practices.

In selecting the theories to review for this chapter, we took a decidedly micro-organizational behavior viewpoint; therefore, we began with the understanding that there are macro-organizational theory essentials beyond this chapter of which the human resource manager should be aware, especially those that inform human resource strategy and organizational design decisions. Knowing that we would be ultimately deficient in our selection of essential behavioral perspectives, we were encouraged by an article (Miner, 2003) that surveyed and rated the importance of organizational behavior theories. Of the seven theoretical perspectives that we reviewed for this chapter, five of them were included in the article, and four of those were in an elite group of theories that achieved average scores above five on a seven-point scale. The article did not include or rate the remaining perspectives that we selected, leaving us satisfied in the knowledge that no listing of organizational behavior theories will likely be complete enough to satisfy everyone. More significantly however, because Miner's (2003) purpose was to inform management educators about the importance of various organizational behavior topics for inclusion in courses and textbooks, the omissions suggested to us that there are theoretical perspectives outside of the mainstream organizational behavior conversation that are necessary for human resource faculty and practitioners to bring forth for discussion, lest they be left out of the education and development of human resource professionals.

Our approach to selecting theoretical perspectives especially important to human resource management was to identify the common HRM functions, and within each function to list those theories that support the development of policies, programs, and procedures. Although the list of functions and their associated theories was extensive, there was duplication in theoretical perspectives among functions. Consequently, we chose to present the theories that we view as most important within three functional contexts: staffing, compensation, and performance management. The theoretical perspectives we identified as essential were interactional psychology and the behavioral notion of "fit," attribution theories, organizational justice theories, expectancy and reinforcement theories, the job characteristics model, and goal-setting theory. Accordingly, the following discussion reviews each perspective and concludes by identifying some of the implications of each for HRM.

Behavioral Theories Relevant to Staffing

We related the behavioral notion of "fit" and attribution theories to the staffing process. First, we used interactional psychology and the attraction-selection-attrition framework to examine the issue of which individuals are attracted to, selected into, or withdraw from organizations. Second, in the context of selection interviews, we employed attribution theory to look at the issue of how social situations are perceived and cause is attributed.

Interactional Psychology and the Notion of "Fit"

Human resource managers likely are familiar with the scenario of selecting candidates for positions inside the organization. Historically, industrial psychology has dominated this process with its emphasis on selection tests and job analysis for the measurement and fit of the person to the job. Recent research by a variety of scholars, guided by an interactional psychology perspective, however, has made great strides toward explaining the behavioral processes underlying an individual's attraction to, selection into, and withdrawal from jobs and organizations. Hand in hand with this burgeoning research stream has been the growing recognition of the importance of person-organization fit and its effects on organizational homogeneity and performance outcomes (Bretz, Ash, & Dreher, 1989; O'Reilly & Pfeffer, 2000; Schneider, 1983a, 1987; Schneider, Smith, Taylor, & Fleenor, 1998).

Contemporary discussion of interactional psychology among researchers studying organizational behavior has its roots in the work of Mischel (1968), Bowers (1973), and Schneider (1983a, 1983b). Interactional psychology grew out of the debate among psychologists regarding whether behavior is primarily a function of individual traits or of situational determinants. Interactional psychology recognized that behavior is wholly determined by neither the trait nor the situation, but instead is a function of the trait-holder acting within, or responding to, the environmental context; that is, behavior is a complex function of the interaction between the person and the situation.

Organizational researchers have discussed interaction as person-job and person-organization interaction. These discussions have been influenced by vocational psychologists who have long recognized the important role of person-occupation, person-job, and person-job environment fit (e.g., Dawis, England, & Lofquist, 1964; Dawis & Lofquist, 1984; Holland, 1985; Super, 1953). An extension of the discussion has been the development of the attraction-selection-attrition framework, which has taken the interaction concept from the individual to the organizational level (Schneider, 1983b, 1987). We present the research related to the person-job fit and the person-organization fit next and subsequently discuss implications of this research to HRM.

PERSON-JOB FIT

The notion that individuals who possess characteristics (e.g., abilities, knowledge, skills, personality traits) that closely address the characteristics of the job will be better performers in the job has held a prominent position in staffing textbooks (e.g., Gatewood & Field, 2001; Heneman & Judge, 2003), in scholarly articles (Caldwell & O'Reilly, 1990; Edwards, 1991; Judge & Ferris, 1992; Kristof-Brown, 2000; Rynes & Gerhart, 1990; Schneider, 1978; cf. Cable & DeRue, 2002; Lauver & Kristof-Brown, 2001), and in government regulation (e.g., *Uniform Guidelines on Employee Selection Procedures,* EEOC). Likewise, there has been some evidence that when the job rewards address the needs and desires of the individual, they enhance the level of satisfaction, commitment, or performance (Cable & DeRue, 2002; Dawis, 1996; Edwards, 1991; Schneider, 1978). This acceptance and understanding of person-job fit principles has been evident in job analysis (Gatewood & Field, 2001; Heneman & Judge, 2003), job rewards analysis (Heneman & Judge, 2003), and validation of selection and performance appraisal instruments (Gatewood & Field, 2001). However, supporting evidence has not been as strong as desirable (e.g., Scarpello & Campbell, 1983). One reason for this lack of consistent support is the fact that organizational researchers have largely ignored the contribution of person-occupation fit to the individual's level of job satisfaction and perhaps commitment and performance (Scarpello & Hayton, 2002).

Interactional psychology distinguishes between the role of an individual's personal characteristics and the fit of those characteristics to the job. For example, several individual differences, such as general cognitive ability and conscientiousness, have been demonstrated to predict performance across a wide variety of jobs and organizations. Therefore, regardless of specific fit to a particular job or type of job, these characteristics generally affect the level and quality of individuals' work outcomes. Alternatively, there are differences in individuals with respect to service orientation, firm-specific knowledge, physical abilities, and personality traits that predict performance or behavior in some jobs, but not in others, depending on the requirements and rewards of the particular job.

Ability

Traditionally, the generally accepted formula for job performance has been (performance = ability × motivation). Organizations were advised that to influence performance they must affect ability levels of employees through training and the like. Although this continues to be good advice, we now know that ability may also interact with job and work characteristics to determine work attitudes and behavior. Specifically, in his review of the ability-situation interaction research, Schneider (1978) set the stage for identifying job dimensions that interact with ability to differentially determine job performance and satisfaction. Specifically, his review identified the job components of incentive system, difficulty or enrichment of the job, and facilitative climate as interacting with ability to predict job outcomes. Identifying *ability* as an individual difference component in the person-job interaction, however, has been too broad a designation for understanding its role in organizational outcomes. It has been further classified into physical, cognitive, psychomotor, and sensory/perceptual (Heneman & Judge, 2003). Of these classifications, cognitive ability has been shown to have differential impact on performance depending on the complexity of the jobs. That is, although cognitive ability is generally predictive, it has a stronger relationship to performance for more complex than for less complex jobs (Hunter, 1986).

Knowledge and Skills

Technical and professional knowledge and skill are dimensions thought to determine work behavior and outcomes through fit with the job. Indeed, selection processes attempt to assess the extent to which an applicant's technical or professional knowledge and skill match the requirements of the job to which they are applying (see Judge & Ferris, 1992, for fit model and hypothesis). However, job knowledge has not demonstrated incremental validity beyond what is explained by cognitive ability (Ree, Carretta, & Teachout, 1995); therefore, the specificity of knowledge interacting with a particular job may not be useful in understanding future job performance (Heneman & Judge, 2003).

An important development in the knowledge and skills components of person-job fit is the role of competencies. Competencies are job-related skills or knowledge of a general nature that extend across jobs within a single organization and are related to both job performance and organizational success (Heneman & Judge, 2003). They represent person-job fit, despite applying to multiple jobs, because they are directly relevant to the design, characteristics, and performance of an individual's current job. Moreover, they are organization-specific to the extent that what is needed for organizational success is idiosyncratic to an organization, such that the competencies that are important in an organization's workers will not necessarily have the same impact or importance to another organization, even among direct competitors within a single industry. For example, Southwest Airlines is reported to have more teamwork activity and flexible job rules among its cabin crews, baggage handlers, and agents than other major air carriers. Therefore, competencies such as interpersonal or teamwork skills, cross-job knowledge, and adaptability may have a differentially greater impact on job and organizational outcomes at Southwest than at United, Delta, Continental, or American, which have stricter work rules and do not extensively cross-utilize workers among jobs (O'Reilly & Pfeffer, 2000).

Personality

Intuitively, managers have always believed that personality is an important dimension of job performance. Academicians, on the other hand, have questioned its use in selection because of measurement and criterion-related validity issues. Today, researchers have identified some personality traits that have demonstrated validity when the trait is matched to the job. Hough and Schneider's (1996) review of the personality literature identified several individual differences that interacted with the job and job characteristics in their effects on behavior and performance. First, they found that extraversion interacted with job type and job autonomy, such that it was more important to performance in managerial and sales jobs versus other professional and skilled or semiskilled jobs and it differentially related to performance in jobs composed of different levels of autonomy (cf. Barrick & Mount, 1991, 1993). Second, they found that agreeableness interacted with job type and job autonomy or complexity, such that it had a stronger association with job proficiency for healthcare workers than managers and executives (cf. Hough, 1992), and it differentially related to performance in jobs composed of different levels of autonomy or job complexity (cf. Barrick & Mount, 1993). Third, they found that compound or job-customized measures of personality, those that combine elements of two or more distinct personality constructs, could be developed such that they predicted performance for a specific job or job family. For example, they reviewed validity evidence supporting compound or job-customized personality measures related to integrity, customer service, management, and sales potential as predictors of performance in specific job types.

The abilities, knowledge, skills, and personality traits discussed to this point reflect one dimension of person-job fit, which is sometimes referred to as *demands-abilities fit*. It is supplemented by a second dimension that refers to the needs possessed by the individual that are fulfilled by a particular job within a particular organizational context (Cable & DeRue, 2002; Edwards, 1991), which is referred to as *needs-supplies fit*. The job-related characteristics that are thought to address employee needs may include a host of monetary and nonmonetary rewards that employees within a specific organization or job group desire and value. Cable and DeRue (2002) demonstrated that when needs-supplies fit was present for individuals, it was related to job satisfaction, career satisfaction, and organizational commitment outcomes. Schneider (1978) showed that the needs-supplies fit dimensions of incentive systems, job characteristics, and management philosophy moderated demands-abilities effects. Therefore, needs-supplies fit not only determines important outcomes in its own right, it also interacts to determine the effect of other forms of person-job fit on work outcomes.

PERSON-ORGANIZATION FIT

Person-organization fit has attracted a great deal of recent attention. Among the issues researchers have addressed have been its definition (Chatman, 1989; Kristof, 1996), its dimensionality (Cable & DeRue, 2002), its measurement (Kristoff, 1996; O'Reilly, Chatman, & Caldwell, 1991), its determinants (Chatman, 1991; Kristof-Brown, 2000; Rynes & Gerhart, 1990), and its outcomes or implications for staffing and socialization (Cable & DeRue, 2002; Cable & Judge, 1996; Chatman, 1989, 1991; Judge & Cable, 1997; O'Reilly et al., 1991; Posner, 1992). Drawing on this flurry of research activity, HRM professionals may ask: what is person-organization fit, how will I know it when I see it, and why should I be concerned about it?

A number of researchers (e.g., Cable & DeRue, 2002; Cable & Judge, 1996; Posner, 1992) have adopted Chatman's (1989) definition of person-organization fit as "the congruence between the norms and values of organizations and the values of persons" (p. 339). Within the *Organizational Culture Profile* instrument, O'Reilly and colleagues operationalized the norms and values of the organization into dimensions of innovation and risk-taking, attention to detail, outcome orientation, aggressiveness and competitiveness, supportiveness, emphasis on growth and rewards, collaborative and team orientation, and decisiveness (O'Reilly et al., 1991). The values of the person that have been captured and correlated with these organizational values have been defined as motivational needs (e.g., need for achievement, need for autonomy) or more directly as preferences for the particular values as reported by the worker (O'Reilly et al., 1991). Person-organization fit can be measured by having individuals sort organizational culture statements according to personal preference and correlating for each individual the relationship to a sorting that describes the organization. The greater the correlation, the better is the fit (Chatman, 1991). Alternatively, it can be measured by the individual's perception of fit to a particular organization (Judge & Cable, 1997). The important outcomes that have been related to person-organization fit include organization attraction, job satisfaction, increased organizational identification and commitment, turnover behavior, and faster adjustment to a new job and organization (Cable & DeRue, 2002; Chatman, 1991; Judge & Cable, 1997; O'Reilly et al., 1991).

ATTRACTION-SELECTION-ATTRITION FRAMEWORK

Building on the work of interactional psychologists, Schneider (1983a, 1983b, 1987) developed a framework to explain the movement of individuals into and out of organizations, the homogeneity of organizational members' characteristics, and the outcomes of homogeneity for the organization. Specifically, Schneider proposed that organizations are systems of people who make decisions about the form and behaviors of the organization. These decisions are initiated or led by the organization founder and are perpetuated by the selection of other individuals into the organization who share common personalities or ideals. Persons external to the organization are attracted to it to the extent that they perceive that the organization members' personalities and values are similar to their own.

Persons internal to the organization evaluate the congruence of their own personality and values relative to their coworkers, and when they find incongruence, they self-select themselves out of the organization. Schneider proposed that this attraction-selection-attrition cycle would yield organizations composed of individuals who are homogeneous in their personalities and values. He also proposed a number of important organizational outcomes arising from homogeneity, including a decreased organizational ability to respond to environmental change, a restriction in applicant pool characteristics that limits the utility of personality measures as selection tools, and enhanced organizational ability to create and sustain culture characteristics (Schneider, 1983a, 1987).

Research testing the framework has provided support for the homogeneity hypothesis. Bretz and colleagues (1989) demonstrated that individuals were attracted to organizations as a function of the fit between the organization's reward system and their need for achievement. Turban and Keon (1993) found that individuals were attracted to organizations on the basis of the fit between their self-esteem needs and the organization's structure. Additionally, Schneider, Goldstein, and Smith (1995) reviewed a series of studies that provided support for the long-term effect of the founder's characteristics on the organization and for homogeneity of personalities within the organizations. Using a sample of 13,000 managers from 142 organizations, Schneider and colleagues (1998) provided further evidence of personality homogeneity within organizations and industries. Finally, Van Vianen (2000) conducted perhaps the most direct test of the homogeneity hypothesis within the selection and attrition functions. Specifically, Van Vianen demonstrated that where there was fit of personality, defined as concern for people, between the employee and the supervisor who recruited and hired him or her, the employee reported greater organization commitment and fewer turnover intentions.

IMPLICATIONS FOR HRM

Taken together, the preceding discussion of interactional psychology can inform human resource managers in a number of ways. Specifically, they can profit from the research using the interactionist framework by considering the following implications for staffing:

- Recruitment should be actively managed to control the level of homogeneity of individuals attracted and selected into the organization. Severe homogeneity may have a negative impact on organizational adaptability in turbulent environments (Schneider, 1983a, 1983b, 1987; Schneider et al., 1995).

- An important function of the selection program may be to evaluate and to select for value congruence (Chatman, 1989).

- Increased prehire activity may yield greater value congruence for those individuals who are hired by the organization and elect to join (Chatman, 1989; O'Reilly & Pfeffer, 2000).

- In addition to the more traditional assessment of demands-abilities fit for job applicants, hiring managers should also assess needs-supplies and person-organization fit, because these types of fit are related to important attitudinal and retention outcomes (Cable & DeRue, 2002; O'Reilly et al., 1991).

- Personality, because it can be measured, may play an important part for the hiring organization in determining an applicant's fit to the organization (Judge & Cable, 1997).

- Interviewers are able to distinguish among, and evaluate for, different types of fit in the selection process (Rynes & Gerhart, 1990).

- Organizational newcomers' value development, fit perceptions, and resulting behavior or outcomes can be managed during the socialization process (Chatman, 1991).

Two cautions stand out among these recommendations. First, although there is some evidence that a fit between an individual's reward preferences and rewards offered on the job enhances job satisfaction, and at times enhances commitment and job performance, this evidence should be viewed with caution. Some research over the years has shown that the above fit does not correlate with job satisfaction for a large proportion of employees. Some research also fails to show that there is a relationship between job satisfaction and job performance. Obviously researchers must explain these discrepant findings before organizations can have confidence in using research results.

Second, organizations must validate personality measures in their organizations before applying them in the selection process. However, because many personality characteristics are abstract constructs (unobservable attributes) that a test is attempting to measure, EEOC Uniform Guidelines require the employer to present not only evidence for construct validity but also evidence that the construct is actually correlated with a job-related criterion (such as performance ratings). These EEOC constraints therefore limit the use of personality tests in organizations wishing to minimize vulnerability to EEO litigation suits (Scarpello, Ledvinka, & Bergmann, 1995).

Attribution Theory and the Selection Process

Human resource managers, and managers in general, are likely aware of the challenge of determining where fault or credit should lie in situations of job applicants' claims of achievement, performance problems and successes, and disciplinary or termination decisions. For example, when an applicant claims that he increased the revenue performance of his department by 50%, should he be credited with extraordinary personal traits that make him an outstanding performer, or was he the serendipitous recipient of the fruits of a vibrant economy that would have benefited anyone managing his department? These types of questions are especially difficult not only because there are limitations to the information available to the decision maker, but also because there are some common biases that decision makers exhibit when faced with attributing credit or blame to the person or the situation. Research in organizations is especially useful to HRM in this regard because it has highlighted an area of social psychology research defining the attribution-of-cause process and its attributional outcomes.

Attribution theory is a family of hypotheses and principles regarding the perceptual and cognitive process in which people engage to determine the source of cause behind their own and others' behaviors. Technically, there is no one *attribution theory,* but rather there is a set of theories related to the antecedents to which a person ascribes cause, and a second set related to the outcomes of a particular causal attribution. The former are referred to as the *attribution* theories, while the latter are referred to as the *attributional* theories (Harvey & Weary, 1984; Kelley & Michela, 1980).

NAÏVE PSYCHOLOGY

Prominent among the attribution theories are Heider's (1958) naïve or common-sense psychology, Jones and Davis's (1965) correspondent inferences theory, and Kelley's (1967) covariation principles. Heider's common-sense psychology has at its core the proposition that individuals willingly and commonly read their environment and process the information to determine why others act the way that they do, much like a scientist might approach studying the cause underlying some phenomenon. He argued that individuals have a need or desire to make their environment more predictable by understanding the processes that drive others' behaviors. His approach suggested that individuals analyze the behavior of others by determining whether the person had the intention to behave or cause outcomes and whether he or she had the knowledge or ability to cause outcomes. These principles were summed up in the ideas of can, want, try, and ought. In Heider's approach, *can* referred to the ability to cause an event to occur. *Want* referred to the intention of the individual toward the behavior and outcome. *Try* referred to the attempt to cause the behavior and outcome. *Ought* referred to the standards of legitimate or appropriate behavior. In Heider's approach, the observer asked whether the individual had the ability and knowledge to cause an action, whether the individual tried to cause the action or was it a matter of circumstance, and whether there were social rules driving the individual's behavior versus some innate disposition. Heider's common-sense psychologist wants to know why the individual acts and why he chooses particular actions. The contribution that the human resource manager can take away from Heider's perspective is the understanding that an individual's evaluation of another's behavior searches for specific enabling characteristics of the other person (e.g., knowledge, ability), determinative characteristics of the environment (e.g., social rules), and indications whether the cause is innate to the person (internal attribution) or present in the environment (external attribution).

CORRESPONDENT INFERENCES THEORY

Arguing that Heider's approach lacked a cohesive structure necessary to the development of testable hypotheses and to be useful for organizing knowledge about causal inferences, Jones and Davis (1965) developed a theory of correspondent inferences that "accounts for a perceiver's inferences about what an actor was trying to achieve by a particular action" (p. 222). At the core of this theory lay the proposition that correspondence increases to the extent that the observed action and an underlying individual disposition are closely related, and decreases to the extent that the observed action is more closely related to a cause external to the individual or that the environment constrains the individual's expression of his or her disposition. Correspondence, then, is concerned with determining the extent to which an individual's disposition is the cause of his or her action—the greater the correspondence, the greater the attribution to an internal or dispositional cause of the action.

Kelly and Michela (1980) summarized correspondent inferences theory as, "The fewer distinctive reasons an actor has for an action and the less these reasons are widely shared in the culture, the more informative is that action about the identifying dispositions of the actor" (p. 461). They concluded from this proposition that the key concepts are *information* and *beliefs*. They defined the important types of information to include non-common effects, similarity and contiguity information, salience, primacy, and covariation, which we discuss subsequently as Kelley's covariation principles.

Non-common effects were described by Jones and Davis (1965) as those outcomes that result from, and are distinctive to, an action. They proposed that information about an individual's disposition is contained in the non-common or distinctive effects particular to an action; that is, the outcomes that are common across different actions do not provide information that helps to understand the individual's underlying disposition. However, as the number of non-common effects increases, the less the observer is able to infer the particular cause of the action. Jones and Davis also described the non-common effects in terms of their desirability. They proposed that the more the effects were desired by members of society in general, the less informative those effects were for inferring the particular dispositional traits of the actor.

Beyond Jones and Davis's non-common effects, Kelly and Michela (1980) reviewed research regarding the similarity, contiguity, salience, and primacy of information and their respective roles in attribution. First, they summarized the *similarity rule* as "properties of the cause are assumed to be similar to the properties of the observed effect (Shultz & Ravinsky, 1977), so that the latter can be used to infer the former" (p. 466). For example, effects of great magnitude will be associated with causes of great magnitude, whereas trivial effects will be associated with insignificant or trivial causes. Second, they described the *spatial contiguity principle* as the need for the cause and effect to have contact. Related to this idea, they defined a *temporal contiguity principle* as the need for the cause and effect to occur at the same point in time, and where there are multiple probable causes, the rule of temporal precedence defined the cause to be an event that directly preceded the effect. Third, they defined the *salience principle* as "an effect is attributed to the first cause that comes to mind when the attribution question is raised, or at least the first one that provides a 'sufficient' explanation" (p. 467). Fourth, they identified the *primacy effect* as the predominance of information that is received early during the attribution process over information received later in determining cause. However, they also reviewed research that demonstrated that when graphic information is presented that shows both early and subsequent information, a *recency effect* dominates over a primacy effect in the person's attribution process.

Jones and Davis's (1965) theory also recognized the role of the observer as an active participant. Specifically, they considered the scenario when the action had a positive or negative consequence for the observer. Referred to as *hedonic relevance*, the effect of an action having personal consequences for the observer was proposed to bias the observer to attribute a greater inference of the cause to the internal disposition of the actor when the effect was positive for the observer. They also stated that this attribution would be determined by *personalism*, which they defined as the actor's intention to benefit or harm the observer. They proposed that when the action had hedonic relevance, the correspondence would be greater when it was also perceived that the action was intentional.

KELLEY'S COVARIATION PRINCIPLES

Kelley's covariation model of attribution has been reviewed by a number of authors (e.g., Fiske & Taylor, 1991; Harvey & Weary, 1984; Kelley & Michela, 1980; Ross & Fletcher, 1985), and has played an important part in generating theory and research regarding attributions of internal versus external causes of behavior. The covariation model proposes that an "effect is attributed to the factor with which it covaries" (Kelley & Michela, 1980, p. 462). Kelley's model goes on to propose specific elements of situations that help to define when observers make internal versus external attributions about the underlying cause of an actor's behavior. These elements include *consensus,* which is the extent to which other members of the population would agree or act in the same manner; *consistency,* which is the extent to which the actor responds in the same manner whenever faced with the same situation; and *distinctiveness,* which is the extent to which the actor responds in a similar manner to other situations.

Ross and Fletcher (1985) concluded that three particular patterns of elements were important to understanding attributions. First, they proposed that high consensus, distinctiveness, and consistency are important to understanding the external environment as the source of cause. For example, if an applicant's interview responses credit him with achieving good customer satisfaction ratings, it is important to know that customer service providers at his former place of employment received high ratings in general, the applicant has not demonstrated high service ratings from other employers, and he received high ratings across all customers at that employer. This level of consensus, distinctiveness, and consistency would suggest that the customer service ratings are somehow due to the circumstances of the former employer, its products or services, its service evaluation process, or its customers.

Second, they proposed that low consensus and distinctiveness with high consistency point toward factors internal to the actor as causes of behavior and outcomes. For example, if the applicant who reported high customer satisfaction ratings formerly worked for the Department of Motor Vehicles, for which there were many unhappy customers and workers received few accolades from customers, has a record of positive customer satisfaction across other former employers, and consistently ranked highly in customer satisfaction at his former employer, then the observer should conclude that this person possesses characteristics enabling him to provide superior customer service.

Third, they proposed that when there is low consensus and consistency, but high distinctiveness, the attribution is likely to be toward the situation. For example, if the person works in a situation where customers tend to be unhappy, and there has been variability in customer feedback about the service provided by the candidate, but the candidate won an award for outstanding service, above and beyond the call of duty, for helping a particular customer with an unusual problem, then the likely attribution would be toward the unusual circumstance rather than toward an individual characteristic that makes the person an outstanding service provider.

Closely aligned with the covariation principle are the discounting and augmentation principles. The *discounting principle* states that when there are multiple potential causes of an effect, the strength of the attribution afforded to any particular cause is decreased (Kelley, 1972). For example, if a job candidate provides evidence that he had an outstanding sales year, but the interviewer also knows that the candidate's former employer was a market leader, that the product was one of the few available on the market, that the candidate was given extensive sales training, that the candidate had years of related sales experience, that the candidate demonstrates good interpersonal skills, and that the economy has been favorable, then any one internal or external cause is discounted in its overall contribution as the cause of the candidate's excellent sales performance. The *augmentation principle* states that if two antecedents are present for an outcome, where the first facilitates the outcome and the second inhibits the outcome, then the facilitating antecedent is attributed greater causal strength than it would have been had the inhibitory antecedent not been present (Kelley, 1972). For example, if a job candidate reports an excellent sales year, but the interviewer knows that the economy and the particular product market were unfavorable, then the interviewer is likely to ascribe a greater attribution of sales ability toward the candidate than if the candidate had worked in a favorable economy and market.

OTHER ATTRIBUTION RESEARCH

Fiske and Taylor (1991) reviewed additional principles and attribution phenomenon that reflect biases or tendencies in how individuals attribute cause. First among these principles is the *fundamental attribution error,* which they defined as the tendency of the individual to attribute cause internally to the actor to a greater extent than externally to the situation or environment (cf. Heider, 1958; Ross, 1977). Second, they described the *actor-observer effect,* which is a tendency on the part of the observer to assign cause internally to the actor, whereas cause for one's own behavior is assigned externally. Third, they defined a *false consensus effect,* such that the observer, assuming that he or she is typical of the population, concludes that others in the population would have a similar response when faced with the situation as he or she has. Fourth, they described a *self-serving bias,* such that internal attributions are made for personal success, whereas external attributions are made for personal failure. Fifth, they identified a *self-centered bias,* which is a tendency to attribute greater cause internally to oneself than what is warranted when there are multiple contributors to the behavior and outcomes.

Fiske and Taylor (1991) also reviewed a stream of dispositional and individual difference research that is especially important to human resource managers. Specifically, they identified research that demonstrated that individuals possess dispositions toward internal or external explanations of cause, which is commonly referred to as *locus of control* (cf. Rotter, 1966). They also identified research that has demonstrated *attributional styles,* which are behavioral tendencies on the part of individuals to exhibit patterns of attributions across situations. Finally, they described research on attempts toward *reattribution training.* They concluded that there is evidence to support changes arising from counseling and training in how people think and behave relative to attributions.

IMPLICATIONS FOR HRM

Knowledge of attribution theories and research results is useful for HR managers for assessing their own biases, understanding the affects of applicant and employee attributions, and training interviewers as well as other managers responsible for conducting employment-related interviews with employees. Some of the theoretical models and research conclusions especially important for assessing and minimizing decision-making biases include the following:

- Correspondent inferences theory alerts the manager to how information is used and how he or she may be biased by the effect of outcomes on him or her. Hiring managers should be aware that they are searching, either implicitly or explicitly, for distinctive outcome effects that they use to infer traits of the individual. They should also be aware that their search for information about the effects and causes may be limited by the knowledge and resources they have available to them (i.e., salient information), and that they process information relative to time (i.e., both the timing of the cause-effect relationship, contiguity, and the timing of information, primacy). Finally, accurate attributions regarding individual traits and motives cannot be made except on the basis of how they deviate from what the typical person would do in a like situation. When the person acts in a socially typical manner, then the observing manager learns little or nothing about the true underlying traits of the individual.

- Kelley's covariation model gives understanding of how individuals combine information to reach conclusions about the person- or situation-based causes of behaviors and outcomes, and of how conflicting or multiple explanations interact to determine why some causes are given more or less weight as explanations of behavior. Managers, whether they are evaluating job applicants, assessing employee performance, or investigating employee discipline cases, may draw on information regarding the consensus, consistency, and distinctiveness that defines the person, situation, and behavior to help ensure less biased and therefore more accurate decision making. Additionally, they may play pieces of information off one another to determine the relative extent of the cause's influence on the outcome.

- Atttribution theory tells us that interviewers rate candidates more positively when they make internal, controllable attributions regarding causes of negative information about their job performance or behavior (Silvester, Anderson-Gough, Anderson, & Mohamed, 2002).

- Interviewers who are external in locus of control rate applicant responses differently from those who are internal in locus of control. Specifically, externals rate applicants' external, controllable attributions equally positive whereas internals differentiate between the responses when rating applicants (Silvester et al., 2002).

- Interviewers share a common understanding about the "rules" that applicants should follow in interviews. When applicants break general, interpersonal rules, interviewers tend to attribute the cause of the rule-breaking to the situation. When applicants break rules specific to interviews—for example, when applicants fail to clarify and present career goals—interviewers tend to attribute these to internal causes (e.g., lack of effort or ability). Rule-breaking on the part of applicants has an overall negative effect on "hireability" ratings assigned by interviewers (Ramsay, Gallois, & Callan, 1997).

- When rating females, males exhibit greater internal attribution toward female success in nontraditional roles, but exhibit greater external attribution toward female success in traditional roles (Reid, Kleiman, & Travis, 1986).

- Preinterview information biases the attributions and conclusions that interviewers make about applicants during the subsequent interview (Knouse, 1989).

- Applicants make internal attributions for job search success and external attributions for job search failure. The more involved the job applicant is in the job search, the more likely he or she makes internal attributions regarding improving chances of success (Knouse, 1989).

- Employees who make external attributions for why they were hired have a greater likelihood of turnover (Knouse, 1989).

Organizational Behavior and Compensation Administration

Compensation decision making is the one area of HRM that is truly multi-disciplinary. The key disciplines contributing to the understanding and design of compensation systems include economics, sociology, and psychology. Yet, the recipient of compensation is the individual. Research has demonstrated that an organization's compensation policies and practices represent one the most influential factors affecting employee attitudes and behaviors (Gerhart, Minkoff, & Olsen, 1995). Therefore, understanding how an individual or group may react to an organization's compensation policies and practices is an important input in designing and administering systems that will contribute to desired organizational outcomes and thus a return on its compensation investments. In this section, we discuss three psychological theories that provide insight into the individual's reactions to pay: justice theory, expectancy theory, and reinforcement theory. Understanding the essential characteristics of these theories increases the organization's ability to influence desirable individuals to join, stay in, and perform for the organization by explaining how individuals may react. Additionally, they help the organization to minimize perceptions of injustice, as these perceptions have been shown to influence a host of undesirable and organizationally harmful behaviors (e.g., Dulebohn & Martocchio, 1998; Mowday, 1991).

Justice Theory

In lay terms, the term *justice* is a synonym for fairness and equity. Traditionally, distributive equity has been the concern for compensation decision makers. However, it is now recognized that justice reactions have three facets:

- Distributive justice, or the fairness of the pay allocations (outcomes).

- Procedural justice, or the fairness of the procedures used to arrive at those outcomes.

- Interactional justice, or the fairness of the treatment received during the application of the procedures when interacting with the organizational agent responsible for said application.

DISTRIBUTIVE JUSTICE

Distributive justice refers to comparison-based theories that explain how individuals determine whether the distributions of outcomes they receive are "fair." There are a number of distributive justice theory formulations. One of the earliest can be attributed to Aristotle. He differentiated between two types of fair outcome allocations: (a) justice in general, or equality, and (b) justice in particular, or equity. Both forms are used in compensation decision making. However, in the design of pay plans, and in contemporary American psychological research, the dominant formulation of distributive justice is Adams's formulation of equity theory.

Adams (1963, 1965) developed a general theory of social inequity to explain causes and consequences of the absence of equity in human exchange relationships. Adams's theory of inequity focused on the causes and effects of wage inequity. He posited that individuals evaluate the fairness of their outcomes using an equity rule whereby they compare their own input-outcome ratios to a referent or comparable other. Individuals perceive equity or fairness when the ratio or balance of their outcomes to their inputs is equal. In contrast, inequity exists when the ratios are perceived as unequal. Furthermore, he asserted that perceptions of unequal ratios (resulting from either under- or overpayment) result in a state of inequity distress or psychological uneasiness that motivates individuals to engage in actions that will remove the dissonance and restore perceptions of equity. Some of these actions may include altering inputs, altering outcomes, adjusting their evaluations of their inputs and outputs, using a different comparison other, using psychological justifications, or withdrawing from the organization (e.g., engaging in negative behavior or quitting). In contrast, perceptions of a balance between input and output ratios result in evaluations that an outcome distribution is equitable, and this evaluation contributes to satisfaction.

An abundance of research has been conducted on equity theory (Deutsch, 1985). The research has generally supported the theory's prediction that employees take action to restore equity (Gerhart et al., 1995). For example, research has demonstrated that when subjects perceive they have been overpaid they try to improve their work and when they perceive they have been underpaid they decrease their inputs or engage in various negative behavior such as sabotage, stealing, or decreasing commitment to work (e.g., Cowherd & Levine, 1992; Pfeffer & Langton, 1993). Research support for reactions to underpayment is more consistent than for overpayment (Mowday, 1991).

PROCEDURAL JUSTICE

Whereas distributive justice focuses on the fairness of pay outcomes, procedural justice focuses on the processes leading up to those outcomes. Research on procedural justice began with Thibaut and Walker's (1975) series of dispute resolution studies within the judicial context. In organizational research, concern for procedural justice surfaced in 1985, when Rowland and Ferris's *Research in Personnel and Human Resources Management* included a monograph by Folger and Greenberg, which suggested that the concept of procedural justice was relevant to performance evaluations and pay system interventions (Folger & Greenberg, 1985).

In their original work on procedural justice, Thibaut and Walker (1975) found that the disputants' satisfaction with legal proceedings, the presiding judge, and their verdict were influenced by perceived fairness of the procedures used to arrive at the verdict, independent of verdict favorability (i.e., innocent or guilty) or perceptions of the verdict's (outcome's) fairness. Specifically, these researchers found that procedures that provided individuals with an opportunity to have process control through input into the proceedings were perceived as more fair and led to a greater acceptance of even unfavorable outcomes. The majority of subsequent research confirmed their finding that process control (or voice) enhances fairness perceptions, independent of the particular outcome.

Leventhal and colleagues (Leventhal, 1980; Leventhal, Karuza, & Fry, 1980) also significantly contributed to the procedural justice literature. They identified structural components that individuals use to evaluate the fairness of procedures. Specifically, they proposed that procedures are fair to the extent that they are consistent, suppress bias, use accurate information, are correctable, represent the interests of the recipients, and are based on ethical standards.

Empirical research, subsequently, has demonstrated the importance of procedural fairness in compensation (Dulebohn & Martocchio, 1998; Greenberg, 1987; Jones & Scarpello, 1999). Compensation research has found that employees are concerned about process fairness, they view process fairness and outcome fairness separately, and procedures that include structural aspects, such as those identified by Leventhal, contribute to perceptions of procedural fairness as well as the acceptance of outcomes (Dulebohn, 1997; Greenberg, 1990; Lind & Tyler, 1988; Scarpello & Jones, 1996). Research also has shown that the pay determination, performance appraisal, pay communication, and appeal procedures are differentially related to satisfaction with pay, supervision, and organizational commitment. Specifically, relative to other pay procedures, perceived fairness of pay determination procedures was found to be the strongest predictor of pay satisfaction; perceived fairness of performance appraisal procedures was the only significant predictor of satisfaction with supervision; and three sets of pay procedures (pay determination, performance appraisal, and pay communications) were significant predictors of organizational commitment (Jones & Scarpello, 1996).

A theory called *referent cognitions* (Folger, 1986, 1987) attempts to explain the observed interactive effects between perceptions of procedural and distributive justice. With respect to compensation procedures, this happens with the interactions between the individual and the person(s) evaluating and communicating the evaluation of the performance appraisal process to the employee. Folger's (1986, 1987) referent cognitions theory suggests that people generate mental simulations (called referent cognitions) about alternative circumstances that might have resulted in fairer outcomes. Thus, Folger and colleagues (Folger, 1986, 1987; Cropanzano & Folger, 1989) assert that resentment over a less-than-anticipated pay increase will be greatest when the individual perceives that the performance appraisal process could have been fairer. In contrast, such resentment is minimized when the procedure is perceived as completely fair.

IMPLICATIONS FOR HRM

Justice theories and related research provide guidelines for examining what applicants and employees may consider when making decisions to join the organization, remain in the organization, and perform for the organization. Additionally, understanding how individuals may react to injustice helps the organization evaluate risks associated with its compensation decision making. Knowing the potentially negative consequences of eliciting perceptions of unfairness in their pay practices, organizations attempt to provide fair pay. Within budget constraints, compensation plans are designed to provide fair pay for the work performed within the organization. Organizations use the concept of equity to develop, administer, and monitor the effectiveness of their pay plans and to evaluate the extent to which applicants and employees will perceive the pay offered by the organization to be fair and acceptable. (e.g., Bergmann & Scarpello, 2001; Milkovich & Newman, 1996). They tend to operationalize the equity concept relative to three referents: external equity, internal job equity, and individual equity. Specific procedures are used to assess each form of equity and then to decide the degree and the method for applying each form to the organization's pay practices.

External equity refers to assessments of the pay competitors in the labor or product markets are offering for identical jobs.

Internal job equity represents assessments of the fairness of pay among jobs within the organization, relative to the worth of each job to the organization.

Individual equity represents assessments of the fairness of pay and pay raises among individuals performing the same job within the organization. This assessment best reflects Adams's description of equity because the referent represents a comparable other. With respect to pay, accurately and consistently measuring and rewarding individual performance and contributions contribute to employee perceptions of individual pay equity.

Although organizations have traditionally focused on outcome fairness, research now suggests that procedural fairness is an important variable to consider. Although research continues to find that distributive justice perceptions are more strongly focused on evaluations of outcomes, procedural justice perceptions have been found to be more strongly focused on evaluations of the institution and the agents responsible for those outcomes. Thus, acceptance of procedures appears to be as important for obtaining desirable behavior as is acceptance of outcomes. Additionally, it appears that organizations monitor the fairness of each of their pay procedures as procedures have been shown to have differential effects on attitudes and behaviors. Moreover, the way the performance appraisal procedure is applied also appears to interact with acceptance of the pay outcome. Taken together, psychological theories of justice help assess the extent to which justice perceptions may affect desirable behaviors and thus the extent to which the organization can get a positive return for their compensation outlays.

Expectancy and Reinforcement Models of Motivation

Motivation is defined as goal-directed behavior. Although motivation is a property of the individual, organizations can influence motivation by their policies and practices. The topic is complex and worthy of in-depth study. In this section, we introduce two motivation models: expectancy and reinforcement, that have provided guidance to the development of various forms of compensation.

EXPECTANCY MODEL

Expectancy models are explanations of energizing factors that motivate effort. They help us understand how people make decisions regarding behavioral alternatives (e.g., Lewin, 1936; Rotter, 1964). Although there are a number of expectancy formulations, the formulation proposed by Victor Vroom (1964) dominates research in American applied psychology.

In 1964, Victor Vroom proposed that people are driven by expectations that their behavior will produce results. For example, the desire for a performance-based pay outcome will result in high performance only if the person possesses a strong expectation that his or her performance will lead to the payout and he or she is capable of achieving the required performance. Accordingly, expectancy theory posits that individual behavior results from deliberate choices among alternatives with the purpose of maximizing self-interest.

Vroom's model has three key components: expectancy, instrumentality, and valence. Each of these constructs represents a belief. *Expectancy* is the individual's "momentary belief of the likelihood that a particular act will be followed by a particular outcome" (Vroom, 1964, p. 17). *Instrumentality* is the degree to which the individual believes that the particular outcome will lead to a secondary outcome. *Valence* is the value the individual places on the secondary outcome.

The model is summarized in terms of Effort, where effort can be computed by the following formula: Effort = Expectancy $\times \Sigma$ (Instrumentality $\times$ Valence). An example of how this theory may be applied is an automobile dealership's bonus plan for salespeople. The sales manager announces that a $10,000 bonus will be awarded to the car salesperson who demonstrates the greatest dollar amount of sales for a particular period. The motivational impact of this bonus pay plan would depend on an individual salesperson's expectancy (i.e., perception of the likelihood of being the top salesperson), instrumentality (i.e., belief that the dealership will actually award the bonus), and valence (i.e., the extent to which the individual values this outcome above other possible outcomes). It is unlikely in this example that the bonus will be perceived as attainable by the majority of salespeople, and therefore, the expectancy of achieving the "top" salesperson slot is not likely to be high. If one of the expectancy components is low, one can expect little effort will be expended, even if the other components are high. Thus, in this example, the dealership's bonus plan will not be successful in generating the desired effort.

Although expectancy theory has received more research support than content theories of motivation (e.g., Maslow's hierarchy of needs theory and Hertzberg's motivation-hygiene theory; Miller & Grush, 1988; Mitchell,

Wabba, & House, 1974), research has not provided consistent evidence to support the overall validity of the model (Van Eerde & Thierry, 1996). This may be partly due to researchers' failure to recognize the perspective of social learning theorist J. Rotter (1964). Like Vroom, Rotter emphasized that behavioral potential is a function of both the expectancy that an outcome will follow the behavior and the value the outcome has for the person; however, Rotter believed that the value of an outcome *is not based on what the person experiences in the current situation* but on what the outcome's realized value had been to the person in the past in similar situations. The difference in the valence calculation, consequently, may explain the weak or inconsistent expectancy theory research results.

REINFORCEMENT MODEL

The concept of reinforcement is based on the work of B. F. Skinner. The principle of reinforcement states simply that behavior that is rewarded in a particular situation tends to be repeated in a similar situation and behavior that is not rewarded tends not to be repeated. Reinforcement, also called behavior modification, involves three elements: (1) the stimulus, (2) the response, and (3) the consequences.

Skinner's concept of operant conditioning is relevant in work organizations. Operant behavior is voluntary behavior, as opposed to classical conditioning, which refers to a reflex behavior. Operant conditioning assumes that human beings explore their environment and act on it. The initial behavior may be random or a test of what the consequences may be. If one wants to influence behavior, one must be able to manipulate the consequences of the behavior (Skinner, 1969). This requires familiarity with the effects of four types of contingency arrangements: positive reinforcement, avoidance learning, extinction, and punishment. Positive reinforcement and avoidance learning are methods to strengthen desired behaviors, whereas extinction and punishment are methods to weaken undesired behavior.

Once the contingencies arrangements are chosen, they must be applied with appropriate timing (called a schedule of reinforcement). A reinforcement schedule is a specification of the occurrence of the reinforcer in relation to the behavior one wants to influence. Choice of schedule also determines the longer term effectiveness of the influence. Schedules of reinforcement may be continuous or partial. In a continuous schedule, a reward is applied every time the desired behavior is performed. In a partial schedule, the reward is applied less frequently. Ferster and Skinner (1957) described four basic types of partial reinforcers: fixed interval, variable interval, fixed ratio, and variable ratio. These schedules of reinforcement affect the speed with which learning takes place as well as the strength of the learning's retention. The strongest form of retention is "habit." Although reinforcement model ideas are simple, effective implementation requires considerable understanding of the nuances of reinforcement and consistency in application. The references in this section provide good sources for learning more about reinforcement.

IMPLICATIONS FOR HRM

Expectancy and reinforcement models both involve behavior-reward contingencies. Expectancy theory suggests that behavior is a consequence of conscious choice, whereas reinforcement theory suggests that behavior is a function of repeated pairings of behavior and rewards, and thus, habit. Although motivation is goal-directed behavior, people have choices as to which goals to pursue and how much effort to expend on those goals. Often, people have to choose between a number of relatively attractive behaviors. Whereas expectancy theory predicts that individuals would choose to behave in whatever way has the highest motivational force, the reinforcement model would say that they would behave in a habitual way. Thus, in the case of expectancy theory, managers may encounter variability in performance depending on the expectancy, instrumentality, and value the individual perceives in the performance, whereas in the case of reinforcement, managers may encounter relatively more static performance based on habit. In either case, the organization's compensation outlays will be more effective if the organization does the following:

- Provides incentives for work that will be perceived as highly attractive and salient to employees (valence).

- Ensures that rewards offered for good performance are significantly different from those offered for mediocre performance.

- Ensures that the required behaviors for the rewards are clear to employees and they perceive a clear link between their performance and the rewards (instrumentality).

- Ensures that the measure of performance is within the employee's ability to affect (expectancy).

- Ensures that the rewards are offered in a consistent manner, using the appropriate schedule of reinforcement.

Organizational Behavior and Performance Management

In performance management, the human resource practitioner is involved in developing systems for managing individual behavior. Traditionally, performance management has been thought of in terms of the individual, and the focus has been on the appraisal of the individual's behaviors or performance in the job. However, because of the central role human resource managers often play in interventions to enhance organizational performance and competitiveness, attention has turned toward activities beyond performance appraisal system design to programs such as job design and goal-setting that influence individual and organization performance. Accordingly, we describe the job characteristics model and goal-setting theory as two important organizational behavior perspectives. The former is relevant to informing job redesign to improve the motivational aspects of the job, enhancing worker and organizational productivity. The latter is relevant for teaching line managers to effectively manage the performance of individuals and teams.

Job Redesign and the Job Characteristics Model

Although a number of distinct approaches to job design are used in various employment settings (e.g., motivational, ergonomics, sociotechnical, human factors; Scarpello et al., 1995), the primary theoretical approach to enhancing lower level employee satisfaction and motivation through job redesign has been provided by Hackman and Oldham's job characteristics model. This model is based on the premise that when aspects of a job satisfy a worker's psychological needs, the worker is motivated to perform the job effectively. The model has three components: *core job dimensions* that lead to *critical psychological states* that result in positive *work outcomes.*

The job characteristics model states that three critical psychological states (experienced meaningfulness of the job or work, experienced responsibility for outcomes of the work, knowledge of the results of the work activities) are affected by the five defining characteristics of a job (skill variety, task identity, task significance, feedback, autonomy; Hackman & Oldham, 1976, 1980).

There have been over 200 published empirical studies and at least three comprehensive reviews of Hackman and Oldham's (1976) job characteristics model (Renn & Vandenberg, 1995). The reviews indicated that most studies have supported the multidimensionality of the job characteristics model's core job dimensions, although there has not been consistent agreement on the number of dimensions (Fried & Ferris, 1987; Roberts & Glick, 1981). As proposed in the model, job characteristics have been found to be related to both psychological and behavioral outcomes. Further, Fried and Ferris (1987) noted that the mediating role of psychological states between job characteristics and personal outcomes has received support as well.

IMPLICATIONS FOR HRM

By understanding the impact of job characteristics on the critical psychological states and the relationship between psychological states and positive work outcomes, human resource practitioners can work to ensure that when jobs are created, redesigned, or evaluated, high levels of the core job characteristics are present in the job. Once it has been determined that jobs need to be redesigned, a number of interventions have been suggested to enhance the core job dimensions (Hackman & Oldham, 1976, Luthans, Kemmerer, Paul, & Taylor, 1987; Robbins, 1992):

- Job enlargement involves adding a number of similar tasks to a job. This may enhance the job's skill variety by increasing the number of different motions or activities in which the worker engages. To the extent that switching among tasks activates or cognitively excites the worker, it has the potential to reduce repetition and monotony that occurs from a lesser number of tasks.

- Job enrichment involves increasing the amount of responsibility by increasing the range and complexity of tasks associated with the job and by also increasing decision-making authority (this is also suggested by motivation-hygiene theory). This intervention has been found to affect skill variety, task identity, and autonomy.

- Interrelated tasks, which may have been performed by more than one worker in an assembly line fashion, may be combined so that a single employee is able to work on an identifiable product, thus affecting task identity.

- Opening feedback channels provides workers with increased feedback and knowledge of the results of their work.

- Other interventions to increase the levels of core job dimensions are available such as forming work teams to provide workers with more autonomy and the opportunity to work on a meaningful unit of work, as well as job rotation, which is similar to job enlargement, in that it increases the activities of a worker by moving him or her to different assignments.

Goal-Setting Theory

Goal-setting theory has been described as having "more scientific validity to date than any other theory or approach to work motivation" (Pinder, 1984, p. 169). Goal-setting theory is the family of propositions that link an individual's consequent level of performance on a task to explicit intentions toward the completion of the task or toward the achievement of an outcome related to the task. It includes hypotheses regarding the existence versus absence of goals, the specificity of goals, the difficulty of goals, the commitment toward goal attainment, the role of feedback during task completion, the presence of incentives, and the role of participation in the setting of goals.

Organizational goal-setting theory's roots have been attributed to the mid-20th century work of psychologist E. A. Locke (1968). However, Locke and Latham (1990) traced its dual origins to the applied work of individuals including F. W. Taylor, P. Dupont, A. Sloan, and P. Drucker, among others, and to the experimental psychology work of O. Kulpe, K. Lewin, C. A. Mace, and T. A. Ryan, among others. As evidence of the former, they pointed out how goals and goal-setting have played parts in both scientific management's task concept and the popular management by objectives (MBO) technique. As evidence of the latter, they showed how the constructs of effort and difficulty levels, intention, goal specificity and challenge, and incentives were related to performance in psychological studies. Subsequent to Locke's groundbreaking integration of the fields and his explication of the goal-setting process, a substantial amount of research-based evidence has accumulated that supports many of his initial and later propositions, as evidenced in a number of qualitative and quantitative reviews (e.g., Latham & Locke, 1979; Latham & Yukl, 1975; Locke & Latham, 1990; Tubbs, 1986). In a review of goal-setting research, Latham and Locke (1979) concluded the following:

- The presence of goals leads to higher performance levels.

- Challenging goals yield better performance than easier goals but incentives or feedback yield better performance only to the extent that they encourage the setting of more challenging goals.

- The underlying mechanisms that link goal-setting to performance are its effect on enriched job design, its role in facilitating job performance by defining job expectations, and its motivational effects related to achievement motives.

- Little of the difference in the performance outcomes from goal-setting is based on how the goals are determined (e.g., assigned or determined participatively).

Although Latham and Locke (1979) had suggested that specific goals yield better performance than vague goals, they later recognized that the specificity or generality of the goals depends on the nature of the subordinate's job. On relatively stable and structured jobs, specifically stated goals will increase performance. On the other hand, on relatively unstable and unstructured jobs, specific goal-setting may be counterproductive and inhibit innovation and creative problem-solving (Locke, Shaw, Saari, & Latham, 1981).

Individual difference variables have also been demonstrated to influence the goal-setting process. Of these variables, self-esteem and self-efficacy have received the most attention and consistent support. In general, research has related these variables to individuals' levels of goal difficulty and commitment (Brown & Latham, 2000; Wofford, Goodwin, & Premack,

1992). By influencing these two factors, higher self-esteem or self-efficacy led to the setting of higher goals, and subsequently to higher performance. At the individual level, Cederblom's (1982) review of research on the performance appraisal interview concluded that goal-setting during the appraisal interview was related to interview satisfaction, perceived fairness and accuracy, utility, mutual understanding of the interview content, and intended and actual performance improvement.

Research regarding goal-setting theory has extended beyond the confines of the model and the study of individual behavior to its role in the performance management system and its impact on organizational performance. For example, Hall, Posner, and Harder (1989) interviewed representatives of 36 firms and found that goal-setting was ranked as the third most important objective of the companies' performance appraisal systems, subordinate only to reviewing and rewarding past performance. They also found that it was larger and more established firms that espoused the goal-setting purpose for their systems. Additionally, more than 80% of the firms set goals during the appraisal interview, and most respondents reported that the goal-setting was participative, rather than assigned. Terpstra and Rozell (1994) surveyed 201 midsize to large organizations and found that more than 60% used formal goal-setting in their performance management system. Most importantly, the use of goal-setting significantly correlated with both annual profit and profit growth for the organizations across all industries.

IMPLICATIONS FOR HRM

Given the apparent efficacy of goal-setting techniques for improving individual performance and their role in performance management systems, the theory has important implications for the design of human resource programs (Latham & Locke, 1979; Locke, Latham, & Erez, 1988; Pritchard, Roth, Jones, Galgay, & Watson, 1988), including the following:

- The specificity or generality of the agreed-on goals should vary with the nature of the subordinate's job (stable and structured versus relatively unstable and unstructured).

- Goals should able to be accurately measured and reflect the entirety of the job. Goals should include quality controls and not be so narrow as to focus effort on some tasks at the expense of other necessary tasks.

- Goals should be neither too easy nor seemingly impossible to achieve. They should be "difficult but attainable."

- Managers should be trained to include a discussion of goal attainment and difficulty during performance appraisal interviews.

- Goal-setting tactics that can be used include targeted goal-setting for special needs improvement and overall goal-setting for unit performance improvement.

- The performance and feedback time period for goal-setting should be based on the job cycle and the availability of performance measures.

- Managers should be taught that goal commitment can be facilitated by providing the employee with necessary information, positive support, legitimate authority, influence, internal and external rewards, participation, and competition.

- Managers should provide their employees with the resources necessary to achieve their goals.

What Do Human Resource Managers *Really* Need to Know About Organizational Behavior?

Reflecting back on the theoretical perspectives we deemed essential to the practice of HRM, some points of common wisdom stood out for us and may be useful for practitioners to take to heart.

OUTCOMES MATTER

People will invest effort and demonstrate performance for those outcomes to which they are committed and that provide value to them. This value-directed, goal-directed behavior, however, is moderated by their expectations that they will be able to achieve or receive the outcome if they put forth the effort and are able to perform. Human resource managers can design goal-setting, appraisal, and reward systems that direct the attention and interest of employees toward organizationally important outcomes and increase performance.

SOCIAL PERCEPTIONS MATTER

People want to understand their world, and when it is important to them, they are quite systematic in deducing the cause or reason why others behave the way that they do. Human resource managers can build this psychological tendency into their selection and appraisal interviews, their discipline and investigation processes, and their management development programs in a manner that facilitates decision making and limits the impact of biases.

Corollary

Fairness matters—people perceive and evaluate fairness in terms of processes and outcomes. People react to fairness perceptions, actively through changes in effort or behavior toward others and the organization, or passively through withdrawal or cognitive distortion. Human resource managers can design processes and determine outcomes that are perceived as fair by working within the guidelines established from the existing research.

FIT MATTERS

People are attracted to other people (or jobs, or organizations) who provide value to them—that is, others who espouse similar values or personalities that reinforce their own, jobs that evoke their interest and allow them to be successful, or situations that provide rewards and opportunities important to their needs and desires. When people are not able to satisfy their needs or wants, they will withdraw or exit from the situation to the extent that they are able. Human resource managers can influence this attraction through managing culture, systems, and job design.

Corollary

Individual differences matter—people have different styles or dispositions in how they perceive situations that determine the decisions or attributions they make. Likewise, on the basis of their individual characteristics, people react differently to, or perform differentially under, alternative job designs, organizational reward systems, goals, cultures, and other variables. Human resource managers face the complex task of identifying and developing the right person for the right situation—or of identifying and designing the right situation for the right person.

References

Adams, J. S. (1963). Toward an understanding of inequity. *Journal of Abnormal and Social Psychology, 47,* 422–436.

Adams, J. S. (1965). Inequity in social exchange. In L. Berkowitz (Ed.), *Advances in experimental social psychology* (pp. 267–299). New York: Academic Press.

Barrick, M. R., & Mount, M. K. (1991). The big five personality dimensions and job performance: A meta-analysis. *Personnel Psychology, 44,* 1–26.

Barrick, M. R., & Mount, M. K. (1993). Autonomy as a moderator of the relationships between the big five personality dimensions and job performance. *Journal of Applied Psychology, 78,* 111–118.

Bergmann, T. J., & Scarpello, V. G. (2001). *Compensation decision-making.* Fort Worth, TX: Harcourt College Publishers.

Bowers, K. S. (1973). Situationism in psychology: An analysis and critique. *Psychological Review, 80,* 307–336.

Bretz, R. D., Ash, R. A., & Dreher, G. F. (1989). Do people make the place? An examination of the attraction-selection-attrition hypothesis. *Personnel Psychology, 42,* 561–581.

Brown, T. C., & Latham, G. P. (2000). The effects of goal setting and self-instruction training on the performance of unionized employees. *Relations Industrielles, 55*(1), 80–95.

Cable, D. M., & DeRue, D. S. (2002). The convergent and discriminant validity of subjective fit perceptions. *Journal of Applied Psychology, 87*(5), 875–884.

Cable, D. M., & Judge, T. A. (1996). Person-organization fit, job choice decisions, and organizational entry. *Organizational Behavior and Human Decision Processes, 67*(3), 294–311.

Caldwell, D. F., & O'Reilly, C. A. (1990). Measuring person-job fit with a profile-comparison process. *Journal of Applied Psychology, 75*(6), 648–657.

Cederblom, D. (1982). The performance appraisal interview: A review, implications, and suggestions. *Academy of Management Review, 7*(2), 219–227.

Chatman, J. A. (1989). Improving interactional organizational research: A model of person-organization fit. *Academy of Management Review, 14*(3), 333–349.

Chatman, J. A. (1991). Matching people and organizations: Selection and socialization in public accounting firms. *Administrative Science Quarterly, 36*(3), 459–484.

Cowherd, D. M., & Levine, D. L. (1992). Product quality and pay equity between lower-level employees and top management: An investigation of distributive justice theory. *Administrative Science Quarterly, 37,* 302–320.

Cropanzano, R., & Folger, R. (1989). Referent cognitions and task decision autonomy: Beyond equity theory. *Journal of Applied Psychology, 74,* 293–299.

Dawis, R. V. (1996). The theory of work adjustment and person-environment-correspondence counseling. In D. Brown, L. Brooks, & Associates (Eds.), *Career choice and development* (pp. 75–120). San Francisco, CA: Jossey-Bass.

Dawis, R. V., England, G. W., & Lofquist, L. H. (1964). A theory of work adjustment. *Minnesota Studies in Vocational Rehabilitation, XV,* 1–27.

Dawis, R. V., & Lofquist, L. H. (1984). *A psychological theory of work adjustment.* Minneapolis: University of Minnesota Press.

Deutsch, M. (1985). *Distributive justice.* New Haven, CT: Yale University Press.

Dulebohn, J. H. (1997). Social influence in organizational justice evaluations of processes and outcomes of human resources systems. In G. R. Ferris (Ed.), *Research in personnel and human resources management* (Vol. 15, pp. 241–291). Greenwich, CT: JAI Press.

Dulebohn, J. H., & Martocchio, J. J. (1998). Employees' evaluations of the fairness of work group incentive pay plans. *Journal of Management, 24*(4), 469–488.

Edwards, J. R. (1991). Person-job fit: A conceptual integration, literature review, and methodological critique. *International Review of Industrial and Organizational Psychology, 6,* 283–357.

Ferster, C. B., & Skinner, B. F. (1957). *Schedules of reinforcement.* New York: Appleton-Century-Crofts.

Fiske, S. T., & Taylor, S. E. (1991). *Social cognition* (2nd ed.). New York: McGraw-Hill.

Folger, R. (1986). A referent cognitions theory of relative deprivation. In J. M. Olson, C. P. Herman, & M. P. Zanna (Eds.), *Social comparison and relative deprivation: The Ontario symposium* (pp. 33–55). Hillsdale, NJ: Erlbaum.

Folger, R. (1987). Relative deprivation and referent cognitions: Reformulating the preconditions of resentment. In J. C. Masters & W. P. Smith (Eds.), *Social comparison, justice, and relative deprivation: Theoretical, empirical, and policy perspectives* (pp. 183–215). Hillsdale, NJ: Erlbaum.

Folger, R., & Greenberg, J. (1985). Procedural justice: An interpretive analysis of personnel systems. In K. M. Rowland & G. R. Ferris (Eds.), *Research in personnel and human resource management* (pp. 115–139). Greenwich, CT: JAI Press.

Fried, Y., & Ferris, G. R. (1987). The validity of the job characteristics model: A review and meta-analysis. *Personnel Psychology, 40*(2), 287–322.

Gatewood, R. D., & Field, H. S. (2001). *Human resource selection* (5th ed.). Orlando, FL: Dryden Press/Harcourt Brace & Company.

Gerhart, B., Minkoff, H. B., & Olsen, R. N. (1995). Employee compensation: Theory, practice, and evidence. In G. R. Ferris, S. D. Rosen, & D. T. Barnum (Eds.), *Handbook of human resource management* (pp. 528–547). Oxford: Blackwell.

Greenberg, J. (1987). Reactions to procedural injustice in payment distributions: Do the means justify the ends? *Journal of Applied Psychology, 72*(1), 55–61.

Greenberg, J. (1990). Organizational justice: Yesterday, today, and tomorrow. *Journal of Management, 16,* 399–432.

Hall, J. L., Posner, B. Z., & Harder, J. W. (1989). Performance appraisal systems: Matching practice with theory. *Group & Organization Management, 14*(1), 51–69.

Hackman, J. R., & Oldham, G. R. (1976). Motivation through the design of work: Test of a theory. *Organizational Behavior and Human Performance, 16*(2), 250–279.

Hackman, J. R., & Oldham, G. R. (1980). *Work redesign.* Reading, MA: Addison Wesley.

Harvey, J. H., & Weary, G. (1984). Current issues in attribution theory and research. *Annual Review of Psychology, 35,* 427–459.

Heider, F. (1958). *The psychology of interpersonal relations.* New York: Wiley.

Heneman, H. G., & Judge, T. A. (2003). *Staffing organizations* (4th ed.). Middleton, WI: Mendota House/McGraw-Hill/Irwin.

Holland, J. L. (1985). *Making vocational choices: A theory of vocational personalities and work environments* (2nd ed.). Englewood Cliffs, NJ: Prentice Hall.

Hough, L. M. (1992). The "big five" personality variables—Construct confusion: Description versus prediction. *Human Performance, 5,* 139–155.

Hough, L. M., & Schneider, B. (1996). Personality traits, taxonomies, and applications in organizations. In K. R. Murphy (Ed.), *Individual differences and behavior in organizations* (pp. 31–38). San Francisco, CA: Jossey-Bass.

Hunter, J. E. (1986). Cognitive ability, cognitive aptitudes, job knowledge, and job performance. *Journal of Vocational Behavior, 29,* 379–410.

Jones, E. E., & Davis, K. E. (1965). From acts to dispositions: The attribution process in person perception. *Advances in Experimental Social Psychology, 2,* 219–266.

Jones, F. F., & Scarpello, V. (1999). Pay procedures: What makes them fair? *Journal of Occupational and Organizational Psychology, 72,* 129–145.

Judge, T. A., & Cable, D. M. (1997). Applicant personality, organizational culture, and organization attraction. *Personnel Psychology, 50,* 359–394.

Judge, T. A., & Ferris, G. R. (1992). The elusive criterion of fit in human resources staffing decisions. *Human Resource Planning, 15*(4), 47–67.

Kelley, H. H. (1967). Attribution theory in social psychology. *Nebraska Symposium on Motivation, 15,* 620–623.

Kelley, H. H. (1972). Attribution in social interaction. In E. E. Jones, D. E. Kanouse, H. H. Kelly, R. E. Nisbett, S. Valins, & B. Weiner (Eds.), *Attribution: Perceiving the causes of behavior* (pp. 1–26). Morristown, NJ: General Learning Press.

Kelley, H. H., & Michela, J. L. (1980). Attribution theory and research. *Annual Review of Psychology, 31,* 457–501.

Knouse, S. B. (1989). The role of attribution theory in personnel employment selection: A review of the recent literature. *The Journal of General Psychology, 116*(2), 183–196.

Kristof, A. L. (1996). Person-organization fit: An integrative review of its conceptualizations, measurement, and implications. *Personnel Psychology, 49,* 1–49.

Kristof-Brown, A. L. (2000). Perceived applicant fit: Distinguishing between recruiters' perceptions of person-job and person-organization fit. *Personnel Psychology, 53,* 643–671.

Latham, G. P., & Locke, E. A. (1979). Goal setting—A motivational technique that works. *Organizational Dynamics, 8*(2), 68–80.

Latham, G. P., & Yukl, G. A. (1975). A review of research on the application of goal setting in organizations. *Academy of Management Journal, 18,* 824–845.

Lauver, K. J., & Kristof-Brown, A. L. (2001). Distinguishing between employees' perceptions of person-job and person-organization fit. *Journal of Vocational Behavior, 59,* 454–470.

Leventhal, G. S. (1980). What should be done with equity theory? In K. J. Gergen, M. S. Greenberg, & R. H. Willis (Eds.), *Social exchange: Advances in theory and research* (pp. 27–55). New York: Plenum.

Leventhal, G. S., Karuza, J., & Fry, W. R. (1980). Beyond fairness: A theory of allocation preferences. In G. Mikula (Ed.), *Justice and social interaction: Experimental and theoretical contributions from psychological research* (pp. 167–218). New York: Hans Huber.

Lewin, K. (1936). *Principles of topological psychology.* New York: McGraw-Hill.

Lind, E. A., & Tyler, T. (1988). *The social psychology of procedural justice.* New York: Plenum.

Locke, E. A. (1968). Toward a theory of task motivation and incentives. *Organization Behavior and Human Performance, 3,* 157–189.

Locke, E. A., & Latham, G. P. (1990). *A theory of goal setting and test performance.* Upper Saddle River, NJ: Prentice Hall.

Locke, E. A., Latham, G. P., & Erez, M. (1988). The determinants of goal commitment. *Academy of Management Review, 13*(1), 23–39.

Locke, E. A., Shaw, K. N., Saari, L. M., & Latham, G. P. (1981). Goal setting and task performance: 1969–1980. *Psychology Bulletin, 90,* 125–152.

Luthans, F., Kemmerer, B., Paul, R., & Taylor, L. (1987). The impact of a job redesign intervention on salespersons' observed performance behaviors: A field experiment. *Group & Organization Studies, 12*(1), 55–72

Miller, L. E., & Grush, J. E. (1988). Improving predictions in expectancy theory research: Effects of personality, expectancies, and norms. *Academy of Management Journal, 31*(1), 107–123.

Milkovich, G. T., & Newman, J. M. (1996). *Compensation.* Boston: BPI-Irwin.

Miner, J. B. (2003). The rated importance, scientific validity, and practical usefulness of organizational behavior theories: A quantitative review. *Academy of Management Learning & Education, 2*(3), 250–268.

Mischel, W. (1968). *Personality and assessment.* New York: Wiley.

Mitchell, T. R., Wabba, M. A., & House, R. J. (1974). Expectancy theory in work motivation: Some logical and methodological issues. *Human Relations, 27*(2), 121–147.

Mowday, R. T. (1991). Equity theory predictions of behavior in organizations. In R. Steers & L. Porter (Eds.), *Motivation and work behavior* (pp. 111–131). New York: McGraw-Hill.

O'Reilly, C. A., Chatman, J., & Caldwell, D. F. (1991). People and organizational culture: A profile comparison approach to assessing person-organization fit. *Academy of Management Journal, 34*(3), 487–516.

O'Reilly, C. A., & Pfeffer, J. (2000). *Hidden value: How great companies achieve extraordinary results with ordinary people.* Boston, MA: Harvard Business School Publishing.

Pfeffer, J., & Langton, N. (1993). The effect of wage dispersion on satisfaction, productivity, and working collaboratively: Evidence from college and university faculty. *Administrative Science Quarterly, 38,* 382–407.

Pinder, C. C. (1984). *Work motivation.* Glenview, IL: Scott, Foresman.

Posner, B. Z. (1992). Person-organization values congruence: No support for individual differences as a moderating influence. *Human Relations, 45*(4), 351–362.

Pritchard, R. D., Roth, P. L., Jones, S. D., Galgay, P. J., & Watson, M. D. (1988). Designing a goal-setting system to enhance performance: A practical guide. *Organizational Dynamics, 17*(1), 69–78.

Ramsay, S., Gallois, C., & Callan, V. J. (1997). Social rules and attributions in the personnel selection interview. *Journal of Occupational and Organizational Psychology, 70,* 189–203.

Ree, M. J., Carretta, T. R., & Teachout, M. S. (1995). Role of ability and prior job knowledge in complex training performance. *Journal of Applied Psychology, 80,* 721–730.

Reid, P. T., Kleiman, L. S., & Travis, C. B. (1986). Attribution and sex differences in the employment interview. *The Journal of Social Psychology, 126*(2), 205–212.

Renn, R. W., & Vandenberg, R.J. (1995). The critical psychological states: An underrepresented component in job characteristics model research. *Journal of Management, 21*(2), 279–303.

Robbins, S. P. (1992). *Essentials of organizational behavior.* New York: Prentice Hall.

Roberts, K. H., & Glick, W. (1981). The job characteristics approach to task design: A critical review. *Journal of Applied Psychology, 66*(2), 193–219.

Ross, L. (1977). The intuitive psychologist and his shortcomings: Distortions in the attribution process. In L. Berkowitz (Ed.), *Advances in experimental social psychology.* New York: Academic Press.

Ross, M., & Fletcher, G. J. O. (1985). Attribution and social perception. In G. Lindzey & E. Aronson (Eds.), *The handbook of social psychology* (pp. 73–122). New York: Random House.

Rotter, J. B. (1964). *Clinical psychology.* Englewood Cliffs, NJ: Prentice Hall.

Rotter, J. B. (1966). Generalized expectancies for internal versus external control reinforcement. *Psychological Monographs, 80,* 1–28.

Rynes, S., & Gerhart, B. (1990). Interviewer assessments of applicant "fit": An exploratory investigation. *Personnel Psychology, 43,* 13–35.

Scarpello, V., & Campbell, J. P. (1983). Job satisfaction and the fit between individual needs and organizational rewards. *Journal of Occupational Psychology, 56,* 315–328.

Scarpello, V., & Hayton, J. (2002). Assessing the nonequivalence of job satisfaction measures. In C. A. Schriesheim & L. L. Neider (Eds.), *Research in management* (pp. 131–160). Greenwich, CT: Information Age Publishing.

Scarpello, V., & Jones, F. F. (1996). Why justice matters in compensation decision-making. *Journal of Organizational Behavior, 17*(3), 285–301.

Scarpello, V., Ledvinka, J., & Bergmann T. J. (1995). *Human resource management.* Cincinnati, OH: South-Western Publishing.

Schneider, B. (1978). Person-situation selection: A review of some ability-situation interaction research. *Personnel Psychology, 31,* 281–297.

Schneider, B. (1983a). An interactionist perspective on organizational effectiveness. In K. S. Cameron & D. S. Whetten (Eds.), *Organizational effectiveness: A comparison of multiple models* (pp. 27–54). New York: Academic Press.

Schneider, B. (1983b). Interactional psychology and organizational behavior. In L. L. Cummings & B. M. Staw (Eds.), *Research in organizational behavior* (pp. 1–31). Greenwich, CT: JAI Press.

Schneider, B. (1987). The people make the place. *Personnel Psychology, 40,* 437–453.

Schneider, B., Goldstein, H. W., & Smith, D. B. (1995). The ASA framework: An update. *Personnel Psychology, 48,* 747–773.

Schneider, B., Smith, D. B., Taylor, S., & Fleenor, J. (1998). Personality and organizations: A test of the homogeneity of personality hypothesis. *Journal of Applied Psychology, 83*(3), 462–470.

Shultz, T. R., & Ravinsky, R. B. (1977). Similarity as a principle of causal inference. *Child Development, 48,* 1552–1558.

Skinner, B. F. (1969). *Contingencies of reinforcement.* New York: Appleton-Century-Crofts.

Silvester, J., Anderson-Gough, F. M., Anderson, N. R., & Mohamed, A. R. (2002). Locus of control, attributions and impression management in the selection interview. *Journal of Occupational and Organizational Psychology, 75,* 59–76.

Super, D. E. (1953). A theory of vocational development. *American Psychologist, 8,* 185–190.

Terpstra, D. E., & Rozell, E. J. (1994). The relationship of goal setting to organizational profitability. *Group & Organization Management, 19*(3), 285–294.

Thibaut, J., & Walker, L. (1975). *Procedural justice: A psychological analysis.* Hillsdale, NJ: Erlbaum.

Tubbs, M. E. (1986). Goal setting: A meta-analytic examination of the empirical evidence. *Journal of Applied Psychology, 71*(3), 474–483.

Turban, D. B., & Keon, T. L. (1993). Organizational attractiveness: An interactionist perspective. *Journal of Applied Psychology, 78*(2), 184–193.

Van Eerde, W., & Thierry, H. (1996). Vroom's expectancy models and work-related criteria: A meta-analysis. *Journal of Applied Psychology, 81*(5), 575–586.

Van Vianen, A. E. M. (2000). Person-organization fit: The match between newcomers' and recruiters' preferences for organizational cultures. *Personnel Psychology, 53,* 113–149.

Vroom, V. H. (1964). *Work and motivation.* New York: Wiley.

Wofford, J. C., Goodwin, V. L., & Premack, S. (1992). Meta-analysis of the antecedents of personal goal level and of the antecedents and consequences of goal commitment. *Journal of Management, 18*(3), 595–615.

Fundamentals of Organizing 15

Structural Design and Its Implications for HRM Practices

Vida Gulbinas Scarpello

The curriculum for coursework in HRM has focused mainly on functional knowledge and skill acquisition necessary to practice within an undifferentiated organizational structure. There is growing evidence, however, that expanding the HRM curriculum to include more extensive coverage of organization theory—particularly elements of organization design and structure—will be a necessary requirement of the future for HR professionals within large and global organizations (e.g., Child & McGrath, 2001; Dijksterhuis, VandenBosch, & Volberda, 1999; Goold & Campbell, 2002; Lewin, Long, & Carroll, 1999).

This chapter's focus is the structure of organizations and its implications for HRM. Although organizations emerge in different historical times and face varying contingencies, the characteristics of their structures tend to flow from a relatively limited set of concerns, such as distribution of decision-making responsibilities and authority, the rules and procedures necessary to handle contingencies, and complexity (occupational specialties within the organization and within its divisions, the number of divisions, the scope of its domain; e.g., Hall, 1999). Those characteristics vary among organizations, and that variability results in different choices of common structural forms. An organization's configuration reflects the form or combination of forms it chooses to use in arranging its parts in ways that will ensure achievement of purpose.

AUTHOR'S NOTE: I wish to thank Professor Christine Quinn Trank for very helpful comments on earlier versions of this chapter.

Organizational structures have consequences for organizations, the people within them, the people who have contact with the organization, and the society of which they are a part (Hall, 1991). Consequently, understanding the common structural forms and their current variants as well as understanding why organizations and their subunits structure their activities the way they do has important implications for the management of human resources. Specifically, to achieve efficient and effective management of people, the HRM function should develop policies, plans, and programs that fit the shape of the organization's structure or, in the case of a diversified or global firm, the shape of each subsystem within the organizational system (e.g., Hall, 1962; Litwak, 1961).

This chapter is organized into three sections. The first section presents three basic structures and their modifications. The second section discusses research on the determinants of the organization's structure and presents a conceptual framework for understanding structural variations. The third section discusses implications for HRM.

Three Basic Structures and Their Modifications

This section examines three common structural forms: functional, divisional, and matrix. I start with the functional structure, as this has been the dominant structure since the Industrial Revolution. This form has been modified and continues to be modified as the competitive environments change and the need arises to adapt to those changes. I discuss modifications to the functional form last, as these modifications also apply to the structures of all three organizational forms discussed in this section. Figures 15.1, 15.2, and 15.3 graphically represent the three structures.

FUNCTIONAL ORGANIZATION

The functional form is sometimes called *centralized, bureaucratic, classic,* and *mechanistic.* It is a formal arrangement that divides labor by grouping activities by the input necessary for performance of *specialized* tasks or functions. The principle guiding this form of organizing is *specialization,* with each function—production, finance, marketing, sales, and so on— focusing on the efficient performance of the function's assigned work. In a functional organization, specialized departments work independently of other departments, and their activities are coordinated through a management hierarchy. Top management makes major decisions about the organization's offerings. Hence, the functional structure is called *centralized.* It is also called *bureaucratic* because the organization is managed by prespecified

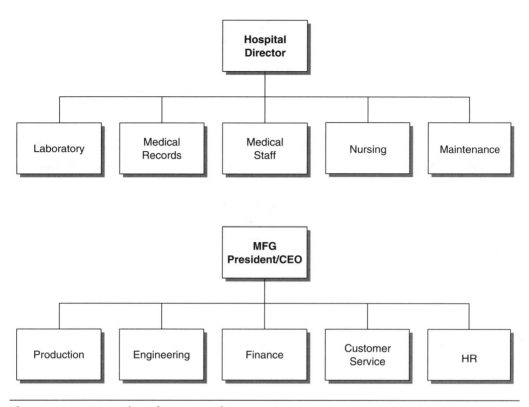

Figure 15.1   Examples of Functional Structures

Note: The functional structure is further divided by specialization. For example, the laboratory function is staffed by laboratory workers and the nursing function is staffed by nurses. The production function is staffed by production workers, and the HR function is staffed by HR workers.

rules and procedures and an authority hierarchy. It is called *classic* because it is the traditional form that came into existence from growth of smaller organizations into large industrial ones (see Weber, 1946; Fayol, 1916/1949; Taylor, 1911/1942). It is called *mechanistic* because people are expected to follow the rules and procedures in doing their work and refer unique problems to their immediate managers for resolution. If those managers cannot resolve the problems, they will send them up the chain of command for resolution. Ideally, this results in an organization that functions efficiently, much like a smooth-running machine.

As industrial organizations spread throughout modern societies, the functional structure became more differentiated horizontally, with each role and each unit becoming more specialized and thus more efficient (Blau, 1970, 1972). Efficient combination of resources in a relatively stable and predictable economy, a concomitant belief that the goals of employees and management were the same, and the belief that conflict can be eliminated through use of rational governing rules and a rational authority

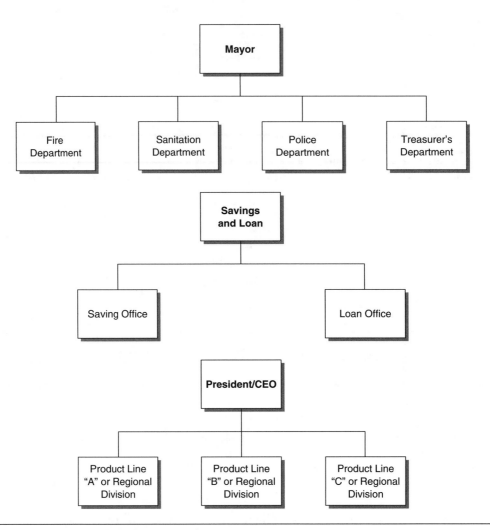

Figure 15.2   Examples of Divisional Structures

Note: Under each division, functional specialization is likely. For example, in the city government, the police department is likely to be organized into functional specialties (e.g., police—street, juvenile, homicide; administrative—accounting, clerical, human resources, customer service.). In the production organization, each product line is also likely to be organized functionally (e.g., production, finance, quality control, engineering and maintenance, physical distribution, etc.). Each of these functional departments will employ functional specialists.

structure, led management to the belief that the functional organization form was the best way of organizing.

That belief started to weaken when tensions between individual and organizational goals surfaced. Those tensions were somewhat contained by use of human relations interventions (such as supervisory training in communication skills and showing concern for employee welfare and job satisfaction). Continuing technological and scientific developments ultimately led to a recognition that those interventions could not ensure the effectiveness of the organization, and further, that the functional structure may not be the best way of organizing in *all* situations.

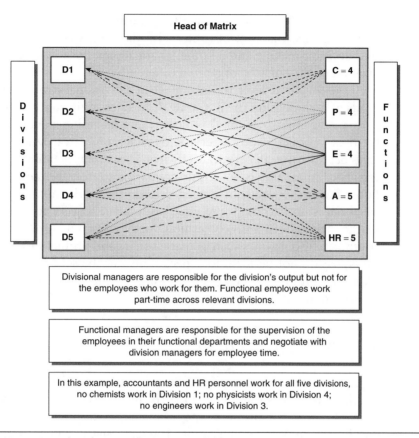

Figure 15.3 Example of a Two-Dimensional Matrix Structure

Note: Divisions may be small projects or large, self-contained units of a corporation. The head of the matrix organization is outside the matrix.

DIVISIONAL ORGANIZATION

This structure is a formal arrangement that divides labor by grouping activities not by specialization but by the desired market outcome (e.g., product, service, process, geographical coverage). In a divisional structure all functional activities are contained within the division. For example, car manufacturers have separate divisions for their product lines, and large savings and loan organizations separate their savings subunits from their loan subunits. Divisions may also be geographically organized. For example, Coca Cola's geographic divisions distribute Cokes whose formulas are adapted to the tastes of customers within diverse geographic regions of the world. This structure is common in organizations with unrelated product or service lines or those functioning in diverse geographic markets with unique customer requirements.

Divisional structures are sometimes called *decentralized* because corporate management delegates business decisions to each division's general manager. Sometimes divisions are completely independent subsidiaries, whereas sometimes they are more closely aligned to the corporation. In any case, division heads manage their businesses, with the corporation exercising financial controls. Internally, divisions may maintain centralized decision making and all other characteristics of the functional organization or they may be organized differently.

At the corporate level, the advantage of a divisional structure is that the heads of each division (be it a strategic business unit, subsidiary, or small, permanent, cross-functional project team) make independent decisions for their product, process, service, or geographic area. Divisional structures decrease overall corporate efficiency because functional activities are replicated in each division, requiring more resources for the outputs produced (such as more people needed to do the work). Yet, they allow the corporation to become more effective in achieving its goals by meeting market demands in a timely fashion. At the corporate level, divisions are controlled by outcomes such as market share and profitability. Those divisions that do not perform to expectations may be sold or otherwise disposed of, without affecting the workings of the rest of the corporation (Scarpello, Ledvinka, & Bergmann, 1995).

MATRIX ORGANIZATION

The matrix is a combination of the functional and divisional structure. It is a *dual authority* structure. In a matrix, managerial power is balanced and shared between two or more types of managers, each representing a different dimension of the organization. The term matrix comes from its initial use in the U.S. aerospace industry, as this gridlike structure evolved from project groupings (i.e., small divisions) during the 1940s and 1950s. Later, the matrix came to be used in other industries (Davis & Lawrence, 1977). Early examples of matrix use include TRW systems, Texas Instruments, NASA, Scandia, Citibank, and Dow Corning. The first Boeing 707 jet also was built using a matrix structure. In the mid 1990s more organizations started to implement matrix structures, and also implemented matrix structures within their divisions. For example, in the mid 1990s AT&T implemented the matrix in its public relations division.

In a matrix structure, there are managers in charge of the functional areas, and there are also managers in charge of the divisions (such as products, services, projects, and geographic areas). Thus, a matrix can have multiple dimensions. Its complexity comes from the fact that one type of manager is not subordinate to the other type—both are at the same organizational level, reporting to the head of the matrix, who is outside the matrix (although matrix organizations are often managed on a team basis). Functional managers are responsible for managing complex technical issues and the employees who are functional experts. On the division side, project managers are responsible for the particular product, service, or geographic area but do not employ their own workforces. Rather, employees within functional departments are shared among the division managers. Thus, matrix employees have at least two bosses: a functional manager who is responsible for the employee's technical performance and a divisional manager who is responsible for meeting unique customer requirements, where customers may also be geographically dispersed. The matrix managers negotiate employee workloads, and employees may work on multiple projects part-time.

Just like the functional and divisional structures involve the management of systems, culture, and behavior, so does the matrix structure. With respect to these issues, the matrix structure is exceptionally complex. This may be one reason the matrix is sometimes not fully implemented. When fully implemented, the dual-authority structure requires that management systems (such as planning, control, appraisal, reward, and others) operate simultaneously along functional and divisional lines. The culture of the matrix is ambiguous, fast changing, complex, and team based.

This is one reason matrix structures have been called organic (Burns & Stalker, 1961). Organic systems are characterized by less-formal job descriptions, great emphasis on adaptability, team decision making, and shared authority. The matrix makes heavy demands on employee and managerial behavior. Because of fast-changing, uncertain, and interdependent work processes, matrix organizations demand that employees and managers alike have extraordinarily flexible personalities capable of dealing constructively with conflicts inherent in a changeable and unstructured work environment in which work is negotiated rather than assigned.

Although matrix structures are becoming commonplace, their complexity has led experts in the past to caution against implementing them unless three conditions are present simultaneously (Davis & Lawrence, 1977). Because relatively less is known about the matrix than about the two less-complex forms discussed above, I will describe conditions for a matrix in detail.

Condition 1: Outside Pressure for Dual Focus. The organization needs to focus simultaneously on achieving high performance goals and satisfying many unique customer requirements. This requirement cautions the organization against using only a functional structure (which achieves high performance, because the work is done by experts) or only a divisional structure (which focuses on customers and markets). By simultaneously using both organizational structures and giving equal power to both functional and divisional managers, the matrix ensures the maintenance of a dual focus.

Condition 2: Pressures for High Information-Processing Capacity. These pressures come from three sources: environmental dynamism, where environmental demands are continuously changing; complexity of tasks; and interdependence among people on highly interrelated tasks.

All three sources have to be examined. If all three are high, conventional ways of handling information are inadequate and tend to break down, requiring the development of more open and complex decision-making processes. The environmental dynamism variable is particularly important to understand, as this produces a need for constant vigilance. For example, there may be sudden changes in market demand, unanticipated moves by competition, political changes that affect global markets, unpredictable technological advances (which leads to task uncertainty), and currency and stock market fluctuations. The key here is that the changes cannot be anticipated, even in the short run—they are surprises. To deal with such surprises, the coordination mechanisms inside the organization must get the available information to the right people in time to influence their decisions. Although computers may help with some information processing, often it is not known which people have the needed information as well as which people need speedy access to the information. To process information quickly and efficiently, employees with high levels of technical knowledge and skill work across the organization's divisional groupings. Thus, in a matrix, employees, rather than managers, are the main coordination mechanisms.

Condition 3: Pressures for Shared Resources. This means that the organization cannot find or cannot afford to duplicate the highly flexible, expensive, and talented human resources it needs to accomplish its work. It must achieve economies of scale in human terms and high performance in terms of both costs and benefits. This results in having matrix employees work part-time for many managers on many projects. In many instances current employees have to be retrained. This can include the acquisition of additional graduate degrees in new technical fields.

Unless all three conditions are overwhelmingly present, simpler modifications can be made to existing structures. For example, without pressure for dual focus and high information-processing requirements (Conditions 1 and 2), an organization can accept a lower level of performance by introducing slack or by organizing into divisions. With the presence of only Condition 1 and/or 3, the organization can create a small top-management team to represent the dual focus and generate high quality and timely decisions. If only Conditions 2 and/or 3 are present, the organization can assign the task of monitoring environmental conditions to boundary spanners, make the managers within the chain of command responsible for maintaining critical channels of communication, and use matrix overlays (discussed below) to share critical resources (Davis & Lawrence, 1977).

MODIFICATIONS TO THE FUNCTIONAL ORGANIZATION

Modifications of the functional structure are common in U.S. industry. They were first described in academic outlets by Jay Galbraith (1973) in his book *Designing Complex Organizations*. His work alerted readers to the functional organization's information-processing problems and ways to resolve those problems. Galbraith observed that as task uncertainty increased, more and more issues were referred up the chain of command for resolution. This resulted in an information overload and inability of top management to respond in a timely manner. Galbraith suggested that the way to deal with this problem was to delegate decision making down to the level where the information originates. Yet, this solution posed problems. Increasing the amount of discretion of low-skilled workers increases the organization's vulnerability to ineffective decision outcomes. On the other hand, increasing the amount of discretion of workers who controlled their work processes, such as craft and professional workers, was feasible if the organization controlled its desired outcomes by setting goals and targets for the completion of work. Goal-setting serves two purposes: (a) it helps coordinate interdependent subtasks and (b) it allows discretion at the local subtask level. Although Galbraith didn't use the term "knowledge worker"[1] in 1973, he was clearly referring to such workers. He further noted that if goal setting did not alleviate the overload problem, the organization can implement one of two strategies: reduce the need for processing information or increase capacity to do so. Structural options for the former strategy are to introduce slack or create self-contained units, and for the latter, to invest in vertical information systems or horizontal communication channels, which he called "lateral relations."

In fast-changing business environments, the slack strategy is rarely available. However, organizations are creating self-contained units (e.g., divisions) of varying size and are delegating decision-making authority to those units. Today, writers in the popular press call them "new" organizations (e.g., Stewart 1992). Most contemporary organizations have invested in real-time computer information systems of varied sophistication. Large and small organizations have also established lateral relations, which we refer to as *structural overlays*. These overlays are used with all organizational forms (functional, divisional, matrix).

Structural overlays complement rather than displace the power of the organization's vertical authority structure. Their purpose is to reduce the number of decisions being referred up the organization's hierarchy. They accomplish this purpose by increasing discretion at lower levels of the organization and allowing decision making at the point where information relevant to the problem originates (Galbraith, 1973). Although organizing into self-contained units (such as large and small divisions or permanent workgroups) also brings decision-making authority down the chain of command, this strategy applies only when work performed by the subunit is *not interdependent* with the work of other subunits. When work is *interdependent*, establishing lateral decision-making processes allows for horizontal communication and information sharing as well as more efficient decision making.

Structural overlays can arise spontaneously. However, when the participants differ in their orientations to tasks for such reasons as occupation, cultural background, and the like or are separated geographically, effective use of group decision making requires formally designed processes.

Formal lateral processes include liaison roles, task forces, teams, integrative manager and linking manager roles, and matrix overlays (Galbraith, 1973). Liaison roles are specialized roles "designed to facilitate communication between two interdependent functional departments and thus to bypass referral of problems up the chain of command" (p. 51). Groups structures (such as taskforces and teams) allow the organization to delegate some decision making to groups made up of representatives from all relevant functions. Taskforces (also called temporary cross-functional teams) and semipermanent teams address specific problems that affect multiple organizational units. Taskforce members represent their units and continue to work in them while on the taskforce. The taskforce disbands when it solves the problem. In semipermanent teams, members are assigned full-time to solve frequently occurring cross-functional problems. Typically, they report to a top executive (in a functional organization), to a general manager (in a divisional organization), or to a top management team (in a matrix organization). Team leaders may have influence power only when they have the expertise and interpersonal skill to ensure that decision making satisfies organizational requirements (to describe such leadership, Galbraith uses the term integrative manager). However, when influence power is insufficient to motivate team agreement, the organization may give the team leader budget control and thus decision-making authority (Galbraith calls this team leader a linking manger).

Sometimes organizations may wish to establish permanent teams to either work on special projects or work on solving ongoing cross functional problems. These small teams consist of employees drawn from the relevant functions. In effect, they become small divisions. The divisions typically report directly to the top of the organization and thus bypass the organizational hierarchy. When the project involves an idea for a new product, a successful team may evolve into a product division. When solving ongoing problems, teams may be mini-divisions or they may be a matrix overlay. For example, at Hallmark Cards teams are assigned to develop and make decisions about cards for a particular holiday. Team members are drawn from the functional areas and may work on a variety of card projects (e.g., Stewart, 1992).

The matrix overlay (not to be confused with a matrix organization) is a structural overlay that enhances the ability to solve complex cross-functional issues on an ongoing basis. As an overlay, the matrix enables members of one functional department to work as needed with other departments or to work full-time in other organizational units while retaining reporting relationships to the home department. Besides the Hallmark Card example, matrix overlays are common in large organizations. For example, HR professionals may work across the organization on issues relevant to a variety of functional managers, or they may work within a division and report to a divisional head as well as to corporate HR. Similar matrix overlays are common in other functional departments (e.g., information systems).

In summary, I described three basic structures and examined modifications to the functional structure. These modifications may be found in any organizational configuration. All three structures can be seen singularly or in combination in today's organizations. Examination of these structures should alert the reader to the fact that there is no best way to organize. The functional organization's focus on specialization ensures efficiency in operations. The divisional organization's focus on outcomes helps ensure effectiveness in attaining market goals. The matrix organization is a combination of functional and divisional forms, yet is qualitatively different from its parts. Its primary focus is survival. Although each of these three structures may be seen in three different organizations, it is common to see all three structures in organizational units of large and complex organizations. It is also increasingly common to see new variants of these structural configurations. Two variants are the customer-product structure and the network structure.

The *customer-product* structure (also called front-back structure; Galbraith, 1998b) is a complex, multidimensional hybrid. Like the matrix, the objective of this structure is to achieve simultaneously customer focus and responsiveness and product excellence and scale. Depending on how the company segments its markets, the front end focuses on customers, customer segments, channels, industries, or geographies. The back end focuses on products and technologies. This structure is being used by organizations whose products or services are bundled and have a very short life cycle; whose commercial *and* individual buyer segments are continuously demanding new and unique types of products or services; who have a great many competitors that can fill customer demand; and who find it impossible to get all activities aligned with and dedicated to one customer segment without losing market share to speedier innovations by competitors. Thus, the structure is intended to adapt to constant innovation and fast product or service obsolescence.

The *network* is a structure composed of independent, yet *interdependent* organizations. It is a structure *of* organizations. This structure is sometimes called an "unbundled corporation," a "broker corporation," and other names. As a structure of organizations it requires control and coordination of independent organizations, which individually are organized in ways discussed in this chapter. Instead of owning all of the necessary activities (from raw materials to contact with customers) that make up a business, the company or government agency managing the network contracts many of its activities to outside organizations. As a result, the networked organization is a network of independent companies, each doing what it does best (Galbraith, 1998a). Success depends on trust among partners (Williamson, 1975). Appendix A further discusses the network and its variants.

Research on Organizational Structures

Why do organizations structure their activities the way they do? There are a number of different answers to this question (see Miller, 1987). A broadly held view is that structure is the mechanism for implementing strategy.

More than 40 years ago, organizational scholar Chandler (1962) proposed that the organization's structure follows its strategy. Yet, the use of strategy as a determinant of structure is problematic. Because strategy is developed at three levels—corporate, business (which is also the corporate level in nondiversified firms), and function—it is not clear at what level the linkage to structure should be made. Furthermore, not all corporate strategies are relevant to organizational structure decisions. For example, how should a corporate R&D strategy affect the organization's authority structure? Does it matter if the R&D strategy is demand driven or supply driven? Sometimes a corporate R&D strategy may affect another function's strategy, such as, for example, HRM if the strategy involves retraining employees. In some cases, the relationship between strategy and organizational structure is clearer. If the organization's market strategy is to diversity into unrelated products or services, it is likely to move away from a functional structure to a divisional structure. However, knowing this fact doesn't tell the designer how to structure each division or the units within each division. The relationship between strategy and structure is more complex.

On the one hand, structure may follow strategy, and on the other hand, strategy may follow structure. In the former case, although strategy doesn't tell the organization which structure to implement, it tells it that structure is a tool it can manipulate to accomplish its goals. In the latter case, if the organization is wedded to a certain structure, then its strategy options will be constrained by its structure and thus structure will follow strategy.[2]

Today, there is general agreement that the organization is a system of interrelated parts (called functions, subsystems, units, or divisions), each of which operates in an external environment that varies in predictability and hence affects the conditions for internal decision making. The structural configuration adopted must therefore *fit* the environmental contingencies within each of the organization's units (Hall, 1962). It is also said that it must *fit* the technology used to transform inputs into outputs.

ENVIRONMENT

The term *environment* sounds straightforward, but there is considerable ambiguity as to its meaning. Some authors suggest it is "all phenomena that are external to and potentially or actually influence the population under study" (i.e., the organization; Hawley, 1968, p. 330). A few prominent researchers have been inconsistent in their use of the term and have included task uncertainty and internal organizational characteristics as part of their definition.[3] Others have suggested that complex contemporary organizations have no boundaries and therefore are part of the environment. Yet, corporations and most managers agree that there is an environment outside the organization that affects organizational decision making (e.g., Child & McGrath, 2001; Tosi, 1992).

The nature of the relationship between the environment and structure has received considerable scholarly attention. Some theorists suggest that the organization controls its environment (e.g., Pfeffer & Salancik,1978), whereas others suggest that the organization is controlled by it and therefore must adapt to environmental contingencies (e.g., McNeil, 1978; Perrow, 1979). Some indicate that the environment itself is not important—what is important are the sectors the organization selects to deal with (e.g., Starbuck, 1976).

Sociologists and administrative scientists have conducted a considerable amount of research in attempts to characterize the *dimensions* of organizational environments (e.g., Aldrich, 1979; Champagne, Neef, & Nagel, 1981; Dess & Beard, 1984; Lawrence & Lorsch, 1967; McCaffrey, 1982; Perrow, 1967). They also have described the *characteristics* of the environment, such as interdependencies of sectors (Emery & Trist, 1965; Terryberry, 1968), its richness with respect to resource availability and range of activities relevant to an organization's operations (Child, 1972), and predictability and rate of change in environmental sectors (e.g., Aldrich, 1979; Dess & Beard, 1984). As multinational structures evolve, researchers are proposing that "specific institutional systems defining each form of capitalism both enables [sic] and restrict the adaptation and development of organizational forms within individual nation states" (Lewin et al.,1999, p. 542).[4]

Management scholars generally agree that an organization's environment can be categorized into three levels: general, industry, and task. Within the voluminous literature on the environment, however, two concepts, task environment and environmental uncertainty, emerge as key in determining the "best fit" between the organization's structure and its environment.

Task Environment. The general and industry environments affect the organization's functioning in various ways; however, William R. Dill (1958) was the first organizational scholar to define sectors in the environment relevant to organizational decision making. Dill (1958) called these sectors the organization's task environment—that segment of the general and industry environment that has a direct effect on the firm's operations and thus its performance. The task environment is critical to strategic decision making and to analysis of the appropriateness of the organization's structure or that of its units. Normally, the sectors that make up the task environment are customers, competitors, regulatory agencies, sociopolitical groups (unions, special interest groups, nation states), suppliers (financial, material, human), and technological innovations. Sometimes, additional sectors may be considered, depending on their relevance to the organization's operations.

Environmental uncertainty refers to the degree to which the task environment affects decision making under conditions of certainty or uncertainty. Two variables are key: (1) homogeneity or heterogeneity of the task environment and (2) the stability or dynamism of the task environment.

Homogeneity or heterogeneity is a function of the number and variety of products or services offered by the organization and the diversity of geographic regions serviced. The task environment is relatively homogeneous when the organization offers a limited number of products or services and serves relatively undifferentiated geographic regions. This is because it has a limited set of customers, competitors, regulatory agencies, sociopolitical groups, suppliers, and technologies to deal with. It is heterogeneous when the organization offers a wide range of differentiated product or services in differentiated geographic regions and thus has to deal with a wide range of environmental sectors.

Stability or dynamism of the task environment refers to the frequency and speed of changes in its sectors and the ability of the organization to predict those changes ahead of their occurrence. If the organization has one or a limited set of related product or service offerings and it can predict environmental changes ahead of time, it functions in a relatively certain decision-making environment. If not, it functions in an uncertain decision-making environment. The organization's task environment can range from certain to hyperturbulent (as is the case in front-back organizations). Figure 15.4 shows the determinants of perceived environmental uncertainty.

Task Environment Sector	Certain Environment	Uncertain Environment
Customers	One type (e.g., preschool children) or limited types (e.g., preschool and K–8)	Many types (women, children, men, seniors, physically handicapped, culturally and/or geographically diverse)
Competitors	Few, or markets are regulated, or markets are open	Many competitors; markets are saturated
Government influence or regulation	Limited	Numerous and may be different for each product or service line and across geographic regions
Technology	Known	Innovations frequent or continuous
Suppliers	Few or can be managed	Many and/or difficult to manage
Sociopolitical groups	Limited influence	Multiple with varied influence
Economy (sometimes important)	Limited influence	Variable influence

Figure 15.4   Determinants of Perceived Environmental Uncertainty

Knowing the determinants of environmental uncertainty is relatively easy, but assessing their behavior is not. The process is subjective, and its accuracy is highly dependent on the cognitive bounds of the assessors (March & Simon, 1958). Operationally, a wide range of questions related to the behavior in each sector may be asked, such as economic and market trends that may affect customers, competitors, suppliers, or sociopolitical groups; technological advances and their applications; worldwide trends of importance to the business; and availability of needed material, financial, and human resources. Management must determine the content of the information relevant to each sector. As a guide, it is useful for management to ask about the areas of operations in which the organization or its units are most vulnerable (Cyert & March, 1963). Completion of a global index of perceived environmental uncertainty may also be useful. Rockmore (1992) developed such an index, which is shown in Appendix B.

TECHNOLOGY

This variable has been subject to much research and continues to be discussed as one determinant of structure of networked organizations (e.g., Child & McGrath, 2001). Yet, the different ways it has been conceptualized have confused rather than informed its relationship to the organizational structure. We can conceptualize technology relevant to this discussion in one of two ways: as a sector in the organization's external environment (as used by researchers studying network organizations) and as the process organizations use to change inputs into outputs. Technological revolutions, such as those associated with the information age or the introduction of new technologies, certainly change organizational functioning and for a time create decision-making uncertainty as well as task uncertainty. Two highly regarded organization theorists, Lawrence and Lorsch (1967), showed that organizational units operating in uncertain and dynamic technological environments exhibit departmental structures that are different from those of units operating in more certain and unchanging technological situations. Jay Galbraith (1973) specifically noted that the key variable in structural design is task uncertainty because it requires a greater amount of information to be processed among decision makers during task execution to achieve a given level of performance. Prominent sociologists (e.g., Dornbush & Scott, 1975) also pointed out that a variety of tasks performed in essence is an admission that the organization has to deal with multiple technologies and thus must structure its subunits according to the uncertainty of the task within the unit. Tasks high on clarity, predictability, and efficiency can be allocated by directive, and those low on these variables, by delegation. Dornbush and Scott make a distinction between mechanistic and organic organizational cultures. Other researchers reasoned that if the technology used to convert inputs into outputs affects the organization's control and coordination mechanisms, then technology determines the organization's structure. This idea was first proposed by Joan Woodward (1958). In her research with 100 companies in Great Britain, Woodward found that the production process was the most important single determinant of an organization's structure. This finding led to much sociological research attempting to find a relationship between technology and the organization's structure. To date, this research has produced inconsistent results.

It is clear to me that technology is not the determinant of the organization's vertical authority structure but is the determinant of its horizontal workflow structure. In the last 15 or so years, practicing HRM professionals have developed expertise in changing the organization's workflow structure. Management consultants Hammer and Champy (1993) discuss this structure in their book *Reengineering the Corporation*. Indeed, their definition of reengineering is "the fundamental rethinking and radical redesign of business processes to achieve dramatic improvements in critical, contemporary measures of performance, such as cost, quality, service, and speed" (p. 32).

In manufacturing, the technology used to transform inputs into outputs is called *flexible manufacturing*. Computers are used to automate and integrate manufacturing components to allow for mass customization. Using this technology alters the workflow structure within departments. There are fewer rules than in traditional manufacturing, decision making within the department is decentralized and team oriented, and communication is face to face and horizontal. In services, it may be necessary to get feedback from the person or object before choosing the tools or processes one should use to do the work. Thompson (1967) called this technology *intensive*.[5] One example of *intensive* technology is that used in the emergency room of a hospital. Here, doctors will first examine the patient and on the basis of feedback from the examination will decide which medical process to apply. Another example is that used by a building contractor who must first examine the land on which the building will sit before deciding how to apply its foundation.

Besides *intensive* technology Thompson described two other technology types he observed in society: (1) long linked, as in serial control by a machine, and (2) mediating, as in a technology that links material, people, and systems. Use of these technologies requires standardized ways of handling categories of inputs. For example, on an assembly line, the worker handles the line and material in a prescribed way. In mediating technology, categories of products or services are also handled in a standard way. For example, the post office links people across time and space. The cost of a "first class" postage stamp is standard for everyone in the country buying this stamp. Similarly, insurance companies group customers into risk categories, and the premium charged is a function of membership in a certain category.

Other technology theorists have proposed different schemes. One who bears mention is Charles Perrow (1967). He views the process of transforming inputs into outputs as a problem-solving process and defines four problem-solving technologies in terms of the "raw material" the organization manipulates. That raw material may be humans, a symbol, or an inanimate object. "People are raw materials in people-changing or people-processing organizations; symbols are materials in banks, advertising agencies and some research organization; and inanimate objects are manipulated in various production situations" (Perrow, 1967, p. 195). Figure 15.5 shows Perrow's technology classification.

Notice that Perrow views problem-solving requirements as a function of (a) the number of exceptional cases or unknowns the worker encounters when working with the raw materials and (b) the method or process the worker uses to solve problems encountered by those exceptional cases. For example, few exceptional cases are encountered when the object is inanimate, as these do not vary in their consistency or malleability over time. In contrast, many exceptions are encountered in human beings and their interactions or in less obvious cases of craft workers or scientists conducting nonprogrammed work. Similarly, the way individuals will solve the problems encountered by these exceptional cases can range from logical and analytical to use of intuition, inspiration, guesswork, or other similar nonstandardized procedures. Using these two dimensions, Perrow classifies problem-solving technologies as "routine," "nonroutine," "engineering," and "craft." Although Thompson's (1967) technology classifications are similar to Perrow's, they are not equivalent. For example, if we say that an emergency room uses

Number of Exceptional Cases Encountered

	Few	Many
Known Ways of Solving Problems	**Routine Technology** Tasks are programmed and few exceptions to standard ways of performing those tasks are encountered. When exceptions occur, problems are solved by following established standards and procedures.	**Engineering Technology** Tasks are variable, and new problems requiring solutions are frequently encountered. When problems occur, they can be solved by using known engineering standards and processes.
Unknown Ways of Solving Problems	**Craft Technology** Tasks are variable, but new problems requiring solutions are seldom encountered. When new problems occur, the ways of solving them may require use of intuition, experimentation, or discovery.	**Nonroutine Technology** Tasks are variable, and new problems requiring solutions are frequently encountered. When new problems occur, the ways of solving them may require use of intuition, experimentation, or discovery.

Figure 15.5 Perrow's Technology Classifications

Source: From *Organization Analysis,* 1st edition by Perrow, Charles. 1970. Reprinted with permission of Wadsworth, a division of Thomson Learning: www.thomsonrights.com. Fax 800 730–2215.

"intensive" technology in its work, what is the equivalent problem-solving technology in Perrow's classification? Is it routine, craft, engineering, or non-routine? In practice, it could be any one of Perrow's classifications, as it would depend on the needs of the particular patient in the emergency room. If we combine Thompson's and Perrow's classifications, we see that long-linked, mediating, and routine technologies all require the standardization of work processes, whereas intensive, craft, engineering, and nonroutine technologies all require allowing workers some control over the way they perform their work. In the latter group of technologies, academic consultants and profes-sionals in private consulting firms can help organizations decide how much discretion to permit workers. This is exactly what Hammer and Champy do in "reengineering." Through their defined process, the organization is able to determine how to transform its inputs into outputs by reengineering its workflow processes. For HRM, reengineering know-how is critical, as it affects the work lives of employees and thus affects the effectiveness of HRM policies and programs. As Hammer and Champy (1993) note, when many processes are reengineered a company may have to "redesign its job-rating (evaluation) schemes, compensation policies, career paths, recruitment and training programs, promotion policies—practically every management sys-tem . . . in order to support the new process designs" (p. 204). Hammer and Champy (1993) also note that reengineering efforts *sometimes* trigger changes in organizational structures.

The key word is "sometimes." Consistent with Hammer and Champy (1993), Thompson (1967) informed us that departmental interdepen-dence can be correlated with workflow structures. When work does not flow between departments (pooled interdependence), the organization can coordinate the work through the managerial authority structure. When the outputs from one department are inputs for another depart-ment, work can be coordinated by the managers of the two departments through face-to-face contact or by establishing a liaison role between the two departments. When departments are totally interdependent, in that work done in one department affects the work done in many departments, the workflow structure may require the use of cross-functional semiper-manent or permanent teams and matrices. If feasible, it may also be dealt with by decreasing performance through use of slack. However, if the organization has many unrelated products or services and its external environment also is dynamic and unpredictable, information bottlenecks in the authority structure may motivate the organization to consider changing its organizational structure in ways that will either decrease or increase the flow of information (Galbraith, 1973).

Implications for HRM

Research focused on finding out the reasons for the variability in organi-zational structures and their units has identified two important structures within the organization and the determinants of each. The label *organizational structure* has traditionally referred to the vertical authority structure. It appears that the organization's authority structure is a function of the certainty or uncertainty of decision making resulting from developments in the organization's or its units' task environments. The horizontal structure is a function of the process used to transform inputs into outputs (i.e., workflow) and the sum of information necessary to bring decision authority down to the point in the organization where the information originates (i.e., structural overlays). At times, the workflow structure correlates with the vertical authority structure because "task uncertainty" produced by changes in the technological sector of the environment also increases decision-making uncertainty for the organization's management. Nevertheless, the *horizontal structure* supports the *vertical authority structure* but does not supplant it. Figure 15.6 shows the relationships discussed or inferred from this chapter's discussion. This figure suggests that it is useful to view the organization and its processes as a system. Specifically, Figure 15.6 is a heuristic representation of relationships between uncertainty of decision making and predictability of events in the task environment, the inferred competitive environment, type of planning used, appropriate organization structure, and corresponding workflow technology.

Although I have not discussed the organization's competitive environment and type of planning used, these variables can be inferred from the current discussion. Although only slightly touched on by Galbraith, control over the workflow process is a function of employee (or group) skill levels. When workers control the way work is performed, the organization can delegate decision making to them, provided controls of goals and timetables for work completion are instituted. The glue that connects the vertical structure to the horizontal structure is the skill level of the employee or workgroup. In mechanistic organizations the proportions of employee skill categories differ from the proportions in organic organizations or their units. Those differences suggest that organizations employing higher skilled workers (so-called knowledge workers) will exhibit a greater degree of horizontal structure than organizations employing lower skilled workers. Figure 15.7 shows proportions of worker skill levels across major job categories in mechanistic and organic organizations. Despite this generalization, even in mechanistic organizations there are situations that require delegation of decision making to workgroups whose members are unskilled and whose work is routine. Here, the worker does not control the way work is performed. Rather, complete information about the way work is performed is contained within the group of employees who complete the total task or work process. In such situations, decisions on how to improve efficiency and quality of output can be delegated to the workgroup through use of quality circles and total-quality management methods. If linked appropriately to motivational HRM incentives, the use of quality circles and total-quality management processes can be instrumental in motivating worker interest in work and thus good citizenship behaviors.

Decision-Making Uncertainty and Task Environment	Organization's Competitive Environment	Type of Planning Used	Appropriate Organization Structure	Technology (workflow)
Certain—homogeneous, stable, predictable; events occur randomly	Organization controls market, which is either regulated or open	None, reacts to environmental demands; focus on internal efficiency	Functional	Generally routine but can occasionally vary
Certain, but events tend to cluster into "good" and "not so good" areas to pursue	Imperfect competition	Long range	Functional with structural overlays. Some delegation of decision making to individuals and groups	Routine with exceptions for craft, technical, engineering, nonroutine, personnel
Changeable	Saturated markets	Strategic at corporate level—may include scenario planning and short-term adaptive planning. Variable at the unit level	Divisional (can vary within divisions)	Variable across divisions
Turbulent (rapid and interrelated changes in sectors); surprises are the rule.	Turbulent—saturated markets	Turbulent—short-term adaptive planning	Turbulent—matrix or with matrix overlays	Turbulent—nonroutine
Hyperturbulent (very short product life cycles)	Hyperturbulent—emerging markets with many competitors	Hyperturbulent—continuous reinvention through planned obsolescence-new product introduction cycles	Hyperturbulent—matrix or may include several forms within the overall configuration	Hyperturbulent—variable Routine (for programmed work) Craft (for exceptions to programmed work) Engineering (for exceptions to programmed work) Nonroutine—for nonprogrammed work

Figure 15.6   Relationships Between Key Components of the Organizational System

Employee Category	Proportion in Mechanistic Organizations	Proportion in Organic Organizations
Managerial[a]	Moderate to high	Moderate to high
Professional	Low	High
Technical/craft	Moderate	High[b]
Clerical/semiskilled	High	Low
Unskilled	High	Low

[a]Proportion of managerial personnel are similar in both types of organizations but the reasons differ. In mechanistic organizations the proportion depends on the height of the hierarchy, as span of control is typically large. In organic organizations the span of control is smaller, as managers have a "facilitator" rather than a supervisory role. Also, many more managers are needed to manage projects and systems rather than people.

[b]Technicians are skilled and in high demand across industries. They were always considered important but in today's economy their attraction and retention is critical, and sophisticated selection systems are used. Between 1950 and 1994 the number of technicians increased 30% (triple the growth of the labor force; see Richman, 1994).

Figure 15.7   Employee Category Proportions in Mechanistic and Organic Organizations

The following propositions summarize the main implications of research on organizational structures for HRM:

Proposition 1: HRM executives and professionals should assess the fit between the organization structure and that of its units and the dynamism of the task environment in which the organization or unit operates before deciding on HRM policies, plans, and programs.

Proposition 2: The HRM function should be organized in such a way as to support the needs of the organization and its units in an efficient and effective manner.

Proposition 3: HRM policies, plans, and programs must match the requirements of the organizational structure in which HRM operates. As there is no one best way of organizing, there is no one best HRM practice.

Proposition 4: HRM activities must ensure that the workflow structures support the organization's information-processing and decision-making requirements and the nature of interdependencies within these structures.

Proposition 5: HRM activities should support the cultural requirements of workflow structures without unnecessarily sacrificing efficiency.

Each of the organizational structures this chapter discusses has important implications for HRM, as does the horizontal structure.

FUNCTIONAL ORGANIZATIONS OR FUNCTIONAL SUBUNITS OF ORGANIZATIONS

The functional structure is the most efficient form of organization and is effective in relatively stable and predictable task environments. Because of environmental certainty, the distribution channels for the organization's product or service are fairly well defined and standardized. The production system consists of activities that have narrow task scope and short time cycles (Tosi, 1999). Activities are preplanned and can be performed by use of standard operating procedures and other rules. Employees within the production system are not highly skilled. If decision making is brought to this level, it must reflect the information available within the workgroup rather than within individual workers. In this situation, work is generally structured because it is routine, but the workgroup has opportunities to make relevant input to management. If the organization employs craft and professional workers, the workflow structure should ensure that workers exercise discretion within budget constraints and goals and timetables for task completion. In this situation, the organizational structure remains formal but the horizontal structure is less formal. The degree of informality is likely to vary, depending on interdependencies required to accomplish work. The culture within the unit will also vary along with the degree of required interdependence. Complexity increases when the work requires cooperation among individuals in a team. Teamwork necessitates close examination of the technical composition of the team, the possible individual and group contributions to team outcomes, and the problem-solving technologies that will have to be used to achieve the team's outcomes. Examination of the competencies required for team performance goes beyond the analysis of a given job (who does what, why, how, and under what working conditions) to the analysis of the individuals on the team, the requirements of the work, and the fit between the composition of the team and the work. Such an analysis has implications for staffing, base compensation and pay raise criteria, performance evaluation criteria and standards, and the promotion readiness of individual team members. Management of HRM in horizontal team situations increases complexity for HRM but does not imply nonstandardization and flexibility in HRM practices. Rather, it implies developing policies, plans, and programs that maximize the effectiveness of the horizontal structure (i.e., workflow and structural overlays) and consistently reward effective outcomes, which must also be specified beforehand.

In functional organizations and functionally organized divisions, the main HRM responsibility is to improve the smooth running of the bureaucracy. It is in these organizations that traditional HRM practices are most effective. The closer HRM practices are to Max Weber's (1946) ideal bureaucracy and Henri Fayol's (1916/1949) principles of management, the greater the contribution HRM will make to its organization and to its employees. The major HRM task is to standardize programs and maintain consistent and fair treatment to all employee categories. The functional organization will run more smoothly when HRM policies and practices are clearly specified and performance is monitored with respect to organizationally desired behaviors such as compliance to work schedules, good citizenship, and the like. Adherence to HRM policies and procedures is necessary for efficient and effective HRM systems. Yet, it is equally important that HRM incorporate an "exceptions" policy whereby individuals and groups are rewarded for exceptional contributions to organizational goal achievement, even in situations where the established goals and rules are not followed or achieved. Functional structures may be present in nondiversified firms and in divisions of diversified firms. When observed in divisions, it is first important to determine whether the division's structure fits its task environment. If it does, the HRM systems should operate as they do in the functional organization.

DIVISIONAL ORGANIZATIONS

At the corporate level, divisional organizations increase the complexity of managing human resources in various ways. For example, the knowledge and skill requirements for jobs across divisions may not be comparable. This reduces the ability to transfer personnel across divisions, which may negatively affect the organization's pool of future corporate executives. This potential problem suggests the development of cross-divisional experiences for employees who make up the high-potential executive candidate pool. Some divisions may be unionized, others not. This raises the question of whether to provide the same HRM benefits to workers in unionized and non-unionized divisions. Divisions may operate in different stages of the product life cycle. Some may be start-ups, some may be expanding, others may focus on maintaining market or be in a state of decline, which means they will probably be operating in different task environments. Product life-cycle differences have one major implication for HRM, which is the development of flexible HRM programs. Although these cannot be specified in advance, some of the issues to address include development of managerial compensation schemes that fit the demands of the product life cycle and development of managerial promotion and transfer programs that consider the fit between the stage of the product life cycle and the potential candidate's breadth of business knowledge and skill as well as personal characteristics (e.g., open to experience). The pay form (proportion of base pay to incentives and type of incentive, market based or not) should be examined to ensure that it fits the stage of the product life cycle (e.g., Bergmann & Scarpello, 2001; Ellig, 1982). Product life cycles also have implications for training and development programs.

Besides matching HRM programs to the demands of each division, questions also have to be asked and answered about how to organize the HRM function. Should it be centralized or decentralized or some combination of the two approaches? How will the organization form affect internal efficiency and effectiveness of HRM? Will one form of organization increase corporate vulnerability to employee litigation suits more than another form? To answer these questions, the HRM function will have to conduct its own SWOT (internal strengths and weaknesses and external opportunities and threats) analysis and relate the outcome of this analysis to the needs of the diverse units it serves.

MATRIX ORGANIZATIONS

The matrix organization is a clear example of an organic structure. It is flexible vertically as well as horizontally. The key implications for HRM are nonstandardization and flexibility. Complexity of matrix organizations suggests the following:

1. All HRM policies and systems must be flexible to support the changing business objectives and its adaptive strategies.

2. Job descriptions cannot be specified precisely; however, technical competence in the relevant field and the personal characteristics related to the workflow structure are essential to specify.

3. Sophisticated selection tools must be developed to address both technical and personality characteristics needed to work effectively in fast-changing and unstructured environments.

4. Selection processes must be team based. Interviewers should be trained in effective group interview processes.

5. Individual performance evaluations must be conducted by all managers for whom the employee works. Although the 360-degree feedback process may be useful, it is likely that functional managers and divisional managers will focus on differing effectiveness criteria (e.g., quality of performance versus speed of performance). When this happens, processes for reconciliation of those differences must be established. Citizenship and team work performance issues must be evaluated as well.

6. Pay allocation decisions must take into consideration both the individual's contribution and contributions made by the individual's workgroups.

7. Knowledge and skill training must be provided on a continuing basis to update technical skills.

8. Organizational development activities should be ongoing to help manage complex technical, administrative, and interpersonal relationships that come with an organization in which work is often negotiated rather than assigned.

CUSTOMER-PRODUCT ORGANIZATION

Increasingly, HRM professionals must understand and work within this structure, as it is common in many information technology firms with software as well as hardware products. It is also seen, on occasion, in large food chains and other retail establishments. In this structure, HRM practices will include those used in mechanistic as well as in organic organizations. The key will be to select the practice that is appropriate (see Herbold, 2002). Galbraith (1998b) proposed the following four HRM implications:

1. Staffing of marketing jobs. Marketing must be placed in the front and back. Each requires different foci. In the front end, product marketing focuses on product features, positioning, pricing, and new product development.

2. Clarifying roles and responsibilities. Unlike the traditional matrix, in which roles are changeable and ambiguous, in this structure they must be clarified for the front and back end, otherwise the potential for conflict is great. Questions as to who will set prices, do forecasts, be responsible for inventory, and be designated as a profit center have to be answered. If both ends are profit centers, they can be managed as a matrix. This will establish a consistent set of targets for both sides to try to meet and for which both are accountable.

3. Managing conflict. The issue here is employee focus. The front end focuses on markets and wants unique things for its customers, and the back end focuses on product and wants scale and equal treatment of all customers. Structural overlays must be created to learn about customer and product needs to resolve issues in a timely fashion. Organizational development activities such as teambuilding and process consultation may be particularly relevant to help the two groups work together (see Scarpello et al., 1995). A tight linkage between the front and back ends must be established for key workflow processes. This will help manage conflict and clarify roles and responsibilities.

4. As in a matrix, HRM policies, plans, and programs may have to take on an adaptive orientation. In some industries (e.g., software development) there may also be a need to retain key personnel through new and innovative incentive schemes, including but not limited to ensuring a fun work culture.

NETWORK STRUCTURE

The main implication for HRM is that there are no new implications, apart from those already discussed. Within the network, HRM is handled by each independent organization. In some cases, it is handled by vendors.

Discussion and Conclusion

Much like the "Parable of the Spindle" (Porter, 1962), scholars from different disciplines and fields generally agree that organizational structure is a function of the external environment in which the organization operates. For networked organizations, it is also a function of interdependencies among the network partners (i.e., workflow interdependencies). For the most part, these interdependencies have little influence on HRM practice, as the goal of network structures is to "link" independent organization. Thus, each will have an independent structure, which will likely take the form of one discussed in this chapter or a configuration of structural forms discussed here.

This chapter's presentation does not explain all determinants of structure, such as the top manager's personality, the influence of family members in a small or large family-owned business, the influence of tradition, the influence of competitor structures, and the like. However, the chapter does explain two important determinants, dynamism of task environment and technology. This knowledge can help HRM increase its understanding of organizations and thus improve its efficiency and effectiveness.

I identified two types of structures, the vertical authority structure and the horizontal workflow structure. Some writers suggest that the authority structure is disappearing from organizational life. Others note that it is always present (e.g., Hirschhorn & Gilmore, 1992). However, the way traditional and contemporary managers exercise authority differs in predictable ways (e.g., Scarpello et al., 1995). Specifically, the values and ways of interpreting things that a group of people share and by so doing establish agreed-on standards or norms for behavior is called *culture*. Today's culture in the United States is egalitarian. This is one reason for the reduced emphasis on status in many organizations. Perhaps a more important reason is the need to empower employees in ways that bring new ideas and innovation into the work setting. This has reduced the use of top management directives as mechanisms of control and has led management to exercise control by more acceptable means such as goal and target setting and other unobtrusive means (see Simons, 1995). HRM involvement in culture change is one way for increasing unobtrusive controls. When managing cultural change, HRM should also implement incentives to maintain the desired change. Similarly, HRM has a large role in managing structural overlays and workflow processes to ensure efficient and effective results. To manage effectively, it is necessary to understand the underlying bases for effective decision making. For example, bringing decision making down to lower levels in the organization for the purpose of "unclogging" bottlenecks in the authority structure requires the assignment of clear roles and responsibilities to the new decision makers (see Rogers & Blenko, 2006). Other issues related to group behavior and group composition are also important for the structuring of overlays.

In summary, this chapter attempted to increase understanding of organizational structures. Effective and efficient HRM practice requires the *selective* use of HRM tools within a particular organizational structure. Indeed, the complexity of modern organizational life demands that HR executives, managers, and professionals possess not only business knowledge but also organizational knowledge and a *broader and deeper* set of HRM functional knowledge, skills, and tools than required in the recent past.

Notes

1. Some readers may suggest that today's knowledge workers are different as "new" organizations require the worker to focus on customization rather than codification. I do not share this view, as professional and craft employees have always focused on solving three types of problems: unique problems with known methods, known problems with unique methods, or unique problems with innovative methods. I recognize that there are situations in which the craft or professional employee may perform routine work (e.g., PhD chemist analyzing analytical properties). In these situations, the worker codifies. Similarly, programmers codify, and systems analyst customize and codify. Thus, knowledge workers have always existed in work organizations. Today's technologies, however, require more knowledge from a greater number of workers than in the past.

2. A firm may maintain a particular structure even when its not the appropriate structure. Some reasons include the owner's personality and desires, tradition, and the fact that competitors have the same structure. Any of these reasons may therefore constrain strategy.

3. Lawrence and Lorsch (1967) noted that in the plastics industry executives told them that the most uncertain aspect of their external environment was scientific knowledge (i.e., technology; p. 25). They measured "task uncertainty" within the research units. They also included *internal production characteristics* in their

definition of environment. They noted, "While what we call 'environment' is fairly self-evident as applied to research, use of this term in relation to production requires some explanation. Contrary to conventional usage, we have chosen to conceive of the physical machinery, the nonhuman aspect of production, as part of its environment" (p. 27).

4. These proposals seem to acknowledge the relevance of the sociopolitical environmental sector to internal decision-making conditions and hence, structure.

5. Thompson's notion of "intensive technology" is used by researchers in their study of "interdependent" global network organizations.

Appendix A

The purpose of the network is to make the core organization (company or government agency) more competitive and more flexible. Flexibility is gained through the use of partnerships to develop suppliers and distribution channels. Once the organization decides its role in the network, it needs to design processes for coordinating activities among its network partners. The same techniques of structural overlays as well as workflow structures used within one organization can be applied to manage the interdependence among the organizations in the network. The organization managing the network coordinates the activities of the independent contract organizations from a small headquarters (hub). The hub organization chooses which activities it will perform, own, and control. Typically, those activities are based on its purpose and perceived competitive advantage and may include activities for which there are few outside suppliers, such as activities that involve scale, that are central to the product's performance, that influence the brand, and that its customers find important (Galbraith, 1998b). Two examples of organizations that are hubs within their networks are Boeing and NASA. Boeing manages the systems-integration function for its aircraft, as well as customer relations, the manufacture of the cockpit, and much of the wing manufacturing. It subcontracts the rest of the work to specialists and low-cost assemblers around the world. In this manner, Boeing performs about 20% of the actual work but is strategically positioned to integrate its business in every aspect (Galbraith, 1998b). NASA is an organization whose boundaries are impossible to specify, from which came the notion of a boundaryless organization. Other examples of network organizations that tie together small manufacturers across the world but have no factories themselves are Nike and Benetton.

Further development of network organizations includes virtual corporations and economic webs:

Virtual corporations are continually evolving group of companies that unite temporarily to exploit specific opportunities and disband when objectives are met. In this arrangement, each independent company gives up some control to temporarily become part of a new organization.

Economic webs are clusters of corporations that cooperate around a technology or a set of customers. Although cooperating at one level, companies within the web continue to compete at other levels.

Network arrangements have several advantages for companies, the most important of which are (a) ability to compete in global markets more efficiently and effectively because of reduced transaction costs through time savings and (b) flexibility to shift strategy.

The key risk is potential loss of proprietary knowledge to partners who prove to be untrustworthy. There are also problems associated with difficulties in holding the network together and lack of total control.

Appendix B: Rockmore's (1992) Perceived Environmental Uncertainty Index

Perceived index of environmental uncertainty is the sum of uncertainty of each sector in the organization's task environment. Each sector's environmental uncertainty index is summed to produce the environmental uncertainty index for the organization or its unit.

The assessors to which the environmental uncertainty questionnaire is given are executives who are knowledgeable of the business strategies, relevant task environment sectors, changes in the sectors over a five-year period, and the importance of each sector to the organization's operations.

The environmental uncertainty index can be obtained by constructing a questionnaire consisting of three sections:

1. Specification of relevant environmental sectors (task environment).

2. Rating of change in each of the sectors over the past five-year period.

3. Rating of importance of each sector for developing or reevaluating the unit's business strategies over the past five-year period.

Each rating can be done using a 1–5 rating scale. For rating of change, the scale's anchors are 1 = no change, 2 = some change, 3 = moderate degree of change, 4 = a high degree of change, and 5 = a very high degree of change. For importance, the scale's anchors are 1 = not important, 2 = slightly important, 3 = moderately important, 4 = important, and 5 = very important.

Calculation of environmental uncertainty is as follows:

(a) Index of environmental uncertainty for each sector in the task environment = rate of change in sector over past 5 years × rating of sector's importance

(b) uncertainty of task environment = sum of sector environmental uncertainty scores

The questionnaire can be developed to assess future environmental uncertainty by changing "past five years" to "future five years". This may suggest whether or not a structural change is in order, and the direction of that change.

Source: Shown by permission of B. W. Rockmore (1992). *The relationship between business unit performance and pay plan design: An environmental perspective.* PhD dissertation, University of Georgia, Management Department.

References

Aldrich, H. E. (1979). *Organizations and environments.* Englewood Cliffs, NJ: Prentice Hall.

Bergmann, T. J., & Scarpello, V. G. (2001). *Compensation decision making* (4th ed.). Fort Worth, TX: Harcourt College Publishers.

Blau, P. M. (1970). A formal theory of differentiation in organizations. *American Sociological Review, 35,* 201–218.

Blau, P. M. (1972). Interdependence and hierarchy in organizations. *Social Science Research, 1,* 1–24.

Burns, T., & Stalker, G. M. (1961). *The management of innovation.* London: Tavistock.

Champagne, A., Neef, M., & Nagel, S. (1981). *Laws, organizations and judiciary.* In P. C. Nystrom and W. H. Starbuck (Eds.), *Handbook of organizational design* (pp. 187–209). New York: Oxford University Press.

Chandler, A. D., Jr. (1962). *Strategy and structure.* Cambridge, MA: MIT Press.

Child, J. (1972). Organization structure, environment, and performance: The role of strategic choice. *Sociology, 6,* 1–22.

Child, J., & McGrath, R. G. (2001). Organizations unfettered: Organizational form in an information intensive economy. *Academy of Management Journal, 44*(6), 1135–1148.

Cyert, R. M., & March, J. G. (1963). *A behavioral theory of the firm.* New York: Prentice Hall.

Davis, S. M., & Lawrence, P. R. (1977). *Matrix.* New York: Addison-Wesley.

Dess, G. G., & Beard, D. W. (1984). Dimensions of organizational task environment. *Administrative Science Quarterly, 29,* 52–73.

Dijksterhuis, M., Van Den Bosch, F. A. J., & Volberda, H. W. (1999). Where do new organizational forms come from? Management logics as a source of coevolution. *Organization Science, 10*(5), 569–582.

Dill, W. R. (1958). Environment as an influence on managerial autonomy. *Administrative Science Quarterly, 2*, 409–443.

Dornbush, S. M., & Scott, W. R. (1975). *Evaluation and exercise of authority.* New York: Basic Books.

Ellig, B. R. (1982). *Executive compensation: A total pay perspective.* New York: McGraw-Hill.

Emery, F. E., & Trist, E. L. (1965). The causal texture of organizational environments. *Human Relations, 18,* 21–32.

Fayol, H. (1949). *General and industrial management* (C. Storr, Trans.). London: Pitman. (Original work published 1916.)

Galbraith, J. R. (1973). *Designing complex organizations.* Reading, MA: Addison-Wesley.

Galbraith, J. R. (1998a). Designing the networked organization. In S. A. Mohrman, J. R. Galbraith, E. E. Lawler, III, & Associates (Eds.), *Tomorrow's organizations* (pp. 76–102). San Francisco: Jossey-Bass.

Galbraith, J. R. (1998b). Linking customers and products. In S. A. Mohrman, J. R. Galbraith, E. E. Lawler, III, & Associates (Eds.), *Tomorrow's organizations* (pp. 51–75). San Francisco: Jossey-Bass.

Goold, M., & Campbell, A. (2002, March). Do you have a well designed organization? *Harvard Business Review, 80*(3), 117–124.

Hall, R. H. (1962). Intraorganizational structural variation: Application of the bureaucratic model. *Administrative Science Quarterly, 7,* 295–308.

Hall, R. H. (1991). *Organizations: Structures, processes, and outcomes* (5th ed.). Englewood Cliffs, NJ: Prentice Hall.

Hall, R. H. (l999). *Organizations: Structures, processes, and outcomes* (7th ed.) Englewood Cliffs, NJ: Prentice Hall

Hammer, M., & Champy, J. (1993). *Reengineering the corporation.* New York: Harper Business.

Hawley, A. H. (1968). Human ecology. In D. L. Sills (Ed.), *International encyclopedia of social sciences* (p. 330). New York: Macmillan.

Herbold, R. (2002, January). Inside Microsoft: Balancing creativity and discipline. *Harvard Business Review, 80,* 73–79.

Hirschhorn, L., & Gilmore, T. (1992, May/June). The new boundaries of the "boundaryless" company. *Harvard Business Review, 70,* 104–115.

Lawrence, P. R., & Lorsch, J. W. (1967). *Organization and environment.* Cambridge, MA: MIT Press.

Lewin, A. Y., Long, C. P., & Carroll, T. N. (1999). The coevolution of new organizational forms. *Organization Science, 10*(5), 535–550.

Litwak, E. (1961). Models of organizations which permit conflict. *American Journal of Sociology, 76,* 177–184.

March, J. G., & Simon, H. A. (1958). *Organizations.* New York: Wiley.

McCaffrey, D. P. (1982). *OSHA and the politics of health regulation.* New York: Plenum.

McNeil, K. (1978). Understanding organizational power: Building on the Weberian legacy. *Administrative Science Quarterly, 25,* 65–90.

Miller, D. (1987). Genesis of configuration. *Academy of Management Review, 12*(4), 686–701.

Perrow, C. (1967). A framework for the comparative analysis of organizations. *American Sociological Review, 32,* 194–208.

Perrow, C. (1970). *Organizational analysis: A sociological view.* Belmont, CA: Wadsworth.

Perrow, C. (1979). *Complex organizations: A critical essay* (2nd ed.). Glenview, IL: Scott, Foresman.

Pfeffer, J., & Salancik, G. R. (1978). *The external control of organizations: A resource dependence perspective.* New York: Harper and Row.

Porter, E. H. (1962, May/June). The parable of the spindle. *Harvard Business Review, 40*(3), 58–66.

Richman, L. S. (1994, August 22). The new worker elite. *Fortune, 130,* 56–66.

Rockmore, B. W. (1992). The relationship between business unit performance and pay plan design: An environmental perspective. PhD dissertation, University of Georgia, Management Department.

Rogers, P., & Blenko, M. (2006). Who has the D? How clear decision roles enhance organizational performance. *Harvard Business Review, 84,* 53–61.

Scarpello, V. G., Ledvinka, J., & Bergmann, T. J. (1995). *Human resource management: Environments and functions* (2nd ed.). Mason, OH: South-Western College Publishing.

Simons, R. (1995, March/April). Control in the age of empowerment. *Harvard Business Review, 73,* 80–88.

Starbuck, W. H. (1976). Organizations and their environments. In M.D. Dunnette (Ed.), *Handbook of industrial and organizational psychology* (pp. 1069–1124). Chicago: Rand McNally.

Stewart, T. A. (1992, May 18). The search for the organization of tomorrow. *Fortune, 125,* 93–98.

Taylor, F. W. (1947). *Scientific management.* New York: Harper & Row. (Original work published 1911.)

Terryberry, S. (1968). The evolution of organizational environments. *Administrative Science Quarterly, 12,* 590–613.

Thompson, J. D. (1967). *Organizations in action.* New York: McGraw-Hill.

Tosi, H. L. (1992). *The environment/organization/person contingency model: A meso approach to the study of organizations.* Greenwich, CT: JAI Press.

Weber, M. (1946). Bureaucracy. In H. H. Gerth & C. W. Mills (Eds. and Trans.), *From Max Weber: Essays in sociology* (pp. 196–244). New York: Oxford University Press.

Williamson, O. (1975). *Markets and hierarchies: Analysis and antitrust implications.* New York: Free Press.

Woodward, J. (1958). *Management and technology.* London: HMSO.

SECTION 7

Stakeholder Views
of HRM Education

The three chapters in this section report on interview and other data gathered from HR executives, labor leaders, and an SHRM survey.

In Chapter 16, Shore, Lynch, and Dookeran report the results of a survey and interviews with HR executives about their views of the importance of formal HRM education for applicants they hire to fill professional HRM jobs. Although their interviews represented a small sample of HR executives, the sampled executives manage 652 HRM employees across 14 organizations in two states. Shore and colleagues provide numerous insights about the state of HRM in business organizations. They conclude that "HRM is atrophying and dying from disuse, misuse, and a lack of care" (p. 308). Explaining why they reach such a pessimistic conclusion, they make several recommendations for training HR professionals in business schools. The authors also challenge HR managers and HR academics to reawaken the HRM field.

In Chapter 17, Graham and McHugh used interviews, focus groups, and a written survey to gather the views of a number of national and local union leaders and unionized employees about their perception of current strengths and weaknesses of the HR professionals with whom they work. They also asked their subjects for recommendations about important HRM competencies. From those responses, they extracted implications for graduate HRM education.

In Chapter 18, Cohen describes the process universities use to develop curricula and the role of accreditation bodies in the core business school curricula. She also explains the role faculty in a specialized field play in the development of the curriculum for a college major or a concentration area. Given the potential variability in "major" requirements and the fact that a full complement of HRM courses cannot be taught at the under-graduate level, Cohen reports the results of a study SHRM conducted to explore which HRM topics or issues an undergraduate-degreed individual must understand to set a foundation for a long-term career in HRM and to be successful in an entry-level HRM job. SHRM's study also discovered that there may be a disconnect between what the practitioner needs to know and what students may be learning.

HR Executives' Views of HRM Education

16

Do Hiring Managers Really Care What Education HRM Applicants Have?

Lynn M. Shore

Patricia Lynch

Debra Dookeran

A s educators in the field of HRM, we believe in the value of HRM training for Master's students, but we wonder if the business community shares our perception. That is, does the business community view Master's-level HRM education as valuable, and in fact, do applicants with this type of training have a competitive advantage in the job market? Although much has been written about HRM education in the last 10 years (e.g., Adler & Lawler, 1999; Brockbank, Ulrich, & Beatty, 1999; Heneman, 1999; Kaufman, 1999; Langbert, 2005; Sincoff & Owen, 2004; Thacker, 2002; Wooten & Elden, 2001), there has been limited exploration of the perspectives of typical HR managers and executives regarding the adequacy of HRM education provided in business school settings. We consider this an important omission, as these are the individuals who are in positions to create policies that affect the hiring of students whom we train in the

AUTHOR'S NOTE: The authors wish to express their thanks to the HR executives who were so generous with their time and thoughts, making this chapter possible. Also, we wish to acknowledge Ted Shore for the helpful suggestions on earlier drafts of this chapter.

business school. Thus, the purpose of this chapter is to look specifically at HR executives' views of the relevance of Master's-level education in HRM in the business school setting. The questions we set out to address include the following: (1) Is there a gap between the knowledge, skills, abilities, and competencies that employers require of HR professionals and the HRM education and training that students receive in HRM Master's programs? (2) If there is a gap, what is its nature? (3) What are potential solutions for closing such a gap and how can HRM academics and practitioners work together to implement the identified solutions? (4) After summarizing the executives' perspectives, what reflections and suggestions can we provide for improving HRM education in the business school?

Methodology

In searching for the answers to these questions, we sought the help of HR managers and executives who we know through consulting or teaching experiences, or who have a connection with one of our respective schools. We administered a survey via e-mail to 14 HR managers and executives who agreed in advance to complete a questionnaire and subsequently to be interviewed. The purpose of the questionnaire was to learn about the backgrounds of the participants and their current employees and to identify core competencies (i.e., knowledge, skills, abilities) they seek when hiring or promoting candidates into HRM positions in their respective organizations. Appendix A contains the items in the questionnaire completed by the HR managers and executives, and Appendix B displays the interview questions that we asked the study participants. Our purpose in conducting the interviews was to allow the managers and executives to elaborate on some of their questionnaire responses to provide us with a more in-depth understanding of issues relevant to HRM education at the Master's level. Below, we include some quotes from the HR managers and executives that we consider especially informative as well as summaries of the themes that were apparent across the surveys and interviews.

The 14 HR executives represent many different types of organizations, and they have quite varied backgrounds. They have spent 21 years on average in the HRM field (with a range of 12–32 years), and they have held an average of five HRM positions during their careers. Ten of the participants (71%) have the title of HR director or vice president. Three participants work in the public sector, one works in a nonprofit organization, and 10 work in for-profit companies. Although all of the executives have college degrees, 10 out of the 14 executives (71%) also have graduate degrees: one MBA, one MBA and JD, one JD, one MPA, three Master's in HRM, one Master's in Communication, one PhD in Human Resource Development, and one PhD in Instructional Design.

The executives noted that very few of their employees who work in HRM have had formal HRM training in either their undergraduate or their graduate education. This fact is particularly striking because 28% of the HRM employees in the executives' firms hold supervisory, middle management, or upper management positions in their respective organizations. In examining the education levels of HRM employees with whom the executives worked, we found that 59% had bachelor's degrees on average (range, 25%–99% across the 14 organizations), and only 14% had Master's degrees on average (range, 0%–38% across the 14 organizations). Of the 14% of HRM employees with Master's degrees (consisting of 652 HRM employees across the 14 organizations), only five HRM employees had an MBA with an HRM major, two had MBAs (not HRM), 15 employees had an MS in HRM from a college of business, four had Master's degrees in HR from a college of education, and one had a Master's degree in I/O psychology. Thus, only 4% of those with Master's degrees had formal education in HRM. Although we don't have data on education levels of employees in these organizations who work outside of HRM for comparison purposes, we were surprised at the generally low levels of education (41% did not even have college degrees) in the HRM function, and also the few who had formal education in the field of HRM.

Findings

To better report our HR executives' views regarding the education and development of HR professionals, we have organized our discussion below into two major categories: (1) the role of the organizational context in influencing HR activities and (2) the core competencies for employees in HRM. The organizational context category includes both the general environment in which HR professionals work and the demands and challenges they face in their own organizational settings. The core competencies category addresses the executives' perceived gaps between the knowledge, skills, and abilities necessary for employees in HRM positions and the competencies their HRM employees actually possess.

ORGANIZATIONAL CONTEXT

To provide some context for the executives' responses, we asked the participants questions about how they define HRM, how much autonomy and power HR professionals in their respective organizations enjoy, and how they believe the field has changed over time. In general, the respondents seemed to find it challenging to define HRM as a field. Some described it in narrow operational terms (e.g., listing its important functional areas, explaining how HRM is structured in a given company, describing it as managing people or as attracting, motivating, and retaining people), whereas others painted a more strategic picture of HRM's role as pushing forward the organizational agenda. There was some distinction between the role HRM plays and the role the executives feel it should play. For example, many respondents believe that HR professionals should be strategic partners and have a seat at the strategic planning table; however, that scenario often does not occur. One person used an analogy to describe HRM's role, suggesting that even though it is the "heart" of the organization, when it comes to decision making "it is the tail, not the dog."

The answers to our question about how much autonomy HR professionals have in each respondent's organization to pursue their ideas and strategies indicate that although they generally have a fair degree of autonomy, often the answer depends on the individual(s) involved or the organizational culture. That is, the more credible the HR professional is within his or her organization, the more autonomy he or she enjoys. Regarding how much power HR professionals in the organization have to influence management decisions, responses indicate that such power is contingent on a variety of factors. For example, HR professionals who effectively make persuasive recommendations, who "know their stuff" and give viable options, who are viewed as credible by their clients, and whose top management supports the HRM area are viewed as having more power to influence management decisions than those professionals who lack these characteristics.

To get an idea of what the future holds for HR professionals, we asked the managers and executives about changes in the field of HRM in the last 10 years. All the respondents agreed that the field has changed significantly and has resulted in gains in credibility for HRM in their organizations. The two areas cited most frequently as being responsible for the changes were the proliferation in the number of employment-related laws and regulations and the increased amount of change and level of complexity that today's organizations face. Several respondents suggested that the former is responsible for the heightened level of respect for HRM in the workplace; others attributed the increased credibility of HRM to both the need for legal compliance and a rise in the level of professionalism of people in the field. A third reason given for the perceived increase in HRM's value is that changing labor market conditions (e.g., labor shortages, skill shortages, multiple generations of workers) mean that organizations need more help with workforce planning now than they did earlier. One study participant summed up the changes overall by saying that HRM has "gone from being administrator of the handbook and benefits to being a core member of the leadership team."

CORE COMPETENCIES

To assess the existence and nature of a gap between the knowledge, skills, and abilities (KSAs) and competencies that employers require of HR professionals and the HRM education and training that students receive in HRM Master's programs, we asked the managers and executives a series of questions about (a) the HRM and general business competencies they consider when hiring and promoting HR professionals and (b) their evaluations of the extent to which the HR employees with Master's degrees possess these competencies in their respective organizations. The question about the core HRM competencies for HR professionals fell into three general categories: HRM functional competencies, business competencies, and general competencies.

Desired Competencies. When asked which HRM functional competencies they look for when hiring, participants identified recruitment and selection (50%), labor and employee relations (43%), compensation (29%), and legal issues (4%). In addition, 14% reported that they seek HRM functional competencies that match the position, and 50% listed multiple competency areas or said they prefer an HR generalist who knows all functional areas. When asked which HRM functional areas they look for when promoting employees, the HR managers and executives said their criteria are very similar to those used for selection. Additional promotion criteria that some participants listed include a higher level of skills and stronger technical skills in the appropriate specialty area (e.g., compensation) than those required at the lower level, and good employee relations skills. Finally, several respondents noted that they consider general managerial skills as well as written and oral communication skills for promotion to HR manager positions.

Next we asked our managers and executives what business knowledge or skills they look for when hiring employees in HRM. They listed finance (50%), budgeting or accounting (36%), database management or IT systems (21%), and strategic thinking, reasoning, and problem solving (21%). Other business-related criteria listed include project management, knowledge of operations, a clear understanding of HRM and business measurement, and an understanding of HRM's role as a business partner. Responses regarding business knowledge and skills considered when making promotion decisions were quite similar to those used for hiring with a few exceptions. For example, 21% of the HR managers and executives seek general management skills or experience, and 14% listed awareness and sensitivity to organizational culture as an important characteristic. Other promotion criteria included knowledge of business operations, interpersonal skills, written and oral communication skills, and an internal knowledge of the organization. When asked what schools or HRM programs they favor when hiring "new" graduates, the majority of the participants stated no particular preference. In fact, most stated that they prefer to hire individuals who had worked in the HRM field, regardless of educational background.

A variety of other general business competencies, most of which are thought to be learned primarily through experience, were viewed as important by executives. These include leadership skills, strategic thinking, and proactive planning. Some of our executives suggested that HRM programs include workshops for students that focus on skill development in these "softer" areas, because they assumed these types of skills are rarely included in the HRM curriculum. For example, one executive commented that

> It is easier to hire someone who has consulting skills and teach them technical skills. The toughest thing is being able to think at a broad strategic level about how the function fits into the corporate structure; the role they need to play/are playing; the ability to change all those things; systems thinking; good conceptual thinking; the ability to conceive things abstractly and discern things which may not be obvious, and turn them into something practical.

When asked what new competencies HR professionals will need in the future, the respondents listed contracting skills, ability to obtain resources, ability to handle numbers and budgets, an understanding of the financial impact of HRM actions, an understanding of what motivates people, and negotiation skills.

Actual Competencies. The final focus of evaluating employee competencies is the assessment of current HR employees who have Master's degrees in HRM. Many of the respondents were not able to address these questions because their employees do not have such degrees. Of those who could answer, however, the majority indicated that they are very satisfied or extremely satisfied with both their employees' HRM competencies and their knowledge of HRM functional areas. On the other hand, they were not satisfied with their employees' general business knowledge. One respondent specified that her employees lacked knowledge of contracts and budgets; another stated that her employees' knowledge "could be better," especially in the areas of finance, financial reports, statistical knowledge, and general economics. When asked what skills their current HR professionals lack, the respondents identified the following: general business knowledge, an understanding of the organization's business needs, basic management skills (outside of HRM skills), good writing skills, ability to communicate their ideas effectively, ability to be persuasive, listening skills (one executive commented that HR people "tend to do a quick fix" instead of listening to what people are really saying), critical thinking, ability to take the complex and make it simple for their "customers," ability to multitask, strategic thinking, and organizational development skills. In short, the responses suggest that there is a sizable gap between the business and general competencies that the executives said are required of HR professionals in their organizations and those that their current HR employees with Master's degrees possess.

PERCEIVED GAPS IN MASTER'S-LEVEL HRM PROGRAMS

After asking the executives to identify the KSAs and competencies required of HR professionals and to assess the extent to which their own HR employees with Master's degrees meet those requirements, we asked some questions to determine the gaps that they perceive in HRM Master's-level education in general. Perhaps the most direct and telling statement was made by the executive who said, "There's a reason why the Operations Vice President is tapped as the HR Vice President: the HRM people can't solve business problems." To address the perceived gaps in HRM education, the executives offered various suggestions. First, they addressed the question of whether business schools are doing a good job of preparing HR professionals for the future. The overall theme of the answers was that there is too much theory and not enough practical knowledge and skills. For example, one respondent was concerned that graduates don't seem to have a "good sense" approach to business—i.e., they are unable to relate HRM to the business or to what is going on in the organization. Another suggested that the schools are doing a "reasonably good job within the parameters of academics. However, much of what is needed can be learned only on the job." Other "missing links" in HRM education, as perceived by the respondents, include the following: strategic approaches to HRM; exposure to handling conflict (viewed as an important omission because of the amount of conflict HR professional have to manage); a realistic picture of HRM's role in an organization (several participants emphasized that they have no use for people who want to enter the HRM field because they "like people"); ability to relate to the diversity of the workforce, particularly in terms of language and culture; the practical versus theoretical side of HRM; the business side of organizations; business strategy, economics, and statistics; real-life business scenarios; and measurement.

The executives' responses to the question of how business schools could better prepare students at the Master's level revealed a number of themes. One of the most frequently mentioned was the importance of practical experience. The key issue they raised was that educators should emphasize the application of classroom knowledge. Specifically, they suggested that academics consider (a) including case analyses, applied projects in organizations, and HR practitioner involvement (e.g., to review course content or as speakers) as part of the curriculum, and (b) hiring faculty with applied HRM experience. They also identified internship and practicum experiences as important learning tools.

It was no surprise that the respondents' list of KSAs and competencies that they believe should be part of a good HRM Master's-level curriculum reflect the perceived deficiencies listed above. This list includes interpersonal skills; persuasiveness; applied experience (i.e., internship); written and oral communication; understanding of the technical principles of

HRM (especially compensation and benefits because of the tremendous cost impact they have on organizations); the business side of organizations; how HRM fits into the business, and how it can help advance the organization's agenda; HRM metrics and accounting; business strategy; economics; statistics; leadership and critical thinking skills; conflict management; and finance (especially the ability to turn data into return on investment (ROI) and to talk in ROI and benchmarking terms).

One of the themes that was apparent in the interviews was that many managers view the Society for Human Resource Management (SHRM) as the major source of training and development for HRM functional knowledge and skills. The majority of managers viewed SHRM certification along with work experience in HRM as adequate for learning the functional aspects of the field. However, some of the participants commented on the inadequacy of SHRM and the American Society for Training and Development (ASTD) for higher level managers and executives in HRM.

> At one time, ASTD and SHRM were very fulfilling for me. But now, I have to prepare white papers for my ideas. I am in a more strategic role and these organizations are incredibly ineffective for me. It is too low level now . . . it's about learning through collaboration, storytelling about when things have gone wrong [and] when they have gone right.

Likewise, many of the HR managers argued for the importance of understanding the business or organization. A criticism of traditional HRM education was the emphasis on teaching HRM functional skills to the exclusion of business knowledge and skills. Below are some representative comments.

> It is important to understand what drives business decisions or have the ability to learn how a business functions. One disconnect of HR: great ideas but do not understand what's driving costs [and] constraints, and [who] values business processes. They must tailor what they say and do into the organizational context. I would prefer someone with a business and HR combination.

> Master's education programs are getting very specialized . . . being too narrowly focused is not good, need to encourage connectivity. HR needs to know HR, but also needs to know business—specifically, *your* business. HR professionals need to get out, walk around, check out new equipment, learn people's names. These things help if later you have to displace people—you know what they've been doing. You can't be isolated in an HR strategic tower; have to balance strategy with operations.

The HR managers also had concerns about traditional MBA education, which often does not include a required HRM course. They were concerned that this makes the value of HRM less apparent to many people in business.

> Most MBAs are in finance. They don't see HR as an integral part of strategy and planning. MBAs don't get the "soft" costs of labor vacancies, shortages (e.g., worker's compensation, replacement costs, lost productivity, training, etc.). They look at the bottom line only, while the "real" costs may be three times those numbers. ROI models are the biggest frustration. Finance people want to hear financial terms so HR professionals need to speak this language and use these models.

Analysis and Discussion

Our analysis of the executives' views reflects our own orientation to HRM graduate education. Specifically, we view HRM as having an interdisciplinary foundation, but as a distinct field with an identifiable knowledge and theory base that should define the education of HR academics and practitioners. In this section, we respond to the information shared by the executives about their employees and the practice of HRM in their organizations, as well as their perspectives on the field of HRM. As part of our discussion, we make a number of recommendations for academics and practitioners alike.

HRM AS A DISTINCT FIELD

One surprising result was the difficulty that the HR executives in this sample had in defining the field of HRM. Even when they did define it, their descriptions varied widely as noted. In retrospect, this point may be the cause of some of the other issues that we discuss below. Because of this confusion, we would like to begin our analysis by making the case for HRM as a distinct field.

Before we can make the case that HRM is a field unto itself we have to be clear about what it is and what it is not—e.g., it is *not* organizational behavior (OB) or the legal field or industrial and organizational psychology or management, although all those areas influence HRM. However, defining the field of HRM and drawing clear boundaries between it and each of the other related fields poses an immediate challenge to HR academics and practitioners.

As a starting point, we draw on the Academy of Management (AOM), the major professional organization for academics in the business discipline of management. Members of the AOM draw a clear distinction between HRM and OB, as demonstrated by the descriptions of each field on its Web site:

> The Human Resource Division is dedicated to a better understanding of how work organizations can perform more effectively by better management of their human resources. That is, we are interested in understanding, identifying, and improving the effectiveness of HR practices . . . in the various functions and activities carried out as part of HR and determining the optimal fit between these practices and organizational strategies, cultures, and performance. (AOM, 2006)

In contrast, the domain statement of the Organizational Behavior Division is "the study of individuals and groups within an organizational context, and the study of internal processes and practices as they affect individuals and groups" (AOM, 2006). Clearly, management scholars view HRM's domain as encompassing the functional aspects of HRM and how they advance organizational goals, and OB's focus domain as examining individual and group processes and behavior within organizations. The fact that HR executives do not see such distinctions challenges HR scholars to more clearly communicate, through multiple forums, the domain of the HRM field and the value of business education as a means of developing the competencies specified in the domain.

An important question is why the HRM discipline suffers from a lack of clarity. One reason for this turn of events is the relative supply of, and demand for, academics trained in functional HRM as compared with those trained in related areas such as OB. Professors in management departments who have not received training in HRM may have little understanding of the field and may assume that anyone trained in a behavioral science discipline, such as psychology or sociology, is qualified to teach HRM courses. Another reason for the confusion is the diversity of academic programs that label themselves as "HRM." Currently in programs across the U.S. there are different versions of professional HRM education, all subsumed under the HRM name (Langbert, 2005). These programs are presented through schools of business, industrial relations, psychology, and education. Each type of school has a different focus, and in turn, its graduates may have different strengths and weaknesses. Most importantly, many programs with HR labels do not train individuals across the entire HRM field, limiting the contributions that both academics and practitioners from these programs can offer organizations with complex human resource and business problems. This diversity in HRM programs contributes to confusion among managers in the field with regard to what HRM education has to offer their organizations.

What can we do? First, academics and practitioners must define the HRM field and its boundaries and develop programs that reflect this definition. Second, academics and practitioners must communicate that information clearly to the public. Partnerships between academics and practitioner professional associations such as SHRM, the ASTD, the Human Resource Planning Society, and WorldatWork could help to achieve this goal to the benefit of academics, practitioners, and ultimately to employees and organizations. Third, HR executives need to get involved in business schools, making clear the value of HRM-trained graduate students for their organizations. In short, they must create a demand for the courses and programs that will educate future HR employees in the areas that organizations require. Fourth, academics and practitioners should put pressure on so-called HRM programs (i.e., those who offer few or no HRM functional courses) either to overhaul those programs so that they do include the functional HRM areas or at least to define clearly what domains they do and do not represent. A consensus on standardized HRM training seems critical. It is necessary for leaders in the HRM field, both academic and practitioner, to agree on the major core content of qualified HRM programs in order to ensure consistency in the graduates they produce. This outcome will help to clarify for executives and prospective HR professionals the value of HRM Master's graduates to organizations.

CREATING "BUY-IN" FOR HRM MASTER'S DEGREE PROGRAMS

Before we leave this topic we would like to offer our own view of how HRM should be defined. We would like to see HRM perceived and operationalized as a recognized partner in an organization's leadership structure. The reason HRM exists is to help the organization achieve its goals, which means that it is concerned with every aspect of the business. One HR executive in our sample provided the following example of what such a vision would look like: if an HR manager asks a production manager what keeps her up at night and the response is, "I've got 10 defects per 100 items and I need to get it down to 1," the HR manager can help *if* that manager knows that this may at least partially be an HRM problem and is willing and able to explore a variety of alternatives to address it. Another executive reported that despite one applicant's relative lack of HRM experience, he hired her on the spot because she understood HRM's role in the organization. Specifically, in response to his question about why she wanted to get into HRM, the applicant replied that HRM is the only function that touches all areas of the business. In this response lies the key to the reawakening of HRM.

Another finding of our study that was quite thought-provoking was the low number of HR employees with college degrees, particularly advanced degrees. This implies that HRM remains one of the business areas in which lower levels of knowledge and fewer competencies are accepted than in other areas. On the basis of the conversations with the executives, there appear to be a number of reasons why they do not hire HRM-trained applicants for HRM jobs. One is that non-HRM-trained employees do a "good enough" job and either bring other skills to the table or are trainable, so they see no need to seek out HRM graduates. Another is a perception that HRM graduates don't add value, as demonstrated by comments that indicate that such individuals are focused too narrowly on HRM or they don't know the business of the organization and cannot or will not be open to framing business issues as HRM issues. As a point of departure, we recommend that greater emphasis on education for hiring and promoting people in HRM would have multiple benefits for organizations. Better educated HR employees are likely to have broader exposure to a variety of disciplines, as well as have greater knowledge and skill. More highly educated HR employees will have greater credibility in the organization. With low education requirements for its jobs, HRM is likely to continue to be viewed as an administrative function rather than as a strategic function.

A related concern is that students may not perceive HRM as a path to a successful business career, so in their graduate programs they do not specialize or concentrate in HRM. Although there are many successful business executives with HRM backgrounds, students seem to need more convincing that HRM is a worthy path to a successful business career. For example, compared to graduate HRM programs, MBA programs are marketed more aggressively as the path to success in the corporate world. Additionally, the financial, operations, and marketing backgrounds of the top chief executive officers may lead students to believe that these paths are the only valid means to the top of the corporate world. The regular appearance of HRM issues in the courts may also add to the perception of incompetence of HR professionals. This perception suggests that HRM program content must be more explicit about the impact HR professionals can make in organizations and engage students in mentoring relationships early in their programs.

We were struck by the small number of HR employees within executives' organizations who have advanced degrees in HRM. This may be due partially to the locations in which we conducted our interviews (Georgia and California). There are few MBA and MS programs in HRM in either state, and California has only *one* stand-alone industrial relations program. Because all of our HR managers recruit locally, they likely are used to hiring individuals without degrees in HRM. This suggests the importance of degree programs in HRM throughout all regions of the U.S. if the desire is to professionalize the field.

An alternative explanation for the low number of HRM degrees among employees in participants' organizations lies in the background and experience of the executives themselves. The lack of HRM education, in fact, reflects the career experience of many of our participants. Most of those individuals who had either MBAs or MS degrees in HRM worked in the field of HRM prior to obtaining those degrees. Thus, the graduate degrees likely were not for the purpose of working in HRM, but for moving into managerial positions. One unstated possibility is that some executives may believe that because they didn't need an HRM education, neither do their employees. Consciously or unconsciously, they are hiring those who are similar to themselves. On the other hand, one private-sector executive who started her career by working as a secretary with a high-school degree and ended up as a vice president of HR reported that she will recommend strongly that her successor be someone with HRM education and experience. Thus, we must ask whether there is a market for people with business degrees who specialize in functional HRM. Although we didn't investigate the market-related issues discussed in other chapters, those of us who teach HRM in business schools need to consider these issues.

Related to the above point, we were troubled by the executives' stated preference for hiring individuals who have worked in the HRM field regardless of their educational backgrounds. Such a preference is problematic for two reasons. First, on-the-job training necessarily involves trial and error, so one cannot assume that everything an individual has learned by this method is correct. Even if it is "correct," it may not be acceptable to the hiring organization. Second, the discussion above shows clearly that executives have very different ideas about how to define the field of HRM. Thus, there is no guarantee that their views are shared by individuals who were trained in other organizations. Far from having a competitive advantage, such candidates may have to be reeducated in some or all areas of HRM to fit the hiring organization's needs.

Finally, we noted an almost universal view that functional HRM could be learned through SHRM courses combined with on-the-job experience. For the reasons described below, we explain why we have a different view.

According to its mission statement, SHRM is "committed to advancing the human resource profession and the capabilities of all human resource professionals to ensure that HRM is an essential and effective partner in developing and executing organizational strategy" (SHRM, 2006). In order to do this, SHRM offers a variety of educational programs for HR practitioners from beginners through executives. Although information about the programs on SHRM's Web site indicates that some programs are taught or facilitated by academics, most instructors seem to be practitioners, some of whom have earned the SPHR certification. In spite of such a varied set of offerings, SHRM, although it has a major role in training HR professionals and adds value, cannot replace HRM education.

The primary reason for making the above statement is illustrated by examining the variety of activities that are included when training is viewed in its broadest sense—i.e., as incorporating all forms of planned learning experiences and activities whose purpose is to effect changes in performance and other behavior through the acquisition of new knowledge, skills, beliefs, values, and attitudes (Scarpello, Ledvinka, & Bergmann, 1995). Although training prepares people to work and helps increase their worth to their employer and to themselves (Bass & Vaughan, 1966), Scarpello et al. (1995)

note that the following activities should be included in personnel training: traditional training, education, vocational training, and management development. Traditional training, which generally takes the form of courses provided by an organization, is meant to promote the learning of specific, factual, and narrow-range content to facilitate or improve performance in the employee's current job (Campbell, Dunnette, Lawler, & Weick, 1970; Laird, 1983). Education, by contrast, is broader, providing experiences that improve employees' overall competence in a specific direction (Campbell et al., 1970; Laird, 1983). Vocational education falls between these two points, as its scope is broader than training yet narrower than education. It may include activities such as apprenticeships and occupational training (Scarpello et al., 1995). Finally, management development includes both education and training whose purpose is to improve managerial skills such as decision making (Campbell et al., 1970; Laird, 1983).

Education, which generally is associated with colleges and universities, is broad in scope and teaches competencies such as critical thinking and decision making. On the other hand, training, vocational training, and management development, which normally are provided by the organization, provide hands-on opportunities to apply the knowledge gained through education. Thus, each form of training has value for its specific area, and together the various forms complement one another. A problem occurs when people perceive these activities to be interchangeable, such that each activity provides comparable knowledge and skills. Especially in HRM, which is such an applied field, there is a need for HR professionals to have a deep understanding of both theory and the knowledge base of the field and how they can be applied to help organizations effectively manage human resource issues when faced with complex and challenging situations. We believe that a combination of education and traditional training, coupled with vocational training or management development, provides the optimal background for HR practitioners. For example, although SHRM teaches technical skills, education addresses the reasons why those techniques are used. SHRM's value lies in its ability to improve the skills of noneducated HR administrators, to provide coursework in areas missed by variable university programs, and as a continuing education forum for HR professionals aspiring to higher levels in the organization. An important limitation for the development of HR professionals is that SHRM does not provide the conceptual understanding that is the hallmark of university education. HR faculty who are on the cutting edge of theory and research development can provide this information in their classroom to HR students.

Another reason why SHRM cannot replace education is that unlike students in a Master's program at a university who either take a set of required HRM courses or select from a narrow list of HRM courses, attendees at SHRM conferences, seminars, and programs pick and choose the programs that they will attend. One problem with this approach is that individuals may overlook or ignore important topic areas. That is, in an

HRM Master's program, faculty and sometimes practitioners determine the courses that are important to an educated person who works in HRM. A "capstone" course that integrates the various functional areas or a final project that is designed to have students apply their cumulative knowledge is often required, encouraging an integrated view of the HRM field and its application to business problems. Thus, although SHRM programs may be sound educationally, individuals who take a series of SHRM courses still may lack comprehensive training in important areas. In addition, courses in an HRM Master's degree program generally are grounded in theory and a body of knowledge based on an accumulation of research evidence. Although practitioners complain about how "theoretical" university courses are, the fact is that good management practices have sound theoretical bases. Our recommendations here are that academics continue to teach the theory but also emphasize its application in the workplace so that practitioners recognize the value that theoretically sound practices bring to the organization. SHRM seems to be addressing some of the above issues. SHRM Academy, for example, offers a structure similar to that of a Master's degree program (i.e., topic areas are identified and the courses required to earn a certificate of completion must be selected from those areas), and the courses are taught by university faculty members.

Relying on the above distinctions among the types of HRM training available, it appears that Master's degree programs can offer content, scope, and structure that SHRM and on-the-job training cannot. However, education and training can complement one another. For example, the accounting field offers a certification that is similar in some ways to the HRM certifications, namely the Certified Public Accountant (CPA). Although people who sit for this exam often take CPA review classes, those training classes do not take the place of university accounting courses. Further, an accounting degree from an accredited university is required before an individual can take the CPA exam. This approach to certification is one that HR professionals should consider, as HR professionals would receive education and a degree in their field followed by specialized training to prepare for certification exams.

DEVELOPING THE "THINKING" PRACTITIONER IN MASTER'S PROGRAMS

Many of the managers questioned universities' ability to teach skills such as critical thinking and decision making. Both of these skills, which contribute to the ability to think strategically, can be developed through classroom and applied experiences. In the classroom, case analyses and field research projects are both methods that can help to develop strategic and analytical skills. Another suggestion is to introduce a series within a program that allows for deeper analysis and understanding of organizational problems, such as a content course followed by a required practice module. Outside the classroom, internships provide students with an opportunity to develop these skills. Not all Master's programs require an internship in their HRM programs, although the more innovative graduate HRM programs do have an internship or a field requirement. There certainly is a need for schools to partner more aggressively with organizations to place students in internships before they graduate so that they can obtain experience with HRM issues. Some schools have been more successful than others in partnering with organizations, although many need to work harder on this area. However, such skill development outside the classroom is time intensive, requiring the supervision of a professor with applied experience or a highly experienced HR practitioner who is educated in HRM. University programs that include internships for their graduate students are needed to provide faculty with sufficient resources to manage the programs, such as release time from their regular course loads.

According to our HR executives, flexibility in thinking and openness to experience are critical for a successful career in HRM. Many of the managers reflected on the importance of being open to learning new things and having a flexible approach to the work environment and the people in that environment. Many HRM graduate programs offer technical expertise in which they emphasize that there is a "right way" to carry out the HR profession. A common emphasis on "best practices" may suggest to students and professionals in HRM that there are correct solutions that cross situations. Academics need to consider whether our emphasis on technical expertise in functional HRM socializes our students into rigid approaches to solving organizational problems. Emphasizing realism in the classroom and providing forums for creative solutions to complex organizational problems are both important for HRM graduate training. This point is illustrated by a comment of one of the HR executives:

> The best HR people are ones who have done things not always HR-oriented . . . people who have spent time in the field with manufacturing. Understanding the business, not ivory tower. . . . Ineffective people are image focused, sit in the office. They make decisions in big boxes that impact people and that will fail. They are too far removed from people. They have no credibility because they lack information.

The latter point in the above quote about getting to know people at all levels has implications for both the education and socialization of HR students. First, through training in the scientific method and measurement, HR students can learn the value of information and data for understanding organizational problems. This is a skill set that is rare in many organizations, so it can provide a basis for improving the marketability of HR students. Second, HR students need to be trained in the area of change management, including an understanding of the roles of organizational design and human systems. All managers are involved in change management today, and HR graduates should have the skills to help managers realize both the importance of their employees for effective change and how HRM systems need to be aligned with the change process.

A common reason the executives gave for not hiring graduates of HRM Master's programs is that faculty lack "real world" HRM experience, so their courses emphasize theory over practice. Although we agree that there is some basis in fact for this perception, we believe it is an overgeneralization. It is true that at some universities, and research institutions in particular (i.e., universities that emphasize research over teaching), the application of research and theory to organizations is not as valued as publishing research in scholarly journals. However, most scholarly journals in HRM require authors to discuss the implications of their research for practice. Likewise, there are many HR faculty who have HRM knowledge, skills, and abilities that they obtained through work in the HRM field, through consulting opportunities, or through research projects in which the results were applied to organizational issues. These projects allow academics to gain practical HRM experience and provide the organizations with sound results and recommendations. Academics then bring this experience and knowledge into the classroom and pass it along to aspiring HR practitioners. All parties win in this type of arrangement. There are a number of well-known HR academics (e.g., Wayne Cascio, George Milkovich) who have achieved recognition by practitioners because of their applied expertise in the field. Still other academics have earned certifications in HRM such as the Professional in Human Resources (PHR) and the Senior Professional in Human Resources (SPHR), both of which require a certain amount of HRM experience before they are granted. Both designations require recertification every three years either by engaging in approved HRM professional development activities or by retaking the certification exam. Thus, academics must remain current in the HRM field in order to maintain their professional certifications.

With over 180,000 members worldwide, SHRM is the largest HRM professional organization in the world (SHRM, 2006). As of April, 2004, 1,082 of those members listed their job title as "academician." Although numerically the academic members are outweighed in this organization, their impact is not insignificant. For example, until SHRM's 2003 restructuring that did away with a committee system, most if not all of the committees had academic members. The Human Resource Certification Institute panels that write and review questions for the PHR and SPHR certification exams have a balance of academic and practitioner members. When SHRM solicits proposals for research projects, it insists that the results be disseminated in practitioner-oriented publications so that those in the HRM field can benefit from the application of theoretical concepts. The current Vice President of Knowledge in charge of the research activities at SHRM is a former HR professor.

One of the possible reasons why there are not more academics involved in applied HRM research is that research institutions do not reward faculty for disseminating practical knowledge. Schools may want to rethink their culture because of faculty shortages and a demand for graduates with practical HRM knowledge and skills. In fact, some schools have created "clinical" faculty positions for experienced practitioners who have teaching responsibilities but no research and publication requirements. Although this may be a positive step forward, the results of our admittedly unscientific sample suggest that HRM programs may want to approach such an alternative with caution. That is, if the HR executives hired in such "clinical" positions have not been trained in HRM, then we may be perpetuating the current situation.

Despite the involvement of academics in the application of HRM in organizations, much more remains to be done. First, there must be more communication between academics and practitioners. Each side needs the other to complement its respective strengths and offset the other's weaknesses. Second, the future of our field depends on both sides taking responsibility and being accountable to each other. For example, practitioners need to tell academics what their needs are, and academics must be responsive to those needs. Responsiveness includes designing and offering HRM courses that reflect current and future organizational requirements as well as making research results available in language that practitioners can understand and use. Practitioners must provide feedback about how well our graduate programs are meeting their needs for competent HR employees. Such feedback should be constructive, identifying specific deficiencies or highlights and suggesting how to improve our programs as the executives in our study have done. Practitioners also can provide opportunities to partner with academics so that both can benefit in the ways described above.

In order to increase the number of academics who have HRM experience, we challenge HR executives to help them gain such experience. Internships, consultancies, summer employment, and research opportunities offer the potential for a synergistic relationship that will benefit faculty, students, and employers in both the short run and the long run. Similarly, HR executives can help by joining the Academy of Management's HR Division and engaging in a dialogue about HRM research. As of April 2004, fewer than 10% of the division's 3,000 members are "executive" members (AOM, 2006). Although the Academy's mission is to support management-related scholarship, interaction with HR executives may help inform that scholarly work.

Conclusions

On the basis of the results of our study of how HR executives view HRM Master's-level education, we may conclude that HRM is atrophying and dying from disuse, misuse, and a lack of care. Although this statement seems harsh, let us review briefly what led us to make this statement.

We believe that many of the problems in HRM education at the Master's level identified by the HR executives are related to the confusion over how the HRM field is defined. When academics and practitioners don't ensure that the boundaries between HRM and other disciplines are defined clearly and communicated widely, we should not be surprised when people misuse or disuse HRM programs, concepts, and practices. MBA graduates who do not take HRM courses during their programs will be uninformed practitioners. The fact that many businesspeople are not educated about HRM's strategic importance should be a wake-up call to HR academics and practitioners alike.

In part, we can attribute the lack of care that contributes to the atrophy in our field to either an undersupply of HRM-educated PhDs, misinformation among many business school faculty as to the domain of the HRM profession, or expediency among hiring committees. For example, when schools cannot find, or do not take the time to find, faculty who are trained in functional HRM, they hire non-HRM-trained faculty members who cannot adequately educate students because they don't know the profession or understand it. Schools that fail to set and enforce standards, both for admission to HRM programs and for completing the course of graduate study in a manner consistent with the HRM profession, display a lack of caring for the field of HRM. On the practitioner side, it is much easier to take a few courses here and there than to take the time to complete a Master's-level program in HRM. This natural tendency for individuals to make choices that easily fit into a busy work and personal life needs to be offset by HR faculty and practitioners who are committed to setting and maintaining educational and professional standards.

To reverse the misuse and disuse of HRM, faculty need to develop strong relations with the business community so that we can stay informed about the challenges that organizations face. This will allow HR faculty to be better educators and advocates for Master's students. Likewise, HR professionals need to provide their perspectives and articulate their needs by serving on business school or department advisory boards and offering to speak to school groups. The misuse and disuse of HRM is reflected in the stories we see daily in the media about organizations that are paying huge settlements in overtime and discrimination cases. The resulting negative publicity is another outcome of a lack of knowledgeable HR practitioners. One can only hope that these cases will serve as a wake-up call to organizations that they need to care about HRM.

Building credibility, with both executives and employees, is viewed as one of the most valuable competencies an HR professional can possess. Many of the HR managers described gains and losses in credibility as dependent on changes in organizational leadership. Although this is an inevitable part of organizational life, we argue that the business school has an important role in contributing to the credibility of the HRM field generally, and the credibility of our graduates specifically. The field of HRM has knowledge and skill bases that are grounded in science and a strong history of practice. The unique role of HRM in organizations requires HR professionals to have both business training and specialized HRM training to be effective "players" in organizational decision making.

In addition to making the above recommendations for training HR professionals in colleges and schools of business, we have made suggestions for HR managers and for HR academics. HR managers are critically placed in organizations for upgrading the practice of HRM by hiring the best trained and most qualified individuals. HR managers would be wise to consider whether the individuals they hire and promote are as well trained as needed for effectiveness in the HRM roles they play. It is important for HR academics to examine our programs and to determine whether we are training practitioners to be effective in the types of roles and organizations that they will work in during their careers. It is especially critical to consider the development of competencies that cannot be trained easily either on the job or through courses offered by SHRM. Critical competencies that ensure the continued success of organizations that hire our business graduates in HRM will provide us with the best basis for marketing our graduates.

Although our research provides many insights into challenges faced by HR educators, we acknowledge that there are limitations to our study, including the use of a convenience sample, the involvement of executives located in Georgia and California, and a relatively small sample size. Likewise, we conducted qualitative interviews that allowed for some variability in interviewer's responses along with our own qualitative interpretations. Nonetheless, we found our results to be consistent with a study by Langbert (2005), which suggests the significance of our results. He found that executives in the New York City area emphasized that although they view an MS in HRM degree with emphasis in traditional HRM functional topics as excellent preparation for HR professionals, they also would like the students from these programs to obtain general business knowledge and interpersonal, change management, and technical skills.

Our discussions with executives led us to the conclusion that *now* is the time to revitalize the HRM field by taking it back from those who would distort it and dilute its strengths. We can teach and practice HRM in ways that highlight its strategic importance in organizations. We and our HR executives have provided many examples of how such revitalization could occur in Master's-level HRM programs. We challenge academics and practitioners alike to seize this opportunity to examine other aspects of HRM education and experience, to make suggestions for change, and to act on them. It is time for us to reawaken the HRM field.

The principal goal of education is to create men who are capable of doing new things, not simply of repeating what other generations have done—men who are creative, inventive and discoverers.

—Jean Piaget

Appendix A

1. How many years have you worked in the field of HR?

2. What is your educational background?

3. What roles/positions have you held in HR?
   In business?
   In other types of organizations?

4. What are the HR functions and departments in your organization?

5. How many HR employees work in your organization?

6. What percentage of HR employees do you currently employ that have Master's degrees?

7. What types of Master's degrees do they have? (please indicate percentages)
   a. % MBAs majoring in HR =
   b. % MBAs majoring in other fields (not HR) =
   c. % Master of Science in HR from a college of business =
   d. % Master's in HR from a college of education =
   e. % Master's in industrial/organizational psychology =
   f. % Master's in other areas of psychology =
   g. % Master's in a field unrelated to HR =

8. What percentage of HR employees do you currently employ that have undergraduate degrees?

9. How many HR professionals do you have at the following levels?
   Staff level =
   First-level supervisors =
   Middle management =
   Upper management =

10. What would you say are the most sought after *HR competencies* you look for when **hiring** Human Resource professionals/graduates? (e.g., compensation, benefits, selection, recruitment)

11. What would you say are the most sought after *HR competencies* you look for when **promoting** Human Resource professionals/ graduates? (e.g., compensation, benefits, selection, recruitment)

12. What would you say are the most sought after *business competencies* you look for when **hiring** Human Resource professionals/ graduates? (e.g., accounting, finance)

13. What would you say are the most sought after *business competencies* you look for when **promoting** Human Resource professionals/ graduates? (e.g., accounting, finance)

14. What would you say are the most sought after *competencies* you look for when **hiring** Human Resource professionals/graduates (e.g., critical thinking, project management, problem-solving skills)?

15. What would you say are the most sought after *competencies* you look for when **promoting** Human Resource professionals/graduates (e.g., critical thinking, project management, problem-solving skills)?

16. From which schools do you regularly recruit employees for HR positions?

Appendix B

1. How would you define human resource management, in general?

2. What do you define as the core HR competencies for an HR professional?

3. How satisfied are you with the HR competencies of your employees who have Masters' degrees in HR?

4. Would you include employee advocacy (i.e., looking out for the interests of workers) as one of the roles of the HR professional?

5. How satisfied are you with the general business knowledge of your employees who have Masters' degrees in HR?

6. How satisfied are you with the level of knowledge in HR functional areas of your employees who have Master's degrees in HR?

7. How could business schools better prepare students in the Master's level education programs (MS and MBA)?

8. For your HR employees, what kind of background experience and education are most strongly associated with success in your firm?

9. How much autonomy do HR professionals have to pursue their ideas and strategies in your organization?

10. How much power do HR professionals in your organization have to influence management decisions?

11. In your opinion, has the field of HR changed significantly over the last 10 years and in what ways?

12. Are business schools doing a good job of preparing HR professionals for these changes? Why or why not?

13. Do you outsource HR activities? If so approximately what percent? And which specific functions or activities do you outsource?

14. When you outsource HR functions, how do you choose the outsourcing firm? How successful have HR outsourcing experiences been?

15. In what ways has outsourcing changed the way you think about the HR professionals in your organization (e.g., the knowledge, skills, abilities, and competencies they need now versus those required before outsourcing)?

16. What would you say are the missing links in HR education today? In your opinion, what is not stressed enough? What is irrelevant?

17. What knowledge, skills, abilities and competencies do you think should be included in an effective Master's level curriculum for HR professionals?

18. At what level(s) do you think it is most useful (to future employers) to educate Master's level students interested in entering the HR field: entry, specialist, generalist, managerial? Operational versus strategic? Why?

19. Looking at your current HR professionals, what skills would you like them to have that they don't currently have?

20. Looking to the future, do you believe that HR professionals need new competencies and which ones would you suggest?

References

Academy of Management. (2006). Retrieved May 6, 2007, from http://www.aom.pace.edu

Adler, P. S., & Lawler, E. E., III. (1999). Who needs MBAs in HR? USC's strategic human resource management MBA concentration. *Human Resource Management, 38,* 125–130.

Bass, B. M., & Vaughan, J. A. (1966). *Training in industry: The management of learning.* Belmont, CA: Wadsworth.

Brockbank, W., Ulrich, D., & Beatty, R. W. (1999). HR professional development: Creating the future creators at the University of Michigan business school. *Human Resource Management, 38,* 111–118.

Campbell, J. P., Dunnette, M. D., Lawler, E. E., & Weick, K. E. (1970). *Managerial behavior, performance, and effectiveness.* New York: McGraw-Hill.

Heneman, R. L. (1999). Emphasizing analytical skills in HR graduate education: The Ohio State University MLHR program. *Human Resource Management, 38,* 131–134.

Laird, D. (1983). *Approaches to training and development.* Reading, MA: Addison-Wesley.

Langbert, M. (2005). The Master's degree in HRM: Midwife to a new profession? *Academy of Management Learning and Education, 4,* 434–450.

Kaufman, B. E. (1999). Evolution and current status of university HR programs. *Human Resource Management, 38,* 103–110.

Sincoff, M. S., & Owen, C. L. (2004). Content guidelines for an undergraduate human resources curriculum: Recommendations from human resources professionals. *Journal of Education for Business, 80,* 80–85.

Scarpello, V. G., Ledvinka, J., & Bergmann, T. (1995). *Human resource management* (2nd ed.). Cincinnati, OH: South-Western College Publishing.

Society for Human Resource Management. (2006). Retrieved May 6, 2007, from http://www.shrm.org

Thacker, R. A. (2002). Revising the HR curriculum: An academic/practitioner partnership. *Education & Training, 44,* 31–39.

Wooten, K. C., & Elden, M. (2001). Cogenerating a competency-based HRM degree: A model and some lessons from experience. *Journal of Management Education, 25,* 231–257.

Labor Stakeholder Views of HR Professionals 17

Implications for Graduate HR Education

Mary E. Graham

Patrick P. McHugh

The HRM profession and the roles of HR professionals in firms have changed dramatically over the last two decades. HR academics and HR professional organizations such as the Society for Human Resource Management advocate and describe enhanced strategic roles for HR professionals (e.g., Becker & Huselid, 1999; SHRM, 2004). Perhaps relatedly, and in response to competitive pressures, globalization, technological change, and other environmental factors, the outsourcing of HR tasks and jobs that are considered to be "noncore" has become a common phenomenon (Bureau of National Affairs, 2003). Thus, the knowledge, skills, abilities, and other qualifications needed by remaining in-house HR professionals differ substantially from before. Furthermore, the newly desired competencies of

AUTHOR'S NOTE: The authors would like to thank Nancy Dellamattera and Rick Welsh for helpful comments and suggestions on earlier drafts. The authors also thank Vida Scarpello, editor of this volume, for insightful feedback that greatly strengthened the final version.

strategic leadership and decision making contrast sharply with the view of HR as primarily a cost center with little responsibility for enhancing firm performance (Mohrman & Lawler, 1999; Truss, Gratton, Hope-Hailey, Stiles, & Zaleska, 2002).

There is some evidence that graduate programs in HRM recognize this important role shift in their curricula (SHRM, 2002). For example, the Master's of Human Resource Management Program at Rutgers University includes course requirements such as "Human Resource Strategy" and "HR Decision-Making" (SHRM, 2002). Moreover, executives, managers, and HR professionals themselves have informed the discussion regarding the competencies or individual knowledge, skills, and abilities HR professionals need (e.g., Becker, Huselid, & Ulrich, 2001). However, to our knowledge, there has been no consideration of another key stakeholder group—the workers who interact with HR professionals in firms—regarding the competencies that HR professionals need and by extension, regarding HR graduate program design.[1] Our purpose was to begin to understand the views and perspectives of workers, particularly those represented by unions, to augment the discussion on the needed competencies of HR professionals. We take the view that unionized contexts present special challenges and therefore require special competencies for HR professionals. In addition, unionized workers may view themselves as a collective more so than nonunionized workers, perhaps necessitating a management approach tailored to this perspective. Thus, in this chapter we focus on the graduate education of HR professionals, although our recommendations will likely have implications for undergraduate HR education. We make the assumption that the competencies can be taught, or at least enhanced for most students.

Through interviews, focus groups, and a written survey, we asked a number of labor union leaders and unionized workers to consider the current strengths and weaknesses of the HR professionals with whom they work. We also asked for their recommendations regarding important HR competencies. From those responses, we extracted implications for graduate HR education. Competencies are classified into three categories: (1) strategic competencies representing long-term, global approaches to managing people, (2) process competencies representing general business skills, and (3) functional competencies, which are the technical aspects of HR program design. Such an approach is consistent with other recent work on HR competencies (e.g., Adler & Lawler, 1999; Chapter 16 of this volume).

The chapter begins with a discussion of the importance of including organized labor's perspective when considering graduate program design. We follow with a discussion of the link between the competencies HR professionals need and HR graduate programs, including a look at HR competencies research. Next, we report our study design and findings, and we conclude with a number of suggestions for HR education at the graduate level.

Why Labor?

There are several reasons why employee and employee representatives' views enhance our understanding of the HR profession. First, it is possible that workers, regardless of union status, have a unique perspective on the competencies needed by the HR professionals with whom they interact. Similar to the potential value of subordinate appraisals in 360-degree appraisal, consideration of workers' views can help reach more valid conclusions. Second, unionized workers may view themselves as a collective rather than as individuals, thereby requiring HR professionals to master alternative approaches to relationship building and managerial decision making. Similarly, firms with organized workplaces or facing organizing drives may need HR professionals with a different skill mix than those in nonunion settings because of more formalized, transparent, and potentially more adversarial relationships between workers and management. Finally, unions' own strategies are affected by the knowledge and skills of the HR professional during organizing drives, collective bargaining, HR program experimentation, and day-to-day operations. For example, HR professionals trained in labor-management relations may more effectively engage in negotiation and grievance processes. Therefore, inclusion of the perspectives of workers and their representatives potentially yields valuable recommendations regarding the future of graduate HR education.

The union workers and other labor representatives with whom we spoke generally confirmed our view of the value of including their perspectives on the knowledge, skills, abilities, and other qualifications needed by HR professionals.

> Because there are a lot of experienced people . . . a lot of senior people [who] have seen how some HR's in the past have actually failed . . . maybe the new ones coming in could learn from someone else's mistakes. [Unionized Worker]

> I wish our [boss] could hear what we are saying in a way . . . I don't think they are even aware of what an HR person could do. [Unionized Worker]

> We offer a perspective if they want a well-rounded and full perspective . . . I'm sure that they would also like to be a stakeholder in conversations about how to make a better union leader as well . . . I think we can learn from each other absolutely. [National Labor Leader]

HR Education and HR Competencies

There is an inherent challenge in studying "HR education" because HR-related programs exist in a variety of units within universities, including schools or departments of business, industrial and organizational psychology, and industrial relations, and in industry-specific programs such as healthcare and public administration. Adding to this challenge is the fact that HR education not only facilitates the development and training of HR professionals, but also encompasses the development of general people management skills for those in a wide range of professions. This chapter focuses on the former—graduate programs designed for aspiring HR professionals. We believe that the implications of our findings will be relevant for most academic programs that serve this purpose. Additionally, the information in this chapter is relevant to practicing HR professionals within and outside unionized settings.

Recent trends in HR curricula include a more strategic perspective on HR activities to complement technical training in program design (e.g., compensation systems, selection methods), greater consideration of the integration of high-performance work practices to affect firm performance, and a lesser emphasis on traditional labor-management relations than in the past (Heneman, 1999; SHRM, 2002). At a glance, these changes appear consistent with the important competencies (i.e., individual knowledge, skills, and abilities) HR professionals need. Becker et al. (2001), in their review of existing competency studies and their own large-scale research, identify five competency domains: knowledge of the business, professional mastery of HR, change management, culture management, and personal credibility, with credibility ranked as the most important competency by HR professionals. SHRM certification tests for HR professionals focus on the technical mastery of HR activities such as employee and labor relations and compensation and benefits; however, the exams also emphasize strategic management, particularly for the senior-level certification (Weinberg, 2002).

In summary, the HR competencies reflected in academic curriculums, competency studies, and SHRM HR certification exam appear representative of the today's HR professionals need. However, one or more key competencies may have been overlooked because the views of all stakeholders, in this case employees and organized labor, have not been considered. In this preliminary examination of the issue, we talked with national union leaders, local labor leaders, and unionized workers.

Methodology

INTERVIEWS AND FOCUS-GROUP RESULTS

We conducted five individual interviews—two with national labor leaders and three with local labor leaders. At the national level, leaders' titles were International President and Strategic Resources Director. Both individuals held leadership positions in large international unions with more than

30,000 members. The local labor leaders' job titles were President of the Union Local (two interviewees) and Executive Board Member (one interviewee). Leaders are affiliated with the following unions: International Association of Machinists and Aerospace Workers, United Food and Commercial Workers Union, United Steelworkers of America, Association of Flight Attendants, Communication Workers of America, and the New York State United Teachers.

We also conducted two focus groups with workers; one group consisted of four elementary public school teachers, and the second group comprised eight production employees at a Fortune 500 manufacturing firm. All of the workers were members of one of the unions listed above. We asked the following questions:

1. How would you define human resource management, in general?

2. If we define core competency as a key area of skill and competence required to ensure the success of the organization (Milkovich & Newman, 2002, p. 152), what do you identify as the core competencies or skills for a human resources professional?

3. Looking at the current HRM professionals with whom you have recently dealt, what knowledge and skills would you like them to have that they don't currently have?

4. How much autonomy and power do HR professionals have to pursue their ideas and strategies in organizations?

5. Looking to the future, do you believe that HR professionals will need new competencies? Which competencies would you suggest?

The HR Domain. Almost all responses by interviewees and focus group participants to Question 1 pertained to the functional aspects of HRM, with employee relations and mediation and employee benefits administration mentioned most frequently. Labor leaders identified a greater variety of functional areas than did workers.

HR Competencies. In response to the remaining questions, study participants identified strategic, process, and functional HR competencies, and the competencies were spread fairly evenly across all three categories. With a couple of exceptions (i.e., opposition to globalization, support for egalitarianism), the competencies did not appear to be uniquely identified with organized labor. Table 17.1 reports all of the competencies mentioned by the interviewees and focus group participants, by competency category

Strategic HR competencies included strategic thinking, partnering with management, leadership, and change management. Process competencies included communication skills and problem-solving ability. The following quotes illustrate some of the process competencies.

Table 17.1 Important HR Competencies Identified by Labor Stakeholders

Strategic	Process	Functional
Change Management Skills	Communication Skills	Ability to Address Morale Problems
Ability to Motivate, Empower Workers	Credibility	Ability to Assist With Personal Problems
Committed Stakeholder of Firm	Egalitarianism	
	Ethics	Negotiation Skills
High-Performance Work System Development	Interpersonal Skills	Recruitment, Retention Skills
	Integrity	
Institutional Knowledge	Objectivity, Neutrality	Knowledge
Interest in Cooperative Relations	Opposition to Globalization	Benefits Law
		Complex Grievance Precedents
Knowledge of Industry, Business	Political Skills	
	Power and Awareness of Power	Labor Law
Knowledge of Profession		Labor Relations
Knowledge of Firm Goals, Mission	Problem-Solving Ability	Legal Knowledge by Sector
	Public Relations Skills	
Leadership	Relationship-Building Skills	National Union
Partnering With Management		Retirement and 401(k) Plans
	Respect, Care for People	
Results-Oriented		Union Contract
Understanding of Internal Firm Processes	Responsiveness	Union Governance
	Sincerity, Genuineness	
Understanding of the Union Environment	Supervisory Experience	
Visibility	Trustworthy, Fair, Honest	

Relationship-Building Skills: They don't get out of their office enough . . . it would give them a better understanding. [Local Leader]

Care/Concern for People: You have got to be able to treat the people . . . with some dignity, respect . . . treat them the way you would like to be treated yourself. [Worker]

Political Skills: They have to be able to get along politically within their own organization, because . . . there are competing interests . . . So they have to be able to operate internally and have their own power base so that they can be effective. [Local Leader]

The functional competencies identified included recruitment and retention, labor relations, employee relations, and employee benefits. The labor stakeholders did not discuss the full range of HR activities in their responses. Perhaps they did not observe the HR professionals conducting all of their responsibilities, or perhaps the HR professionals with whom they interacted were specialists rather than generalists. Not unexpectedly, responses heavily emphasized labor relations knowledge and skills; however, in unionized contexts, labor relations qualifications frequently encompass competencies in other functional areas such as compensation, working hours, and other terms and conditions of employment. Several examples illustrate that the labor stakeholders recognize the value and potential of functional HRM competencies:

> There is a certain technique in picking great people and retaining people. [Worker]

> That's something that we really lost here—we have no one . . . [who knows] our benefits package. [Worker]

> It's really understanding the dynamics of collective bargaining, sitting across the table and keeping the process moving. How to use certain levers to move it further without actually stalling it . . . being able to read and understand the people sitting across the table. [National Leader]

To get a sense of the relative importance of the competencies, we grouped similar competencies and counted the numbers of times they were mentioned in the interview and focus group transcripts. Table 17.2 reports competencies that were mentioned most frequently by a particular group (i.e., workers, local leaders, national leaders).

Table 17.2   Most Frequently Identified Competency Areas, by Stakeholder Group

Unionized Workers (n = 12)	Local Labor Leaders (n = 3)	National Labor Leaders (n = 2)
Knowledge of Union Contract and Labor Relations	Knowledge of Unions and Labor Relations	Negotiations and Collective Bargaining Skills
Communications, Interpersonal Skills	Communications, Interpersonal Skills	Communications, Interpersonal Skills
Credibility/Integrity	Credibility/Integrity	Knowledge of the Business
Recruitment and Retention Skills	Responsive and Results-Oriented	Strategic HR Skills (e.g., employee motivation, high-performance work system design)

There was substantial overlap in the most frequently mentioned competencies across the labor stakeholder groups. All three identified communications/interpersonal skills as a key competency for HR professionals. Sample quotes include the following:

> I think you shouldn't always be afraid that you could get yelled at [by the HR professional]. [Worker]

> Even though we had heated battles there was just this ability to communicate and there was a mutual respect. [National Leader]

Similarly, each labor stakeholder group identified specific or general knowledge of unions, union contracts, labor relations, or negotiations and bargaining. In fact, labor relations competencies were mentioned most frequently across all groups.

Two of the groups—unionized workers and local labor leaders—identified credibility/integrity as an important competency for HR professionals. For example,

> When last year I was still [deciding] whether to stay or go, he was very complimentary, but . . . general compliments . . . How do you know that I'm such a good [employee]—how do you know that? Never seen me [perform job duties], never spoken to me about my [job duties] . . . I didn't feel like I wanted to hear it from him because it didn't mean anything coming from him. [Worker]

Competencies that only one group or another emphasized appeared to correspond to the particular roles of the three labor stakeholder groups. Only the workers identified recruitment and retention skills as among the most important competencies, and local leaders alone emphasized the importance of responsiveness and results-oriented HR professionals. National labor leaders uniquely identified strategic HR skills such as high-performance work system design.

Constraints to HR Competency Application. Unfortunately, the development of important competencies may not be enough to enhance the effectiveness of the HR professional in some firms because of organizational constraints. The consensus of the focus groups was that their HR professionals had little power and autonomy in making major decisions such as grievance handling, negotiations, or addressing significant HR problems, but that they had more authority over minor decisions. With the exception of one local labor leader who thought that HR professionals had "some" power and autonomy, the labor leaders we interviewed concurred that HR professionals have little job discretion. Personal characteristics of the HR professionals themselves may exacerbate this problem. Observations from each of the local labor leaders illustrate these points:

> How much they will be allowed to run with the ball, well, we'll probably have to see how secure [top management] is.

[It] doesn't matter how knowledgeable you are if your stand is to do whatever operating management wants.

[HR professional] knows his boundaries.

There's a lack of authority to settle the grievance.

In short, it may be necessary to address these organizational and personal constraints on HR professionals in developing suggested sets of competencies for them.

SURVEY RESULTS

Focus-group participants and labor leaders also completed a survey regarding the competencies possessed by the HR professionals in their firms. We created 13 competency descriptions based on representative items for important HR competencies identified by Becker et al. (2001). The survey items were modified on the basis of suggestions from a Fortune 500 labor relations professional. Twelve focus-group members and three local labor leaders responded to the final set of items using a 1 (strongly disagree) to 5 (strongly agree) scale. Table 17.3 presents the means (M) and standard deviations (SD) for the 13 preestablished HR competencies.

Table 17.3   Ratings of HR Professionals' Competencies

Competency	Employees Mean (SD) (n = 12)	Local Leaders Mean (SD) (n = 3)
Has personal credibility	3.25 (0.97)	4.00 (0.82)
Has a track record of success	3.00 (0.85)	3.17 (0.58)
Has earned the trust of workers	2.75 (1.14)	2.92 (0.83)
Is able to manage change	3.00 (1.04)	3.50 (0.58)
Has ideas for the future	3.00 (0.74)	3.33 (0.47)
Takes a proactive role in bringing about change	2.75 (0.87)	3.08 (0.83)
Is able to manage firm culture	2.75 (1.14)	3.00 (1.00)
Shares knowledge across organizational boundaries	2.67 (1.15)	3.75 (0.50)
Encourages management to practice what they preach	2.08 (0.90)	3.58 (0.83)
Delivers effective human resource management programs	2.50 (1.00)	3.33 (0.58)
Expresses effective verbal communication	2.83 (1.40)	3.25 (0.96)
Sends clear and consistent messages	2.50 (1.31)	2.50 (1.00)
Understands the business in which our firm operates	2.75 (1.36)	3.83 (0.58)

Note: Responses were on a 5-point scale ranging from 1 = strongly disagree to 5 = strongly agree.

Overall, HR professionals do not appear to be performing well on these competencies in the eyes of the workers we surveyed. The highest score pertained to personal credibility, which has been identified as one of the most important competencies for an HR professional to possess (Becker et al., 2001). However, no average item response from employees reached a score of 4 (i.e., somewhat agree), and low scores on the "delivers effective human resource management programs" (M = 2.50, SD = 1.00) and "sends clear and consistent messages" (M = 2.50, SD = 1.31) are somewhat troubling given their centrality to a successful HR function.

In general, local labor leaders evaluate HR professionals' competencies somewhat more favorably than the employees. Local labor leaders evaluate HR professionals relatively highly on personal credibility and also recognize HR professionals' degree of understanding of the business of their firms. Like employees, however, local leaders do not perceive that HR professionals are sending clear and consistent messages (M = 2.50, SD = 1.00), nor do they evaluate them particularly favorably on HR program delivery (M = 3.33, SD = 0.58).

Given our unique opportunity to examine the views of organized labor, we took the opportunity to ask study participants to evaluate HR professionals on preestablished labor relations competencies as well. We created 11 labor relations competency descriptions based on representative labor relations content from HR textbooks. The survey items were modified on the basis of suggestions from a Fortune 500 labor relations professional, and used a 1 (strongly disagree) to 5 (strongly agree) scale. Table 17.4 presents the means and standard deviations for the labor relations competencies.

Table 17.4 Ratings of HR Professionals' Labor Relations Competencies

"The HR professionals with whom you interact have the knowledge and skills to . . ."	Employees Mean (SD) (n = 12)	Local Leaders Mean (SD) (n = 3)
Participate in the collective bargaining process	3.00 (0.85)	4.42 (0.69)
Conduct negotiations with union representatives	3.17 (1.11)	3.92 (0.16)
Facilitate cooperative labor-management relationships	3.27 (1.01)	3.92 (0.96)
Achieve labor-management cooperation	2.82 (1.17)	3.75 (0.96)
Facilitate meaningful worker input and participation	2.75 (1.29)	3.75 (1.50)
Incorporate worker suggestions into firm operations	2.58 (1.16)	3.75 (1.26)
Deal with workers fairly and legally during a union organizing drive	2.64 (0.92)	2.67 (1.53)
Follow labor laws during a union organizing campaign	2.82 (0.98)	2.67 (1.53)
Follow labor laws, in general	3.33 (0.89)	4.33 (0.47)
Deal with day-to-day disputes at the workplace	2.83 (1.11)	4.42 (0.50)
Manage the grievance process	3.08 (1.08)	3.75 (0.50)

Note: Responses were on a 5-point scale ranging from 1 = strongly disagree to 5 = strongly agree.

Again, employees tended to evaluate the HR professionals relatively unfavorably overall regarding labor relations competencies. Particular problem areas seemed to be the knowledge and skills necessary to facilitate worker participation and input, dealing with workers fairly and legally during a union organizing drive, and dealing with day-to-day disputes at the workplace. Local labor leaders concurred, indicating that labor relations competencies pertaining to management conduct during organizing drives were lacking. However, the leaders evaluated HR professionals quite favorably on their knowledge and skills used in the collective bargaining process, following labor laws in general, and in dealing with day-to-day disputes. There were large gaps in the views of employees versus local labor leaders (i.e., employees rated HR professionals more unfavorably) on collective bargaining competencies, skill related to incorporating worker input and suggestions, following labor laws in general, and daily dispute handling. This may be due to the small sample size or the nonrandom nature of the survey; however, these initial results raise interesting questions.

Implications for HR Education

The information provided by the labor stakeholders with whom we spoke has implications for the design of graduate programs in human resource management. HR professionals with labor relations responsibilities need labor relations competencies and advanced competencies in several areas, one route to which is graduate HR education. Most of the competencies offered by labor stakeholders overlapped competencies considered important by other stakeholders (Becker et al., 2001; Heneman, 1999). Our initial study results indicate that HR professionals have not yet mastered these important competencies.

Our inquiry also generated several new suggestions for HR graduate education, highlighting the importance of consulting the views of workers in developing competency inventories for HR professionals. For one, the labor stakeholders do not appear to emphasize analytical skills to the degree that management does (Heneman, 1999). The worker perspective also generated suggestions in the areas of credibility, labor relations, interpersonal skills, and recruitment and retention, as detailed next. Not surprisingly, these findings revolve around the process and functional competency categories, rather than those at the strategic level.

Autonomy, Power, and Credibility. While conducting the focus groups we became aware of the influence of structural constraints that hinder HR professionals in their use of the important competencies they have developed (Legge, 1978; Truss et al., 2002). We suggest that graduate programs in HR prepare students to operate professionally within potentially challenging contexts in which HR has little authority or autonomy. HR competency use, particularly in the strategic category, may require creativity, communication, change management, and political skills aimed at advancing the HR profession and HR professionals' own credibility in organizations. Although there is undoubtedly some content in this regard incorporated into current HR courses, we feel there is a need for a more concerted emphasis on advancing the HR profession and the status of HR professionals in order to enhance the efficacy of the efforts of HR professionals.

On a related note, there is a clear need for graduate programs in HR to address the development of the credibility/integrity competency. Becker and colleagues (2001) outline three dimensions of the personal credibility competency: (1) living the firm's values and keeping the culture, (2) relationships with colleagues are founded on trust, and (3) being an important player in the business (see also Ulrich & Beatty, 2001). In our results, we observed comments from workers and labor leaders that fell into all three dimensions of this definition; however, from workers' perspectives, credibility may rest more heavily on the degree to which they trust their HR professionals and the degree of perceived commitment on the part of the HR professional to them. This is not to suggest that management interests and employee interests will always coincide, yet it is the responsibility of the HR professional to manage and balance stakeholder relationships, including those with workers (Scarpello & Ledvinka, 1988; Kochan, 1997).

Graduate programs in HR can begin to develop the credibility competency in students by emphasizing its importance to professional success. The competency of responsiveness/results-oriented emphasized by the local labor leaders (presented in Table 17.2) may be a good starting point as well, as this potential correlate of credibility appears fairly teachable. On the other hand, the credibility competency may present the largest challenge to graduate HR education because it may comprise multiple competencies (e.g., HR program delivery and interpersonal skills). In addition, individual personality characteristics (e.g., conscientiousness) may be important determinants, suggesting that the selection of HR students and professionals might be especially important here. Moreover, an HR professional's credibility may be affected by organizational contexts such as the centralization of HRM decisions or the status of the human resource function within particular firms, to a greater degree than other competencies.

> Quite frankly most of [the HR professionals] are not allowed to speak; the corporate guys—sometimes it is actually amusing for us to watch, as painful as it is . . . to sit across from [HR] people that we deal with on a daily basis that we know are strong, good, straightforward people and they are not allowed to speak. [Local Leader]

It is clear that changes to graduate education are only a partial solution to the credibility, autonomy, and power problems faced by HR professionals.

By definition, professions are "high status, knowledge-based occupations" characterized by autonomy and authority over clients and subordinate occupational groups, among other features (Hodson & Sullivan, 2002, p. 282). Therefore, the success of improvements to graduate HR education rests at least partially on the general development of the HR profession. Thus, we recommend a three-pronged approach to addressing these issues: (1) national professional organizations such as SHRM should continue to advocate for the HR profession's strategic and technical capabilities; (2) top management should begin vesting strategic and program responsibility in their HR professionals at all levels so that HR can add value to the firm more readily and enhance its credibility in the eyes of employees; and (3) graduate HR education should emphasize competencies in the areas of politics, communications, and change management that will assist HR professionals in carrying out their professional duties.

Labor Relations Content. A second suggestion for graduate HR education is that curricula for HR professionals maintain or enhance their labor relations content. Although this may seem counterintuitive given the decline in unionization rates in the U.S., knowledge about labor history, unions, collective bargaining, and negotiation and dispute resolution represent essential skills and knowledge for the HR professional seeking cooperative and productive partnerships with workers in organized and unorganized settings (Foulkes, 1980; Shore et al., 2008). Such understandings form the basis for recognizing and dealing with the work-related concerns of all employees and for developing fair processes for managing any workforce. Reinforcing this point is evidence that a majority of workers desire some form of representation in the workplace (Freeman & Rogers, 1999). For multinationals, labor relations content may be especially critical given the globalization of business and the fact that unionization rates in other countries are typically much higher than in the U.S. (Dowling, Welch, & Schuler, 1999).

Within unionized settings, labor relations competencies are critical, as suggested by the following statements:

> They have got to be able to do both [labor relations and human resources] . . . We've had managers over there in human resources that could only do one or the other. [Local Leader]

> You have got to know the union contract. [Worker]

> The history of the union and so you have a little more sense of why it is so near and dear to a whole bunch of people . . . so when we are arguing about things you know that it might seem emotional or unfounded . . . It is real important to a lot of people. A lot of people say they will die union. [Local Leader]

Communications and Interpersonal Skills. We also suggest that HR educators focus on communication skills, in theory and practice. The communication skills that all three labor stakeholder groups identified reinforce the notion that HR involves the management of relationships in organizations both to ensure the effectiveness of HR program delivery but also to ensure that firm strategy is implemented. Consistent with this point, communications and interpersonal competencies are central components of the change management and culture management competencies identified in recent research (Becker et al., 2001).

> So being able to communicate and understand the signals that are being sent from one side to the other are absolutely essential. [National Leader]

> Somebody that can make good eye contact and . . . personable, someone that people can feel comfortable talking with. [Local Leader]

> Really good [manager] . . . walks around and talks to [employees] . . . he is not just sitting there in his office. [Worker]

Recruitment and Retention. Finally, the workers in the focus groups understood the value of recruiting and retaining high-quality individuals (see Table 17.2). Several group members recognized that there are specific recruitment and selection techniques, and they expected a high level of technical proficiency in this area from their HR professionals. These findings parallel recent calls for using recruiting and retaining talent as a means of enhancing firm performance (e.g., Kaye & Jordan-Evans, 2002). Hence, graduate programs in HRM should ensure that their staffing content is current and that sufficient attention is paid to the retention of high-quality or highly skilled workers. This recommendation supports the development of the culture management HR competency described by Becker and colleagues (2001).

In summary, we recommend that graduate HR education place greater emphasis on ways to address and work within the structural constraints HR professionals face in their organizations, as well as on the interpersonal skills required to build relationships with important stakeholders in firms. In addition, we advocate a continued emphasis on labor relations content and an enhanced focus on the recruitment and retention of valuable employees.

Conclusion

This chapter seeks to add a fresh perspective to the discussion regarding the design of HR programs at the graduate level of study. By consulting unionized workers and national and local labor leaders, we generated several new insights, including the need for HR education to address structural constraints on HR competency application and the continued importance of labor relations competencies. Whereas the labor stakeholders confirmed the importance of technical HR competencies such as recruitment and retention of workers, they also stressed the importance of competencies in the area of interpersonal communications and the credibility of HR professionals. We encourage educators in the HRM field at the graduate level to seriously consider these findings in their continuous improvement or redesign efforts of graduate programs in HR.

Note

1. For case studies on worker reactions to HR interventions, see Mabey, Skinner, & Clark (1998).

References

Adler, P. S., & Lawler, E. E., III. (1999). Who needs MBAs in HR? USC's strategic human resource management MBA concentration. *Human Resource Management, 38*, 125–129.

Becker, B. E., & Huselid, M. A. (1999). Overview: Strategic human resource management at five leading firms. *Human Resource Management, 38*, 287–301

Becker, B. E., Huselid, M. A., & Ulrich, D. (2001). *The HR scorecard.* Cambridge, MA: Harvard University Press.

Bureau of National Affairs. (2003). *HR department benchmarks and analysis* [Executive Summary]. Washington, DC: BNA, SHRM co-produced.

Dowling, P. J., Welch, D. E., & Schuler, R. S. (1999). *International human resource management* (3rd ed.). Cincinnati, OH: South-Western College Publishing.

Foulkes, F. K. (1980). *Personnel policies in large nonunion companies.* Englewood Cliffs, NJ: Prentice Hall.

Freeman, R. B., & Rogers, J. (1999). *What workers want.* Ithaca, NY: Cornell University Press.

Heneman, R. L. (1999). Emphasizing analytical skills in HR graduate education: The Ohio State University MLHR program. *Human Resource Management, 38*, 131–134.

Hodson, R., & Sullivan, T. A. (2002). *The social organization of work.* Belmont, CA: Wadsworth/Thompson Learning.

Kaye, B., & Jordan-Evans, S. (2002). Retention in tough times. *T & D, 56*, 32–37.

Kochan, T. A. (1997). Rebalancing the role of human resources. *Human Resource Management, 36*, 121–127.

Legge, K. (1978). *Power, innovation, and problem-solving in personnel management.* London: McGraw-Hill.

Mabey, C., Skinner, D., & Clark, T. (Eds.). (1998). *Experiencing human resource management.* London: Sage.

Milkovich, G. T., & Newman, J. M. (2002). *Compensation* (7th ed.). Boston: McGraw-Hill Irwin.

Mohrman, S. A., & Lawler, E. E. (1999). The new human resources management: Creating the strategic business partnership. In R. Schuler & S. Jackson (Eds.), *Strategic human resource management* (pp. 433–447). Oxford: Blackwell.

Scarpello, V., & Ledvinka, J. (1988). *Personnel/human resource management: Environments and functions.* Boston: PWS Kent.

Shore, L. M., Lynch, P., & Dookeran, D. (2008). HR executives' views of HR education: Do hiring managers really care what education HR applicants have? In V. Scarpello (Ed.), *The handbook of human resource management education,* (pp. 291–314). Thousand Oaks, CA: Sage.

Society for Human Resource Management. (2002). Profiles: HR graduate programs. Retrieved February 17, 2004, from http://www.shrm.org/foundation/directory/profiles.asp

Society for Human Resource Management. (2004). *The maturing profession of human resources in the United States of America Survey Report.* Alexandria, VA: Author.

Truss, C., Gratton, L., Hope-Hailey, V., Stiles, P., & Zaleska, J. (2002). Paying the piper: Choice and constraint in changing HR functional roles. *Human Resource Management Journal, 12,* 39–63.

Ulrich, D., & Beatty, R. W. (2001). From partners to players: Extending the HR playing field. *Human Resource Management, 40,* 293–307.

Weinberg, R. B. (2002). *Certification guide.* Alexandria, VA: Human Resource Certification Institute.

Strategic Partnerships Between Academia and Practice

18

The Case for Nurturing Undergraduate HR Education

Debra J. Cohen

HRM has evolved to become both a science and an art. Even so, today HR is a profession in transition. Most HR professionals need to be skilled in all the technical aspects of HR, especially compliance, but they also need to understand the strategic importance of HR and be able to participate and contribute on an advanced level to an organization's success. HR is widely recognized as an important organizational function, but it is not always valued as a profession that contributes to the strategic success of an organization. To have an effective partnership and contribute to strategic discussions, HR must be seen as a credible, knowledgeable, influential partner not only in core HR issues but also in all areas of business. A solid educational foundation can create the base on which the knowledge, skills, and abilities for this contribution are built.

For HR professionals, both education and experience are imperative at all levels if we are to be valued as strategic partners. Both education and experience can be powerful tools for the HR profession in influencing and affecting an organization. One way to begin developing this expertise is by studying HR in a university setting.[1]

AUTHOR'S NOTE: The research presented here was made possible by the valuable contributions of Letty Kluttz, PHR, Knowledge Manager at the Society for Human Resource Management.

Although many professionals today have advanced degrees in HR or business or came to the profession via other areas of study, a steady stream of students are studying HR at the undergraduate level. HR degrees do not rival such fields as accounting, finance, or international business in terms of enrollment, but with 10,000 student members annually in the Society for Human Resource Management (SHRM), the world's largest HR management association, one could surmise that there are minds to mold and an opportunity to influence the shaping of future HR professionals.

SHRM is the leading voice of the human resource profession. SHRM provides education and information services, conferences and seminars, government and media representation, online services, and publications to more than 210,000 professional and student members throughout the world. SHRM is committed to advancing the HR profession and the capabilities of all HR professionals to ensure that HR is an essential and effective partner in developing and executing organizational strategy and to serving the needs of the HRM professional by providing the most essential and comprehensive set of resources available.

Most universities that offer undergraduate concentrations in HRM do so as a subspecialty to a broader business degree. In addition, because most universities have some form of accreditation, either regional, national, or both, they usually adhere to a specific set of rules regarding foundation courses and specified formulas and categories of courses that students and advisors must follow. Typically, these rules ensure that students receive a broad and varied set of courses and content and that appropriate rigor and depth are accomplished.

Schools that have AACSB (Association to Advance Collegiate Schools of Business, formerly the American Assembly of Collegiate Schools of Business) accreditation or some other form of accreditation follow a common set of requirements of core classes and electives. Schools that have regional accreditation also follow a set of common denominators but may not have the same level or type of requirements. Regardless of the review process, curriculum requirements, and course mix that a university follows, there is usually some flexibility in the electives and the field of concentration that a school offers. Qualitative and anecdotal research, however, shows that most schools offer only between four and six courses in HR and that the requirements are usually fairly loose. That is, there may be some required courses, such as an HR overview course, an advanced or case course, or a strategic HR course, but most have a set of electives that are fairly fluid depending on staffing levels of faculty and their teaching preferences.

Business schools will usually have similar types of offerings around such curricula as marketing, finance, accounting, information systems, and so forth. Typically, the faculty at the university will define the specific courses that might encompass the program, specifying the number of credits, prerequisites, or capstone courses and whether or not an internship, co-op experience, or some requirements are necessary for fulfillment of a degree.

Thus, the mix of courses and requirements is dictated by what academicians believe is necessary. Moreover, this mix is likely dictated by the preferences of the faculty for the type and content of the core courses for any given field of concentration (i.e., major). Rarely are internships *required,* and in some cases, when offered as electives, they may be difficult to obtain.

To take the case further, if faculty expertise and interest exist in staffing or HR information systems (HRIS), then there is likely to be a course covering these topics in the curriculum. If expertise and preference exist for international HR or compensation, courses in these areas may be offered instead of courses in staffing or HRIS. The potential problem is that although all the topics are important and interesting, it may be that a course in HRIS is more important than a course in international HR. Given limited resources, most schools can't offer all the "slices" of HR that exist. Moreover, the curriculum process at most universities is fairly slow, and it may be difficult to modify curriculum as quickly as HR practice may indicate.

SHRM, guided by its mission to both serve the professional and advance the profession, has recently asked the question: *What HR knowledge do undergraduates need to start a career in HR?* Specifically, SHRM has set out to explore what key HR topics or issues a degreed undergraduate[2] student must posses in order to be successful in an entry-level HR job and set a foundation for a long-term career in HR.

To answer this question, a qualitative analysis of select universities was completed,[3] along with an analysis of various career content sources such as the Department of Labor (Bureau of Labor Statistics) occupational outlook information, the body of knowledge outline from the Human Resource Certification Institute (HRCI), a review of entry-level HR jobs listings, and the most frequently asked questions from HR professionals. In addition, a series of focus groups with students, faculty, and HR practitioners were held.

The Bureau of Labor Statistics (BLS) provides detailed information about various occupations and summarizes the types of courses students might undertake in these fields to be successful. In reference to entry-level HR positions, the BLS recommends prospective HR specialists to take courses in the following subjects:

- Compensation
- Recruitment
- Training and development
- Performance appraisal
- Principles of management
- Organizational structure
- Industrial psychology

Although they are sometimes offered as electives, most schools generally do not require these courses. Indeed, with only four to six courses available for a concentration, it would be impossible to provide a sufficient introduction to HR and then cover all of these topics in depth.

The Human Resource Certification Institute (HRCI) is a credentialing organization that works to define the HR body of knowledge and assess candidates on their mastery of that body of knowledge. HRCI provides a body of knowledge outline based on a detailed practice analysis conducted every three to five years to codify the responsibilities of entry-level and senior HR professionals. This outline provides the weighting of each area, and the certification examination follows these weightings with the appropriate number of questions. The practice analysis gathers information on the contemporary practice patterns of Professionals in Human Resources (PHRs) and Senior Professionals in Human Resources (SPHRs). It was designed to provide comprehensive descriptions of the functional areas and responsibilities performed in actual practice and the knowledge required in actual practice. The PHR and SPHR certifications indicate that the holder has demonstrated mastery of the HR body of knowledge and accepted the personal challenge to stay informed of new developments in the HR field. To be successful in their jobs, HR professionals must know how to deal effectively with strategic management and planning issues, international competition, management staffing, and family and social issues that affect the workplace. Table 18.1 shows the current outline and weightings for the two certifications.

Table 18.1   HRCI Body of Knowledge Outline Through 2006

Topic Area	PHR	SPHR
Strategic Management	12%	26%
Workforce Planning and Employment	26%	16%
Human Resource Development	15%	13%
Compensation and Benefits	20%	16%
Employee and Labor Relations	21%	24%
Occupational Health, Safety, and Security	6%	5%

HRCI Body of Knowledge Outline Beginning 2007		
Topic Area	PHR	SPHR
Strategic Management	12%	26%
Workforce Planning and Employment	26%	17%
Human Resource Development	17%	17%
Total Rewards	16%	12%
Employee and Labor Relations	22%	18%
Risk Management	7%	7%

Source: HRCI Body of Knowledge Outline. Used with permission of the Society for Human Resource Management.

Another reflection of the educational needs or knowledge requirements for HR professionals is related to the use of SHRM Information Center. Staffed with over a dozen information specialists, knowledge managers, and librarians, the Information Center fields over 185,000 inquiries via e-mail, live chat, and telephone by HR professionals each year. Over the years in which the Center has been operating, definitive themes have emerged with regard to the types and topics of typical questions. Summed up in a single word—compliance—these questions cover a variety of important employment law issues. Moreover, there are certain laws or topics that clearly stand out as the most troubling or at least as the most asked about. Table 18.2 shows that for a recent three-month period, the Fair Labor Standards Act (FLSA) and the Family and Medical Leave Act (FMLA) have evoked the most questions from HR professionals. The questions are varied, of course, but the list in Table 18.2 shows the range.

Questions reflect a lack of depth of understanding of employment laws. Although their conceptual understanding is clear, the day-to-day workings or implications of the laws are not apparent to them, nor are the differences by state. For example, one request was for documented information to verify that companies must pay overtime after eight hours worked in a day, as learned in college. However, federal FLSA regulations mandate the payment of overtime after 40 hours are worked in a workweek, not after eight hours in a day, which is only a provision in some states. For example, the state of California mandates overtime after eight hours on a daily basis. Another caller wanted to find out where in the regulation he could find proof that if employees on FMLA leave used paid sick leave for part of the leave, it extended the number of weeks of leave by that amount of paid leave, as he learned in college. Section 825.207 of the law states that "FMLA permits an eligible employee to choose to *substitute* paid leave for FMLA leave, and an

Table 18.2   SHRM Information Center: Top 10 Topics July–September 2006

Topic	Number of Questions
FMLA	1875
FLSA	1085
Records and Record Keeping	636
Termination	635
Policies and Manuals, Handbooks	511
I-9	434
COBRA	392
Reference Checking/Investigation	373
Other Benefits	347
Americans With Disabilities Act	305

Source: SHRM Information Center. Used with permission of the Society for Human Resource Management.

employer to require an employee to *substitute* paid leave for FMLA leave." The key word is "substitute." Paid time is taken concurrently with unpaid leave under FMLA so that the total leave granted does not exceed 12 weeks. The leave entitlement is not extended by the use of paid leave.

This raises the question of how much and what type of education students receive regarding employment law. Although laws such as the FMLA and the FLSA are undoubtedly covered in introductory courses, the level of detail that is needed to apply them to organizations on a day-to-day basis is far greater than a conceptual understanding. Table 18.3 shows the required and elective courses in HR uncovered during the qualitative analysis of HR programs. A little less than 20% of the schools require a course in employment law and a little less than 10% offer such course as an elective. For laws such as the FMLA and FLSA, it may be that details will be learned in compensation and benefits courses, but as can also be seen in Table 18.3, these courses are not required nor offered with any regularity at most universities reviewed. It is not possible for most universities to offer all of the "slices" of HR topics, given the number of courses after accreditation requirements that they can offer. However, it may be that, if HR courses are offered on the basis of teaching preferences or availability of teaching expertise, there is somewhat of a disconnect between what practitioners need to know and what students are learning. As a result, it may be wise to develop a system whereby schools and universities have a better understanding of what practitioners face on a day-to-day basis to help guide curriculum development.

On the basis of these qualitative analyses, several conclusions emerged. Specifically, these data indicate that, given many different approaches, there is a certain level of confusion for both students and employers. Students don't know what to look for or what they are qualified to do, whereas employers don't know if they can find what they want or need and, therefore, have to be willing to train and develop an entry-level student. There seems to be an inconsistent message from academia because there is no common set of knowledge or courses delivered. More importantly, the depth of information required to be a successful practitioner may not be provided, as illustrated by student questions to the Information Center.

Although there are differences in where a degree in HR resides (differences were noted in departments and schools), what the degree is called (e.g., BA, BBA, BSBA, etc.), and whether it is considered a "major," a "concentration," or an "emphasis," it is clear that undergraduate degrees in HR are possible and readily available across the U.S. Most of these degrees appear to reside within a business school and, as a result, have the advantage of course requirements in a variety of business disciplines. On the flip side of universities perhaps not recognizing all of the practical needs of students who plan a career in HR, those who hire these new graduates may not recognize the value of a broad business degree. For example, students who graduate with a business degree with a concentration in HR will have taken

Table 18.3 Required and Elective Courses

Course Description/Title	Number of Schools Where Course Is Required	Number of Schools Where Course Is Elective
Collective Bargaining	4	3
Compensation and Benefits	4	7
Compensation and Benefits, Advanced	0	1
Current Issues in HR Management	2	5
HR Management, Advanced	4	2
Human Resource Management	18	2
Industrial and Labor Relations	3	3
Industrial/Organizational Behavior	1	0
Industrial/Organizational Psychology	1	1
Internship	3	8
Labor and Employment Law	6	3
Labor Relations	3	8
Organizational Behavior	12	2
Performance Management and Compensation	1	1
Recruitment and Selection	2	3
Training and Development	2	9

courses in accounting, finance, marketing, international business, management, and so forth. This business acumen will serve them well and should help bring a perspective to the HR function that practitioners today recognize as critically important. Studies about HR competencies (Brockbank, Ulrich, & Beatty, 1999; Ulrich, Brockbank, Yeung, & Lake, 1995) clearly indicate the need for HR professionals to posses business acumen and expertise. As with HR content, these students may lack the immediate practical application of business acumen, but a broad understanding of the language of business and how various disciplines complement and depend on one another is necessary.

Core courses in HR should be grouped and designed to provide broad functional knowledge in the HR discipline. The classroom experience should equally prepare students to be successful in their chosen discipline. How much of what an entry-level HR professional needs to know should be learned in the classroom versus on the job? SHRM is committed to participating in the process that will lead to the effective development of curriculum and assisting with the timely modification of classroom content to reflect current business and HR issues. It is our goal to provide input and assist HR academicians with the difficult task of organizing an effective curriculum.

As a result of the questions raised in the initial review of curriculum, SHRM embarked on a process to dig a bit deeper and learn what students, faculty, and practitioners thought about the issue of undergraduate education. A series of focus groups were conducted with these three constituencies. A moderator guide was developed, and participants were taken through a series of questions and given an opportunity to comment. Figures 18.1, 18.2, and 18.3 show the detailed summary results. Overall, practitioners concluded that although book knowledge is great, practical hands-on experience is imperative. Students who come in with a view that HR is based on book definitions miss the point of how dynamic it is in the work environment and how the practice actually occurs.

---

1. Internships should be required for all undergraduate HR students.

2. An undergraduate degree is preferable for entry-level workers.
   - An undergraduate degree gives students a foundation and assists them in their career and understanding of HR.

3. Students need to learn practical application, not just theory.
   - They need to know how what they are learning can be applied to the workplace.

4. It is important to expose students to all areas of business.
   - Companies should have students shadow the CFO, VP of HR, etc., to see what issues come up on a daily basis: perception versus reality.

5. Practitioners see a culture shift in HR, and the following HR-related skills were defined as necessary for a successful career in HR:
   - Change management.
   - Presentation and oral skills.
   - Statistics and economics understanding.
   - Business writing.
   - Communication skills.
   - Consulting skills.

6. An entry-level position was defined as an exempt-level position that requires a bachelor's degree and three years of experience.
   - The size of the company plays a significant role in what is required or needed in an entry-level position.
     - In smaller companies, an entry-level position exposes students to more areas of HR, whereas in a larger company, an entry-level position might be more of a stereotypical support role.

Figure 18.1 Focus Group Results: Practitioners

Academicians, on the other hand, talked about the difficulty of incorporating practical experience into their curriculum. Although some universities have a commitment to internship programs, most find it difficult to help students secure the necessary experience and thus designate internships as optional. In addition, many academicians talked about their desire for a course template they could follow. Some believe that a template based on industry interface would assist at their university because an independent body would show curriculum committees what students need to succeed. Finally, much of the discussion centered on the need for broad business background as well as HR-specific information to be competitive in today's business environment. Figure 18.2 shows the detailed summary from this focus group.

In many ways, students echoed the comments of practitioners and academicians. They understand the need for practical experience but are concerned about how to obtain it in a meaningful and affordable way. Their perspective on how to acquire the requisite experience was a little different. They believe that working in an organization while in school would be

---

1. Schools would be interested in a template for an undergraduate degree that showed what classes should be taught.
   - This template should be based on the competencies for HR professionals.
   - All students regardless of their major should take a basic HRM course.
   - Students should be required to take a communications course, public-speaking course, and a business-writing course.
   - Academics need to listen more to practitioners' needs.
   - Internships should be part of the curriculum.
   - It would be helpful if SHRM formatted guidelines for internships.

2. Basic background in Management is also seen as important and may be confused by some hiring managers as not being part of HRM.

3. Experience and internships are critical.
   - Wide variations exist from school to school about requirements and parameters for internships.
   - Employers also differ in terms of internship requirements and guidelines.

4. There is a need to develop templates, guidelines and parameters.
   - Need to "push" this out to the practitioner.
   - Consider using SHRM chapter structure to lend assistance for helping students get the requisite experience they need to supplement their HR education.
   - Consider a tie-in with certification.
   - Consider developing grant programs to help.

Figure 18.2 Focus Group Results: Academicians

a meaningful experience unless they are asked to do menial or administrative tasks. Thus, they place a higher value on the contribution they can make to an organization than practitioners do and believe that, as a learning experience, this is something to which they are entitled. Students also discussed the need for faculty to have real-world experiences as well to aid their professors in using realistic examples and conveying more than textbook information as they teach HR courses. Figure 18.3 summarizes the details from this focus group.

---

1. Internships should be required, but students want to learn something while interning.
    - Internships should not be about grunt work.
    - Students want to be able to shadow their supervisors to see what they do.
    - Students also need to take the initiative and show what skills they have and what they can bring to the table.

2. Students want more practical application in their classes, as (it is their belief) they do not use theories in the real world.

3. Students believed that an Employment Law class is an imperative part of a curriculum.

4. Faculty "internships" would be extremely beneficial to get the professors connected to the real working world and bring real-life experiences into the classroom.

5. Students thought that a degree was not necessary for an entry-level job, which they viewed as someone having zero years of work experience.
    - They did view the degree as an investment that will help them further their careers.

Figure 18.3   Focus Group Results: Students

Summary and Conclusions

There are some clear common denominators that have come from this research, as well as some clear action steps that can be taken. Implications for future research indicate that more than just anecdotal information should be collected to understand existing differences and to help build bridges between academia, business, and students. Implications for practice indicate that a neutral body, such as SHRM, is in a perfect position to facilitate the action steps necessary to advance the HR profession by helping all three constituencies to better understand one another and to serve the needs of one another.

As a profession, we've come a long way, but SHRM also recognizes the need to go further. HR is at a crossroads where HR professionals must recognize the importance of influence in business discussions and the value that HR can bring to the strategic process. More importantly, HR professionals, through their knowledge, credibility, and influence, must help all business leaders to see the relevance and value of HR. In practice, this means basing our decisions on sound, concrete research and with financially analyzed solutions and suggestions. Yes, HR professionals are in the "people business," but being strategic business partners means that we need to be analytical in our approach as we help drive the business forward in pursuit of shareholder and stakeholder value.

The future is bright for HR, and a key to this success will be continued knowledge development for HR professionals and students. Our profession will grow stronger through dedication to HR education. HR will strengthen its contribution to strategic decision making with a commitment to business and HR education. In the future the expectation for well-trained and business-literate HR professionals will be the norm rather than the exception. A profession that does not seriously train and educate its newest entrants may not survive as a profession at all.

Notes

1. An earlier version of this chapter was presented at the 2002 HR Town Meeting, at the Academy of Management Meetings in Denver. Although some factual material has been updated, for SHRM's HR Curriculum Guideline and Templates and current work please visit www.shrm.org or link to it directly at http://www.shrm.org/hrresources/surveys_published/SHRM%20HR%20Curriculum%20Guidebook%20&Templates%20for%20Undergraduate%20and%20Graduate%20Programs.pdf.

2. Although graduate degree programs are important, as are degree programs from around the globe, it was our intention to begin by looking at undergraduate programs in the U.S. before considering a project with a wider scope.

3. The following schools were reviewed by examining the curriculum on their Web sites and calling or e-mailing individuals at the school to verify and update information: American U, Washington, D.C.; Arcadia U, Glenside, PA; Barton College, Wilson, NC; Baylor U, Waco, TX; Boston College, Chestnut Hill, MA; Clemson U, Clemson, SC; Cornell U, Ithaca, NY; DePaul U, Chicago, IL; Florida State U, Tallahassee, FL; George Washington U, Washington, D.C.; Hawaii Pacific U, Honolulu, HI; Idaho State U, Pocatello, ID; Indiana U of Pennsylvania, Indiana, PA; James Madison U, Harrisonburg, VA; Kansas State U, Manhattan, KS; Loyola U of Chicago, Chicago, IL; Marquette U, Milwaukee, WI; Marymount U, Arlington, VA; Michigan State U, East Lansing, MI; North Carolina State U, Raleigh, NC; Northeastern U, Boston, MA; Ohio State U, Columbus, OH; San Francisco State U, San Francisco, CA; U of Central Florida, Orlando, FL; U of Colorado at Denver, Denver, CO; U of Maryland, College Park, MD; U of Minnesota–Twin Cities, Minneapolis, MN; U of Nevada, Las Vegas, Las Vegas, NV; U of Pennsylvania, Philadelphia, PA; U of Pittsburgh, Pittsburgh, PA; U of Wisconsin–Whitewater, Whitewater, WI.

4. See http://www.shrm.org/students/intern_published for a detailed discussion of internship guidelines and suggestions.

References

Brockbank, W., Ulrich, D., & Beatty, R. (1999). HR professional development: Creating the future creators at the University of Michigan Business School. *Human Resource Management, 38,* 111–118.

Ulrich, D., Brockbank, W., Yeung, A., & Lake, D. (1995). Human resource competencies: An empirical assessment. *Human Resource Management, 34,* 473–496.

SECTION 8

HR Success Constraints

The three chapters in this section focus on constraints to success that HRM education and HRM practitioners face. Chapter 19 discusses external reasons for the problems HR graduate programs face in business schools. Chapter 20 suggests that the nature of the HRM occupation and its current practitioners argues against the involvement of HRM executives in the organization's strategic process. Chapter 21 takes an opposing position but argues that to do so requires changes in HRM education and the business knowledge base of its practitioners.

In Chapter 19, Rynes, Owens, and Trank begin by noting that a study commissioned by the American Assembly of Collegiate Schools of Business (AACSB) found that within 65 MBA programs and a sample of 3500 full-time MBA students, HR ranked last among 12 business disciplines in terms of perceived importance to the curriculum. Although OB came in at 10th, the core OB course ranked first in terms of the perception that it currently receives "too much coverage." The authors follow up on the AACSB findings by reporting results of a study that more closely explores the dimensions of student perceptions about HR. The results seem to indicate that failure to produce more positive attitudes toward HR has negative short-term and long-term consequences for practicing HR professionals. The authors describe the demise of the HRM program, first at the MA level and later at the MBA level, at the University of Iowa business school; discuss some of the difficulties HR instructors and students experience in business schools; and speculate about the underlying causes for those problems. They conclude by suggesting that the crisis HRM faces in business schools can be attributed to the (often hypocritical) practices of business itself.

In Chapter 20, Bereman and Graham present a general view of HRM that exists in practice. They note that, for the most part, the involvement of HR professionals in significant strategic management has not materialized to any great degree. They propose three reasons for this state of affairs: (1) natural forces of strategic management are centered in markets whereas HR decisions are responses to market opportunity, (2) differences in vocational interests and orientations between HR managers and executives involved in the strategic management process, and (3) occupational preparation and background of HR practitioners. Although the authors' presentation is pessimistic about the future of HRM, there is a glimmer of optimism when they note that the HR skill requirements contained in the *Dictionary of Occupational Titles* are not very important for executives. This suggests that corporate executives may hire unqualified HR personnel because they do not know what competencies to expect of HR. This theme is echoed in Chapter 21.

In Chapter 21, Theeke suggests that HR will not become part of the organization's strategic planning process as long as the HR practitioner is perceived by other functional managers as less skilled and as having less understanding of the breadth of standard business processes. He proposes two reasons for this perception: (a) the variety of educational backgrounds of HR professionals and (b) confusion of business executives as to the competencies required for professional work in HR. Next, he discusses the business skills HR professionals need to acquire to garner equal status with other business professionals. Theeke proposes that joining a strategic planning team without the requisite skills will not serve the HRM field's interest. The HR profession will not advance if non-HR managers in the organization continue to say that HR managers are nice people who are quantitatively challenged and know little about business functions.

"Be There, or Be in HR!" 19

The Trials and Tribulations of Human Resource Management in Business Schools

Sara L. Rynes

Skip Owens

Christine Quinn Trank

> *"Be there, or be in HR!"*
>
> —Recruitment poster for the organizational meeting of the
> MBA Graduate Financial Management Association

E ver since publication of Schuler's (1990) seminal article, "Repositioning the HR Function: Transformation or Demise?" it has become increasingly recognized that the HR function is at a critical juncture. Acknowledgment of a crisis in HR has led to an outpouring of research, experimentation, and dialogue about how to reposition HR in a way that will unmistakably add value to organizations (e.g., Beatty & Schneier, 1997; Beer, 1997; Csoka, 1995; Ulrich, 1998; Ulrich & Losey, 1997).

What has received far less attention is the fact that HR faces a similar crisis in business schools. A 1997 study commissioned by the American Assembly of Collegiate Schools of Business (AACSB) found that among a sample of 3500 full-time students in 65 MBA programs, HR ranked dead last (12th of 12 disciplines) in terms of perceived importance to the curriculum

(Educational Benchmarking Inc., 1997). In addition, the course most closely related to HR, organizational behavior, was ranked 10th in terms of importance and first in terms of perceptions that it currently receives "too much coverage" in the curriculum. (Perhaps the only thing saving HR from this dubious distinction is the fact that it is not even taught in many MBA programs; e.g., Freedman, 1990; Myers, 1990).

The fact that HR has credibility problems in most (though not all) business programs has at least two serious consequences. First, unless HR can create a more positive image among business students, business programs will continue to turn out future managers and technical professionals (e.g., financial analysts, management consultants, information systems designers) who have negative attitudes toward HR professionals and little appreciation of what effective HR practices can contribute to organizational success. Given that today's business students are tomorrow's business leaders, failure to produce more positive attitudes toward HR portends continuing problems for HR professionals considerably into the future. In this very real sense, discussions of HR transformation in business organizations are incomplete without discussions of what is occurring with HR in business schools.

Second, negative student attitudes toward HR are likely to deter the "best and brightest" business students from pursuing careers in HR, or even from taking elective HR coursework. Although it is true that many HR professionals are educated in places other than business schools (e.g., Freedman, 1990), the fact that HR professionals are increasingly expected to be "business people first" (Schuler, 1990) makes a compelling case for educating future HR professionals who are strong in *both* general business and HR (see also Ulrich, Brockbank, Yeung, & Lake, 1995; Wilhelm, 1995). In addition, because possession of an MBA is increasingly becoming a prerequisite for upward career mobility in organizations, failure to have MBA-trained HR managers may further limit the career paths of HR professionals (HR career paths are already truncated relative to paths in most other functional areas; Kanter, 1977; Pfeffer, 1994).

For these reasons, the discussions that have occurred around the HR crisis in business need to be extended to include business schools as well. To date, however, there has been little discussion of the challenges confronting HR education, other than to speculate about the types of knowledge, skills, competencies, and coursework that HR students should be provided (e.g. Burke, 1997; Csoka, 1995; Freedman, 1990; Van Eynde & Tucker, 1997). Although this is a valuable dialogue, the relatively poor standing of HR in business schools suggests that student attitudes and motivation—not just knowledge and skills—also need to be considered.

In this chapter, we describe some of the difficulties that HR experiences in business schools and speculate about the underlying sources of the problem. We believe that until the root causes of our problem (and all the accompanying symptoms) are looked squarely in the eye, any "solutions" that might be attempted are likely to prove ineffective.

Nature of the Problem

We first became interested in this problem as a result of a curricular change implemented in our own business school, the Tippie College of Business at the University of Iowa. Until 1993, Iowa was one of several schools (like Wisconsin and Minnesota) that had a formal MA program in human resources and industrial relations (HR/IR) that was partly separate from and partly integrated with the MBA program. For example, HR faculty taught combined MA-MBA courses, and MA students took many of their courses with MBA students. By combining MA and MBA students in elective offerings, we were able to offer a wide variety of HR specialty courses such as staffing, compensation, and training and development.

However, by the early 1990s, the University's central administration (and subsequently, our deans) gave us a mandate to improve student quality in the MA program and make it more profitable, or to abolish it entirely. However, because we had no discretionary resources with which to improve student quality (e.g., marketing or student recruiting budgets), success seemed unlikely.

In addition, we were all aware of the popular press claim that what HR departments needed now was "business people first" and HR people second. As a result, our department decided to abolish the MA in HR/IR and to replace it with an MBA concentration in HR. At the time, we had little doubt that we were doing the correct thing—we would winnow out the weaker students from HR/IR (especially those who were math-phobic, as they would now have to take finance, accounting, and so on), and we would be educating the type of student that business claimed it desperately needed—the "business person with HR knowledge and skills."

Within a year or two, however, it became clear that the anticipated benefits of our strategic decision had failed to emerge. First, we found that the vast majority of applicants who had wanted to apply for the (newly abolished) MA program were uninterested in getting an MBA. Even more distressingly, we found that almost no one who applied for the MBA was interested in majoring in HR. Thus, we rapidly went from a department with a steady cohort of 20–30 Master's students to one with only a handful of students with serious career interests in HR. As enrollments in our HR electives declined, we became more of a "service" department, providing courses in general management and organizational behavior for students who were destined to major in something else (usually finance). Faculty found themselves having to "retool" toward organizational behavior and OB electives, and the number of faculty in the department was cut back rather dramatically. A few years later, the HR course was "merged" with the OB course in the MBA core, giving each only half its previous coverage.

How could such a seemingly sensible change strategy have gone so wrong? In order to find out why so few business students were majoring in HR, we conducted a survey of student perceptions among both BBA and

MBA students. Generally speaking, the survey was designed around expectancy theory concepts. Specifically, we wanted to know whether the problem was one of *expectancy* (student uncertainty about the availability of HR jobs or their ability to be successful in HR coursework), *instrumentality* (perceptions of the rewards of HR careers relative to those in other functional areas), or both.

Tables 19.1 and 19.2 report the perceptions of BBA and MBA students, respectively, with respect to HR versus other majors. Our results clearly show that most business students have negative impressions of careers in HR, relative to those associated with other functional areas.[1] For example, in terms of instrumentality, results showed that both BBAs (n = 387) and MBAs (n = 160) perceived HR to offer the lowest starting salaries, lowest 10-year salaries, and lowest salaries for top people in the field of all majors.[2] HR was also perceived to have the poorest opportunities for advancement and the lowest likelihood of providing a fast track up the corporate hierarchy. Finally, careers in HR were believed to have the lowest impact on organizations of any function (except accounting, among MBAs only) and to be significantly less "interesting" and "meaningful" than careers in finance and marketing. These are important disadvantages in a culture where income and hierarchy are primary sources not only of material comfort, but also of social status and judgments of relative worth (e.g., Bok, 1993; Frank, 1985).

Table 19.1   BBA Perceptions of Six Business Careers

Variable	HR	Accounting	Finance	MIS	Marketing	Operations
Job availability	2.76	3.50**	2.96**	3.68***	2.68	2.74
Number of job offers	3.69	5.80**	4.46*	6.09**	4.00	3.73
Successfully complete requirements	4.49	3.57**	4.17**	3.61**	4.49	3.90**
Graduated at top of class	3.39	2.50**	3.01**	2.66**	3.42	2.97**
Starting salary	31,666	40,290**	36,506**	40,189**	33,238**	35,158**
10-year salary	56,628	75,202**	69,442**	74,187**	61,789**	64,254**
Salary of top people	136,425	246,462**	326,305**	251,996**	223,293**	198,372**
Opportunity for advancement	3.00	3.90**	4.06**	3.94**	3.68**	3.64**
Have impact on organization	4.05	4.08	4.33**	4.19*	4.40**	4.28**
Fast-track to top	2.71	3.42**	3.68**	3.46**	3.28**	3.50**
Interesting work	3.41	2.79**	3.69	3.06**	3.68**	2.92**
Meaningful work	3.40	3.05*	3.65*	3.23	3.56	2.98**

*different from HR at $p < .01$.
**different from HR at $p < .001$.

Table 19.2 MBA Perceptions of Six Business Careers

Perception	HR	Accounting	Finance	MIS	Marketing	Operations
Job availability	2.84	3.61**	3.56**	4.06**	2.93	3.07*
Number of job offers	2.64	3.59**	3.81**	4.24**	3.03*	2.85
Ability to complete requirements	4.36	3.85**	4.17	3.84**	4.32	4.06**
Ability to graduate at top of class	3.68	23.03**	3.34*	3.15**	3.69	3.34*
Starting salary	51,735	56,529**	61,926**	59,872**	54,976**	56,117**
10-year salary	81,444	91,872**	106,939**	96,486**	96,486**	91,612**
Salary of top people	200,316	303,069**	575,591**	296,331**	157,576**	260,166**
Opportunity for advancement	2.91	3.27*	4.22**	3.63**	3.86**	3.50**
Impact on organization	3.71	3.58	4.33**	4.03**	4.45**	4.14**
Fast-track to top	2.60	3.08**	4.47**	3.20**	3.70**	3.56**
Interesting work	3.03	2.45**	3.74**	3.06	3.74**	3.08
Meaningful work	3.20	2.62**	3.80**	3.29	3.84**	3.24

*different from HR at $p < .01$.
**different from HR at $p < .001$.

In terms of expectancies, HR was also perceived to have the fewest entry-level vacancies of any field except marketing. However, students did not have low expectancies with respect to their perceived ability to successfully handle HR coursework. Indeed, expectancies of being able to complete HR coursework and graduate at the top of the major were higher in HR than in any other discipline except marketing.

Root Causes

As Kochan (2002) reminds us, we are unlikely to generate appropriate solutions to problems if we do not understand their root causes. Here, we examine four factors that we believe represent fairly "deep" causes of the bind in which we find ourselves. We begin with the one that, above all, we believe to be most central—the value placed by business on people in general, and on the HR function in particular.

TAKING THEIR CUES FROM BUSINESS

Business students attempt to prepare themselves in ways that will increase their attractiveness to prospective employers (Gutek, 1997). Because of this, business norms and practices provide important signals to students concerning the skills, behaviors, and attitudes that are truly valued in organizations, and the credentials that are most likely to produce the best prospects for initial employment and continued career advancement. This observation has led Stone (1991) to argue that "for many executives, the most effective way to change what happens inside the schools is to change what happens inside their own companies" (p. 62). Therefore, it is instructive to analyze current business norms in terms of what they communicate to students about the importance of human resources in business, and human resource knowledge and skills in business careers.

On the face of it, it might appear that businesses are transmitting very positive messages to students in this regard. For example, many businesses have adopted values statement such as "People are our most important asset" or "The customer comes second (after employees)." In addition, surveys of recruiters and employers consistently conclude that businesses want graduates with enhanced leadership, teamwork, and communication skills (e.g., Byrne, Leonhardt, Bongiorno, & Jespersen, 1996; Cappelli, 1995; Green & Seymour, 1991; Porter & McKibbin, 1988).

On the other hand, students have also become accustomed to seeing headlines suggesting that business behavior often diverges considerably from business rhetoric. For example, a Towers Perrin survey showed that whereas 73% of executives claimed that employees were their company's most important investment, employees came in second to last in terms of plans for actual strategic expenditures (Swoboda, 1995). Similarly, Luthans, Hodgetts, and Rosenkrantz (1988) found that managers who received the most promotions were those who spent the least time working with people.

In addition, the popular business press routinely reports on businesses that conduct repeated waves of downsizing and plant relocations, even under profitable conditions (e.g., Murray, 1995). *Fortune* has proclaimed that corporate "loyalty is for suckers" (Munk, 1998, p. 72), even as we attempt to convince employers (and students) that the most effective HR practices to be centered on high employee involvement, performance-based rewards, and strong commitments to job security (e.g., Arthur, 1994; MacDuffie, 1995; Pfeffer, 1998; Reichheld, 1996).

The end result of actual corporate behavior (as opposed to corporate rhetoric) is that many business students—who are much more likely than other students to have business experience and to read the business press—come to the classroom with considerable cynicism about the value that organizations place on both people *per se* and "people knowledge and skills" (Rynes & Trank, 1999). For example, Dean, Brandes, and Dharwadkar (1998) have written about the difficulty of teaching topics such as "teamwork" to part-time MBAs who hold full-time jobs in real organizations:

> The students could see the benefits of teamwork in theory but perceived it, in practice, as merely a slogan used by their organizations

to appear progressive, without changing anything about how work actually gets done ... one young woman was so appalled by her organization that she thought she must be part of "some huge experiment on demotivating employees." (p. 341)

Consistent with this view, Badaracco and Webb (1995) report that in most of the companies joined by graduating Harvard MBA students, managers are perceived as being able to treat employees almost any way they want—not only rudely, but also unethically or even illegally—so long as they "make their numbers." Both empirical research (Miceli & Near, 1992) and the recent experiences of whistleblowers at Enron, Worldcom, and the FBI (Lacayo & Ripley, 2002) show that employees who attempt to expose wrongdoing in their own organizations are far more likely to suffer discrimination than to receive praise or thanks.

A second important way in which corporations transmit their values to students is through the skills and credentials they look for in graduating students. Despite companies' professed desire for HR and people-related related knowledge and skills, in reality, many companies are looking first and foremost for people with technical skills who can immediately fill functional specialist roles without additional training (e.g., Allen, 1998). Moreover, recent research suggests that recruiters' actual screening decisions are quite different from their verbal accounts.

For example, Rynes, Trank, Mullenix, and Ilies (2003) recently asked recruiters whether they would prefer to hire students who majored only in a single functional area of business (e.g., finance, management information systems (MIS), or accounting), versus students with double majors—one in a functional area and the other in general management (including such courses as leadership, human resource management, organizational change and development, teams, negotiation, and ethics). When asked directly, 75% of recruiters said they preferred students with double majors. However, in a carefully controlled experiment where all characteristics of student resumes were controlled except for double versus single major (and corresponding lists of coursework), addition of the general management major made *no difference whatsoever* to recruiters' willingness to interview students. Instead, decisions to interview were overwhelmingly dominated by the previous work experience of the candidate—in other words, credentials that were acquired completely outside of the educational experience.

These realities are not lost on students. For example, *Business Week* recently linked corporate hiring behaviors to students' lack of interest in ethics instruction: "This past semester, even as billions of shareholder dollars were evaporating in corporate scandals, [only] about two dozen students signed up for [MIT's ethics] class—no more than the usual number. [The instructor] says a dozen other students pre-registered for ethics but ultimately decided against the course *in favor of the hard-skills classes that catch the eye of recruiters. The students didn't have jobs yet; they wanted something recruiters perceived as directly relevant*" (Hindo, 2002).

Similarly, in *Snapshots From Hell: The Making of an MBA,* Peter Robinson (1994) described the "tiering" that occurs in MBA summer internship hiring at Stanford, based on students' prior finance or banking experience. He also recorded the following exchange from his own interview with McKinsey:

> "I see you have no quantitative background to speak of" [said the partner]. My political background was impressive, he said, and [his firm] did value what he termed people skills, especially at the higher levels of the firm . . . "But I have to be frank. In my judgment, we'd have to spend too much of the summer training you." (p. 164–167)

Robinson also noted that students with weak mathematical backgrounds were required to attend a remedial "math camp" and were branded for the duration of the program as "poets." In contrast, it almost goes without saying that students who were weak in communication, interpersonal, or political skills, or who lacked background in psychology or sociology, were not subjected to similar remedial procedures.

A final way in which many businesses demonstrate the low value they place on HR is through the salaries and career opportunities they extend to HR practitioners. For example, 1998 *Business Week* data for graduating male MBAs showed that HR grads averaged $62,000 as compared with $90,000 for consulting, $79,000 for information technology, $75,000 for finance and operations, and $70,000 for marketing and accounting. Surveys by the National Association for Colleges and Employers (NACE, 1996, 1997) reveal the same patterns at the undergraduate level. Moreover, both the NACE and the *Business Week* surveys show that, as our students suspected, there are far fewer jobs for business graduates in HR than in other functional areas. For example, fewer than 1% of MBAs were hired into HR in 1998, as compared with 35% in finance, 28% in consulting, and 15% in marketing ("The MBA road," 1998).

Moreover, these career disadvantages persist over time, with HR professionals having shorter career paths, smaller chances of becoming a CEO, and significantly lower VP-level salaries than professionals in finance, marketing, or operations (Kanter, 1977; Pfeffer, 1994). These characteristics of HR careers, combined with the uncertain value of HR coursework for attaining other types of business positions, have negative implications for business students' choice of majors, enrollment in HR electives, and motivation to perform well in HR core courses (assuming they are even offered).

LACK OF BUSINESS SCHOOL ADMINISTRATIVE SUPPORT

The statistics cited in the preceding section have serious implications for the administrative support that business schools are likely to provide

HR students. The implications cover the gamut of admissions, advising, and placement activities.

In particular, the advent of various media rankings of business school "quality" have disadvantaged majors that have low relative starting salaries, small numbers of vacancies, or both—conditions that clearly apply to positions in HR. Given the increasing popularity of *Business Week* and *U.S. News & World Report* rankings (which are based on such factors as student and recruiter opinions as well as placement rates, starting salaries for graduates, and salary increments over preeducational salary), schools have a substantial interest in admitting students who are likely to have the most, and the most lucrative, opportunities after graduation. This means that admissions officers, student advisors, and placement officials all steer aspiring and current business school students to areas such as consulting, finance, and information technology, rather than HR, nonprofits, or operations. This same bias extends to the way in which students are viewed as potential future donors; it is much easier to envision getting large sums of money from individuals working on Wall Street or at McKinsey than as the HR director for a manufacturing firm or, even worse, a low-paying nonprofit agency.

Under this type of a reward structure, admissions officers are not likely to go out of their way to admit applicants who aspire to HR positions, and career advisors are not likely to steer them toward the major. For that matter, neither are the second-year MBAs who have a large role in socializing new business school students. In our experience, by the end of orientation week, most students have been persuaded by their elders to major in something else (usually finance). Finally, even if placement officials were eager to place individuals in lower-paying positions, the fact that most schools lack a critical mass of HR students makes it very "expensive" to generate placements for only a handful of students.

Although the reader may think that these experiences are unique to Iowa, we are convinced that they are not. In October 1999, a professor from Wake Forest University posted the following query on the HR Division Network of the Academy of Management:

> I teach in an MBA program in which we don't have a specialization in HR, although we do offer a few HR electives. The majority of our students have no interest in pursuing an HR career. However, every year, two or three students decide that they want to go into HR after graduation, and they seek out my advice for how to get into HR. My question is: What kind of advice should I be giving these students? Are companies hiring MBA graduates for HR positions? What should I suggest these students do to break into HR? I do think their broad-based business education is an asset, but on the other hand, their lack of functional depth and work experience in HR seems to be a limiting factor.

The responses were illuminating. First, virtually all respondents confirmed that they, too, dealt with at most a "handful" of students who were seriously interested in HR as a career. Responses included:

- We have the same challenge here [Wharton] and I don't have a good idea. Sometimes we send them to HR consulting firms (Hay, Towers Perrin, Hewitt) which at least gives them some exposure to the field.

- We have the same situation at Georgia Tech. Some time ago, we tried to build a stronger HR concentration in the school, but never attained more than about six students each year. We had a four-course concentration and tried to place them in some sort of practicum as part of their final year. About two years ago we finally gave it up.

- At UNC we face a similar situation. Only a small number of our MBAs wish to pursue careers in HR.

In a sort of chicken-and-egg process, the small number of students was also seen to be reflective of the hiring practices of employers. Specifically, faculty observed that in contrast to the rhetoric of wanting "business people first" in HR, some recruiters for HR positions really want *HR people first,* especially those with prior experience. Given employer hiring patterns, it is easy to see why business school administrators do not expend much energy trying to build this market:

- My experience while on the faculty at [Michigan State University's] School of Labor and Industrial Relations was that many Fortune 500 companies were primarily recruiting for the specialized degree, but would also include a few MBAs in the pool. Typically, the MBAs that would get picked had prior work experience in HR or HR internships. Still, this is an area where the specialized degree does seem to be the primary avenue when it comes to entry-level corporate recruiting.

- Most employers do not come here [University of North Carolina] specifically seeking MBAs to go into HR jobs—many companies do indeed have these jobs and hire for them, but they go to places like MSU, Cornell, Wisconsin, and Minnesota [note: these are all schools with Industrial and Labor Relations schools rather than MBAs with HR concentrations].

- I could count on one hand the number of HR positions that have been available for our MBA students in the last five years.

NATURE OF BUSINESS STUDENTS

Another challenge for HR instructors is that the material they teach may be inconsistent with students' preexisting values and beliefs, thus creating emotional resistance to HR content. For example, business students have been found to be more materialistic than most other students (Collins, 1996), as well as more individualistic (Frank, Gilovich, & Regan, 1993; Pfeffer, 1994), more politically conservative ("New MBAs," 1997; Sidanius, Pratto, Martin, & Stallworth, 1991), and more resistant to the generally liberalizing effects of higher education with respect to social pluralism (Sidanius et al., 1991). These characteristics are probably exacerbated by admissions decisions that favor applicants expressing interest in finance, MIS, or consulting over lower-paying careers such as HR or management of nonprofits. In any event, these values and beliefs can present formidable challenges to HR instructors, who are more likely than economics, finance, or accounting professors to focus on market and organizational imperfections (e.g., discrimination, cognitive errors, politics, unethical behaviors), as well as to point out the potentially positive effects of employee diversity, teamwork, and cooperative relationships (Dean et al., 1998; Prasad, 1997).

A related challenge is that although many business students attend "schools of management," only a small minority want or expect to become managers (Schein, 1996). In fact, motivation to manage has been dropping among U.S. college students for several decades (Howard & Bray, 1988; Miner, Ebrahimi, & Wachtel, 1995), whereas the attractiveness of occupations offering autonomy, technical challenges, and freedom from managerial responsibility (particularly investment banking and consulting) has been increasing for some time now (Branch, 1998; Howard & Bray, 1988; Schein, 1996). In these jobs, graduates can act as advisors or technical specialists without taking direct responsibility for (or often even seeing) the human consequences of their decisions (Huey, 1993; Mintzberg, 1989; O'Shea & Madigan, 1997). Therefore, although HR instructors (and textbooks) typically assume that most of their business students want to learn about "management," in fact they increasingly want to learn about finance, MIS, or venture capitalism instead (EBI, 1997; Taylor, 1998).

NATURE OF THE SUBJECT MATTER

A final difficulty for HR instructors concerns several features of the subject matter itself. One such characteristic is that business students tend to think of HR and OB as "easy" courses (see Table 19.1) covering topics that are mostly "common sense." Prasad (1997, p. 213) has indicated that students regard OB as "fuzzy" or a "blow-off course," whereas Robinson's (1994) reaction to it at Stanford was that it was a "sham discipline, based on pop psychology and sixties jargon" (p. 59). Given these attitudes, it is sometimes difficult to get students to pay much attention to behavioral coursework or to spend much time on HR assignments. (Data collected a few years ago at Iowa showed that our students spent approximately five times as many hours on homework for the finance core course as on homework for the OB-HR core course.)

Apparently, student overconfidence with respect to behavioral issues has been a longstanding challenge for instructors, as evidenced by this 82-year-old quote: "The beginning student, while willing to admit ignorance on many technical questions, comes . . . with certain concepts of causation in human behavior quite firmly fixed" (Nixon, 1925, p. 418). In addition, because the vast majority of business positions in HR are filled with individuals who do not have a college degree in HR (e.g., Freedman, 1990), questions are raised as to whether HR really reflects a scientific body of knowledge or an academic discipline. Thus, HR instructors face questions of professionalization similar to those confronting their counterparts in business organizations.

Can Industrial Relations Programs Bypass the Problem?

As should be clear by now, we see a rather substantial array of obstacles to HR becoming a "major force" in business schools. In comparison with stand-alone industrial relations programs, nearly all forces in business schools are aligned against having a powerful HR presence—few students with HR (or even management) interests, small numbers of HR jobs and recruiters, poor salaries relative to other MBA career options, poor student word of mouth, and weak administrative support via admissions, advising, and placement.

In all these regards, we would have to say that the future for HR education continues to be much brighter in IR programs, despite business rhetoric that it wants "business people first" in HR positions. Rather, data and experience show that recruiters for HR positions want HR people first, preferably with experience, and preferably trained in the same way that most who have attained college-level training in HR have done so in the past—in specialist bachelor or Master of arts programs in industrial relations and human resources.

In IR programs, HR is "king of the roost," occupying a position akin to finance or consulting in business schools. For example, the vast majority of students enter IR programs with an intrinsic interest in behavioral issues. In addition, relative to majors in labor economics, organizational behavior, or collective bargaining, HR students have the most (and the most lucrative) job prospects. As a result, they also tend to have the most resources and power in IR programs (this is a distinct change from 20 or 30 years ago, partly attributable to the decline of unions).

However, simply continuing to train the "cream of the HR crop" in IR programs does nothing to obviate the problem that HR has a poor reputation in business *per se*. Furthermore, it simply delays the point at which the HR-trained professional will come up, head-to-head, against MBAs with majors in accounting and finance who are likely to treat HR as an expense to be whittled and downsized as each financial quarterly return comes due. The question as to whether IR programs are truly equipping students to deal with these eventual realities is, in our opinion, an open one.

Business schools, rather than IR programs, are the source of the next generation of business leaders. To the extent that business schools turn out graduates who are ignorant, or even disdainful, of HR issues, the negative effects will be felt by HR professionals for a long time to come. Therefore, it is important for academics and professionals to communicate on educational matters and to develop joint solutions to problems in both the classroom and the workplace, because they are inherently interrelated (Dean et al., 1998; Stone, 1991).

We truly wish we had a list of simple "what-to-do" pieces of advice, but we do not. We believe the issues involved are deeply embedded in the way business operates, and we see few signs of benign reversal in the near future. Because of this, the most we hope for is that this article will stimulate further discussion and joint problem solving between academics and practitioners directed toward dealing with this issue. As our evidence makes clear, problems in HR education cannot be solved in isolation from HR's problems in the workplace.

Notes

1. Because we conducted this survey at only one school, there is a possibility that our results are due to weakness of the HR faculty at Iowa. However, at the time the survey was conducted, our faculty included such prolific researchers as Frank Schmidt, Tim Judge, Murray Barrick, and Mick Mount. In addition, the department's teaching evaluations were consistently (and still are) higher than those of other departments in the college.

2. Because the survey was taken several years ago, salary figures have been inflated to 2007 levels using an annual cost-of-living figure provided by the Bureau of Labor Statistics Web site. Even so, it appears that Iowa students have lower salary expectations than those revealed by actual salary surveys of graduating students. However, although our results show salary underestimates in an absolute sense, surveys of actual salaries show that our sample was highly accurate about relative salaries across disciplines, as shown later in the chapter.

References

Allen, C. (1998, March 22). Minding their own business. *Washington Post Magazine*, pp. W18, W28–W30.

Arthur, J. B. (1994). Effects of human resource systems on manufacturing performance and turnover. *Academy of Management Journal, 37,* 670–687.

Badaracco, J. L., & Webb, A. P. (1995). Business ethics: A view from the trenches. *California Management Review, 37*(2), 8–28.

Beatty, R.W., & Schneier, C. E. (1997). New HR roles to impact organizational performance: From partners to players. *Human Resource Management, 36*, 29–38.

Beer, M. (1997). The transformation of the human resource function: Resolving the tension between a traditional administrative and a new strategic role. *Human Resource Management, 36*, 49–56.

Bok, D. (1993). *The cost of talent.* New York: The Free Press.

Branch, S. (1998, March 16). MBAs: What they really want. *Fortune, 137*(5), 167.

Burke, W. W. (1997). What human resources practitioners need to know for the twenty-first century. *Human Resources Management, 36*, 71–79.

Byrne, J. A., Leonhardt, D., Bongiorno, L., & Jespersen, F. (1996, October 21). The best B-schools. *Business Week*, pp. 110–122.

Cappelli, P. (1995). Is the "skills gap" really about attitudes? *California Management Review, 37*, 108–124.

Collins, M. (1996). What are they and what do they want? *Journal of Career Planning and Employment, 57*(1), 41–56.

Csoka, L. S. (1995). *Rethinking human resources* (Report 1124–95-RR). New York: The Conference Board.

Dean, J. W., Brandes, P., & Dharwadkar, R. (1998). Organizational cynicism. *Academy of Management Review, 23*, 341–352.

Educational Benchmarking, Inc. (1997). *1997 AACSB/EBI full-time MBA student satisfaction exit survey.* St Louis, MO: Author.

Frank, R. H. (1985). *Choosing the right pond: Human behavior and the quest for status.* New York: Oxford University Press.

Frank, R. H., Gilovich, T., & Regan, D. T. (1993). Does studying economics inhibit cooperation? *Journal of Economic Perspectives, 7,* 159–171.

Green, K. C., & Seymour, D. T. (1991). *Who's going to run General Motors?* Princeton, NJ: Peterson's Guides.

Gutek, B. A. (1997). Teaching and research: A puzzling dichotomy. In R. Andre & P. Prost (Eds.), *Academics hooked on teaching.* Thousand Oaks, CA: Sage.

Freedman, A. (1990). *The changing human resources function* (Report 950). New York: The Conference Board.

Hindo, B. (2002, June 14). Where can execs learn ethics? *Business Week Online.* Retrieved May 2, 2007, from http://www.businessweek.com/bwdaily/dnflash/jun2002/nf20020613_6153

Howard, A., & Bray, D. 1988. *Managerial lives in transition: Advancing age and changing times.* New York: Guilford.

Huey, J. (1993, November 1). How McKinsey does it. *Fortune, 128*(11), 56–81.

Kanter, R. M. (1977). *Men and women of the corporation.* New York: Basic Books.

Kochan, T. A. (2002). Addressing the crisis in confidence in corporations: Root causes, victims, and strategies for reform. *Academy of Management Executive, 16*, 139–141.

Lacayo, R., & Ripley, A. (2002, December 30). Persons of the year: The whistle-blowers. *Time, 160*(27), 30–60.

Luthans, F., Hodgetts, R. M., & Rosenkrantz, S. A. (1988). *Real managers.* Cambridge, MA: Ballinger.

MacDuffie, J. P. (1995). Human resource bundles and manufacturing performance: Organizational logic and flexible production systems in the world auto industry. *Industrial and Labor Relations Review, 48,* 197–221.

The MBA road. (1998, October 19). *Business Week,* special insert accompanying "The best B-schools."

Miceli, M. P., & Near, J. P. (1992). *Blowing the whistle: The organizational and legal implications for companies and employees.* New York: Lexington.

Miner, J. B., Ebrahimi, B., & Wachtel, J. M. (1995). How deficiencies in motivation to manage contribute to the United States' competitiveness problem (and what can be done about it). *Human Resource Management, 34,* 363–387.

Mintzberg, H. (1989). Society has become unmanageable as a result of "management." In H. Mintzberg, *Mintzberg on management: Inside our strange world of organizations* (pp. 335–373). New York: The Free Press.

Munk, N. (1998, March 16). The new organization man. *Fortune, 137*(5), 62–74.

Murray, M. (1995, May 4). Thanks, goodbye: Amid record profits, companies continue to lay off employees. *The Wall Street Journal,* p. A1.

Myers, D. W. (1990). Business schools lag in HRM offerings. *HRM Magazine, 35*(8), 72–75.

National Association of Colleges and Employers. (1996, September). *$alary $urvey.* Bethlehem, PA: Author.

National Association of Colleges and Employers. (1997, January). *$alary $urvey.* Bethlehem, PA: Author.

New MBAs: Nasty by nature. (1997, February 17). *Fortune, 135*(3), 127.

Nixon, H. K. (1925). Popular answers to some psychological questions. *American Journal of Psychology, 36,* 418–423.

O'Shea, J., & Madigan, C. (1997). *Dangerous company: The consulting powerhouses and the businesses they save and ruin.* New York: Random House.

Pfeffer, J. (1994). *Competitive advantage through people: Unleashing the power of the work force.* Boston: Harvard Business School Press.

Pfeffer, J. (1998). *The human equation: Building profits by putting people first.* Boston: Harvard Business School Press.

Porter, L. W., & McKibbin, L. E. (1988). *Management education and development: Drift or thrust into the 21st century?* New York: McGraw-Hill.

Prasad, P. (1997). Between text and context: Restoring connections in the OB classroom. In R. Andre & P. J. Frost (Eds.), *Researchers hooked on teaching.* Thousand Oaks, CA: Sage.

Reichheld, F. F. (1996). *The loyalty effect.* Boston: Harvard Business School Press.

Robinson, P. (1994). *Snapshots from hell: The making of an MBA.* New York: Warner Books.

Rynes, S. L., & Trank, C. Q. (1999). Behavioral science in the business school curriculum: Teaching in a changing institutional environment. *Academy of Management Review, 24,* 808–824.

Rynes, S. L., Trank, C. Q., Mullenix, A. M., & Ilies, R. (2003). Behavioral coursework in business education: Growing evidence of a legitimacy crisis. *Academy of Management Learning and Education, 2,* 269–283.

Schein, E. H. (1996). Career anchors revisited: Implications for career development in the 21st century. *Academy of Management Executive, 10*(4), 80–88.

Schuler, R. S. (1990). Repositioning the human resource function: Transformation or demise? *Academy of Management Executive, 4*(3), 49–60.

Sidanius, J., Pratto, F., Martin, M., & Stallworth, L. M. (1991). Consensual racism and career track: Some implications of social dominance theory. *Political Psychology, 12,* 691–721.

Stone, N. (1991). Does business have any business in education? *Harvard Business Review, 69*(2), 46–62.

Swoboda, F. (1995, February 5). So, you think you're top dog in the corporate hierarchy? *The Washington Post,* p. H6.

Taylor, A. (1998, April 13). Consultants have a big people problem. *Fortune, 137*(7), 162–165.

Ulrich, D. (1998). *Delivering results: A new mandate for HR professionals.* Boston: Harvard Business School Press.

Ulrich, D., Brockbank, W., Yeung, A. K., & Lake, D. G. (1995). Human resource competencies: An empirical assessment. *Human Resource Management, 34,* 473–495.

Ulrich, D., & Losey, M. (Eds.). (1997). Special issue on the future of human resource management. *Human Resource Management, 36,* 1–179.

Van Eynde, D. F., & Tucker, S. L. (1997). A quality human resource curriculum: Recommendations from leading senior HRM executives. *Human Resource Management, 36,* 397–408.

Wilhelm, W. R. (1995). Response to "Reexamining professional certification in human resource management." *Human Resource Management, 34,* 295–297.

Why Human Resources Managers Fail as Players in the Strategic Management Process

20

Nancy A. Bereman

Gerald H. Graham

How many decades ago was it when a few farsighted academicians made the grand gesture of changing the name, and hopefully the impact, of personnel managers? Personnel management morphed into HRM. The intent was to expand and deepen the role of people who specialized in the personnel function. The vision was for HR managers to grow into partners with CEOs and functional vice presidents in strategic management. The vision was grand. It was exciting, and there is some evidence that professionals who use the HR title are slightly more likely to be involved in strategic planning than those who use the personnel title (Hoque & Noon, 2001). Perhaps the most notable example of HR changing to a strategic role is the admission by General Motors' officials that they understand that they cannot become a truly global corporation without strategic support from HR. GM reports that their HR manager is a functioning member of the company's overall strategy board but admits that HR is still in transformation and there is much room for improvement (Leonard, 2002).

But for the most part, the involvement of HR professionals in significant strategic management has not materialized to any great degree. Most practitioners seem to still be involved primarily in traditional, transactional activities. For instance, a survey of 540 HR practitioners in Canadian organizations reported that only one out of three indicated that they had a role in strategic planning. Only 8% of departments claimed to be "completely" involved in creating the company business plan. Seventy-one percent of CEOs, 74% of line managers, and 77% of employees perceive that HR is still highly transactional (Brown, 2001a; Orr, 2002). Some American critics even suggest that HR practitioners are becoming less influential, as evidenced by companies outsourcing traditional HR functions (Ulrich, 1998). Further, many see HR as a cost center for the organization rather than an integral strategic partner (Caster, 2001; Pelham, 2002). Some suggest that the HR function is at a crossroads. Because of numerous efforts by many, there may be a window of opportunity to move out of the traditional HR function into a more strategic role. However, if HR managers do not take advantage of the opportunity and embrace the wider interdisciplinary approach required for strategic input, HR will run the risk of continuing to be marginalized (Becker & Gerhart, 1996).

This chapter postulates three reasons why human resources managers, in large part, have only limited impact in the strategic management of their organizations. The findings are based on numerous interviews with CEOs of large and small organizations, personal experiences in strategic planning with many organizations as both a consultant and a board member, and personal experience as faculty advisor to undergraduate students wishing to major in HRM at an AACSB-accredited school of business. As appropriate, we have supported our assertions with data from O*Net—the Occupational Information Network.[1]

Reason One: The Natural Forces of Strategic Management

The natural forces of strategic management do not favor human resources functions. Correspondingly, the tools of strategic management relegate human resources activities to a tactical role.

MARKET FORCES DOMINATE STRATEGIC MANAGEMENT

We define strategic management as "the process of selecting and implementing approaches (strategies) to achieve an organization's mission and goals." We assume that organizations exist to achieve a purpose (mission) and that the purpose can be subdivided into goals (outcomes). Strategies then become the means by which the organization achieves its mission and goals.

Successful organizations' missions and goals satisfy market needs. Successful leaders perceive market needs and evolve products and services that serve them. They also implement the means by which the products and services are produced and delivered. Thus, the natural forces of strategic management are centered in markets. The successful identification, interpretation, and satisfaction of market forces determine whether an organization survives, flourishes, or dies. In lay terms, successful managers "find a need and fill it."

The contributions of HR managers, as important as they are, typically are not "drivers." For instance, Bill Gates, apparently after some deliberation, saw a strategic opportunity to develop products and services to appeal to Internet users. Of course, the company had to select and train appropriate personnel to implement the strategy. But the market of potential Internet users was the "driver" in the decision. Neither the method of selecting or training, nor even the decision to add employees, was the driver. Rather the human resources decisions were a response to the market opportunity.

Frequently, companies make decisions to expand products or services, enter new markets or even industries, change distribution methods, utilize new technology, and the like. All of these decisions affect employees. And HR managers rightly involve themselves in the decisions relating to employees. However, it is not typical for employee factors to be significant drivers in strategy execution. For instance, after the recent falloff in airline traffic and the subsequent reduction in orders for large airframes, the Boeing Company did not say, "We have 10% more people than we need. Let's produce more (or different) product so that we can more fully utilize the skills of our people." The reduced demand in the market was a more powerful force than the "extra" employees, and the company responded by downsizing its workforce. In rare cases, leaders might decide to enter an area because employees have particular skills that would make it easy to serve the area. Still, these are exceptions, not the general rule.

STRATEGIC MANAGEMENT TOOLS

Perhaps in part because market forces are so dominant, the tools of strategic management reflect these forces and in so doing, in many organizations, reduce personnel decisions to a more tactical place. Strategic management analysis tools such as business-level strategies, functional-level strategies, global-level strategies, corporate-level strategies, and portfolio analysis are analytical tools for making sense of and responding to market forces. Business-level strategies focus on product or service cost and differentiation—both crucial issues in the marketplace. Functional-level strategies describe operations within a company such as manufacturing, marketing, product development, and customer service. HR functions are certainly a part of these functional-level strategies, but, according to its treatment in most strategic management textbooks, it is not a large part.

A scan of a few books shows very few pages devoted to human resources issues. Although this state of affairs reflects lack of HR knowledge among strategic management academicians, it contributes to perceptions held by non-HR graduates of business schools that HR expertise is not important to strategic decision making.

Corporate-level strategies speak to issues of vertical integration, diversification, alliances, acquisitions, new ventures, and the like. These are tools for analyzing market demands or opportunities. Portfolio analysis provides a way of assessing the current product mix to determine which products to invest in and which to downgrade. Many of these issues may not be directly relevant to HRM. Some could argue that the SWOT (strengths, weaknesses, opportunities, threats), also a strategic management tool, addresses the issue of personnel, especially when looking at strengths and weaknesses. For instance, an organization may have strengths in loyal, motivated, or dedicated workers. Seldom do these human resource strengths translate into strategic drivers. On occasion, though, the knowledge and high level of skill exemplifying the presence of rare and valuable talent may translate into strategic drivers. Unfortunately, the presence of such drivers is seldom recognized by corporate executives and their less-qualified HR heads.

Reason Two: Differences in Vocational Interests and Orientations

Discussions with many chief executive officers and human resources managers as well as observations of students who have selected HRM as a major suggests that, as with most career-choice decisions, a self-selection process operates. That is, individuals select careers according to their own abilities, values, and personality traits. In fact, as advisors to students we encourage this.

The differences between the vocational interests of executives and HR managers can be seen in the information provided on O*Net (2004, 2006b) for the job of Chief Executive and the job of Human Resources (see Table 20.1). As seen from Table 20.1, the patterning of occupational interests between the executives and HR managers differs. Nevertheless, both groups contain individuals who share vocational interests. Executives show somewhat greater interest in enterprising occupations than HR managers do, but enterprising occupations are also of greater interest to HR managers than are the other occupational categories. Neither group is particularly interested in occupations involved with working with ideas and requiring extensive amount of thinking. Yet, executives have greater interest in searching for facts and figuring out problems than do HR managers. Perhaps the main differences between HR managers and executives center on degree of interest in social as opposed to conventional occupations.

Table 20.1   Interests for Chief Executives and Human Resources Managers

HR Managers	Executives	Interests
	Standardized Values	
89	97	Enterprising[a]
50	78	Conventional[b]
67	61	Social[c]
28	36	Investigative[d]

Source: Data for this and subsequent tables are derived from O*Net (2004, 2006b).

[a]Enterprising occupations frequently involve starting up and carrying out projects. These occupations can involve leading people and making many decisions. Sometimes they require risk taking and often deal with business. [b]Conventional occupations frequently involve following set procedures and routines. These occupations can include working with data and details more than with ideas. Usually there is a clear line of authority to follow. [c]Social occupations frequently involve working with, communicating with, and teaching people. These occupations often involve helping or providing service to others. [d]Investigative occupations frequently involve working with ideas and require an extensive amount of thinking. These occupations can involve searching for facts and figuring out problems mentally.

Human resources managers seem to be more relationship oriented than outcomes oriented, whereas the opposite pattern is seen for executives. These differences relate to a fundamental disconnect between the roles and values of both parties. For example, individuals in social occupations tend to be oriented toward helping others and providing service to others. Although this is a positive orientation, HR is a technical area of management rather than a social service occupation. Consequently, a purely social orientation is problematic as it introduces bias in decision making. HR practitioners with a strong social orientation are likely to be less credible with their non-HR peers because at times they put individual issues and concerns ahead of organizational interests.

Successful strategic managers, while considering the impact of their decisions on individuals, focus on alternatives that produce the most favorable outcomes for the organization. For instance, a social orientation would argue for decisions that improve morale, whereas strategic managers may sacrifice morale, at least in the short run, for the purpose of a better competitive position such as reduced costs. There are times when layoffs are necessary, when nonproductive employees should be terminated, and when wayward employees require discipline. HR professionals who are graduates of HR Master's programs in business or in functionally based interdisciplinary industrial relations programs understand these tradeoffs. These professionals often succeed in challenging strategic managers' decisions because their arguments are credible to those managers. HR practitioners who are less knowledgeable about the field of HR, having learned their tasks on the job, may not have the credibility necessary to either challenge or question the decisions made by strategic managers.

HR managers seem less prone to take risks, and their decision making appears to be more cautious. As one CEO reported, "My HR manager would be completely satisfied with a 2%–3% improvement each year. I've got to have more than that." Another CEO reported, "When my HR manager proposed a rather elaborate program to change the culture of our organization, I asked him if he would be willing to 'bet his job' on the results of his efforts. I'm not even sure he understood the point I was making." The more successful strategic managers understand that they live and die by the outcomes of their decisions; the lack of business knowledge and skill of many HR managers appears to lead them to seek status quo and security over risk and uncertainty.

MICRO- VERSUS MACRO-ORIENTATION

In many organizations, the human resources function appears to be more specialized than the functions of marketing, finance, or operations. The specialization seems to draw HR practitioners more into day-to-day "fire-fighting" activities (Brown, 2001b; Legge, 1978). In such organizations, it is more difficult for HR practitioners to fully appreciate the intricate and complex relationships that make up the total organization, and consequently strategic thinking becomes more difficult. Efforts to relate the micro HR variables to financial outcomes necessary for meaningful strategic management input have not been as successful as many had hoped (Wright, Dyer, Boudreau, & Milkovich, 1999).

Examples of what appear to be more micro (transactional) activities include hiring, numerous compliance issues, safety, discipline, pay programs, performance evaluation, employee policies, and employee consultation. It can be argued that these activities affect the total organization, and they do, but they do not seem to have the same organizational reach as the activities of accounting and finance, marketing, and operations. Accounting and financial managers become intimate with the activities of all departments in their analysis of budgets, costs, and the like. But persons responsible for compliance or safety focus first on these issues and second on those aspects of the organization that are most affected by them. Even a function such as performance evaluation, which may be required in most departments, focuses more on the issues and techniques of evaluation that on the intimate details of issues the departments face. Broader HR functions such as cultural change and training and development do involve broad cross-sections of most organizations. Still, the focus is more on the nature of culture and the curriculum and delivery than on departmental issues.

In chiding HR practitioners to prepare themselves to better participate in strategic management, practitioners urge HR managers to know the broader dimensions of the business, including such things as core customer group, price-earnings ratio, cost of capital, markets, profitability, return on investment, leverage ratios, and characteristics of major shareholders. HR needs to focus more on elements of business problems that are likely to impede growth and profitability or diminish shareholder value (Becker, Huselid, Pickus, & Spratt, 1997; Brown, 2001a; Cheddie, 2001). Ann Boswall, vice-president of human resources and one of the six members of top management team at Imperial Tobacco in Montreal, adds, "It is absolutely essential for HR to do a better job of learning about the business outside of their own department" (Brown, 2001a, p. 20). Furthermore, HR people by their role more often act with staff authority, which is to say, they recommend to line managers who have the final say-so for the decision.

Accounting, finance, and economics, truly the language of business, force managers to understand minute aspects of the operations of all departments as well as the relationships between the departments. Marketing professionals, to be successful, must thoroughly understand the organization's product or service, and this forces them to a broader view of the total organization. Operational managers, because they have to understand the impact of costs and revenues, also usually have a broader view. Further, marketing professionals and operational people in effective organizations interact about the core issues involved in finding and filling the needs of their customers, clients, patients, or students.

HARD VERSUS SOFT SKILL ORIENTATION

Table 20.2 provides information from O*Net (2004, 2006b) about the different knowledge sets that are thought to be important for Chief Executives and Human Resources Managers. Some of the striking differences are the high level of importance of administration and management, economics and accounting, and law and government and the low level of importance for personnel and human resources policies and practices for chief executives. By contrast, the top knowledge sets required for human resources managers are personnel and human resources policies and practices, English language, and customer and personal service; a low level of importance is placed on accounting and psychology knowledge sets. Clearly the knowledge sets listed in the *Dictionary of Occupational Titles* (O*Net, 2006a) suggest that HR is a social occupation as well as a nontechnical occupation. This may explain the attraction of HR jobs to individuals with a wide range of occupational preparations

It appears that many HR practitioners select the area because they perceive that their talents and subsequently their success is with the "softer aspects" (communication, listening, people, problem solving, conflict resolution) of organizations. Anecdotally, numerous undergraduate students and practitioners have commented that they chose HRM because it does not require a lot of math, accounting, or engineering or because they "like to work with people." The presence of individuals with a wide range of

Table 20.2   Knowledge Required for Chief Executives and Human Resources Managers

	Chief Executives	
Importance	*Knowledge*	*Description*
86	Admininstration and Management	Knowledge of business and management principles involved in strategic planning, resource allocation, human resources modeling, leadership technique, production methods, and coordination of people and resources.
75	Economics and Accounting	Knowledge of economic and accounting principles and practices, the financial markets, banking, and the analysis and reporting of financial data.
74	Law and Government	Knowledge of laws, legal codes, court procedures, precedents, government regulations, executive orders, agency rules, and the democratic political process.
73	English Language	Knowledge of the structure and content of the English language including the meaning and spelling of words, rules of composition, and grammar.
72	Customer and Personal Service	Knowledge of principles and processes for providing customer and personal services. This includes customer needs assessment, meeting quality standards for services, and evaluation of customer satisfaction.
67	Sales and Marketing	Knowledge of principles and methods for showing, promoting, and selling products or services. This includes marketing strategy and tactics, product demonstration, sales techniques, and sales control systems.
57	Personnel and Human Resources	Knowledge of principles and procedures for personnel recruitment, selection, training, compensation and benefits, labor relations and negotiation, and personnel information systems.
	Human Resources Managers	
Importance	*Knowledge*	*Description*
94	Personnel and Human Resources	Knowledge of policies and practices involved in personnel/human resource functions. This includes recruitment, selection, training, and promotion regulations and procedures;

Importance	Knowledge	Description
		compensation and benefits packages; labor relations and negotiation strategies; and personnel information systems.
82	English Language	Knowledge of the structure and content of the English language including the meaning and spelling of words, rules of composition, and grammar.
80	Customer and Personal Service	Knowledge of principles and processes for providing customer and personal services. This includes customer needs assessment, meeting quality standards for services, and evaluation of customer satisfaction.
74	Administration and Management	Knowledge of business and management principles involved in strategic planning, resource allocation, human resources modeling, leadership technique, production methods, and coordination of people and resources.
71	Law and Government	Knowledge of laws, legal codes, court procedures, precedents, government regulations, executive orders, agency rules, and the democratic political process.
68	Clerical	Knowledge of administrative and clerical procedures and systems such as word processing, managing files and records, stenography and transcription, designing forms, and other office procedures and terminology.
68	Education and Training	Knowledge of principles and methods for curriculum and training design, teaching and instruction for individuals and groups, and the measurement of training effects.
58	Economics and Accounting	Knowledge of economic and accounting principles and practices, the financial markets, banking and the analysis and reporting of financial data.
57	Psychology	Knowledge of human behavior and performance; individual differences in ability, personality, and interests; learning and motivation; psychological research methods; and the assessment and treatment of behavioral and affective disorders.

occupational preparation in HR jobs, however, appears to reflect hiring decisions of non-HR executives and their HR managers. Critics say that HR practitioners do not have very many "numbers," and they are reluctant to place too much emphasis on complex analytical tools that make use of a lot of numbers. With the exception of turnover statistics, many numbers that HR does collect seem to focus on inputs, for instance, number of people trained, applications received, and the like. There are few generic HR metrics that are strictly driven by HR efforts (Brown, 2001b). Successful strategic managers, though, place a premium on hard skills. Sophisticated financial analysis, complex production planning schemes, rigorous marketing research, and the like all require at least an appreciation for the tangible (hard) tools of analysis.

Consistent with the listing of knowledge required for chief executives and HR managers, Table 20.3 provides information from O*Net (2004, 2006b) about the relative importance of different skill sets for the two groups. The most important skills for executives (in descending order of importance) are judgment and decision making, management of financial resources, critical thinking, coordination, negotiation, active listening, monitoring, and complex problem solving. Contrast these "active" skills to the "softer" skills for the HR managers of active listening, management of personnel resources, reading comprehension, writing, speaking, negotiation, time management, and social perceptiveness. Only the skills of "active listening" and "negotiation" are shared between the two groups.

REACTIVE VERSUS PROACTIVE ORIENTATION

Strategic managers must be proactive. Historically, HR actions tended to be more reactive or designed to safeguard the company from possible future harm. An HR executive in a very large company, who had close ties to the president, proudly put it this way: "The president tells me what type of changes he wants in our management culture, and I develop the program to deliver the changes." It did not appear to be an issue with the HR executive that he was simply reacting rather than participating in a strategic decision. Apparently, many HR practitioners have bought into the internal and external customer orientations, and this has put them into a responsive and reactive mode rather than a proactive one. The attitude of too many HR staff seems to be, "Just do what they ask for" (Green, 2002). In governmental organizations, even when HR departments engage in strategic planning for their departments, they tend to focus on what they need to do to serve the broader organizational mission and goals rather than sitting at the table with strategic managers when the company's mission and strategies are debated. Thus, HR is still a passive, reactive member of the team (Tompkins, 2002).

Table 20.3   Skills for Chief Executives and Human Resources Managers

	Chief Executives	
Importance	*Skills*	*Description of Skill*
99	Judgment and Decision Making	Considering the relative costs and benefits of potential actions to choose the most appropriate one.
96	Management of Financial Resources	Determining how money will be spent to get the work done, and accounting for these expenditures.
92	Critical Thinking	Using logic and reasoning to identify the strengths and weaknesses of alternative solutions, conclusions, or approaches to problems.
92	Coordination	Adjusting actions in relation to others' actions.
92	Negotiation	Bringing others together and trying to reconcile differences.
90	Active Listening	Giving full attention to what other people are saying, taking time to understand the points being made, asking questions as appropriate, and not interrupting at inappropriate times.
89	Monitoring	Monitoring/assessing performance of yourself, other individuals, or organizations to make improvements or take corrective action.
87	Complex Problem Solving	Identifying complex problems and reviewing related information to develop and evaluate options and implement solutions.
	Human Resources Managers	
Importance	*Skills*	*Description of Skill*
92	Active Listening	Giving full attention to what other people are saying, taking time to understand the points being made, asking questions as appropriate, and not interrupting at inappropriate times.
89	Management of Personnel Resources	Motivating, developing, and directing people as they work, identifying the best people for the job.
78	Reading Comprehension	Understanding written sentences and paragraphs in work-related documents.
78	Writing	Communicating effectively in writing as appropriate for the needs of the audience.
77	Speaking	Talking to others to convey information effectively.
76	Negotiation	Bringing others together and trying to reconcile differences.
74	Time Management	Managing one's own time and the time of others.
71	Social Perceptiveness	Being aware of others' reactions and understanding why they react as they do.

HR professionals do manpower planning in reaction to growth projections; they develop compliance programs in reaction to regulatory agencies; they train and develop in reaction to perceived skill gaps; and most performance evaluation systems seem to place a lot of emphasis on defensiveness against potential lawsuits as opposed to personnel development (e.g., Hammonds, 2005). Surely, the importance of documentation in most HR functions results more from reactions to real or imagined past injustices than it does to future strategic choices.

Reason Three: Occupational Preparation and Background

Finally, and perhaps most importantly, it appears that the occupational preparation and background of many, if not most, HR practitioners do not lend themselves to the recruitment and development of persons with strategic management talents and orientation.

OVERSPECIALIZATION OF HR

Strategic management requires a broad, overall view of the firm. The majority of current HR practitioners focus on implementation of narrow, specialized tasks, which does not lend itself to the development of strategic managers. It is common to specifically design HR tasks to specialize in such tactical (transactional) activities as recruiters, compliance officers, trainers, wage and salary administration managers, counselors, and the like. Typically, these jobs are very specialized and actually require that the person know very little about the overall operation and products or services of the company. Although it is true that many functions in other areas are also specialized, it appears that most of the orientation in HR remains on narrow, specialized tasks. Roper (2001) encourages HR people to take on more roles outside of their responsibilities by conducting business assessments—research reports that identifies problems and recommends solutions for particular issues. Yet it is difficult to do for individuals who enter HR without HR technical training and without business knowledge or skill.

UNIVERSITY CURRICULA AND EDUCATIONAL BACKGROUND

Writing in *Public Personnel Management*, consultant and trainer Marnie Green (2002) flatly states that the primary reason HR practitioners have not been satisfied with their attempts to participate in strategic management is because they are still trained and reinforced in the traditional, transactional mindset. She adds that the shift from transactional to strategic will not occur until HR staff members are adequately and properly trained for this new role (Green, 2002). Tompkins agrees that training in human resources emphasizes the administration of personnel systems and not general management or organization development (Tompkins, 2002). Although these perceptions may relate to HR practices in public-sector organizations and training in academic programs such as public administration and human resource development, they do not entirely reflect the state of business school curricula. First, it would be difficult to even find a business school program that emphasizes personnel administration. Second, the undergraduate core curriculum in business is the same for all students. Like other business students, HR students are exposed, in the required courses, to the vital concepts of return on investment, cost-benefit analysis, marginal costs, payback period, opportunity costs, and the like. However, those concepts may not be reinforced in the HR courses to the degree they are reinforced in the other functional courses of business. As a result, HR graduates initially may not fully understand the relationships between HRM activities and the activities of other functions. Business graduates in the other functional areas, however, may have even less understanding of the relationships among the business functions and HR because HR is not a core (i.e., required) course in most business schools. These issues ultimately can be resolved because all business graduates understand business. Perhaps more significant criticisms of educational programs revolve around the misunderstanding that HRM programs have common body of knowledge requirements. Although HRM content in business, industrial relations, and industrial and organizational psychology does overlap, it is not identical. Moreover, the label HRM is used for programs in public administration and adult education, which often have very little functional HR content.

Besides variability in educational programs claiming to graduate HR practitioners, an even greater problem is that many practitioners have no educational preparation in HR and are hired into entry-level positions where they learn their HR tasks on the job. Educational backgrounds in a great variety of fields (such as clinical psychology, communications, history, English, adult education, sociology, public administration, and others) appear to qualify applicants for HRM jobs. This may be the cause of the state of HRM practice and the criticism of its practitioners because it leads to few connections between HRM program costs and their benefits. For example, when I asked a training director of a large firm if he could demonstrate the benefits of his very extensive training budget and effort, his reply was, "No, we simply have to keep hoping that the president continues to fund our efforts on faith." It also leads to limited career paths for HRM practitioners. This may also be the effect of corporate executives' lack of expertise in functional HR.

LIMITED CAREER PATH

It appears that a career path is both shorter and more limited in HR than in other functional areas. Additionally, a rotation to HR is not seen as a choice assignment for prospects in management-training programs. HR career paths seem to top out as the top official in the HR department of smaller companies.[2] In very small companies, the HR department might be only two or three people, or even just one person, in which all HR activities are clerical in nature and do not require possession of technical HR knowledge and skill. Larger companies do have much larger HR departments, but it is unusual for the top HR person to be promoted to higher positions in marketing, operations, or finance. It is also rare for an HR person to takes a sideways move to accept a position in these areas. In short, people who get into HR seem to stay in the area, and there does not appear to be an open career path to other functions or to higher positions within the company. In recognizing the inadequacy of career experience for preparing HR to make strategic contributions, Green (2002) argues that companies should implement a job rotation program for HR people to spend 18–24 months in the functional areas of the company. Given the varied educational preparation of HRM practitioners, this is a difficult program to implement. Many organizations have management development programs that rotate promising young prospects among various functional areas and geographic locations within the company. Yet, promising young management candidates do not enthusiastically seek a tour of duty in HR as a "rounding out" of their experiences. They much prefer various operational assignments in which they get to make decisions about some aspects of the production of the company's products or services. They also desire marketing and finance assignments, as these positions allow them to broaden their understanding of the overall company.

A Paradox?

Very successful practicing managers understand the importance of selecting the right talents for their organizations. They know that they must have people who both are talented enough to do the jobs they are hired into and, at the same time, have an ability to work with others in a teamwork environment. Managers also understand that the selection process is critical because it is just not possible to develop people into required strengths of performance and teamwork unless they are somewhat gifted in the desired areas to begin with. Managers recognize the importance of hiring and keeping the right people, and they often build in powerful financial incentives to keep star performers. Market analysts and successful dealmakers also know that the future value of an organization depends heavily on the leadership of the firm and its talent pool. As the legendary basketball coach John Wooden remarked, "Not all coaches with good talent win but all coaches who win have good talent."

It would seem that, because selection and retention strategies are so vital to success, HR professionals would receive greater appreciation from the top management team. But the reality is that many HR executives do not understand their role in this process—that is, to design an effective staffing system and not to make hiring decisions. Company leaders rightly pride themselves in selecting their members, and they do not allow HR professionals to have significant influence. One CEO commented, "So much of who you hire depends upon the personal relationship that you develop with the individual. I don't see how my HR person can assess this relationship better than I can." Down through the ranks, operational managers exert significant influence in hiring decisions, and relationships with mangers are certainly key factors in why talented subordinates stay or leave the firm. HR practitioners get heavily involved in recruiting and screening employees, but they have yet to understand their role within the total staffing system.

Summary

There is little evidence that HR practitioners have taken a seat of equal influence with other managers when it comes to setting the strategic direction of the company. This chapter proposed three reasons why this has not come about: (1) external market forces that dominate strategic management; (2) differences in vocational interests and orientations of executives and HR managers; and (3) occupational preparation and background of HR practitioners. All three reasons correlate with the view outsiders have about HRM. The observation that the HR knowledge and skill requirements listed in O*Net do not reflect the HRM curricula in business or industrial relations educational programs is problematic. Equally problematic is the fact that HR knowledge is not very important to corporate executives. This clearly suggests that HR executives may not know what knowledge and skill to expect from their HR subordinates and managers. In turn, HR managers who are not educated in HRM are likely to hire others similar to them and to devalue formal HR education. Perceptions about HRM practitioners will change if practitioners become academically qualified in business and in HRM and if executives gain an understanding of HRM and of how their organization will benefit from HRM expertise. There are some organizations that contain these elements. The majority, however, do not, and this is the reason why HR managers fail to be players in the strategic management process.

Notes

1. O*Net can be found online at http://www.onetcenter.org. O*Net is a comprehensive database of worker attributes and job characteristics. It is designed to be the replacement for the *Dictionary of Occupational Titles* (DOT) and will be the nation's primary source of occupational information.

2. Even in smaller companies the HR practitioner may not head the function, as it is typical to house HR in the finance department.

References

Becker, B., & Gerhart, B. (1996). The impact of human resource management on organizational performance: Progress and prospects. *Academy of Management Journal, 39*(4), 779–801.

Becker, B., Huselid, M., Pickus, P., & Spratt, M. (1997). HR as a source of shareholder value: Research and recommendations. *Human Resource Management, 36*(1), 39–47.

Brown, D. (2001, November 5). HR's role in business strategy: Still a lot of work to be done. *Canadian HR Reporter, 14*(9), 1, 20, 22.

Brown, D. (2001, November 19). The measure of function. *Canadian HR Reporter, 7*(20), 1, 7.

Caster, M. (2001). How HR can survive and thrive in the organization. *Organization Development Journal, 19*(2), 79–92.

Cheddie, M. (2001, August). How to become a strategic partner. *HR Focus, 1*(8), 1, 13–15.

Green, M. (2002, Spring). Internal human resources consulting: Why doesn't your staff get it? *Public Personnel Management, 31*(1), 111–119.

Hammonds, K. H. (2005, August). Why we hate HR. *Fast Company, 97,* 40–47.

Hoque, K., & Noon, M. (2001). Counting angels: A comparison of personnel and HR specialists. *Human Resource Management Journal, 11*(3), 5–22.

Legge, K. (1978). *Power, innovation and problem-solving in personnel management.* London: McGraw-Hill.

Leonard, B. (2002, March). GM drives HR to the next level. *HRMagazine, 47*(3), 46–50.

O*Net. (2004). *Summary report for human resources managers* (Report no. 11-3040.00). Retrieved December 11, 2006, from http://online.onetcenter .org/ link/summary/11-3040.00

O*Net. (2006a). *Dictionary of occupational titles.* Retrieved December 11, 2006, from http://online.onetcenter.org

O*Net. (2006b). *Summary report for chief executives* (Report no. 11-1011.00). Retrieved December 11, 2006, from http://online.onetcenter.org/link/ summary/11-1011.00

Orr, B. (2002, February 11). Six strategic roles for HR to fill. *Canadian HR Reporter, 15*(3), 7.

Pelham, D. (2002, April). Is it time to outsource HR? *Training, 39*(4), 50–52.

Roper, B. (2001, November). Sizing up business problems. *HR Magazine, 46*(11), 50–56.

Tompkins, J. (2002, Spring). Strategic human resources management in government: Unresolved issues. *Public Personnel Management, 31*(1), 95–110.

Ulrich, D. (1998, January). A new mandate for human resources. *Harvard Business Review, 76*(1), 124–135.

Wright, P., Dyer, L., Boudreau, J., & Milkovich, G. (Eds.). (1999). *Strategic human resources management in the twenty-first century.* Stamford, CT: JAI Press.

Why Knowledge of Core Business Functions Is Crucial for HR Managers

21

Herman A. Theeke

After years of informal discussions with Vida Scarpello, I was grateful when, in 2002, she organized a forum to discuss the HR field and provided me with an opportunity to organize and share my thoughts on the importance of business knowledge and business skills in an HR education. In thinking about how to approach this topic, I decided I really was faced with two choices, one I will call "To Ponder" the other "To Pander." I realized that I could tell readers either what I thought they ought to hear or what I thought they wanted to hear. If I told them what I thought they needed to hear, and it made them uncomfortable, readers could choose either to dismiss my ideas or to ponder the issues that I raised. If I told them what they wanted to hear, such pandering might endear me to readers, but it probably would not lead them to ponder the issues. I knew it would be easier to pander but more rewarding to ponder.

In the years since Professor Scarpello first asked me to share my thoughts about the importance of core business knowledge for HR managers, there have been a few events that seem worth mentioning. At the 2006 Academy of Management meeting, a number of sessions focused on the future of HR management. One session I attended, which seemed to fit into the pander category, was one in which Professors Ulrich and Lawler bemoaned the shortcomings of HR and its failures to meet business's expectations. Another activity that I think has caused HR academics to ponder the future is the 2005 article "Why We Hate HR" by Keith Hammonds. His article represents quite a change in perspective from the 2001 book *The War for Talent* by Michaels, Handfield-Jones, and Axelrod, in which we were told how important the HR function was and would be. Of course, against these events has been the steady outsourcing of the HR administrative trivia and the HR practitioner belief that HR is becoming more and more of a strategic player. Finally, my own pondering about HR has changed my view of the field. In contrast to the paradigm we held in the past, I now suggest that HR should adopt a human resource liability management approach as a replacement for its human resource asset model (Theeke, 2005). These recent events accentuate the importance of the questions Professor Scarpello raised initially in 2002. We still need to decide in what direction HR educators want the occupation to develop. For example, should we, as HR educators, pander to the business conservatives? Simply by railing against government regulation of employment, we can garner much support from human resource and non-human resource business practitioners. It would be easy to implore HR educators to rally against unions and liberal lawmakers. Although such an approach from HR educators might tend to endear HR to some of their business counterparts, it could also reveal an ignorance of international and comparative industrial relations, John Dunlop's (1958) "web of rules," Sidney and Beatrice Webb's (1902) concept of "common rules," and the labor economic foundations that are, in part, the basis for professional HRM practice.

The challenges to HR educators will not be eradicated by pandering to the current practitioners, nor will they be resolved by changing HR's name or replacing it with some other social institution, the government's rules, or the union's rule-making authority. The challenge to HRM is to provide value in addition to and within the framework of those extra-organizationally imposed rules. This value must emanate from the same source as that of the purchasing department or the production department or the engineering department. It must emanate from the provision of an input factor with the proper quality and proper cost that fits with and in the strategic plan of the organization.

Identification of the Issue

This brings us to the subject of this chapter, which is to answer the general question, "What must HR professionals do to become an equal partner in developing corporate strategic plans?" Specifically, I have been charged to suggest the coursework and preparation needed for such participation. As I have pondered this charge, it has occurred to me that perhaps this desire to participate in strategic planning could be considered as a problem, because a problem is an unmet goal or objective. If I am correct, then a problem-solving process can be employed to develop a solution. We all know that the standard problem-solving process is often presented as (1) identify the problem, (2) determine the causes of the problem, (3) generate alternative solutions, (4) evaluate the alternatives, (5) select the best alternative, (6) implement the chosen alternative, and (7) evaluate the effectiveness of the implemented option. Experience probably has taught you that this apparently simple process is really more complex than it first appears. The process really requires an initial questioning (pondering) of the goal that has not been met to determine whether there is really a problem. It requires investigating (pondering) whether the accomplishment of the desired goal will alleviate the underlying problem or generate externalities that will compound the problem, add to it, or create additional problems. Only after this most difficult, problem identification, aspect of the problem-solving process has been completed should the determination of causes of the problem and subsequent steps be undertaken. Therefore, when I entertain the question, "What training and preparation would HR professionals need to participate in strategic planning?" I am compelled to ask "Why do HR professionals want to participate in strategic planning?"

HR Managers' Motives to Engage in Strategic Planning

I believe there are a number of reasons HR professionals want to participate in corporate strategy formulation. Some reasons are driven by the HR profession's desire to secure an equal footing with other business functions and the power that flows from participating in the corporate decision-making process. Some emanate from recent organization pressure on the HR profession to manage its functional area in a manner that parallels the other business functions.

DESIRE FOR EQUAL POWER

Since I became interested some 30 years ago in what then was called the personnel function, I have noted with wonder that human resource employees tended to be paid less than employees in other functions, and the deference paid to HRM practitioners also seems to be less. Over the years I observed that human resource practitioners received little respect. Some of my past observations are summed up in the article "Why We Hate HR" (Hammonds, 2005). Over the years, I have heard and been told by various people that it was their experience that the "HR department was the place where less competent managers were located" and "where you sent the employees who needed personal hygiene or other counseling." I heard other managers complain that all HR did was impede the progress of securing workers by imposing EEOC and affirmative action rules that were stupid and unnecessary and impede production by enforcing unnecessary health and safety rules that were developed by impractical OSHA employees. As a personnel director, I experienced contempt from some other managers when I enforced union contractual obligations, insisted on EEO and affirmative action compliance in hiring and promotion, and so forth. Entering, in the mid-1970s, an industrial relations doctoral program at the University of Minnesota provided some understanding as to the source of negativity toward HRM. In a lecture, Professor Herb Heneman, Jr., suggested that HR was misunderstood by other business functions and as a result corporate decision makers hired untrained and unqualified people to work in the field. He made this point with a fictitious story about the loading dock manager, "Old Joe," upon whose head a load of boxes had fallen and which rendered the man able only to smile and shake hands. Herb said the company's executives decided that because "Old Joe" had been a loyal employee they should find him some other job. You guessed it, they decided his two abilities—smiling and shaking hands—were all that were needed to become the head of HR. This bothered Herb. He explained that his solution was professional certification through the professional association ASPA, which is now known as Society for Human Resource Management (SHRM).

At about this same time, the mid-1970s, I was involved with a group of HR practitioners who were interested in investigating an area called human resource accounting. They found this attractive because they believed that it would allow them, via cost justification and cost-benefit analysis, to compete successfully for their company's resources. They believed that HR programs added value and also believed that if they could demonstrate the value HR brought to the company, then the HR function would have greater value to the organization and receive greater respect. Wayne Cascio (2000) echoes the themes that I encountered in the 1970s in his respected book *Costing Human Resources*. In the preface to the book, he suggests that the reason for wanting to do human resource valuation is so "HR management can compete successfully for resources with the managers of other functional business areas" (p. viii). And he thinks we fail at it because "much of what we do in the human resource management field remains generally misunderstood and underestimated by the organizations we serve" (p. vii). He goes on to state that, "In part, we in the field are responsible for this state of affairs because much of what we do is evaluated only in statistical or behavioral terms, if at all. Like it or not," he writes, "the language of business is dollars, not correlation coefficients" (p. vii). These statements of Cascio's imply to me that HR does not get its share of corporate resources or respect because our practitioners don't employ standard business approaches. I think the preceding demonstrates that, historically and currently, HR practitioners desire better treatment. I think HR practitioners desire to participate in strategic planning because they know the invitation to participate is an indication of an improved level of respect equal to other functional areas. I also think it might be fair to conclude that the contribution and activities of the HR function might not be well understood by the other business functions. If correct, this misunderstanding of the HR function might preclude the transfer of strategic planning skills developed from any new preparation requirements for HR students. I suggest that HR practitioners will not be invited to engage in strategic planning so long as the HR practitioner is perceived by the other functional managers as less skilled and having less understanding of the breadth of standard business processes.

So long as the HR field is perceived as a refuge for people who, like Herb's former loading dock supervisor, don't have the capacity to work on the other "important" business functions, HR practitioners will be paid less and will play a diminished role in corporate strategic plans. I therefore would recharacterize the problem of the profession as "How can HR professionals garner equal status with other business professionals, where indicators of equal status would include comparable compensation, and commensurate functional authority, combined with equality of access and involvement in corporate and strategic decision making?"

ORGANIZATIONAL PRESSURE FOR HR TO PARTICIPATE IN STRATEGIC PLANNING

New corporate emphasis on *knowledge-based* organizations and on the importance of *intellectual capital* is directing the focus of organization strategy to the acquisition retention and motivation of human resources. This new emphasis logically will cause corporate planners to seek participation from human resource practitioners.

In their 2001 book, *The War for Talent,* authors Ed Michaels, Helen Handfield-Jones, and Beth Axelrod contend that HR leaders will be as important as a chief financial officer. They contend that attracting, developing, and retaining talented people is the basis for competitive advantage more so even than financing strategies, tax tactics, and so on. Furthermore, they report that 88% of the corporate officers they surveyed thought it was critical or very important that HR managers be high-impact partners to line managers in strengthening the talent pool, but only 12% strongly agreed that their HR leaders now play that role. Expressing dissatisfaction with that finding, the authors write that each of an organization's divisions and each major location should have a superb HR generalist who is strategic, impact oriented, direct, tough minded, and effective at influencing peers and senior managers. They suggest that this HR person will forge the link between business strategy and talent and become the architect of the development strategy for the top 50–100 managers. They also predict that line leaders will need and welcome a strategic partnership with outstanding HR executives.

THE NEEDED CHANGES

There are two questions that must be answered to accomplish the goal of equal power in the strategic planning process.

1. How does the HR occupation change the perceptions that other functional managers have about HR practitioners?

2. How does the HR occupation change the capabilities of its practitioners so the practitioners have the capacity to effectively participate in strategic planning?

Change in perceptions about HRM probably requires changes in HRM education and the successful learning of business skills. Unless HR capabilities are thought to equal the other functional managers' business skills, it will be difficult to convince the other functional managers to allow HR to participate in strategic planning. The possibility that corporate heads in the future are going to be more prone to invite human resource executives into the strategic planning arena is not a positive development, if the HR executives are under qualified or not qualified in all aspects of business. The worst case for the profession, I fear, would be for corporate heads to perceive that their HR executives are competent when they are not. This would be disastrous because the HR executive would be allowed to participate in strategic planning but would soon be discovered to be incompetent.

Moving Toward the Solution

There seems to be convergence between the desires of HR practitioners to participate in strategic planning and the desire of other organization members to get HR practitioners involved. As noted, for this *new* relationship to come to fruition both perceptions of the HR practitioner's abilities and actual abilities must change. The remainder of this chapter will deal with these two issues.

CHANGING THE PERCEPTION OF HR MANAGERS' ABILITIES

Over the years I have noted that HR practitioners who spoke to the student chapter of SHRM, which I advise, seemed to have quite varied backgrounds. There were directors who had been public school teachers and worked up through a training route. There were directors who had trained as attorneys. Others had no formal training but began as receptionists or administrative employees in an HR office. Some had studied other business functions such as accounting or marketing or finance. Some had degrees in psychology, sociology, speech, or human resource development (HRD). Many had obtained certification from the American Society for Training and Development (ASTD), the American Society for Personnel

Administration (ASPA) or its newer form (SHRM), or the American Compensation Association (currently called WorldatWork). Of course, some were business graduates with HRM majors and some had degrees from the standalone HR/IR graduate programs. Because I knew that practicing accountants, marketing managers, or finance managers don't have the same variety of education and training, I wondered what it was that caused this variation in HR.

One day while thinking about this I remembered Herb Heneman's story of Old Joe on the loading dock. As I thought about this I realized that the people who ran companies were the ones who hired and promoted people in the HR function. I knew that in small and medium-sized businesses the HR director often reported to a Vice President of Finance, and I knew that the people who ran companies and made the HR director hiring decision generally did not have degrees in HR; they probably never even had a course in HR management. They might have a degree in finance or accounting or marketing or supply-chain management depending on what function was the driver of their particular business. Then I wondered, "Why would these people, who wouldn't consider hiring employees who didn't have functional training to work in the other functional areas of business, do so for HR?" I have come to believe that it is because these executives know the requirements for those other functional areas but are confused about the qualifications required for HR.

In business programs, students are generally required to complete what are called the core business courses. The core consists of accounting, finance, marketing, a production or operations course, statistics or quantitative methods, perhaps an information systems course, and an introductory "people" course, which is typically management or organizational behavior. Typically, there is no core requirement of a human resource management course. The students who become the future corporate decision makers have been told that they are required to take these core courses so they have exposure to *all* functional areas. They don't know they haven't taken an HRM course. They think the organization behavior class or the introduction to management class was the human resource class. Their confusion is reinforced when the instructors who teach these courses also teach in the HR major area. Behavioral courses are not functional HR courses and have no quantitative requirements. Hence they are often perceived as "common sense" and "easy." Because these courses are presumed to be HRM, experience in them drives the conclusion that the HR area isn't all that difficult. Adding to the belief that HR isn't demanding is the other students' perception that the HR majors in the business programs don't perform as well as they do in the finance and accounting and production and quantitative or statistics classes but still are able to be outstanding in the HR classes. Basically, the people who will be hiring HR managers conclude that there isn't much that is difficult about HR and that it attracts less-skilled students. This conclusion may be corrected if the business core required an introductory HRM course for all majors and if that course were taught at a level that required business students to use their previous training in accounting and financial decision making as well as statistics.[1] At a minimum, when HRM faculty teach the introductory management course or the required organization behavior course they should explain that this is not an HRM class.

A second part of the problem arises because many non-HRM business graduates assume that all standalone HR/IR graduate programs contain a business core requirement. Many with whom I have talked are surprised to learn that this may not be true.[2] The effect of this assumption is to cause the business graduates to think their HR counterparts, who lack skills in finance and accounting, are less intelligent because "they haven't learned the material, when in reality they just have not been taught it."

The Needed Skills

The simplest reason that HR managers need core business training is that such training allows them to develop the ability to communicate with and understand other functional managers with whom they will interact during strategic planning. This ability is needed to develop the credibility that is required to secure an entry into the strategic planning process and to effectively participate in it. Although it is easy to understand the steps in a strategic planning process, having the skills to complete and comprehend the economic forecasting and financial evaluation of alternatives that are developed using pro forma accounting statements and consideration of various types of risk is not an easy, innate, or intuitive process.

HR practitioners will need to share some common understanding and be comfortable with the definitions of some important business concepts. I don't mean that they have not heard the words before, but rather I mean that they need to understand these words in the way that professionals in the business world understand them. To demonstrate the level of understanding required of HRM practitioners, let me discuss two terms, *asset* and *value*.

"ASSET"

HR managers are very quick to agree and quick to tell others that human resources are the most valuable assets. But many in HR could not even define an asset or explain the concept of value. I contend that when HR managers actually understand the definitional requirements for an asset, the HR field would abandon the human resource asset paradigm in favor of a human resource liability management paradigm (Theeke, 2005). When HR managers insist on incorrect applications of finance and accounting concepts, other business managers question HR capabilities. If an HR manager tells finance managers "people are assets," the HR manager might need to be able to demonstrate it. Instead of HR managers thinking that accountants and finance managers "just don't get it" when we say we manage and create HR assets, maybe we need to realize that finance majors do know the definition of an asset. In their coursework they have been required to study accounting and economic texts such as Pindyck and Rubinfeld (1992), who, in their microeconomics text, write "An asset is something that provides a monetary flow to its owner" (p. 155). A rental unit provides a flow of rent. A savings account provides a flow of interest payments. A share of stock (not the dividend from it) has an implicit flow of capital gains or losses. Or they have read a managerial accounting text similar to the one authored by Ray Garrison (1991), where they learned "A cost is normally viewed as being an asset if it can be shown that it has revenue producing powers or if it can be shown that it will be beneficial in some way to operations in future periods. In short, a cost is an asset if it can be shown that it has *future service potential* that can be identified" (p. 269). Skousen, Stice, and Stice (1998), in their Appendix D, the glossary of their intermediate accounting book, define an asset as follows, "asset. A resource of an entity: technically defined by the FASB 'as a probable future economic benefit obtained or controlled by a particular entity as a result of past transactions or events'" (p. D-2). This definition is international as evidenced by David Alexander and Christopher Nobes (1994), who in their book *European Introduction to Financial Accounting,* enumerate the criteria for determining an asset. They suggest that an asset should provide probable future benefit, be controlled or possessed by the business, and be the result of some earlier event or transaction. On the basis of these definitions, the following are examples of nonassets: the ability to produce a product for which there is no demand (has no probable future value); a societal administered healthcare system that improves the physical well-being of employees (is not controlled or possessed by the business); the value of the experience that might be gained from next year's operations (has no earlier transaction or event).

This concept of *asset* is important for HRM practitioners who want to compete for organization resources by claiming that HRM programs create assets or that the organization's human resources are assets. The definition of an asset requires that there be monetary flows. So, if a researcher or HR practitioner wants to claim that they have an asset in human capital or an asset in intellectual capital or in their organization structure or anything else, business-trained managers who know the definition of an asset are going to ask for a demonstration that there are monetary returns. They know that when one has only the cost and not the returns, one cannot engage in managerial decision making except in that rare instance when one can assume that the benefit flows from all options are equal. I believe that HR practitioners would be better served if they understand these definitions and consider that from the perspective of many other managers, human resources would be better thought of as contingent liabilities (Theeke, 2005). Yet, I am convinced that before HR managers are capable to even consider such a departure from the human resource asset model, they will need to become more generally trained in finance and accounting than is the case at present. Furthermore, to engage in strategic planning, which involves capital budgeting (i.e., the process of deciding where, when, and if one project should be funded over another or at all), the costs and benefits, including estimates of risk and timing of the costs and benefits for all options, are required. This information is needed because strategic business decisions are based on the value estimates of the options.

"VALUE"

One important concept in the valuation process that implicitly defines value is *net present value* (NPV). Brealey and Myers (1996), in Chapter 2 of their text on corporate finance, explain the concept of NPV and suggest that NPV calculations make sense for asset valuation. Later in Chapter 11, these authors discuss the concept of economic rent and its implications for capital budgeting. They explain:

> When an industry settles into long run economic equilibrium, all its assets are expected to earn their opportunity cost of capital—no more and no less. If the assets earned more, firms in the industry would expand or firms outside the industry would try to enter it. Profits that more than cover the opportunity cost of capital are known as economic rents. These rents may be either temporary (in the case of an industry that is not in long run equilibrium) or persistent (in the case of a firm with some degree of monopoly or market power). The NPV of an investment is simply the discounted value of the economic rents it will produce. (p. 276)

The authors caution their readers, the finance students, that when they perform a financial analysis and see a positive NPV, rather than accepting it they should

> probe behind the cash flow estimates and try to understand the source of the economic rent. A positive NPV is only believable if you believe your company has some special advantage. Such advantage can arise in several ways You may be smart or lucky enough to be the first to the market with a new, improved product for which customers are prepared to pay premium prices (until your competitors enter and squeeze out excess profits). You may have a patent, proprietary technology, or production cost advantage that your competitors cannot match at least for several years. You may have some valuable contractual advantage. (p. 276)

The important point here is that for the value to be greater than zero, the present value of the monetary flows that are generated must exceed the cost of acquiring and maintaining the resource. From an economist's perspective, I think this means there must be some market imperfections. These market imperfections are exactly what businesspeople seek because they realize there is no profit in a perfectly competitive market and in the imperfect market they can accumulate these economic rents from their resources.

To try to get HRM practitioners to understand how businesspeople think of value, I tell them the following story. A storeowner has purchased two types of television sets. One hundred dollars was paid for type one and two hundred and fifty was paid for type two. I then ask them to tell me which set has the most value. They look at me as if I am crazy for asking them the obvious question, so I ask for a show of hands. Most of the hands go up for the $250 set. I always worry when a person puts up the hand for the $100 set. But what I am looking for here really is the person who doesn't choose either. Then I hope that choice arose for the right reason, that being, "*The answer cannot be determined from the information given.*" Businesspeople would say the TV that has the highest value is the one that throws off the higher contribution margin or the one that has the higher NPV. So what does this have to do with human resource valuation? Well, if you know only the costs, you cannot calculate value. It is not too far a leap to also realize that you cannot determine value if you know only benefits. Imagine that I tell you I sold two cars, one for $10,000 and the other for $15,000, and ask you which sale had more value. Without the costs for the cars you can't answer. Well, it should be clear that value depends not only on cost but also on benefits. So with this simple understanding of what an asset is and what is required to determine the asset value, we can begin to understand what HR managers must know to interact with other strategic planners trained in finance or accounting.

To be credible with other managers, if we in HRM would like to claim that the costs of our programs or the money spent for our employees is an asset, we must be able to show that the reason we spent these monies was to provide a future monetary flow to the organization. Second, if we want to value our human resource as assets, we will need to determine the value of the current and any future monetary outlays required as well as the periodic returns that will flow from the asset. If HR practitioners and educators understood *accounting concepts* better, they would realize that this approaches the impossible. It will be easier to show non-HR managers the liability they incur from poorly managed HR programs and practices than to ever convince them that you know the asset value of the organization's human resources or its HRM programs. It isn't that non-HRM managers need to be convinced that there is value in human resources. Brealey and Myers, as early as 1984 in the second edition of their corporate finance text, explained the difference between the market value and the value of the firm's tangible assets (book value) with reference to "intangible assets such as accumulated technical expertise, an experienced sales force, or valuable growth opportunities" (p. 408). So, finance students learn that the value of most businesses depends on managers, skilled workers, and engineers. They would have no quarrel with HR here. The rub comes because the human resource asset valuation problem requires isolating the independent effect of the human resource from an interaction effect in order to demonstrate the portion of a value that should be attributed to the human resources.

HOW TO ACQUIRE NEEDED SKILLS

I think there are some immediate things that HRM managers and prospective HRM practitioners can do to acquire the ability to participate in strategic planning. First, study finance, managerial finance, and capital budgeting. Second, study and understand managerial accounting so that terms such as cost, expense, capital, capitalize, asset, liability, relevant cost, fixed cost, variable cost, sunk cost, and opportunity cost have the same meaning when HRM and other people in business use them. HR practitioners need to be grounded in the core business courses and understand terms such as business risk, financial risk, market risk, portfolio risk, and political and foreign government risk. And they need to understand the methods for asset pricing and valuing assets. It seems that at a minimum every HR person should be able to present the formula for NPV calculations and should be familiar with internal rate of return, payback, and return on investment (ROI) methods. HRM practitioners need to understand production and operation precepts to understand the concepts of excess capacity versus buffers, and economic order quantity (EOQ), just-in-time (JIT), statistical process control (SPC) and statistical control processes (SCP), and inventory control, and be able to translate these into HRM consideration such as differential risk exposure within a union environment (that is, different liability exposure). Perhaps HR managers might actually begin to manage some of their own processes such as recruitment and training as if they were production systems.

Strategic planners need to understand statistics and the calculation of risk and had better not create confusion between the estimation of risk and return. If one increases the chance of having a productive employee, you increase the "expected payoff" from the productive employee because the risk of not receiving the payoff has decreased. But you don't increase the value of the payoff. Financial analysts, who do capital budgeting, are decision makers under risk. They estimate payoffs, probability of payoffs, costs, and probability of costs. But they don't think that, because they are estimating, the estimates don't matter. I recall one of psychologists Hunter and Schmidt's statements on utility theory (a topic they focused on in numerous issues of *Journal of Applied Psychology*) in which they reported that, after studying financial decisions, they concluded that those finance people make a lot of guesses. In my recollection, Hunter and Schmidt were saying that the real numbers don't matter to finance people so we don't have to worry too much about how good our numbers are either. Hunter and Schmidt were wrong. Financial analysts, because they know they are estimating, are always asking how good is that estimate, or how do I know that the estimate of the risk and cost and revenues are good. When we want to participate with others in organizations to determine uses of the organization's resources, we are engaging in strategic decisions. People trained in capital budgeting or managerial accounting work from general precepts to determine the relevant costs and returns for specific decisions. For example, Garrison (1991) gives common types of cash flow in his managerial accounting book when he discusses NPV.

He lists cash outflows:

Initial investment (including installation costs).

Increased working capital needs.

Repairs and maintenance.

Incremental operating costs.

He lists cash inflows:

Incremental operating costs.

Reduction in costs.

Salvage value.

Release of working capital (p. 599).

They are instructive for us because if HR managers understand the financial decision makers' requirements and precepts of production/operations, they will understand that HRM information can change the estimates that are the basis of evaluating production processes strategic alternatives. This can change those cash flows that form the basis for NPV calculations. For example, increasing the quality of labor can

1. Reduce a machine constraint by better equipment utilization.

2. Extend the life of equipment by knowledge of correct utilization and maintenance.

3. Increase the capacity of the equipment or processes through better utilization and proper setup.

4. Improve future revenues by increasing the quality of finished goods by working in closer tolerances.

Conclusion

In this chapter, I proposed that the desire for HR involvement in strategic planning has been part of the HRM agenda for a number of years. If my assessment is correct, that desire is beginning to be embraced by other functional areas of the organization. I suggest that there are risks associated with such involvement. These risks emanate from the non-HR functional managers' historic perception that HR managers are not as qualified as other functional managers. I suggest that in some respects this may be true because business decision makers have not required the same business skill level of the HR directors they hire and also because standalone IR/HR programs have not required completion of a business core, common to MBA and other business program graduates.

I have recommended that before HR managers become involved in strategic planning, they should become as well versed in financial decision making, managerial accounting, production planning and operations management, and the other business core courses as are the other functional business managers. I have expressed the fear that joining a strategic planning team without the requisite skills will not serve the HRM field's interest. The HR profession will not advance if the non-HR managers continue to say that HR managers are nice people who are quantitatively challenged and know little about business, business operations, accounting, or finance. I believe we need to develop a base of power by becoming more like other businesspeople. We cannot have members of our profession seen as quantitatively weak with lower than necessary skills in accounting and financial analysis. There is no reason that we should believe that our students would succeed only because they have the people skills and not the business skills. We must be perceived as having *all* of the same skills as other business professionals, with additional expertise in functional HR systems. As I stated before, I believe the best way for us to gain that perception is to really have business skills, not to only acquire the perception of them. Practicing managers will know if HR is faking it. They might not tell you they know, but paying you less, not giving you commensurate functional authority, and not allowing you to participate equally in strategic planning are strong empirical indicators of diminished power.

Notes

1. Often this is not possible as these classes may be taught by faculty who do not have degrees in business and have not acquired business knowledge and skills in their own education preparation outside a business school or through personal initiative.

2. Some IR/HR programs are incorporating accounting and finance courses in their curricula. I argue that all IR programs should incorporate and reinforce through use those courses in their curricula, even if the goal is to prepare students for jobs as regulators or union advocates, as they need the same knowledge of business as the people they hope to regulate or influence. All psychology programs should have the same expectation for students terminating with a Master's in I/O psychology, especially if those graduates seek jobs in HR in business or public-sector organizations.

References

Alexander, D., & Nobes, C. (1994). *European introduction to financial accounting.* New York: Prentice Hall.

Brealey, R. A., & Myers, S. C. (1984). *Principles of corporate finance* (2nd ed.). New York: McGraw-Hill.

Brealey, R. A., & Myers, S. C. (1996). *Principles of corporate finance* (5th ed.). New York: McGraw-Hill.

Cascio, W. F. (2000). *Costing human resources: The financial impact of behavior in organizations* (4th ed.). Cincinnati, OH: South-Western College Publishing.

Dunlop, J. (1958). *Industrial relations systems.* New York: Holt.

Garrison, R. H. (1991). *Managerial accounting: Concepts for planning, control and decision-making* (6th ed.). Boston: Irwin.

Hammonds, K. H. (2005, August). Why we hate HR. *Fast Company, 97,* 40–47.

Lawler, E., III. (2006). Presentation at Academy of Management Meeting, August 2006, Atlanta, GA.

Michaels, E., Handfield-Jones, H., & Axelrod, B. (2001). *The war for talent.* Boston: Harvard Business School Press.

Pindyck, R. S., & Rubinfeld, D. L. (1992). *Microeconomics* (2nd ed.). New York: Macmillan.

Skousen, K. F., Stice, E. K., & Stice, J. D. (1998). *Intermediate accounting* (13th ed.). Cincinnati, OH: South-Western College Publishing.

Theeke, H. A. (2005). A human resource accounting transmission: Shifting from failure to a future. *Journal of Human Resource Costing and Accounting, 9*(1), 40–59.

Ulrich, D. (2006). Presentation at Academy of Management Meeting, August 2006, Atlanta, GA.

Webb, S., & Webb, B. (1902). *Industrial democracy.* London: Longmans, Green.

SECTION 9

HR Professional Success and Parting Thoughts

The book concludes with this section. Chapter 22 delineates success factors for HR executives, and Chapter 23 focuses on the HRM credibility crisis.

In Chapter 22, Pierson identifies the factors that differentiate success from lack of success among HR executives. It is "the bottom line" of all approaches and discussions about HRM education and practice. In a sense, Pierson offers the criteria against which HRM educators may assess their undergraduate and graduate HRM students and programs.

In Chapter 23, Scarpello notes that the book contains chapters on the HRM curriculum and chapters more basic to the present state and future of HRM and HRM education. She first summarizes the four models of HRM education presented in this book and then discusses critical issues in the field and in HRM education. The main focus of the chapter is HRM's credibility problem with its various constituents. She discusses some ideas for gaining (or regaining) HRM credibility.

Human Resource Professional Success 22

David A. Pierson

People have long debated the importance of HRM. Some argue that it is central to a successful, forward-thinking organization, whereas others believe it adds little value and should be largely eliminated except for certain record-keeping tasks best handled by a clerk with a computer. After all, individual managers should manage their people without HR interference. *Fortune* (Stewart & Woods, 1996) even ran a column a number of years ago accusing HR of obstructing successful business practices and creating nothing but roadblocks for managers as they seek to achieve excellence. But there are successful HR executives who add real strategic value to their organizations. The difficulty is identifying the factors that differentiate success from lack of success.

This chapter speculates about some core HR issues regarding success that every HR executive has considered at some time in his or her career. Although I do not attempt to justify the existence of HR, I will present some ideas of what constitutes success in HR, itemize the qualifications that seem to lead to this success, and finally speculate on what all this means for institutions that attempt to train HR professionals, the organizations that employ them, and individuals currently in the field or thinking of joining it. These ideas reflect 25 years of observations accumulated while teaching HR graduate students and consulting with all types of employers, both for profit and not for profit, across a variety of industries and sizes. Some of the concepts I owe directly to colleagues and clients who have graciously shared their opinions and observations with me over the years. The final results are not scientifically derived, but rather experientially gleaned.

Defining HR

HRM means different things to different audiences, and it certainly should function differently in different situations. However, I would define the essential or core competency of HR as providing vital human capital information used in shaping the organization's vision and then helping to execute that vision through the people that make up the organization. This competency is equally important in for-profit businesses and not-for-profit organizations, in both the public and private sectors.

The basis for HR is the people the organization employs, but HR's influence and understanding should not be confined to employees, but rather should include everything influencing or influenced by the employee contract, both strategically and tactically. What differentiates HR from other organizational functions is the basis of information (employees), not the scope of influence or interest, which should be organization-wide. The function exists in every human organization with a mission it seeks to accomplish. The function might be centralized or grouped under the umbrella of a separate structural function, or it might be decentralized across other business functions and roles. But every human organization's vision must be accomplished through the collective efforts of the organization's members. This definition of HR necessarily involves organizational transformation and helps focus the discussion of HR success and who might be good at achieving this success.

Defining HR Success

Individual HR success is most easily defined as simply commanding the top HR slot in a large, successful organization in the same way as a player is deemed successful if he starts on a Super Bowl–winning team. However, many good football players never make it to the Super Bowl, and not all the members of a Super Bowl team excel. So defining HR success is not straightforward. The task of gauging success is made more difficult because success is a moving target: the field is changing, organizations are changing, and people are changing. Success in the 1960s, 1970s, or even 1980s is not success in the 21st century. The field of HRM has evolved from personnel—which was principally administration—to making people happy, to measuring everything, to being strategic, to being in the mahogany suite, to being. . . . This evolution compels HR execs to be either clairvoyants, chameleons, changelings, or contortionists to really understand and enact the role they should play in their organization at a particular time—no small order.

But a number of success criteria appear to stand the test of time and be relevant across organizations:

- *Made a difference*—The organization became a different and better place because of the individual's efforts. This difference can be assessed against the organization's mission or by assessing positive impact on the organization's culture as viewed by its stakeholders. In the end, the yardstick for success has to center around what the individual actually *achieved*.

- *Developed and operated within a moral code*—CEOs and CFOs make the news when they breach society's norms, but HR executive are probably more routinely called on to embody the organization's values and maintain a steady hand on the organization's moral tiller. The public sees the CEO, but the organization's members acutely feel management philosophy and culture, which the HR executive must help shape and maintain.

- *Rose to the top*—The HR tone is established from the top of the function, and success requires the long climb to this position.

- *Recognized by peers*—Over an extended professional career, success should include recognition within the profession. This might include speaking engagements, professional association leadership positions, and chairing various professional committees within professional associations.

- *Advice sought and taken*—Technical experts can influence in isolation, but the HR executive can be successful only if she is sought out for advice, the advice is valued, and the advice is acted on.

- *Navigated the organization around the rocks*—During the history of every organization, rocks will emerge out of nowhere and threaten the achievement of long-term objectives. Successful HR executives see these rocks in the distance and chart a safe course of action around them, while keeping the organization's mission well in view.

- *Professionalism of the function*—Organizations can be differentiated by the professionalism of their HR functions. Roughly defined, HR professionalism is characterized by effectiveness, efficiency, responsiveness, and use of state-of-the-art methods and technology. The successful head of the function establishes this milieu by demanding these outcomes and rewarding their achievement. Successful HR executives surround themselves with talented professionals and allow them to shine both inside and outside the organization.

- *Considered a leader, not just a manager*—Managers direct, leaders get out in front and demonstrate by example how success can be achieved.

- *Had fun*—It is probably impossible to be truly good at something you don't enjoy. It's much easier to be good at things we like doing. Plus, it's better to have fun than not to have fun, so a legitimate success criterion is to have had fun.

What Creates This Success?

Success in HR can be explained both situationally and individually. Given the choice of being lucky or good, most people would choose to be lucky. But this isn't a choice any of us is granted. The only things we can control are the decisions we make and the manner in which we work. From an organizational standpoint, choices are made among candidates on the basis of the perceived value these candidates will potentially add to the organization. In HR, the organization's senior executive attempts to choose the candidate who will most likely be successful as described above.

Success is a function of personal attributes, training, experience, luck, and, perhaps, structure. Let's examine them one by one.

PERSONAL ATTRIBUTES

Researchers have identified competencies that appear to differentiate highly successful HR executives from average ones. Taking a different tack, here are attributes that I and others associate with HR executives whom we believe have achieved success as described above:

- *Decisive*—Does not shy away from making difficult decisions.
- *Fair*—Makes decisions on the basis of clear criteria after weighing all the evidence.
- *Handles complexity*—Able to consider complex issues without needing to overly simplify them.
- *Chooses good people*—Able to accurately assess people and place them into roles where they will be successful and translate that personal success into organizational success.
- *Good networker*—Develops an extensive network of people with different skills and abilities in order to call on the appropriate person for assistance when a particular need arises.
- *Analytic*—Able to carefully sort through myriad details and identify important themes.
- *Grasps the big picture*—Able to rise above the details after sifting through them and recognizes the overall patterns that explain the data.
- *Approachable*—Not aloof.
- *Honest*—Demonstrates complete integrity in all decisions and interactions.
- *Intelligent (cognitively and emotionally)*—Possesses sufficient cognitive ability (IQ) to solve business problems while demonstrating considerable emotional intelligence (EQ) in order to understand people and relate to them at multiple levels.

- *"Grounded"*—Able to place issues in perspective with a "good street sense" about the causes and consequences of various actions and decisions.

- *Ethical*—Maintains a clear moral code that is understandable, straightforward, and clearly evidenced and communicated.

- *Socially secure and adept*—Able to interact with individuals and large groups and people from all backgrounds.

- *Empathetic*—Able to understand others by inserting oneself into the other person's situation and vicariously experiencing that person's perspective and pressures.

On a skill level, HR executive success ultimately depends on highly developed transformational skills. The HR exec is often called on to spearhead change and transform parts or all of the organization. The ability to effect this change without overly ruffling feathers and alienating peers requires considerable skill and interpersonal finesse while remaining focused on the ultimate goal. As one colleague phrased it to me recently, "transactional skills (efficiently handling HR transactions of whatever type) get you in the door, but transformational skills are necessary to be strategically successful."

Appropriate leadership *style* is situational and depends on the needs of the organization at a particular time. Some highly successful HR executives project a hard-headed, no-nonsense persona, whereas others are softer and more caring and spend time getting to know people and understanding their individual needs. Specifying the organizational characteristics that require one style or the other is beyond this chapter, but is very important for each CEO to carefully consider. Anecdotally, one colleague remembered that the hard-headed approach worked well in one situation that was fraught with change, whereas the softer style was highly successful in a situation where the organization was experiencing fewer changes and was much more stable. Phrased differently, in a sailboat race the captain must be decisive and highly directive, whereas the captain of a weekend cruise must be more diplomatic and address the individual needs of each crewmember.

Are these characteristics identical to those that predict success in other functions? There probably is at least an 80% overlap, but the other 20% is critical. Successful HR executives should understand the dynamics of organizational change or transformation better than any other executive. They have to intuitively understand the implications of change long before it occurs and anticipate corrective action before it is needed. They have to fundamentally understand how to align resources—by adding, subtracting, or melding current resources—with the organization's mission in order to better accomplish the organization's vision. Understanding organizational dynamics, not necessarily organizational politics, has to be second nature for HR executive success.

TRAINING

Formal training is important in every professional field, and human resources is no exception. The school of hard knocks leaves many bruises that are clearly evident to anyone observing the embattled graduate. Formal study would have enabled the veteran to know when to duck, when to weave, and how to effectively counter-punch.

Human resources training should include technical human resource curricula as well as general business coursework. It's clear that HR executives have to understand finance, marketing, and operations as well as organizational development, compensation, staffing, and employment. This is the best way to understand the organization's business and recognize how to effectively advance the organization's mission. Graduate school training should include these diverse business topics whether it is an MBA or a specialized HR degree. It is also important to understand metrics. HR professionals must gather, analyze, and summarize diverse information about the organization, its employees, and the larger labor market. Training in statistics and mathematics is invaluable to this end. Finally, it's probably useful to have some general education in the liberal arts. This helps produce a better-rounded individual, able to interact with diverse audiences, place situations into a larger context, and understand them from a broader perspective.

Does all this require graduate training? Probably. But the training does not eliminate the need for extensive experience both inside and outside human resources.

EXPERIENCE

Human resources is somewhat unique among business functions; it's perhaps the only business field that is required to interact with all other elements of the organization on the other person's home field. Finance people interact with all other functions, but using financial language and rules. Human resource people, if they are successful, must interact with other functions using the language and models of these other functions. The important task of HR is to help these functions create value and enhance effectiveness through the efforts of the people working there. Certain governmental regulations and rules have to be followed, but the most important value HR can add to other business functions is to help management and employees throughout the organization work better and create a stronger culture.

The HR executive can accomplish these outcomes only if they truly understand and empathize with all functions in the organization. Much of this understanding can come only from a varied and complete set of experiences that transcend human resources. I contend that the successful HR executive must understand every element of the organization better than nearly any other individual in that organization, perhaps including the CEO.

Individuals can gain this understanding in different ways. Some people gain it by being truly gifted observers. They can watch and observe and gain an understanding nearly as intense as that gained by others actually in the situation. Others must actually take part in the experience in order to understand it. HR executives in this latter group must spend time working in other functions in order to truly understand them. This is a time-consuming, but necessary, way of being able to demonstrate an empathy with fellow executives from across the organization. This empathy becomes invaluable and better enables the successful HR executive to have a chair at the strategic planning table.

Internally within HR, experience is also an issue. As a leader within HR, the executive must also be able to demonstrate a thorough understanding of different functions—in this case the different HR functions. Otherwise, it is difficult for the leader to evaluate HR strategies and alternative actions proposed by members of his or her function. A significant part of this knowledge can come from professional training, but it must also come from actually working within at least several of the different HR functions. Some individuals are able to successfully lead an HR function without having a strong core specialty. However, these individuals must surround themselves with a highly competent and trusted staff that is able to lead functional areas within HR. Finally, it is probably good for the head of HR to have worked in different organizations to experience how HR is practiced elsewhere. This allows the HR executive to better maintain a perspective and judge the likely outcomes of different decisions. A friend tells me that he was told early in his professional life that "good judgment comes from experience and experience comes from bad judgment." Perhaps organizations want to hire HR executives with good judgment honed from experiences and bad judgments made elsewhere.

All of this experience takes time to acquire. Perhaps this is why the HR executive is the person around the table with the most gray hair. There are few HR wunderkinds. Most heads of HR take a while to finally rise to the top chair and provide meaningful influence within major organizations. Each individual makes career decisions one at a time—almost using a random-walk decision model. At each intersection in our career we make what we believe to be the best decision and then move on to the next one. Looking backward, careers are often not straight lines, but rather zigzag paths. We decide whether to change organizations or change focuses and then move on. We only hope that our body of work is deemed adequate to prepare us for the next challenge. Successful HR executives somehow acquire the necessary experience described here and are able to draw on the many lessons learned to help the organization achieve success.

It may be empirically possible to determine whether working in multiple organizations or gaining experience in multiple business functions is better preparation for assuming the top HR hat. But for most people, this isn't how careers are planned. Individuals ascending career ladders in HR must remember to make the most of whatever experiences they encounter. Diverse experiences are generally better than narrow ones. So we must take advantage of opportunities when they arise, but in the meantime, garner as much knowledge as we can from the situation in which we find ourselves.

Operating experience affords the HR executive the benefit of more thoroughly understanding the organization's business. Every executive must actually feel and gain a sixth sense for the organization's business. Because few if any organizations are ultimately in the business of employing and paying people, HR executives are not in the mainstream of most companies. Therefore, to gain a complete understanding of the organization's core business, HR executives must do so either vicariously or by having spent time in operations. A thorough understanding of the business is essential in order to create HR philosophies and strategies that enable the business to better meet its goals. Effective HR programs are really management tools, designed to facilitate managing the organization. It is difficult to formulate effective management tools without completely understanding the organization's business.

Another reason for HR executives to have operating experience is that it provides them with the opportunity to experience HR programs from the other side. Line executives often complain bitterly about how onerous and useless many HR programs are. We claim that the programs we design, from performance management programs to compensation schemes, should be "owned" by management and not be just "another HR program." But without ever experiencing these programs from the non-HR vantage point, the HR executive can never know the impact these programs have on operations or reliably assess whether line management will assume ownership of them. Creating design teams made up of operations people will help, but having operations experience within the HR function is a better solution.

LUCK

Another ingredient to predicting HR success is luck. People find themselves in situations because of happenstance, but they benefit from those situations on the basis of their own efforts. HR executives are no different from anyone else in this regard. People we see as lucky are really people who have made the most of whatever opportunities have come their way. It's good to hire people who are lucky because they have probably worked hard at making their luck work well for them. Consequently, luck is an important ingredient in the HR success formula.

STRUCTURE

The final factor leading to HR success involves the way in which the HR executive structures the HR function in the organization. Structural HR models have evolved over time. The time-honored approach of functionally organizing HR into its classic components of employment, compensation, benefits, training, and the like is hardly exciting and probably eliminates the likelihood of any "systems thinking" occurring. However, structure matters, and the HR executive's probability of success does depend on how well the HR structure aligns with the organization's needs.

Probably the most current thinking is that HR should be integrated into operations by "embedding" HR staff into operations teams. This maximizes HR impact at the level of operational decisions and helps ensure that HR perspectives are incorporated into these decisions rather than having to be shoehorned in later. It also greatly increases the operations knowledge level for the HR professionals who join the operations teams, which, in turn, should result in HR policies and practices that better incorporate operational reality. Although this is an effective approach in many situations, particularly project-driven technology, it requires considerable resources and therefore may not be cost-effective in all environments. As is typical, there is no one best HR structure. But the structure of HR delivery is every bit as important to consider in organizational design as configuring the organization's information system or its financial system. The successful HR executive understands organizational and business realities well enough to design the most effective HR delivery system possible given these opportunities and constraints.

Conclusion

A friend of mine who is not in human resources has had numerous experiences in his career with people from HR—and most of those experiences appear to have been negative. Borrowing a phrase from the military, he refers to human resource people as "HR pukes." Although it's a more colorful phase than many people would use, his feelings are probably shared by many.

The problem he sees with HR is that it usually impedes progress and adds little if any value to the organization. They are like government regulators: they are bureaucratic, have little or no regard for the business, do not think strategically, are overly concerned with rules and regulations, and are just a plain pain. These are not the people my friend would want to run his business or formulate strategic business plans. This is similar to the *Fortune* editor's criticism we referred to in the opening paragraph.

Assuming that HR exists for more than just to keep organizations out of trouble, what can we say to my friend? We can point out that human resources are critical in every organization; it is just that the human resource **function** may not add value to every organization. Management must provide leadership and establish a winning strategy that everyone in the organization can get behind. Part of this leadership and strategy involves establishing a work culture that people enjoy *and* enables the organization to meet its goals and pursue its mission.

Executives will embrace an HR function that successfully assumes a significant portion of the burden of creating this successful work culture. Some line managers could do it all themselves, but it is often more efficient to create an HR function to shoulder some of this burden. This doesn't free managers from managing. Rather, it better **enables** them to manage by providing tools and ideas that multiply management's efforts and enhance the organization's success, benefiting everyone in the organization.

HR success is clearly tied to organization success. HR executive success is clearly linked to enhancing the success of every other executive and nonexecutive in the organization. A successful HR function and executive makes the organization and everyone in it look good. In the end, this is how HR gains entrée to the executive suite.

Reference

Stewart, T., & Woods, W. (1996, January 15). Taking on the last bureaucracy. *Fortune, 133*(1), 105–108.

Parting Thoughts on Human Resource Management Education in the United States 23

Vida Gulbinas Scarpello

The chapters in this handbook contain a wide range of topics written by a large number of HRM experts. Initial chapters describe the multifaceted evolution of the field and its educational programs as well as current HR programs in industrial relations and industrial and organizational psychology. A number of chapters focus specifically on the HRM curriculum. Chapters 5–7 discuss newer approaches to delivery of HRM education in undergraduate programs within business schools. As there is increasing emphasis on international HRM education and few educators have studied this topic in depth, Chapters 8–10 present remarkably consistent approaches to teaching a graduate course in international HRM. Chapters 11–13 discuss topics that are sometimes neglected in HRM education: the role of rewards in job-choice decisions, conceptual tools for analyzing ethical aspects of HRM decisions, and a model of transfer of knowledge in the field of HRM. Chapters 14 and 15 provide brief tutorials on organizational concepts relevant to HRM. Chapter 14 focuses on basic psychological concepts relevant to development of HRM programs, and Chapter 15 focuses on organization structures and their relationships to HRM practice. This work also contains chapters on stakeholder views of HRM education (Chapters 16–18), constraints to HRM success (Chapters 19–21), and determinants of individual success in HRM practice (Chapter 22). Together with the material in the initial chapters, these latter chapters are basic to discussion of the present state and the future of HRM and HRM education. In this closing chapter, I therefore focus on (1) the state of the HR field and HRM education in the United States, (2) credibility of the HR field and HRM education, and (3) some ideas for building a legitimate HRM function and profession.

The State of the HR Field and HRM Education

In the preface, I noted that the book grew out of the first HRM town meeting at the 2002 Academy of Management meeting. The question asked at that meeting was "Is HRM dead or just sleeping?" That question is reminiscent of the question Peter Drucker posed in 1954. He asked, "Is personnel management bankrupt?" He answered it by saying "no, it is just temporarily insolvent." Later, Odiorne (1960) and Dunnette and Bass (1963) echoed that sentiment.

We can safely say that there is a variously labeled field of HRM. This field has existed since the initial employment of people. Today, various groups claim expertise in managing people. Consequently, there is no single identifiable field of HRM nor a single identifiable educational program in HRM. Education in HRM consists of varied, fragmented, yet overlapping coursework that can be categorized into four distinct models of HRM, three of which were presented by Tom Mahoney in Chapter 2.

Models of HRM Education and Their Implementation

INDUSTRIAL RELATIONS (IR) MODEL

This model (Mahoney's Model 1) focuses on management of human resources within any type of work organization. Mahoney notes that this model "implicitly assumes that the practice of HRM requires broad professional development and is independent of the institutional setting" (p. 32; e.g., corporation, law practice, social agency, hospital, university). The IR-HR program at the University of Minnesota, described by Fossum (Chapter 3), is multidisciplinary and includes perspectives from a number of economics subfields as well as labor relations, industrial and organizational psychology, sociology, administrative sciences, law, and other relevant disciplines. IR programs, however, vary in their foci. Although most are heavily influenced by institutional economists, some also tend to emphasize economic factors affecting the employment relationship to a greater extent than organizational, group, and individual factors. Master's programs are the largest programs within IR, and PhD programs are the smallest.

INDUSTRIAL AND ORGANIZATIONAL PSYCHOLOGY (I/O) MODEL

This model draws its curriculum content primarily from industrial, social, and organizational psychology. By definition, I/O programs produce psychologists. The focus is on development of tools for use in the HRM function, a strong emphasis on psychological measurement and testing, and the understanding of individual and group behavior.

HR programs in I/O psychology tend to offer more coherent sets of courses than do programs in IR. This can be partly attributed to the guidance of the Society of Industrial and Organizational Psychology (SIOP) in setting competency requirements for I/O programs. Normally, students are admitted into the PhD program and may terminate with a Master's degree if they no longer wish to pursue the PhD or if they fail to meet the qualifications for further study. The PhD program is therefore the largest program in I/O psychology and the Master's is the smallest. More than half of the new I/O PhDs take a variety of private-sector jobs. I/O psychologists also take jobs within the public sector, often in merit system environments. This may explain the relative familiarity businesses and government have with the benefits of I/O psychology education.

BEHAVIORAL SCIENCES MODEL IN BUSINESS SCHOOLS (OB)

This model (Mahoney's Model 3) focuses on what *behavioral science knowledge* every manager should possess to effectively manage relationships with direct reports and other people within his or her sphere of operations.

The behavioral sciences model is generally implemented as a core organizational behavior (OB) course requirement in MBA programs, or as part of the core management course in the undergraduate business program. With rare exceptions (e.g., Brigham Young University), OB specialization at the Master's level is limited to one to three courses.

HRM MODEL IN BUSINESS SCHOOLS

This model (Mahoney's Model 2) assumes that HRM is a functional specialty of management and that practitioners must know how it relates with and affects other functional specialties of management such as finance, accounting, marketing, and operations. In this model, undergraduate business students fulfill all business core requirements and may declare HRM either as a major or as a concentration area. At the Master's level, MBAs may declare HRM as their concentration area, or the business school may offer an MA degree in HRM. The MA programs may or may not require completion of core business courses. When not required, HR-MA programs in business schools increasingly require their students to take select business courses such as managerial and cost accounting and corporate finance. With few exceptions, PhD specializations in business, including HRM, require students to complete core functional courses in business as part of their PhD degrees.

Causes for the Variability of HRM Educational Programs

As already discussed by Cohen (Chapter 18) and others, educational programs in HRM are quite variable; their content depends on the faculty composition within a particular university unit. Master's and PhD graduates of multidisciplinary IR programs generally have at least four areas of *functional* HR expertise in common: compensation decision making, labor relations, staffing, and training and development. Similarly, although SIOP sets competency requirements for PhD education in I/O psychology, there is considerable flexibility in the content of those programs. Nevertheless, common areas of *functional* HR expertise in I/O psychology are staffing, performance appraisal, and training and development.

In his discussion of the historical evolution of HRM, Mahoney suggested that today's HRM differs from its historic antecedents. In many respects it has "merged interests of labor economics, industrial psychology, human relations and organization theory (sociology and administrative sciences) with a particular focus on the management of organizations" (p. 30). In effect, HRM programs in business have multidisciplinary roots.

The broadly based stakeholder-oriented education PhDs in IR receive through multidisciplinary IR programs has produced four decades of IR-educated HRM faculty who, for the most part, work in management departments of business schools. Business schools have also traditionally employed I/O psychologists, who represent a greater number of HRM faculty, simply because I/O programs traditionally produce more PhDs than do IR programs.

As Fossum (Chapter 3), Cohen (Chapter 18), and others have noted, discipline composition of faculty, discipline dominance in a particular university unit, and faculty's discipline identification influence the HRM curriculum offered within a particular university program. This is the reason Fossum is pessimistic about development of a common HRM curriculum. It may also be the reason why Cohen believes that SHRM is in the best position to unite the various groups in HRM toward a unified curriculum.

I disagree with both perspectives and believe strongly that HRM faculty in business schools are in the best position to develop a unified and effective HRM curriculum. As in other recognized professions (e.g., accounting, finance, engineering, nursing), the role of the professional organizations is to aid, support, and advance the profession through various means, including continuing education, but not to supplant the academic preparation of its practitioners.

Although it is imperfectly applied, the business school model permits I/O psychologists, industrial relations scholars, organizational sociologists and theorists, HRM business school PhD graduates, and scholars from other relevant fields to come together and apply their knowledge and skill to the development of HRM as a functional specialization of business and as a profession with knowledge and skill applicable to any type of work organization. Many HRM faculty in business school programs have MBAs, and others have educated themselves in the business areas most relevant to their academic interests and HRM teaching activities. Thus, with respect to HRM programs in many business schools, the vision of the 1930s that "the future should see a type of instructor who is soundly trained in economic principles, labor economics, production, finance, marketing, insurance, statistics, business law, accounting, sociology, and psychology" (Stockton, 1932, p. 223) has been realized. Indeed, the best interdisciplinary HRM programs in business have far surpassed the expectations of the 1930s, although this fact is not generally known within the employment environment.

Credibility of the Field and HRM Education

The authors in this book have identified numerous issues relevant to further development of the HR field and HRM education. The key issue appears to be "credibility." Although individuals may differ in perceptions as to sources of credibility, I believe credibility is a function of competence and personal integrity. The definitions I use for these terms can be found in the 1980 *Webster's New World Dictionary*.

Webster's defines the term "credible" as "believable, reliable, plausible" and "credibility gap" as "an apparent disparity between what is said and the actual facts, the inability to have one's statements accepted as factual or one's professed motives accepted as the true ones" (p. 332). The term "competent" is defined as "well qualified, capable, fit" (p. 289). The term "integrity" is defined as "the quality of state of being of sound moral principles, uprightness, honesty, and sincerity" (p. 732).

When we hear that HRM education lacks credibility among its constituents, we should clearly take notice that we have a significant problem as a field and as HRM educators. Yet, as Rynes et al. note (Chapter 19), "until the root causes of our problem (and all accompanying symptoms) are looked squarely in the eye, any 'solutions' that might be attempted are likely to prove ineffective" (p. 346). So, what are the root causes?

CREDIBILITY OF HRM AND HRM EDUCATION AS DISCUSSED BY CHAPTER CONTRIBUTORS

Rynes et al. suggest three root causes for lack of HRM credibility. The first is actual corporate behavior as opposed to corporate rhetoric. Citing numerous studies, these researchers show that although corporations say they value people and ethical behavior, their practices say the opposite. Thus, students with business experience come to the classroom with cynicism about the value and importance of people knowledge and skills. Additionally, corporations as well as HR executives place little value on HR educational credentials when making hiring decisions. A second root cause is lack of business school administrative support. This is related to the first root cause. As business schools attempt to satisfy future employers, they place great stock in media rankings of business school "quality." Those rankings provide substantial incentives to admit students who are likely to be in greatest demand and have the greatest number of lucrative opportunities after graduation. In turn, this is perceived as raising the business school's prestige with the business community, and at the same time disadvantages smaller programs within the school. The third root cause is the nature of business students. Rynes et al. suggest that the material taught in HR may be inconsistent with students' preexisting values and beliefs, thus creating emotional resistance to HR content. Many students also don't want to learn management, as they are increasingly more interested in business-related professional and technical occupations. Finally, the subject matter itself is not attractive, as business students tend to think of HR and OB as common sense and easy courses.

On the basis of numerous interviews with CEOs of large and small organizations, personal experiences in strategic planning with many organizations, and personal experiences as faculty, Bereman and Graham (Chapter 20) also give three reasons why HR managers have a limited impact in the strategic management of their organizations. First, they note that successful corporate managers act to satisfy market needs, whereas HR managers react to market opportunities. Second, there are differences between executives and HR managers in vocational interests and orientations. Third, the occupational preparations and backgrounds of HR managers limit their ability to participate in strategic management decisions.

Theeke (Chapter 21) agrees that HRM lacks credibility among business professionals. He attributes this state of affairs to the following three sources: hiring practices of corporate executives and managers, the variety of educational backgrounds of HR executives and professional employees, and lack of business knowledge among HRM practitioners. Theeke notes that corporate executives hire people who have no functional HR training for top HR positions but they don't do so in other functional areas of business. He believes that such hiring decisions stem from confusion about the qualifications required for HR. That confusion can be linked to the executives' own educational backgrounds. Even executives with business degrees are confused. As business majors they had taken an introduction to management course. As MBA students they had taken an organizational behavior course. In either case, they tended to think they had taken an HR course. Thus, when they hire HRM executives, they tend to hire "people-oriented" people and don't have expectations of technical HRM competence. In turn, the non-HRM-educated HRM executives also tend to hire individuals with varied backgrounds.

Theeke's assessment is supported by Shore et al.'s findings (Chapter 16) that few HRM executives have formal HRM education and that these executives are more interested in hiring people with good interpersonal skills who have HRM experience than they are in hiring individuals with HR educational credentials. A recent study also indicates that employers are not even interested in hiring HRM personnel with HR certification. Aquinis, Michaelis, and Jones (2005) analyzed each of 1,873 HR job announcements over a one-week period posted on four Web sites (www.monster.com, www.hotjobs.yahoo.com, www.careerbuilder.com, and www.shrm.org) and found that only *nine* job announcements stated a requirement for HR certification. Only 70 stated a preference for *any type* of certification.

Lack of credibility of HRM managers is also evident in interviews with labor leaders and employees in unionized settings. Graham and McHugh (Chapter 17) found that their subjects perceived HR professionals as having little power and autonomy to make decisions related to important issues such as grievance handling and negotiations. Although local labor leaders recognized that HR professionals had a good understanding of the their firm's business and were personally credible, they also perceived that HR professionals sent unclear and inconsistent messages.

MY ASSESSMENT OF THE CREDIBILITY OF HRM AND HRM EDUCATION

My experience as a professor and consultant leads me to agree with the following:

- Corporate actions are not consistent with corporate rhetoric about the value of people.
- There is a lack of business school support for HRM programs.
- There is a lack of student interest in HRM.
- There may be personality differences between business managers and HRM managers.
- HRM personnel cannot become strategic players and cannot be effective HRM practitioners without as much or more functional business knowledge as possessed by other functional managers, and as Pierson (Chapter 22) suggests, as much as the CEO.

Yet, I also believe strongly that these are not universal truths. In a country as large as the United States, research always uses an accidental sample, and all perspectives and observations can be supported. There are companies who use and value HRM expertise, there are HRM programs that provide students with requisite knowledge and skills, there are many students with prior business experience who are not cynical and value HRM knowledge and skill, and there are many HRM professionals who are exemplars to others, with or without having had formal HRM education. This is not the norm, however. Why not?

To answer this question I draw on my graduate days and classes in sociology. From my formal organization classes in the early 1970s, I learned that corporations were likely to grow globally and eventually the world may be run by global corporations rather than nations—as corporate interests would surpass national interests. We are seeing these developments today. The globalization of industry has changed the nature of business's competitive environment and has increased complexity and ambiguity of doing business. Complexity associated with global expansion has further interacted with ambiguity to produce a situation that enables greed and political behavior to dominate decision making in many corporate contexts. This is clearly evident in the large number of corporate scandals and corporate attempts to sell U.S. technology to nations that are not recognized as sharing our nation's interests. In such an environment, managing human resources efficiently and effectively is not a great concern. Ethical corporate behavior also is not a great concern and, in some instances, results in the punishment of individuals who exhibit such behavior.

Corporate behavior influences business school behavior. As state educational funding decreased, fundraising became a business school dean's primary task. As deans focus on this task their goal is to satisfy the local business community rather than the educational needs of the students. One way of doing this is to rationalize their school's stature by their school's position in media rankings.[1] These attract students and engender local business support, even though the ranking's inaccuracy may be recognized within the affected business school and by its faculty.

Today's deans tend to be externally oriented, not education oriented. Like some of the businesses they attempt to serve, their goals tend to be short-term and motivated by self-interest. Reduced state funding has motivated deans to fill teaching schedules with adjunct or non-tenure-track faculty, who serve at the discretion of the dean and often are less qualified than tenure-track faculty, who are generally not accountable to the dean. The discretionary money deans bring into their colleges is also used to "buy" faculty who will promote the dean's agenda by providing them with extra research money or decreased teaching loads. This environment has decreased collegiality within business schools and decreased the quality of education. Faculty who maintain educational standards sometimes withdraw from participating fully in internal decision making and by so doing unintentionally abdicate their broader educational responsibilities.

Yet, I am not a pessimist. I agree that HR is sleeping, but it can be awakened. We need to awaken to the fact that although HRM is a functional area of management, unlike other functions it has yet to be recognized as legitimate. We also have to awaken to the fact that the world is what it is. The root solution to the credibility problem in HRM education is us, HRM educators.

Some Ideas for Building a Legitimate HRM Function and Profession

This book's contributors chose to write about the topics that interested them. As I researched the evolution of the field and read the works of my HR colleagues, I came to a number of conclusions.

EDUCATION IS A MIND-ALTERING EXPERIENCE

To build a legitimate organizational function and profession, we must think globally and act through our professional association, the HR division of the Academy of Management. We must recognize that there is a great deal of variability in HR programs and that the reasons—(a) discipline composition of faculty, (b) fragmented knowledge of faculty claiming expertise in HR, (c) departmental hiring focused on potential research productivity rather than on HR content expertise, (d) the field's acceptance of self-proclaimed expertise in HR, (e) faculty self-interests are better served through self rather than professional orientation, (f) lack of external standards or controls for the content of HR teaching, and (g) increased reliance on SHRM as the source for professional expertise—all contribute to barriers for the field's development. The field also will not advance if we follow the next management trend, change the field's name, think up new ways to convince business executives of HRM's value, or abdicate our responsibilities as educators to professional associations. To advance the profession of HRM, we must educate our students and help them develop professional values. Those values should serve the multiple constituencies of HRM through delivery of state-of-the-art expertise in functional and organizational activities.

As HRM faculty, we must be competent, exhibit personal integrity, and identify with HRM rather than our individual educational backgrounds. To advance the profession will require a great deal of work and passion for teaching HRM. Relevance and rigor in classes can be achieved only by faculty who are expert in the functional areas of HRM, understand business practices and enjoy interacting with businesses and other types of employing organizations, know how to manage political behavior, and have a passion to educate students for success as practicing professionals. Without faculty expertise and passion, it should be no surprise that students will find HRM courses boring, easy, and useless. It should also be no surprise that students with prior business experience are cynical about HRM— they've experienced incompetence in their employing organizations. We must always remember that our goal and responsibility is to educate and thus to change *minds* during this process.

PASSION—MOTIVATION—CREDIBILITY

Besides expertise, passion for the field is essential to engage students and enable them to learn. It is interesting to note that *Webster's* (1980) dictionary begins to define the term "passion" in terms of suffering, endurance, agony, and martyrdom. If we define "passion" as *Webster's* does later, "enthusiasm, fondness, love, extreme compelling emotion" (p. 1038), then we can relate passion to motivation. As we all know, motivation is goal-directed behavior. Motivation is what energizes, directs, and sustains behavior until the goal is reached. If we are to move our field toward professionalism, it is important to review the role motivation plays in our credibility problems and how we can use motivation to solve those problems.

As noted earlier, employers tend to hire into HRM individuals whom they perceive to be "relationship oriented." This is clearly not a compliment. Psychologist David McClelland (1961, 1965, 1975, 1976) has identified several important motives relevant to the present discussion. These are need for affiliation, need for achievement, need for autonomy, and need for power. McClelland and research in organizational settings clearly indicate that relationship-oriented (high need for affiliation) HR managers are not likely to improve credibility of HRM. People with a high need for affiliation desire the approval of others and often conform to the wishes of those around them. Because they are genuinely concerned with the feelings of others and fear offending managers, coworkers, employees, or union officials, they may not be able to make the hard decisions that often have to be made. Even when they make those decisions to please their managers, they may not be able to communicate their truth to affected employees. This results in credibility problems and diminished trust in HRM.

In settings where individual effort can have considerable impact, such as professional or entrepreneurial jobs, individuals with a high need for achievement have been shown to experience success (McClelland, 1961, 1965, 1976). Clearly, need for achievement is present in all research-oriented faculty. It is also present in competent faculty who have dedicated their lives to developing students, without receiving external reward or recognition. However, a critical motive for achieving organizational success is power. McClelland (1976) identified two forms of power: personal and institutional. Personal power involves the need to control and dominate other people for personal gain. Institutional power also involves a need to control and dominate, but it focuses on the goals of the organization rather than on personal gain. Need for institutional power is increasingly exhibited in faculty who recognize that it is time to take control of and responsibility for further development of the HR field and HRM education. As McClelland and others have shown, corporate leaders are those who possess a high need for institutional power, a high need for achievement, and a low need for affiliation.

We must identify our leaders and assist them. We must also seek help from colleagues whose basic needs are research achievement, personal power, *and* autonomy from administrative control (e.g., Zaleznik, 1970). By remaining outside of the pressures exerted by their college administrators because of their research-based stature, these colleagues have considerable power within their departments and colleges. We must work to solicit the occasional needed support from these highly powerful colleagues to build the profession of HRM. This will not be an easy task, as it is exactly these faculty who allow deans and other administrators to hire less-qualified adjunct or full-time non-tenure-track faculty to teach their courses, which then allows them to have even more autonomy to pursue their research agendas and personal stature. Finally, as HRM faculty we must assess our own contributions to the HRM credibility gap and the role we want to play to close that gap.

Closing the HRM Credibility Gap Requires Developing Professional HRM Programs Across U.S. Universities

Programs across universities vary in relevance and rigor because of the composition of their faculty. Consequently, business school faculty committees composed of IR, I/O, and MBA educated members of the HR Division of the Academy of Management as well as representatives from IR and I/O HRM programs can advance the HRM field to a profession through the following activities:

- Develop common core course requirements for HRM programs, wherever they reside, along with common course titles and content.

- Review the content and accuracy of HRM textbooks and endorse books that pass the academy's review board. Today's textbooks are content deficient and biased. We must encourage authors to represent the content of the whole field without bias. For example, Fossum (Chapter 3) noted that textbook focus is increasingly shifting toward the practices that are of benefit to the employer and away from those that are primarily oriented toward employee welfare. Although he reviewed only a select few textbooks, both of these biases must be recognized and eliminated. As well, textbooks with a distinct disciplinary bias such as economics or psychology must be challenged.

- Develop an accreditation committee to review HRM programs and faculty competence, much like the AACSB does for business school accreditation.

- Develop selection criteria for HR graduate studies that include interest in business, ability to think broadly and creatively, and exhibit personal characteristics of individuality and integrity.

- Sponsor workshops in areas that HRM faculty need to retool or refresh and provide continuing education credits for completion of such workshops.

- Establish working relationships with academic representatives of SIOP and the Industrial Relations Research Association as well as representatives of the three HRM practitioner organizations. Although SHRM was recognized in this book, two other organizations are critical. WorldatWork is the primary organization for compensation professionals (although this organization has expanded its domain) and consultants. Human Resource Planning Society is a relatively elite and somewhat closed organization of top HRM executives.

The easiest aspect of the task is curriculum development, because IR and I/O curricula already overlap. There is one course, however, that I believe is critical to an HRM, MBA, or MA curriculum, does not overlap with content taught in any academic discipline, and is the one HRM course that will instantly improve the credibility of any HRM program. That course, unique to HRM, is *compensation decision making*. It is unique because it is interdisciplinary. It integrates theory and knowledge from economics, sociology, psychology, organization theory and design, and business (finance and accounting), and applies that knowledge to design and administration of compensation programs for executives, all types of employee groups, and all types of work organizations across the globe. I also argue strongly for the method of its teaching.

The method of teaching compensation decision making is significant. I originally took the course, as many Minnesotans have, from Professor George Milkovich. I also worked in compensation administration, consulted in the area, and taught the course to MBA and MA students in three recognized business schools as well as internationally. Additionally, I taught this course to third-year PhD students in I/O psychology. My teaching experiences led me to conclude that the only way to teach this topic, in its complexity, is to have the students master the topic. Anything short of mastery produces technicians who can harm rather than help their organizations and its employees. Mastery can be achieved by having student groups develop and justify a compensation program for a fictitious employer and fictitious employee groups. Mastery teaching also requires a teacher who has mastered the subject matter.

In teaching the course to I/O PhD students, I discovered that although they were very familiar with a large number of tools used in compensation administration, they experienced difficulty in putting the pieces into a whole. I also found that MBA students thought the course was extremely useful and harder than their corporate finance course. MBA graduates applied and obtained jobs as senior compensation analysts (jobs that typically require three years of experience in compensation) when they showed prospective employers their projects. Several MBAs started their own consulting firms, marketing their compensation expertise to small businesses after taking this one course. A number of MBAs were hired into the finance function of medium-sized corporations with chief responsibility for the corporation's compensation activities.[2] Finally, I have received numerous notes from corporate compensation executives thanking me for their new employees.

My experience with this course is not unique. Many colleagues who teach compensation, using the same delivery process, have had similar experiences. The major difficulty in specifying this course as a core HRM course is the limited number of HRM faculty with expertise in the area.

Although some faculty have SHRM certification in compensation, and others have taken a SHRM course, it is my strong belief that faculty wishing to master compensation decision making will be served best by learning its content from qualified academics. Although compensation courses delivered by professional associations are useful for new entrants into the field and can also improve faculty expertise in the area, they are too limiting for faculty wishing to master the area. A compensation course (or several courses) taught by a qualified academic will be broader in theory, provide choices of methodologies as well as critiques of each, and allow for quick adaptation to diverse organizational settings and employee groups. One additional caveat: I have found that reading a compensation text is not a substitute for gaining expertise in compensation decision making. Writers of texts (including myself) appear to have difficulty in communicating all essential information in written form—one has to suffer through the process.

As you can tell, I'm passionate about compensation. I hope that I presented a convincing argument for inclusion of *compensation decision making* into the graduate HR core course requirements group. This is one area where HRM graduates can establish instant professional credibility. It is also the one area that is core to all other HRM functional activities. Indeed, lack of expertise in compensation decision making is a clear indicator of deficiency in HRM knowledge and skill. I also challenge my colleagues to develop new interdisciplinary courses in other basic HRM areas. Currently, they are limiting and thus contribute to misunderstanding of HRM's domain.

Many colleagues are experts in various aspects of HRM, and many have solid expertise in all relevant areas of business. Many colleagues are college administrators, and many have MBAs. Others have specialized expertise in research methodologies relevant to business and all other HR-relevant areas. We must draw on our collective expertise to build a strong HRM profession. A good beginning is to solicit involvement in this task from this handbook's authors, as they demonstrate their commitment to HRM through their present contribution. We must also look within our collective knowledge base to develop the HRM profession rather than continuing to solicit inputs from outside, just because we find others' perspectives interesting and potentially useful. Nevertheless, it also is important to learn from practice and link our knowledge and skill to the needs of practice, as Stone et al. discuss in Chapter 13.

As finance and accounting evolved from economics, marketing from consumer behavior, and operations management from operations research, so too should we evolve our teaching profession from our roots in the disciplines that contribute research knowledge to the field as well as our roots in industrial relations and I/O psychology. We don't need to change the name of the field, but we do have to select faculty colleagues who share the vision of an HRM profession and have a complementary set of functional expertise to cover the content area of our educational endeavor. We also have to organize our course offerings and their content to provide students with the essential HRM core competency.

Pierson (Chapter 22) suggests that HRM's core competency is "providing vital human capital information used in shaping the organization's vision and then helping to execute that vision through the people that make up the organization" (p. 398). He further notes that HR professionalism is "characterized by effectiveness, efficiency, responsiveness, and use of state-of-the-art methods and technology" (p. 399). The successful head of the function establishes this milieu by demanding these outcomes and rewarding their achievement. Successful HR executives surround themselves with talented professionals and allow them to shine both inside and outside the organization. Along with Pierson, I believe this requires competence in the functional areas of HRM, understanding of organizations and organizational behavior, competence in the basic areas of business, personal integrity, and luck. Furthermore, I strongly believe that the role of HRM is to balance the interests of the key stakeholders in the employment exchange: employers, employees, and society (also, see Shultz, 1959).

Developing HRM from a field into a profession and a legitimate function of management will increase the credibility of HRM practitioners because it will increase their competence. Educational programs that develop professional values and select students who exhibit personal integrity will further increase HRM's credibility with its various constituents as well as increase demand for HRM knowledge and skills.

As a cautionary note, HRM faculty should be careful not to take on the values of business. Rather, faculty should practice their academic occupation as it was intended to be practiced. As another Pierson stated in his report to the AACSB nearly 50 years ago (1959):

The feel for the feasible and the relevant in a business environment is a highly desirable quality—in fact, it is essential for effective performance—but it is unlikely that there is any simple means of determining its existence. The opposite danger is probably more serious. Institutions of higher education which prepare for careers in a particular field always court the risk of becoming mere followers of the particular group they serve. In their zeal to please (i.e., to be realistic and practical) they may fail to provide any leadership. In case of business, employers are hardly in need of the practical kind of advice they can derive from their own experience and immediate associates. This emphasis on independent investigation through formal and informal research calls for faculty members who are ready to challenge widely accepted ideas; this is an absolutely essential quality at the graduate level, but a highly desirable one at the undergraduate level too. Business school faculties should strive to break new ground for business, playing the role of informed questioners and constructive critics. . . . Thus, a sense of the practical is desirable only if it does not crowd the element of originality, the very quality which is the hallmark of first-rate academic work. (p. 278)

Pierson challenges HRM business faculty to reinvent itself and look inwardly rather than to the business community and to professional associations for answers.

Having said the above, I now must part. I thank my authors for their commitment to HRM and for contributing their thoughts to this volume. I thank Sage Publishing Company and you, the reader, for allowing me to express my rather strong opinions. I leave you to decide if and how you want to proceed. As I retire from full-time teaching, I end this chapter with the hope for a brighter HRM future.

Be like the bird, who halting in his flight on limb too slight feels it give way beneath him, yet sings knowing he has wings

—Victor Hugo

Notes

1. These are also used in other areas, such as medical schools. Rankings attract students or patients but are not very useful criteria for assessing an educational program's quality.

2. In small and medium-sized corporations in the U.S., the finance department is typically responsible for compensation. I discovered that the finance department and sometimes the corporate planning department has responsibility

for employee compensation in some very large businesses headquartered in Europe, China, and the Middle East. Many executives in various countries read about the credibility problem with HRM and choose to bypass that "problem" by taking another route. I believe they are making a big mistake, but as Theeke notes, they don't know they are doing so.

References

Aquinas, H., Michaelis, S. E., & Jones, N. M. (2005). Demand for certified human resources professionals in internet-based job announcements. *International Journal of Selection and Assessment, 13,* 160–171.

Drucker, P. F. (1954). *The practice of management.* New York: Harper.

Dunnette, M. D., & Bass, B. M. (1963). Behavioral scientists and personnel management. *Industrial Relations, 2,* 115–130.

McClelland, D. C. (1961). *The achieving society.* Princeton, NJ: Van Nostrand.

McClelland, D. C. (1965). Toward a theory of motive acquisition. *American Psychologist, 20,* 321–333.

McClelland, D. C. (1975). *Power the inner experience.* New York: Irvington.

McClelland, D. C. (1976). Power is the great motivator. *Harvard Business Review, 54,* 100–110.

Odiorne, G. S. (1960). Company growth and personnel administration, *Personnel, 37,* 32–41.

Pierson, F. C. (1959). *The education of American businessmen.* New York: McGraw-Hill.

Shultz, G. P. (1959). Personnel management and industrial relations. In. F. C. Pierson (Ed.), *The education of American businessmen* (pp. 452–474). New York: McGraw-Hill.

Stockton, F. T. (1932). Personnel management in collegiate business schools. *Personnel Journal, 11*(4), 220–226.

Zaleznik, A. (1970). Power and politics in organizational life. *Harvard Business Review, 48,* 47–60.

Name Index

Subject Index

431

About the Editor

Vida Gulbinas Scarpello earned her PhD and MA in industrial relations from the University of Minnesota. She served on the faculties of management at the University of Georgia, the University of Florida, and Georgia State University, from which she retired in 2002. She was a visiting professor at Cornell University, the University of Minnesota, and United Arab Emirates University. Dr. Scarpello's graduate-level teaching included courses in organization design, behavior, and change; survey in HRM; strategic and international HRM; compensation theory and administration; labor relations; field research; and seminars in HRM and in organization theory. She was honored at the University of Georgia for outstanding graduate-level teaching and was voted second-year MBA teacher of the year at the University of Florida. Dr. Scarpello has taught in the Executive MBA program at the University of West Indies, the Executive MBA program for physicians at the University of South Florida, and the Executive MBA program at Georgia State University. Dr. Scarpello's research, published in top academic journals, spans a wide range of topics including theory and measurement of job satisfaction; strategic, justice, and measurement issues in compensation; and interorganizational relations. She is the recipient of several multiyear research grants from the National Science Foundation (NSF), has served on the NSF's reviewer panels, and currently serves as evaluator for the NSF's Industry/University Cooperative Research Program. She has also served on the review panel for workplace violence proposals for the Oklahoma City National Institute for Terrorism Prevention. Dr. Scarpello is coauthor of *Personnel/Human Resource Management: Environments and Functions*; *Federal Regulation of Personnel and Human Resource Management*; *Compensation Decision Making*; and *Small Business Management & Entrepreneurship*. She contributed chapters to *Blackwell Dictionary of Human Resources Management*; *Applying Psychology to Business*; and *Research in Management*. Her professional service includes editorial board memberships for the *Academy of Management Journal* (two terms), the *Academy of Management Executive, Journal of Organizational Behavior, Human Resource Management Review,* and *Human Resource Management.* She also served as a regular reviewer for 12 other journals, including *Journal of Applied Psychology, Journal of Applied Social Psychology,* and *Organizational Research Methods.*

Dr. Scarpello is past chair of the Human Resources Division of the Academy of Management, past president of the Southern Management Association, and a fellow of the Southern Management Association. She has served as instructor for many management development programs and as interest arbitrator for wage rate disputes in the telephone industry. She consults with major U.S. corporations and has consulted with state and city governments. Dr. Scarpello has served as an expert witness before Ontario's Pay Equity Tribunal and for a number of employment litigation cases in the United States, including *McKeon Jones & Johnson-Randolph v. CWA and AT&T*; *Carson B. Carmichael et al. v. Martin Marietta Corporation*; *Haynes v. Shoney*; and *Reynolds v. Alabama Department of Transportation*. Currently, she holds a courtesy appointment as professor at the University of Florida.

About the Contributors

David B. Balkin is professor of management and chair of the Management Division at the Leeds School of Business at the University of Colorado-Boulder. He earned his MA and PhD in industrial relations at the University of Minnesota and his BA in political science at UCLA. Professor Balkin is co-author of *Managing Human Resources* and *Management*. He has published over 40 articles in scholarly journals such as *Academy of Management Journal, Personnel Psychology, Industrial Relations,* and *Strategic Management Journal* as well as professional journals such as *Organizational Dynamics, Academy of Management Executive,* and *Compensation and Benefits Review*. Professor Balkin's research focuses on design and performance of strategic reward systems and the management of innovation. Prior to joining the University of Colorado, Boulder, Professor Balkin served on the faculties of Northeastern University and Louisiana State University. He has also been a visiting professor at HEC-Montreal in Canada and Toulouse University in France. He has taught internationally in graduate programs at the University of Aix-en-Provence (France), Carlos III University (Spain), the Norwegian School of Management (Norway), Copenhagen Business School (Denmark), Haifa University (Israel), and Catholic University (Dominican Republic). He has also served as expert witness in pay and employment discrimination litigation and consults with for-profit and nonprofit organizations on pay strategy and pay system design.

Nancy A. Bereman is chair of the Management Department at the W. Frank Barton School of Business at Wichita State University and associate professor of management. She earned her PhD in industrial relations from the University of Minnesota following the MBA and BA in psychology from Wichita State University. She teaches courses in all functional areas of human resource management.

Her research has appeared in *Human Resource Management Review, Public Personnel Management, Journal of Employee Responsibilities and Rights, The Journal of Higher Education, Journal of Management,* and *Journal of Real Estate Education*. She consults with organizations on a variety of human resource management issues, including compensation system design. Dr. Bereman has served as associate dean of the Barton School of Business and as associate dean for academic affairs and undergraduate programs. She also served as assistant dean of faculties for personnel and as university affirmative action officer at Wichita State University. Dr. Bereman is the

1994 recipient of the Wichita State University Board of Trustees teaching award and recipient of the 1987 faculty award for exceptional research published in a refereed journal at the Barton School of Business. She has been faculty advisor for the Wichita State University Student Chapter of the Society for Human Resource Management (SHRM) for 15 years and has guided that chapter to superior merit awards in most of those years. She has served SHRM in a variety of other ways and was elected "Outstanding Student in the Nation" in 1974 by that same organization. Dr. Bereman serves as the Education Advocate for the Wichita Chapter of SHRM and is a member of WorldatWork.

Thomas J. Bergmann earned his PhD in industrial relations from the University of Minnesota and an MS in IR from Loyola University, Chicago. Until his untimely death in 2004, Dr. Bergmann was a professor of management at the University of Wisconsin-Eau Claire. He also served as assistant dean and research director for the College of Business. Dr. Bergmann's primary interests included the human resource areas of compensation, selection, staff readjustment, interpersonal conflict, and employee satisfaction. He is co-author of *Compensation Decision Making* and published over 50 articles in such journals as *Personnel Psychology, Human Resource Management, Compensation and Benefits Review, Compensation and Benefits Management, Journal of Occupational and Organizational Psychology, Human Resource Planning, Journal of Applied Business Research, Journal of Organizational Behavior, Public Personnel Management, Journal of Managerial Issues, Human Relations, Management Communication Quarterly, The Employees' Responsibilities and Rights Journal,* and *Journal of Contemporary Business Issues.* Dr. Bergmann was involved in many professional and academic associations including the American Compensation Association (now WorldatWork), the Society for Human Resource Management (for which he was advisor to the UWEC student chapter), the Academy of Management, and the Industrial Relations Research Association. He also conducted executive workshops in supervisory training, coaching and counseling, hiring, mentoring, and team building. His consulting experiences included job evaluation and performance appraisals, organizational analyses, attitude surveys, and general management advising. In gratitude for his dedication to HRM and HRM education, his friends and colleagues at UWEC have established a yearly HRM scholarship in his name.

Wayne F. Cascio received his PhD in industrial and organizational psychology from the University of Rochester in 1973. Currently he is professor of management and international business at the University of Colorado at Denver. He has taught at Florida International University, the University of California-Berkeley, the University of Hawaii, the University of St. Gallen, Switzerland, the University of Geneva, and the University of Hong Kong. During the academic year 1987–1988 he was a visiting scholar at the Wharton School of the University of Pennsylvania. In 1988 he received the Distinguished Faculty award from the HR Division of the Academy of Management, in 1994 he received the Bemis award for excellence in HRM from the International Personnel Management Association's Assessment Council, and in 1999 he received the Distinguished Career award from the HR Division of the Academy of Management. He has received two "best paper" awards from the *Academy of Management Executive* for his research on downsizing and restructuring (1993 and 2003), and an honorary doctorate from the University of Geneva (Switzerland) in 2004.

He is past chair of the HR Division of the Academy of Management (AOM), a former member of the AOM board of governors, past-president of the Society for Industrial and Organizational Psychology, and chair-elect of the Society for Human Resource Management Foundation (2007). He has authored more than 85 journal articles, 35 book chapters, and 20 books, including *Managing Human Resources: Productivity, Quality of Work Life, Profits* (7th ed., 2006), *Applied Psychology in Human Resource Management* (6th ed., 2005), *Costing Human Resources: The Financial Impact of Behavior in Organizations* (4th ed., 2000), and *Responsible Restructuring: Creative and Profitable Alternatives to Layoffs* (2002).

Dr. Cascio has consulted with more than 150 organizations on six continents. His research on staffing, training, performance management, and the economic impact of HR activities has appeared in a number of scholarly journals. Current and past editorial board memberships include *Journal of Applied Psychology, Academy of Management Review, Journal of Management, Journal of Industrial Psychology* (South Africa), *International Journal of Selection and Assessment* (UK), *Human Performance, Asia-Pacific HRM* (Australia), *Organizational Dynamics, Journal of World Business,* and *Zeitschrift für Personal Psychologie* (Germany). An elected fellow of the Academy of Management, the American Psychological Association, and the National Academy of Human Resources, he currently serves on the boards of directors of CPP, Inc. and the Society for Human Resource Management Foundation.

Debra J. Cohen is the chief knowledge officer, Society of Human Resource Management (SHRM) and is responsible for the Society's Information Center and Research Department. Dr. Cohen joined SHRM in May 2000 as the director of research where she oversaw SHRM's Survey Program, Workplace Trends and Forecasting Program, and other content development initiatives. She received her PhD in management and human resources in 1987 and her Master's degree in labor and human resources (MLHR) in 1982, both from the Ohio State University. She received her bachelor of science in communications from Ohio University. Prior to joining SHRM, Dr. Cohen served as an HRM faculty member at George Washington University (10 years) and at George Mason University (five years). Dr. Cohen has published over 30 articles in such journals as *Personnel Psychology,*

Human Resource Development Quarterly, Journal of Management, Human Resource Management Journal, Journal of Small Business Strategy, Journal of Business and Psychology, Training and Development Journal, Journal of Management Education, and *Journal of Business Ethics.* Prior to her academic career, she was a practicing human resources manager in training and development. Dr. Cohen remains professionally active, having served on the executive board of the HRM Division of the Academy of Management and on the board of the Academic Partnership Network of the American Compensation Association (now WorldatWork). She is currently an associate editor for *Human Resource Management Journal,* serves on the editorial review boards of *Human Resource Management Review* and *The Journal of Management,* and does ad hoc reviewing for *Human Resource Development Quarterly.*

John R. Deckop is associate professor of human resource management in the School of Business at Temple University. He earned his PhD in industrial relations from the University of Minnesota. Before coming to Temple University, he was an assistant professor of management at Vanderbilt University. Other appointments at Temple University have included department chair (1995–2002) and associate director of the Henrietta Frankel Ethics Center (1993–1996). He has also served on several nonprofit boards of directors. Dr. Deckop's teaching interests include reward systems, human resource management, and business ethics. In 1988 he was named Temple University's MBA Professor of the Year. His current research interests include the topics of risk and justice in compensation systems, organizational antecedents and consequences of materialism, reciprocity and organizational citizenship behavior, and the design of human resource management practices to benefit the transition of former welfare clients to the world of work. He was co-principal investigator on a $108,850 grant from the Charles Stewart Mott foundation on the latter topic. He has been quoted in numerous newspaper articles nationwide on the topic of compensation systems, particularly executive compensation systems. Dr. Deckop has published in numerous academic journals, including *Academy of Management Journal, Journal of Management, Industrial and Labor Relations Review, Human Resource Management Review, Human Resource Management, Journal of Business Ethics, Journal of Occupational and Organizational Psychology, International Journal of Manpower,* and *Nonprofit and Voluntary Sector Quarterly,* among others. He is an ad hoc reviewer for several journals, and is a member of the editorial boards of *Academy of Management Journal* (1998 to present) and *Group and Organizational Management* (2003 to present). He is the editor of a 2006 book titled *Human Resource Management Ethics.*

Renée E. DeRouin is a doctoral candidate in the industrial and organizational psychology program at the University of Central Florida. She was the recipient of the Society for Industrial and Organizational Psychology's 2004 Robert J. Wherry Award and the American Psychological

Association/American Psychological Association of Graduate Students' 2005 Distinguished Graduate Student in Professional Psychology Award. Her research interests include training, distance learning, learner control, mentoring, and stereotype threat, and her work has appeared in *Journal of Management, Human Resource Management, Research in Personnel and Human Resource Management, Ergonomics in Design, Advances in Human Performance and Cognitive Engineering Research,* and *Handbook of Human Factors and Ergonomics Methods.*

Debra Dookeran earned her PhD in human resources from the W.T. Beebe Institute of Personnel and Employment Relations at Georgia State University. She earned her MBA from Cardiff University, Wales and BSc. with honors from the University of West Indies. Dr. Dookeran was an assistant professor of management at the Ziklin School of Business at Baruch College until her resignation in 2006. She has taught courses in compensation and human resource management. Her research interests include perceived organizational support, psychological contracts, trust, organizational justice, and corporate social responsibility. Dr. Dookeran has worked in banking and manufacturing in supervisory and management positions and is currently managing the care of her family.

James H. Dulebohn is an associate professor of human resource management and organizational behavior at Michigan State University's School of Labor and Industrial Relations. He earned his PhD and Master's degrees from the University of Illinois at Urbana-Champaign in human resource management. Dr. Dulebohn has held faculty appointments at the University of Texas at San Antonio, Georgia State University, the University of Georgia, the University of Illinois, and Michigan State University. He has taught courses at the graduate and undergraduate levels in human resource management, strategic human resource management, organizational behavior, organizational development and change management, compensation, human resource information systems, and research methods. His research interests include decision making in human resource management systems, compensation and benefits, performance management, and social influence in organizations. His articles have appeared in journals including *Academy of Management Journal, Personnel Psychology, Journal of Management,* and *Journal of Risk and Insurance.* Dr. Dulebohn has consulted in the areas of human resource management, compensation, and benefits for a variety of organizations including Dow Chemical Company, Monsanto, TIAA-CREF, the State of Illinois, the State of Texas, and Marriott.

John A. Fossum is acting associate dean of faculty and research and professor of human resources and industrial relations in the Carlson School of Management at the University of Minnesota. He holds a BA in economics from St. Olaf College, an MA in industrial relations from the University of Minnesota, and a PhD in labor and industrial relations from Michigan State University. He began his academic career at the University of Wyoming in 1972. In 1974, he joined the School of Business Administration at the University of Michigan as an instructor, was promoted to assistant professor in 1975 and associate professor in 1979, and was elected department chair for the organizational behavior and industrial relations area in 1982. In the early 1980s at Michigan he was a faculty associate at the Institute for Social Research and was also actively involved in developing and delivering executive-level human resource management programs.

In 1983, he joined the industrial relations faculty at Minnesota. During his tenure at Minnesota, he was director of graduate studies in industrial relations between 1984 and 1987 and for a transition year in 1997–1998. From 1987 to 1991, 1994 to 1997, and during 2004–2005, he was the director of the Industrial Relations Center (IRC) and chair of the graduate faculty in industrial relations. The IRC operates Master's and doctoral programs with approximately 220 Master's and 15 doctoral students, trains union leaders and members through the Labor Education Service, and produces applied research through the Human Resources Research Institute. While director, he was the chair of the University Council of Industrial Relations and Human Resource Programs (a consortium of schools offering graduate or large undergraduate programs in HR-IR) for a two-year period. He was one of the founding academic members of IRC-GOALS, a joint university-business consortium for recruiting underrepresented minorities into HR-IR graduate programs, and later served as its chair for a three-year term.

He has held visiting faculty positions at UCLA, Cornell, and the Warsaw School of Economics; and has taught in programs offered by the Université Jean Moulin Lyon III (France) and the University of Warmia and Mazury in Olsztyn, Poland. In fall 2001, he was a Fulbright Lecturer at the Warsaw School of Economics. He is the author of *Labor Relations: Development, Structure, Process* (nine editions) and a co-author (with Herbert G. Heneman, III, Donald P. Schwab, and Lee Dyer) of *Personnel/Human Resource Management* (four editions). He is a member of the Academy of Management and the Labor and Employment Research Association and was the chair of the Personnel/Human Resources Division of the Academy in 1981–1982. His research interests involve primarily employee compensation, human resource management and firm performance, and labor-management relations issues. He has published widely in these fields.

Collette A. Frayne is professor of international business and human resource management in the Orfalea College of Business at California Polytechnic State University. From September 2003 to 2005, Dr. Frayne held the Thomas F. Gleed Chair of Business Administration in the Albers School of Business at Seattle University. Dr. Frayne earned her doctorate from the

University of Washington, the MBA from the University of San Diego, and the BS in business administration from the University of Delaware. At Cal Poly, she teaches courses in international business management and international human resource management. She also serves as faculty advisor for the AIESEC international internship program as well as the International Management Concentration. She has also taught at the University of Western Ontario (Canada), Texas Christian University (USA), the University of Washington (USA), the University of Delaware (USA), Institut Pengembangan Manajemen Indonesia (Jakarta), Lajos Kossuth University (Hungary), the Helsinki School of Economics and Business Administration (Helsinki & Mikkeli, Finland), the Monterey Institute of International Studies (USA), Poznan School of Banking (Poland), and Bond University (Australia). Dr. Frayne's teaching, research, and consulting interests have focused on issues of human resource management, self-management, power and influence, and organizational change, particularly in international joint ventures and alliances. She has authored a book and published approximately 70 articles and case studies in outlets such as *Journal of Applied Psychology, Academy of Management Journal, Journal of International Business Studies, Journal of Management Education,* and *Journal of International Management.* Her research has received several "best paper" awards, including the George and Sara McCune Best Paper Award from *Journal of Group and Organization Management.* Currently, Dr. Frayne serves on the editorial boards of *Journal of World Business, Journal of Organizational Behavior, Academy of Management Executive,* and *Journal of Management Inquiry* and has served as a co-chair of the Teaching Committee for the International Management Division of the Academy of Management.

Dr. Frayne is a member of her university's Athletics Governing Board and has served on the University Research Grants Award Committee. She is the recipient of the Dean's Emeritus Award for faculty teaching, research, and service excellence in 1994 and 1999 as well as recipient of two prestigious awards from the Academy of Management and the Society for Industrial/Organizational Psychology for her research in self-management. At the University of Western Ontario she received the Dean's Team distinction for teaching excellence each year from 1987 to 1992 and also the Dean's List commendation for teaching excellence and the Global Perfection Award for teaching in 2001. At Cal Poly she was nominated for the University Distinguished Teacher Award in 1997 and 1998, and received it in 1999. Dr. Frayne also is president and CEO of an international management consulting company where she is actively involved in international management consulting and executive development activities in North America, Europe, and the Asia-Pacific region. Her clients include a variety of domestic and multinational organizations, several Fortune 500 and Fortune Global 500 organizations, and nonprofit organizations. In her management development and training activities she has worked with executives from Nokia Oy, Hewlett Packard, Eastman Kodak,

Cisco, Starbucks, Costco, Safeco, Agilent Technologies, Hewlett Packard, Caterpillar, ITT Sheraton, California Highway Patrol, Rautaruukki Oy, Eastman Chemical Company, Digital Equipment Corporation, AT&T, DuPont, Ericsson, Polartest Oy, DHL Courier International, Corporate Image, Ernst & Young, Valio Oy, and the Ontario Ministry of Industry Trade and Technology. She has also taught in numerous university and corporate executive education programs in Canada, the U.S., Australia, Europe, and Asia.

Gerald H. Graham is the R.P. Clinton Distinguished Professor of Management and former dean of the W. Frank Barton School of Business at Wichita State University. He received his PhD in management from Louisiana State University. Dr. Graham has published four management textbooks and numerous research articles. His research interests include study of nonfinancial incentives, leadership, conflict resolution, employee appraisal, and organizational communication and use of goals and objectives. He has made management presentations to more than 750,000 participants in 46 states, Canada, Mexico, and Slovakia. He also has been the recipient of the Wichita State University Excellence in Teaching and the Barton School of Business Teaching awards. Dr. Graham is past-president of the board of directors of Goodwill Industries of Kansas and former board member of the United Way of the Plains. Besides being an active management consultant, Dr. Graham has facilitated more than 100 partnering workshops with the Army Corps of Engineers, several state agencies, cities, and private firms. He has also delivered more than 30 educational seminars to state departments of transportation and private contractors on the concepts of partnering.

Mary E. Graham is the Newell Associate Professor of Organizational Studies in the School of Business at Clarkson University. She earned her PhD from the School of Industrial and Labor Relations at Cornell University, with a concentration in human resource studies. Dr. Graham teaches courses in introductory and advanced human resource management, change management, rewards management, and organizational behavior. Dr. Graham has published on incentive pay programs, gender-related pay disparities, and perceptions of corporate reputation, in such journals as *Organization Science, Journal of Organizational Behavior, Organizational Research Methods, Eastern Economic Journal,* and *Cornell Journal of Law and Public Policy.* She has served as an associate editor of *Human Resource Management* journal, and she is a member of the editorial review board of *Human Resource Management Review.* Before her academic career, Dr. Graham worked as a tax accountant and earned her CPA, and served as a legislative aide in the U.S. House of Representatives.

Greg Hundley is professor of management in the Krannert School of Management at Purdue University and director of the Center for

International Business Education and Research (CIBER) at Purdue. He earned his PhD and MA in industrial relations from the University of Minnesota and B.Com. degree from the University of Western Australia. Prior to joining Purdue University, Dr. Hundley held faculty appointments at the University of Oregon, where he served as chair of the Department of Management and director of the Institute of Human Resource Management and Industrial Relations and also at the University of Minnesota, the University of Western Australia, and Xavier University. His teaching spans a wide variety of courses at all educational levels and includes human resource management, HR for the general manager, quantitative methods in industrial relations and human resource management, strategic human resource management, compensation theory and administration, employee benefits and risk management, issues in labor markets, management context and environment, labor and employment relations, and management of technology. In recent years, he has focused primarily on teaching international HR. Dr. Hundley's research has been published in many major journals, including *Academy of Management, Strategic Management Journal, British Journal of Industrial Relations, Industrial Relations, Industrial and Labor Relations Review,* and *Journal of Human Resources.* Professor Hundley has served on the editorial board of *Academy of Management Journal* and the *Asia-Pacific Journal of Human Resources.* His current research programs are concerned with the effects of individual values and national culture on HR practices, the transfer of management consequences of self-employment, and the relationship between self-employment and entrepreneurship.

Cameron Klein is a doctoral candidate in the industrial and organizational psychology program at the University of Central Florida (UCF) in Orlando. He is currently employed as a senior graduate research assistant at UCF's Institute for Simulation & Training. He has presented his work at regional and national psychology and management conferences and has published over a dozen journal articles and book chapters. His primary research interests include interpersonal skills, team and individual training, training evaluation, assessment centers, and item development, analysis, and revision, and his work has appeared in *Leadership Quarterly, International Encyclopedia of Ergonomics and Human Factors, International Review of Industrial and Organizational Psychology,* and *Encyclopedia of Applied Psychology.*

Scott Lester is associate professor of management and director of the Center for Leadership at the University of Wisconsin–Eau Claire. He earned his PhD in organizational behavior from the University of South Carolina in 1997. Prior to his doctoral work, he received a BA in psychology and business from the University of Richmond in 1991 and worked for a year as a management and training consultant. Scott teaches organizational behavior and human resource management courses at both the undergraduate and graduate levels. He also facilitates supervisory management workshops for area companies through the University of Wisconsin-Eau Claire's Office of Continuing Education. His current research interests include dyadic trust, psychological contracts, group potency, and other-oriented work values. He has published his research in a variety of journals including *Academy of Management Journal, Journal of Applied Psychology, Organizational Behavior and Human Decision Processes, Journal of Management, Journal of Organizational Behavior, Journal of Management Education, Human Resource Planning, Journal of Occupational and Organizational Psychology, Human Resource Development Quarterly, Journal of Leadership and Organizational Studies,* and *Journal of Managerial Issues.* Dr. Lester is a member of a number of professional organizations including the Academy of Management, the Midwest Academy of Management, the Southern Management Association, and the Society for Human Resource Management (SHRM). He is currently a representative on the executive board of the Midwest Academy of Management. Currently he serves as the faculty advisor for the University of Wisconsin-Eau Claire student chapter of SHRM. He has served as an ad hoc reviewer for a number of journals including *Academy of Management Journal, Organizational Behavior and Human Decision Processes, Journal of Management, Journal of Organizational Behavior, Human Relations,* and *Journal of Managerial Issues.*

Kimberly Lukaszewski is an assistant professor of management at the State University of New York at New Paltz. She earned her MBA in human resources information systems (HRIS) and her doctorate in organizational studies from the State University of New York at Albany. Her research focuses on human resources information systems, information privacy, and the effects of race and disability on employment decisions. Results of her research have been published in such journals such as *Human Resource Management Review* and *International Association for Human Resources Information Management Journal.* She has also written various book chapters that have been published in *Handbook of Workplace Diversity, The Brave New World of eHR: Human Resources Management in the Digital Age,* and *Advances in Human Performance and Cognitive Engineering Research.* She has presented various papers at the annual meetings of the Academy of Management, the Society for Industrial and Organizational Psychology, the Eastern Academy of Management, and the International Association for Human Resource Information Management.

Patricia Lynch, PhD, SPHR, earned her doctorate in human resources, with a minor in employment law, from the W.T. Beebe Institute of Personnel and Employment Relations at Georgia State University. She earned the MBA from University of Memphis and BBA from Smith College. Dr. Lynch is principal of HR Value, a consulting firm in Long Beach, California, that helps clients align employee behaviors and decisions with organizational goals. Dr. Lynch is an expert in measurement and evaluation, compensation, performance management, and employee training and development. Her practical advice and customized interventions enable her clients to leverage their investment in employees to achieve measurable bottom-line outcomes. Dr. Lynch has more than a dozen years of HR experience working with managers at all levels in the public, private, and nonprofit sectors. A former university professor, she has taught courses in human resources such as compensation, labor relations, staffing, performance management, and training at the graduate and undergraduate levels. She has been an instructor, a curriculum designer, and a special project leader for the Los Angeles County Learning Academy for six years. Dr. Lynch has published articles in both academic and practitioner journals and has contributed chapters to two books. Prior to earning her doctorate, she had a successful career as a senior financial analyst for Federal Express Corporation (now FedEx Corporation). Dr. Lynch serves on the Human Resource Certification Institute's (HRCI) Western Region Item Writing Panel, which writes questions for the SPHR and PHR (Professional in Human Resources) exams. Because of her expertise, HRCI has invited her to serve the profession in a number of capacities, including as a reviewer for the HRCI Practice Analysis Task Force, which updated the PHR/SPHR body of knowledge in 2005, as a member of the team that reclassified all items in the PHR and SPHR databases in 2006 following the 2005 update, and as a subject matter expert for the new California Practice Exam that will test individuals' knowledge of California employment law beginning in 2007.

Thomas A. Mahoney (deceased 2004) earned his PhD and MA in economics from the University of Minnesota in 1956 and his BA in economics from Wabash College. He was the Frances Hampton Currey Professor of Organization Studies, Emeritus, Owen Graduate School of Management, Vanderbilt University. From 1956 to 1982, Dr. Mahoney was on the faculty of industrial relations, Graduate School of Management at the University of Minnesota. From 1964 to 1966 he served as director of the Industrial Relations Center at Minnesota. During his career, Dr. Mahoney also held visiting professorships at the Graduate School of Business Administration at the universities of Stellenbosch and Witwatersrand in South Africa; Faculty of Commerce, University of British Columbia; and University of Wisconsin-Milwaukee.

Dr. Mahoney is remembered fondly by his MA and PhD students at the universities of Minnesota and Vanderbilt. Although he taught a wide range of graduate courses, his most memorable courses are in the areas of compensation theory and organization theory and design. During his career he supervised 19 dissertations.

Among his doctoral students are well-known academics such as George T. Milkovich, Marc Wallace, Peter Frost, and Jerry Newman, as well as consultants Norman Crandall, Paul Nystrom, and David Pierson. More recent students include John Deckop, Arlen Honts, and Mary Watson.

Dr. Mahoney is also remembered for his keen intellect and range of knowledge within the field. This range is particularly evident from his published works. During his career, Dr. Mahoney published eight books and monographs and 71 articles and chapters on a wide range of topics in an equally wide range of prestigious academic and professional outlets. For instance, his books and monographs range from the topics of compensation to leadership and executive development to problems of union administration. Among the academic outlets for his work are such prestigious journals as *Administrative Science Quarterly, Academy of Management Journal, Organizational Behavior and Human Performance, Management Science,* and *Industrial Relations.* Professional journal outlets are equally prestigious, such as *Organizational Dynamics, Harvard Business Review, Business Horizons,* and *California Management Review.* Dr. Mahoney also contributed chapters to such outlets as *Research in Organizational Behavior, Frontiers in Industrial/Organizational Psychology: Productivity in Organizations, Publishing in Organizational Sciences,* and *Handbook of Human Resource Management: Compensation and Benefits (BNA),* among others.

Dr. Mahoney's service to the profession includes editorial board membership for *Human Resource Management Review* and *Human Resource Planning Journal.* He served as editor for *Academy of Management Journal* and as ad hoc reviewer for *Administrative Science Quarterly, Journal of Applied Psychology, Industrial & Labor Relations Review, Academy of Management Journal, Management Science, Journal of Management,* and *Personnel Psychology.* Dr. Mahoney served on the board of governors for the Academy of Management and board of directors for the Human Resource Planning Society. Finally, he served as chair of the Human Resource Division of the Academy of Management.

Dr. Mahoney's external activities include consulting, expert testimony, and management and executive development seminar instructor. Among his consulting clients were State Farm Insurance Companies, Honeywell, General Mills, Northern Telecom, Pfizer, J.C. Penny, Peat Marwick & Mitchell, Hay Associates, Manville, NASA, the World Bank, and others. Dr. Mahoney testified in 14 employment discrimination litigation cases involving a wide-ranging group of large employers. His management and executive development seminars were conducted at 11 universities in four countries (U.S., South Africa, Mexico, Canada). U.S. universities include the University of Michigan, the University of Wisconsin, Cornell, Vanderbilt, and the University of Minnesota. Dr. Mahoney was an invited presenter at 19 major university research colloquia.

Last but not least, Dr. Mahoney is listed in *Who's Who in the Management Sciences.* Other honors include five Outstanding Teaching Awards; Academy of Management Career Achievement Award, Human Resources Division; Fellow, Academy of Management; University of South Carolina Human Resource Research Center Special Award; Southern Management Association, Distinguished Last Lecture; and Distinguished Achievement Award, University of Minnesota Alumni Association.

Patrick P. McHugh is an associate professor of employment and labor relations in the Management Department at The George Washington University. Professor McHugh earned his BS in business administration at Bowling Green State University and an MA in economics at Washington State University. He earned his PhD in labor and industrial relations from Michigan State University. He has written more than 30 articles, papers, and book chapters related to employment and labor-management relations, employee participation, collective bargaining, and employment law. His articles have appeared in *Industrial & Labor Relations Review, Human Relations, Industrial Relations (Berkeley), Economic and Industrial Democracy, Journal of Labor Research, Labor Law Journal,* and *Human Resource Planning,* among other publications. He is an editorial board member for *Human Resource Management Journal.* In addition to teaching and writing activities, he has provided technical assistance to the American Pharmacists Association, Federal Mediation and Conciliation Service, Ford Motor Company, United Auto Workers, and the American Federation of State, County, and Municipal Employees.

Brian Murray is an associate professor and associate dean for the College of Business at the University of Dallas. He earned his PhD from Cornell University in human resource studies. He has taught courses in human resource management, HR strategy, compensation, staffing, careers, and organizational behavior. His research has included examinations of skill-based pay, quality awareness training effectiveness, and employee pension choice decisions, and has been published in journals including *Academy of Management Journal, Personnel Psychology,* and *Decision Sciences,* among others. His current research focuses on employee benefits, human resource service quality, and effectiveness. Dr. Murray's consulting includes work in compensation and surveying and has focused on not-for-profit organizations and professional associations, including the University of Texas at San Antonio, the San Antonio Development Agency, the San Antonio Human Resource Management Association, and the San Antonio Manufacturers Association.

Jerry M. Newman is Distinguished Professor of Organization and Human Resources in the School of Management at the State University of New York-Buffalo. He earned his PhD in industrial relations from the University of Minnesota and his BA from the University of Michigan. As a faculty at SUNYAB for 30-plus years, he has received frequent teaching awards, including the Chancellor's Distinguished Teaching Award, State University of New York System. Dr. Newman also served his school as Interim Dean. He is co-author (with George Milkovich) of *Compensation,* author of *My Secret Life on the McJob: Lessons From Behind the Counter Guaranteed to Supersize any Management Style,* and author of 12 book chapters and more than 40 articles on compensation, performance management, and general human resource issues. He has served on editorial boards of *Journal of Contemporary Business Issues* and *Academy of Management Journal* and is a regular reviewer for nine other publications. Dr. Newman has consulted with more than 50 companies nationally and locally on compensation, performance management, and other HR issues. He is a charter member of the Society for Human Resource Management, Buffalo, New York, and in 1993 was named Human Resource Professional of the Year by its Niagara Frontier Chapter.

Skip Owens is a self-employed human resources consultant. He received his MS in management & organizations from the University of Iowa.

David A. Pierson is an independent consultant and founded The Pierson Group in 1997. His general emphasis is human resource consulting with a concentration in diagnosing and designing fixed and variable reward programs for all employee levels. He has extensive experience in developing performance-based compensation programs in a variety of industries including healthcare, medical equipment, electronic, and general manufacturing; finance; distribution; and consumer products. Dr. Pierson earned his PhD and MA in industrial relations and a BME in mechanical engineering, all from the University of Minnesota. He is a member of WorldatWork and has been an instructor in its certification series. He is also the author of various articles on compensation and human resources management and has spoken to numerous groups on these topics. Dr. Pierson has more than 20 years of experience in human resources consulting, most recently with the Hay Group, and prior to that he was a Principal with Towers Perrin. Before entering consulting, he was a tenured faculty member of the Human Resource Administration Department within the School of Business at Temple University, where he currently serves as an adjunct faculty member.

Christine Quinn Trank is an assistant professor in the Rawls College of Business at Texas Tech University, where she teaches general management and organization theory. She earned her PhD in organization studies from the University of Iowa. Her current research examines the intersection of symbolic interaction and institutional theory and the relationship between universities and business from an institutional perspective. She serves on the editorial boards of *Academy of Management Journal* and *Academy of Management Learning and Education.* Prior to receiving her doctorate, she served as an administrator in higher education for a number of years.

Sara L. Rynes is the John F. Murray Professor and Chair of the Department of Management and Organizations at the University of Iowa. She earned her PhD in industrial relations from the University of Wisconsin. Her current research interests include compensation, recruitment, field influences on higher education, and knowledge transfer between academics and practicing professionals. Dr. Rynes is current editor of *Academy of Management*

Journal and previously served two terms on this journal's editorial board. Additionally, she has served on the editorial boards of *Journal of Applied Psychology, Personnel Psychology, Quality Management Journal, Academy of Management Learning and Education,* and *Society for Industrial and Organizational Psychology's Frontier Series.* She is co-author of a compensation book with Barry Gerhart (Sage Publications) and is a Fellow of the American Psychological Association and the Society for Industrial and Organizational Psychology. She is the 2006 recipient of the Career Achievement Award presented by the Human Resources Division of the Academy of Management.

Eduardo Salas is trustee chair and professor of psychology at the University of Central Florida, where he also holds an appointment as program director for the Human Systems Integration Research Department at the Institute of Simulation and Training. He is also the director of UCF's PhD in Applied Experimental & Human Factors Program. Previously, he was a senior research psychologist and head of the Training Technology Development Branch of the naval Air Warfare Center Training Systems Division for 15 years. During this period, Dr. Salas served as a principal investigator for numerous R&D programs focusing on teamwork, team training, advanced training technology, decision making under stress, and performance assessment. He received his PhD (1984) in industrial and organizational psychology from Old Dominion University. Dr. Salas has co-authored over 300 journal articles and book chapters and has co-edited 18 books. He is a current or past member of the editorial boards of *Journal of Applied Psychology, Personnel Psychology, Military Psychology, Interamerican Journal of Psychology, Applied Psychology: An International Journal, International Journal of Aviation Psychology, Group Dynamics,* and *Journal of Organizational Behavior* and is current editor of *Human Factors Journal.* In addition, he has edited special issues in *Human Factors, Military Psychology, Journal of Organizational Behavior,* and *International Journal of Aviation Psychology.* He currently edits the annual series *Advances in Human Performance and Cognitive Engineering Research* (Elsevier). Dr. Salas has held numerous positions in the Human Factors and Ergonomics Society during the past 15 years. He is past chair of the Cognitive Engineering and Decision Making Technical Group and of the Training Technical Group, and served on the executive council. He is a very active member of Society for Industrial and Organizational Psychology (SIOP) and is past series editor for the Professional Practice Book Series. Dr. Salas consults with a variety of manufacturing companies, pharmaceutical laboratories, industrial organizations, and government organizations. He is a fellow of the American Psychological Association (SIOP and Division 21) and the Human Factors and Ergonomics Society.

Leon Schjoedt is an assistant professor of management at Illinois State University. He received his PhD in management from the University of Colorado at Boulder, and received his MBA at the University of

Wisconsin-Oshkosh and his BA at the University of Southern Denmark. He has served on the faculty at the University of Copenhagen.

Lynn M. Shore earned her PhD in industrial and organizational psychology from Colorado State University in 1985. Prior to joining the faculty at San Diego State University, she was on the faculty at the University of California, Irvine, and Georgia State University. Her primary research areas are on the employment relationship and workforce diversity. In the area of employment relationships, she has researched such topics as perceived organizational support, psychological contracts, leader-member exchange, and international aspects of employment relationships. Dr. Shore's work on diversity has examined the impact that composition of the workgroup and employee/supervisor dyads has on the attitudes and performance of workgroups and individual employees. Her work has appeared in elite scholarly journals such as *Academy of Management Journal, Academy of Management Review, Journal of Applied Psychology, Personnel Psychology,* and *Journal of Organizational Behavior.* Professor Shore is an associate editor of *Journal of Applied Psychology* and is a fellow of the American Psychological Association and the Society for Industrial and Organizational Psychology. Professor Shore has held leadership roles in the Academy of Management, having served as chair of the Human Resources Division (2000–2001) and on the executive committee (1995–1998). She has taught a variety of courses in human resource management and organizational behavior at the undergraduate, Master's, and PhD levels.

Kevin C. Stagl has partnered with dozens of organizations over the past decade to cultivate lasting business value via targeted human capital management solutions and decision support. In his current role as an organizational consultant with Assessment Technologies Group (ATG), and formerly as a research scientist at the Institute for Simulation and Training (IST), Dr. Stagl has been fortunate to have had the unique opportunity to learn from, and collaborate with, an influential list of individuals working on the leading edge of organizational science and practice. At IST, Dr. Stagl, with the guidance of his academic mentors, Drs. Eduardo Salas and Barbara A. Fritzsche, initiated a program of research that spans the spectrum of team issues, with an emphasis on fostering leadership, performance, development, and adaptation. The lessons learned and best practices distilled from this effort have appeared in three dozen scholarly outlets, including *Journal of Applied Psychology, Leadership Quarterly, Organizational Frontiers Series, Research in Multilevel Issues,* and *International Review of Industrial and Organizational Psychology.*

Dianna L. Stone earned her PhD from Purdue University and is currently a professor of management at the University of Texas at San Antonio. Her research focuses on employees' reactions to electronic human resources systems, information privacy, and diversity in organizations including issues of race, culture, and disability. Results of her research have been published in *Journal of Applied Psychology, Personnel Psychology, Academy of Management Review, Organizational Behavior and Human Decision Processes,* and *Journal of Management.* She is a fellow of the American Psychological Association and the Society for Industrial and Organizational Psychology. She has served as the chair of the Human Resources Division of the Academy of Management and as financial officer for the Society for Industrial and Organizational Psychology. Dr. Stone serves on the editorial boards of *Human Resources Management Review* and *Human Resources Management Journal.* She has published two books on the topic of electronic human resources management, including *The Brave New World of eHR: Human Resource Management in the Digital Age* (with Hal G. Gueutal) and an edited volume titled *Advances in Human Performance and Cognitive Engineering Research.*

Eugene F. Stone-Romero, PhD (University of California-Irvine), is a professor of management at the University of Texas at San Antonio. He is a fellow of the Society for Industrial and Organizational Psychology, the Association for Psychological Science, and the American Psychological Association. He previously served as the associate editor of *Journal of Applied Psychology* and on the editorial boards for *Academy of Management Journal, Journal of Applied Psychology,* and *Journal of Management.* He is now on the editorial boards of *Personnel Psychology, Organizational Research Methods,* and *Asian Journal of Business and Information Systems.* Dr. Stone-Romero's research interests include unfair discrimination in employment, personality-based biases in selection, cross-cultural issues in organizations, organizational justice, job design, privacy, reactions to feedback, work-related values, and moderator variable detection strategies. The results of his research have been published in such journals as *Journal of Applied Psychology, Personnel Psychology, Academy of Management Journal, Organizational Behavior and Human Decision Processes, Journal of Management,* and *Applied Psychology: An International Review.* He is also the author of numerous book chapters and two books, *Research Methods in Organizational Behavior* and *Job Satisfaction: How People Feel About Their Jobs and How It Affects Their Performance.* Stone-Romero is the 2007 recipient of the T. A. Mahoney Mentoring Award presented by the HR Division of the Academy of Management.

Rebecca A. Thacker is an associate professor of HRM at Ohio University, having received an MBA and a PhD in HRM from Texas A&M University's College of Business. Her publications appear in such journals as *Journal of Management, Human Relations, Human Resource Management Review, Journal of Psychology, HR Magazine, Business Horizons, Training & Development,* and *Employee Responsibilities and Rights Journal.* Dr. Thacker currently serves on the editorial boards of *Human Resource Management* and *Human Resource Management Review* and also serves as chair of the teaching committee of the HR Division of the Academy of Management. She consults with both private- and public-sector organizations and has testified on employment-related issues before a committee of the United States House of Representatives, the Ohio State Senate's Judiciary Committee, and the Ohio Advisory Commission to the U.S. Commission on Civil Rights. Dr. Thacker is professionally certified by the Human Resource Certification Institute of SHRM as a Professional in Human Resources (PHR).

Herman A. Theeke is professor of management and industrial relations in the College of Business at Central Michigan University. He earned his PhD in industrial relations from the University of Minnesota and his MBA from the University of Michigan. Dr. Theeke has worked as the human resource director for a large urban hospital, as the associate director of the University of Michigan's Human Resource Accounting Program, and as the program coordinator for the Human Resource Research Programs at the University of Minnesota. At various times he has served as a consultant to major U.S. corporations, such as General Motors and Ford Motor Company.

Dr. Theeke teaches a variety of management and industrial relations classes and championed an AACSB award winning program that provided the educational model for a new and innovative undergraduate business program. He has also served his College as chair of the Management Department and is an executive board member of the faculty union. His research in the area of human resource accounting includes a recent (2005) award-winning article that proposes abandoning the human resource asset paradigm and replacing it with a human resource liability model.